The Political Soul

The Political Soul

Plato on Thumos, *Spirited Motivation, and the City*

JOSH WILBURN

OXFORD
UNIVERSITY PRESS

OXFORD
UNIVERSITY PRESS

Great Clarendon Street, Oxford, OX2 6DP,
United Kingdom

Oxford University Press is a department of the University of Oxford.
It furthers the University's objective of excellence in research, scholarship,
and education by publishing worldwide. Oxford is a registered trade mark of
Oxford University Press in the UK and in certain other countries

First Edition published in 2021

Impression: 1

Published in the United States of America by Oxford University Press
198 Madison Avenue, New York, NY 10016, United States of America

British Library Cataloguing in Publication Data
Data available

Library of Congress Control Number: 2021942728

ISBN 978–0–19–886186–7

DOI: 10.1093/oso/9780198861867.001.0001

Printed and bound by
CPI Group (UK) Ltd, Croydon, CR0 4YY

For my oikeioi

Contents

PART IV

Acknowledgments

I am grateful to the following for their contributions to this project: my graduate advisors, John Cooper, Alexander Nehamas, and Hendrik Lorenz, who first encouraged my interest in Platonic *thumos*; Rachel Barney, Rachana Kamtekar, Gabriel Richardson Lear, Jessica Moss, and Clerk Shaw, for early feedback on the book proposal; Nicholas D. Smith, for exceptionally kind encouragement throughout my career, and for feedback on an early chapter draft; Kirsty Ironside, Jeremy Reid, Krisanna Scheiter, Rachel Singpurwalla, Christen Zimecki, and an anonymous referee, for reading and providing comments on the manuscript; the published work of those named above, as well as that of (among others) Julia Annas, Cinzia Arruzza, Tad Brennan, Douglas Cairns, Gabriela Roxana Carone, G. R. F. Ferrari, Angela Hobbs, Charles Kahn, Xavier Márquez, Marina McCoy, Andrea Wilson Nightingale, Olivier Renaut, Frisbee Sheffield, Christina Tarnapolsky, Josh Weinstein, and James Wilberding, for providing valuable interpretive resources and insight that contributed greatly to my thinking about various topics in this book, and to which I feel a deep debt (though I do not personally know some of those named, and certainly do not mean to suggest that any of them would endorse specific ideas I defend in this book); Bryan Butts, Kristin Courville, and (again) Christen Zimecki for their critical research assistance in the early stages of the project; the editorial team at Oxford University Press; the support of the Wayne State University Career Development Chair, which facilitated my completion of the book; and my friends, parents, and family, especially my husband David and our spirited pup Lola, for their love and support.

Introduction

When Socrates is asked in Plato's *Phaedrus* whether he believes a certain legend about the wind god Boreas, he responds that he has no time to scrutinize the truth of such stories. "The reason," Socrates explains, "is this":

> I am still unable, as the Delphic inscription orders, to know myself; and it really seems to me ridiculous to look into other things before I have understood that . . . I look not into them, but into my own self: Am I beast more complicated and savage than Typho, or am I a tamer, simpler animal with a share in divine and gentle nature? (229e4–230a6)[1]

The Delphic command to which Socrates refers here is one that Plato clearly took very seriously: it is quoted or cited in six Platonic dialogues.[2] As Socrates' comments in the *Phaedrus* hint, moreover, it is an imperative that Plato took to command examination of one's own *soul*. And indeed, later in the same dialogue, Socrates presents the dazzling mythical image of the human soul as a charioteer and team of two horses, one good horse and one bad. The image depicts Plato's tripartite account of human psychology, which he first introduces in the *Republic* and elaborates in the *Timaeus*, and which constitutes one of his most original and compelling contributions to the task of introspection assigned by the Delphic oracle. According to this theory, the embodied human soul consists of three distinct "parts," each of which is the source of distinctive kinds of motivations—urges, desires, emotions, and the like—that spur human beings to action. The reasoning part (represented by the charioteer) motivates us to pursue wisdom and what is best; the appetitive part (or "bad" horse) motivates us to pursue bodily pleasure and wealth; and, finally, the spirited part (or "good" horse) motivates us to pursue—among

---

[1] Except where noted, translations of Plato are from Cooper and Hutchinson (1997), with my own modifications. Reprinted by permission of Hackett Publishing Company, Inc.

[2] The inscription is cited at *Laws* 923a, *Phil.* 48c–d, and *Prot.* 343b, and is discussed at length at *Charm.* 164c–170a and *Alc.* 124a–129a. Cf. *Hipparch.* 228d–e and *Rival Lovers* 138a, as well as Xenophon, *Mem.* 3.7.9 and 4.2.24.

The Political Soul: Plato on Thumos, *Spirited Motivation, and the City.* Josh Wilburn, Oxford University Press.
© Josh Wilburn 2021. DOI: 10.1093/oso/9780198861867.001.0001

other things, we will see—honor, victory, and a good reputation.[3] This psychological theory provides Plato with powerful philosophical resources for examining and explaining human behavior and ways of life: why people think, act, and live in the different ways they do; what makes them good or bad, virtuous or vicious, decent or dissolute; and how people either fail or succeed in achieving happiness in both their individual and collective moral lives.

This book examines Plato's reflections on the *spirited* part of the soul and spirited motivation over the course of his career. Broadly speaking, my central aims are twofold. First, I will defend and explore the claim that spirit is the distinctively social or political part of the human soul for Plato. By that, I have in mind the idea that spirited motivations are essentially oriented toward the relation of the embodied self to *others*, and that the spirited part is therefore responsible for the desires, emotions, and traits that allow human beings to form relationships with one another, interact politically, and cooperate together in and protect their communities. According to this view, spirit is the source not only of the martial, aggressive, and competitive qualities for which it is well-known, but also for the feelings of affection, love, friendship, and civic fellowship that bind families and communities together and make cities possible in the first place. Because it is the political part of the soul in this sense, moreover, central social and political challenges—in particular, how to educate citizens properly in virtue and how to maintain unity and stability in communities—cannot be addressed and resolved without proper attention to the spirited aspects of human psychology. My second aim, then, is to show how Plato's critical assessments of unjust political conditions and unsuccessful moral education, as well as his constructive political ideas and proposals, are informed by his thinking about spiritedness. I will argue, moreover, that Plato draws attention to the role of spirited motivations in politics and social issues not only in works that feature the tripartite theory, but also, and in ways that are not often recognized, in dialogues that span the whole course of his career.

Although my focus is on the spirited part of the soul, this book will also engage along the way with issues regarding the appetitive and rational parts as well. As the metaphor of the charioteer and two horses suggests, the three parts of the embodied the soul are *interconnected* components of an individual's psychology, such that we cannot examine and understand one part entirely in

---

[3] For the widely (thought not quite universally) accepted view that the charioteer and horses of the *Phaedrus* represent (at least some version of) the tripartite soul of the *Republic*, see, for example, Guthrie (1971a: 235), Hackforth (1952: 72), Irwin (1977: 239), Nicholson (1999: 163–4), Rowe (1986: 177–8), and Taylor (1927: 307).

isolation from the others. Much of tripartition's explanatory and analytical power involves its treatment of the complex and various *relationships* that can develop among the three parts of the soul—how they causally interact, affect, and relate to one another, and how those dynamics influence and determine human actions and life choices in both the private and public spheres. Plato's account of spirit and its role in education, ethics, politics, and social life, consequently, involves careful consideration of its relations (in both ideal and non-ideal cases) to reason and appetite. In the course of studying spirit, therefore, I will also address topics and controversies that concern the other two parts of psychology, as well as the theory of tripartition as a whole.

Plato's spirited part of the soul itself gets its name from the early Greek term *thumos*. His favorite way of referring to it, as we will see, uses the derivative compound word *thumoeides*, and his account of spirit itself owes much to the history and tradition of these two terms and to the Greek concept of *thumos* in particular.[4] Throughout this book I will attempt to situate Plato's views on spirit in their historical and intellectual context by highlighting ways in which they draw on, reflect, or are illuminated by the work of his predecessors and contemporaries. This requires, first and foremost, understanding some of the history Plato invokes in naming the spirited part of psychology. In order to introduce the concept of spirit, then, I begin here by providing some preliminary background on the terms *thumos* and *thumoeides* through a brief survey of their main uses in early Greek literature.

The meanings and connotations of *thumos* are shaped primarily by its usage in early epic and poetic literature. *Thumos* is the single most common psychological term in Homer and is used prolifically throughout the Greek poetic tradition leading up to the time of Plato. Although the term appears informatively in other types of literature as well, writers in the historical, medical, philosophical, and rhetorical prose traditions tend to make use of it less frequently. As a result, by the fourth century the word has come to have something of a poetic or archaic ring to it in most contexts.[5] In adopting *thumos* as a namesake for his spirited element of the soul, therefore, Plato

---

[4] It will be my practice in this book to use English transliterations of Greek in the main text (but more often Greek itself in the notes). When I provide transliterated phrases or individual words for quoted text, I will leave the original Greek grammatical forms intact in the transliteration. Hence we will encounter not just *thumos*, for example, but also its accusative, dative, and genitive forms (*thumon*, *thumōi*, and *thumou*, respectively).

[5] Herodotus provides an instructive example. The term *thumos* occurs relatively infrequently (only about eighteen times) in his prose history, and almost never outside of quoted dialogue in his own narrative voice. Several of its occurrences within quotation, moreover, appear in oracular or prophetic contexts, e.g. at 7.140.16; cf. 1.120.14 and 5.56.4.

chooses a term that calls to mind the world of Homeric heroes and the protagonists of poetry.[6] Although *thumos* has a broad range of meanings in this early Greek literature,[7] three main (rough, sometimes overlapping, and not necessarily exhaustive) categories of its usage are especially noteworthy.[8]

First, *thumos* is used to refer to something like the energizing or animating principle of a person or living thing, or to the source of vital energy, strength, or consciousness.[9] When a Homeric warrior eats, for instance, it is his *thumos* which gains strength.[10] Conversely, *thumos* becomes "weary" as a result of labor; it is weakened by disease; and when a warrior faints or dies he can be said to "lose" his *thumos*.[11] In such uses the term is often translated as "life," "life-force," "soul," or "breath." This conception of *thumos* is closely related to or grounded in its connections with the human body and bodily processes. Indeed, *thumos* is not merely a *psychological* term in early Greek literature. Its meaning also extends into, or at least is nebulously contiguous with, the realm of physiology and anatomy.[12] On the physiological level, *thumos* is strongly associated with the two bodily elements whose loss most conspicuously

---

[6] Cairns (2014: paras. 10, 42), Cooper (1984: 12), Hobbs (2000: 7), Renaut (2014: 14), and Veggeti (1998: 65–6, n. 89) all draw attention to the Homeric connotations of *thumos*.

[7] For further discussion of *thumos* in early Greek literature, see Adkins (1970: Ch. 2), Böhme (1929), Cairns (2014), Caswell (1990), Cheyns (1983), Claus (1981: Chs. 1–2), Dodds (1951: 15–17), Frère (2004: 13–106), Harrison (1960: 65–72), Hobbs (2000: 7–8), Renaut (2014: Ch. 1), Snell (1953: 9–22), and Webster (1957). Sullivan (1981, 1988, 1993a, 1993b, 1993c, 1994a, 1994b, 1995, 1999, and 2000) offers a series of studies of *thumos* and other psychological terms in various early authors. Also relevant is the work of Cairns (1993) on the Greek concept of *aidōs* and North (1947, 1966) on *sōphrosunē*.

[8] Because of *thumos*' rich and layered range of meanings, I tend to think that attempts to identify more precise or finely grained categories of its usage are misguided. For example, the fivefold classification offered by Caswell (1990) seems to me somewhat arbitrary, both in the categories it identifies and in some of its assignments of specific instances of *thumos* to one category rather than another. The deliberately fluid threefold scheme I offer here is actually closer to Böhme's (1929), upon which Caswell takes herself to be improving.

[9] This usage is most common in early writers, especially Homer. Because Plato takes the soul as a whole, not any one part of it, to be the animating principle of living things, this usage of *thumos* has more in common with Plato's notion of the embodied *psuchē* than his notion of the spirited part in particular (although Plato retains, we will see, *thumos*' connections to bodily organs and processes associated with this usage). Frère (1997: 13) similarly finds that Platonic *thumos* does not serve as a Homeric life-principle, but on different grounds: "Le *thumós* est-il, comme chez Homère le *thumós-psyché*, principe de vie? Aucunement. La vie selon Platon se lie essentiellement au troisième type d'âme, à l'âme nutritive."

[10] Eg. *Od.* 5.95, 8.98, 14.28, 14.111; cf. Hesiod, *Th.* 641.

[11] For "weariness," see *Il.* 11.88. Loss of *thumos* at death occurs at *Il.* 16.410, 16.606–7; cf. Hesiod, *Shield* 426–8. When agents regain consciousness after fainting, *thumos* returns to them (e.g. *Il.* 22.475, *Od.* 24.349). *Thumos* is also afflicted by disease, e.g. *Od.* 11.200–1; cf. Mimnermus, fr. 2.15, "thumos-destroying illness" (νοῦσον θυμοφθόρου).

[12] It is debatable whether and to what extent the psychological and physiological are distinct for early authors, particularly Homer, but nothing in this book depends on an answer to that question. It is at least true, as Adkins (1970: 21) comments, that "the line between physiology and psychology is blurred in Homer." For further discussion, see Cairns (2014), Clarke (1999: 106–26), Renaut (2014: 199–206), and Rohde (1925: 50–1, n. 58).

coincides with death: breath and blood.[13] The etymology of the term *thumos* itself may even reflect, or at the very least suggest to Greek thinkers like Plato, some connection with the processes of respiration and circulation. Several philologists propose that *thumos* is cognate with Sanskrit and Latin terms for "smoke" (*dhumas* and *fumus*, respectively) and thus is connected with other phonetically similar Greek terms such as *thumiazō*—"to burn so as to produce smoke." According to this line of analysis, *thumos* may have referred originally to the "hot, swirling, choking and apparently very active" smoke and air produced by fire, and from there evolved into a notion of excited breath or a source of energy associated with breath.[14] Plato offers an alternative etymology, but one which hints at similar physiological underpinnings. In the *Cratylus*, Socrates suggests that *thumos* gets its name "from the raging (*thuseōs*) and boiling (*zeseōs*) of the soul" (419e1-2).[15] The etymological connection Plato has in mind is to the Greek word *thuō* ("to rush along, storm, rage"), and the two Greek terms Socrates uses are often applied to the raging or seething of stormy winds or waters. The imagery suggests that on a metaphorical level, *thumos* is like a tempest within us. This point is confirmed by the fact that epic and poetic writers often liken an enraged *thumos* or spirited anger to violent and irresistible winds or storms.[16] The language of seething may also reflect something more literal, however: that in a person energized by, or "fuming" with, spirited emotion, breath becomes quickened (or "storm-like") and blood becomes warmer (or "boiling").

[13] Some commentators actually identify Homeric *thumos* with forms of breath or blood to various extents. See, for example, Gomperz (1896: 200–1), who refers to it as "der Rauch- oder Blutseele," as well as characterizations in Liddell and Scott (1996; see entry for θυμός), Onians (1954: 48), Redfield (1994: 173–4, cf. 1985: 99–100), Wersinger (2001: 172), and, more cautiously, Webster (1957: 149). For criticism of such identification, see Böhme (1929: 23) and Cairns (2014: para. 32 ff.). I myself am committed only to affirming that *thumos* is *related to* or strongly *associated with* breath and blood, rather than straightforwardly identified with either.

[14] Adkins (1970: 17). As Claus (1981: 15, n. 14) notes, "It is customary to assume a development from 'smoke' to 'breath' and the 'spirit.'" Discussions of the etymology of *thumos* also appear in Böhme (1929: 19–23), Caswell (1990: 7–8), Cheyns (1983: 22–6), Lynch and Miles (1980), and Onians (1954: 44–54).

[15] Cf. Aristotle's reference to the definition of ὀργή offered by natural philosophers: ζέσιν τοῦ περὶ καρδίαν αἵματος καὶ θερμοῦ (*DA* 403a31-b1).

[16] Caswell (1990: Ch. 4) provides a rich study of such parallels and metaphors in Homer; cf. Claus (1981: 21–3) and Webster (1957: 151–2). As Caswell suggests, part of the connection seems to be that *thumos*, with its relation to anger and rage, is characteristically *forceful* in the way that storms can be, and it can also make an agent go "off course," as storms can, by causing rash and imprudent behavior. Ideas of this sort continue to be reflected in metaphors that appear throughout the poetic tradition. For example: "My heart (θυμέ), to what foreign headland are you diverting my ship's course?" (Pindar, *Nem.* 3.26–7); "Take care that your anger (θυμός) doesn't seize you and drive you off course" (Aristophanes, *Frogs* 993–8); and "Flashes of growing anger (θυμῷ) will soon set alight the rising cloud of her lament" (Euripides, *Medea* 98–108).

Whatever the correct etymology or "original" meaning of *thumos*, however, its usage in Homer and later writers clearly reflects strong associations with breathing and blood. The Homeric *thumos*, for example, is frequently described using the language of respiration: characters often "breathe out" (*apopneiōn*, *Il.* 13.654), "exhale" (*aïsthe*, *Il.* 20.403), or "gasp out" (*kekaphēota*, *Od.* 5.468) their *thumos* upon death or loss of consciousness. Hence literal loss and shortness of breath are characterized as conditions that prominently involve the agent's *thumos*.[17] Similarly, the loss of blood in Homer is correlated with a weakening or loss of *thumos*:

...and when [the spear] was drawn out the blood gushed forth and distressed his spirit (*thumon*). (*Il.* 11.456–8)

...and the dark blood welling out from his liver filled his chest, and darkness enfolded his eyes as he lost his spirit (*thumon*). (*Il.* 20.470–2)[18]

Closely related to these physiological connections, finally, is the anatomical association of *thumos* with the lungs and heart. In Homer, *thumos* often appears in tandem with words for the heart and chest or lung area—for example, "and then dread grief came upon his heart (*kradiēn*) and spirit (*thumon*)."[19] Throughout the epic and poetic traditions, moreover, *thumos* is often "located" in the chest, breast, or lung area (*stēthos* and *phrēn* or *phrenes*),[20] and it is frequently used synonymously with various words for the chest area or the heart (such as *kardia* or *ētor*).[21]

---

[17] Cf. *Il.* 3.292–4, 22.475; and Tyrtaeus, fr. 10.24. Conversely, the *excitement* of *thumos* has implied effects on breath at *Od.* 24.318–19: "Odysseus' *thumos* was stirred, and a sharp pang shot up through his nostrils." Similar ideas evidently inform the Greek observation that flared nostrils are indicative of spiritedness and anger, e.g. in the Peripatetic *Physiognomics* 811b3–4; Euripides, *Rhesus* 785; and Xenophon: "Wide open nostrils afford room for freer breathing...For whenever a horse is angry (ὀργίζηται)...or becomes spirited (θυμῶται) under its rider, it dilates its nostrils" (*Eq.* 1.10). Cf. Burnet (1916: 245).

[18] Cf. *Od.* 3.449–55; and Aeschylus, *Ag.* 1388–90: "Fallen thus he gasped away his spirit,...breathing forth quick spurts of blood." Conversely, the coagulation of blood in a wound coincides with the restoration of strength to *thumos* (*Il.* 16.528–9).

[19] This formulaic line appears, for example, at *Il.* 16.52 and *Od.* 18.274. Cf. Hesiod, *WD* 340. The expression κατὰ φρένα καὶ κατὰ θυμόν is another frequently recurring phrase, e.g. at *Il.* 4.163. Cf. Hesiod, *Th.* 611–12.

[20] This occurs repeatedly throughout Homer, e.g. at *Il.* 8.202 and *Od.* 15.165; cf. Hesiod, *Th.* 239, 549.

[21] The interchangeability of *thumos* and "heart" is especially clear in many texts, e.g. at *Od.* 20.5–22. See Ch. 2, n. 13 below for Plato's recognition of this point.

In the second main usage of *thumos*, the term refers to a seat or subject of psychological activity, including volitional,[22] deliberative,[23] and especially *emotional* activity:

> But he went to Pytho, suppressing the unspeakable anger (*cholon*) in his spirit (*thumōi*).   (Pindar, Ol. 6.38)

> Many were the pains (*algea*) he suffered in his spirit (*thumon*) upon the sea.
> (Homer, Od. 1.4)

In these passages *thumos* is the psychological site where anger or pain takes place, or perhaps even the psychic entity that bears or experiences them. In its emotional and volitional usage, *thumos* is well-known for being associated with the motivations, qualities, and virtues of a warrior. In Homer this notably includes, to begin with, emotions and attitudes that express sensitivity to the economy of honor (*timē*), fame (*kleos*), and glory (*kudos*). *Thumos* motivates Homeric heroes to fight for honor and glory, and a warrior's *thumos* becomes "proud" as a result of the honor he receives.[24] Most importantly, Homeric heroes feel the emotion of wrath or anger in response to a perceived *loss* of honor. Thus when Agamemnon takes away Achilles' darling "prize" Briseis, Achilles becomes enraged in his *thumos* and must "check his wrath (*cholon*) and curb his spirit (*thumon*)" (*Il.* 1.192) to prevent himself from killing Agamemnon on the spot.[25] Lest there be any doubt that his anger is concerned with honor and status, his subsequent entreaty to his mother Thetis is clear:

> Mother, since you bore me, though to so brief a span of life, surely the Olympian, Zeus who thunders on high, ought to have granted me honor (*timēn*); but now he has not honored (*etisen*) me at all. In fact, the son of

---

[22] In its volitional usage, *thumos* is commonly the psychic entity responsible for "urging" or "bidding" an agent to do something, e.g.: "And his *thumos* urged (ἀνῆκε) godlike Sarpedon to... demolish the battlements" (Homer, *Il.* 12.307–8). Cf. Verdenius (1985: 18, 31) on this volitional usage in Hesiod.

[23] In Homer, *thumos* is often the *locus* or subject of planning and deliberation, especially when the agent is conflicted, e.g.: "The old man pondered, his *thumos* divided in two ways, whether he should go into the throng of the Danaans of swift steeds, or go find Agamemnon" (*Il.* 14.20–2). Related to its role in internal debate, it can also serve an interlocutory function. Homeric heroes sometimes speak to their *thumos* (e.g. *Il.* 22.98), which can apparently also speak back: the phrase "But why has my *thumos* spoken with me this way?" is a recurring one in Homer (*Il.* 11.407, 17.97, 22.122, 22.385); see Sharples (1983). *Thumos* is never quoted directly in Homer, however, as discussed in Cairns (2014: paras. 39–41). I will say more about spirit's relation to deliberation in Ch. 8.2.

[24] For examples of the role of *thumos* in the pursuit of κλέος, κῦδος, or τιμή, see *Il.* 6.441–6, 12.407, 15.561–4, 20.179–81. *Thumos* is also the source of Zeus' *desire* to grant glory (e.g. *Il.* 12.174, 15.596).

[25] Cf. 1.215: Achilles is θυμῷ κεχολωμένον. On the ethics of honor among Homeric warriors, see Gagarin (1987) and Renaut (2014: 25–8).

Atreus, wide-ruling Agamemnon, has dishonored (*ētimēsen*) me, for he has taken away and holds my prize through his own arrogant act.

(*Il.* 1.352–6)[26]

Closely related to its role in a warrior's concern for honor and glory, *thumos* is also responsible for the rage, fury, or martial energy required for successful fighting. Indeed, one of the paradigmatic expressions of spiritedness, both in Homer and for Greeks in Plato's time, is the passionate anger or vigor associated with effective warriors on the battlefield. *Thumos* is, for example, what warriors in Homeric literature and poetry must rouse in themselves or their fellow soldiers to ready themselves for battle:[27]

My spirit (*thume*), my spirit (*thum'*) . . . rise up and defend yourself: set your breast against your foes as they lie in ambush and stand steadfastly against the enemy nearby. (Archilochus, fr. 128.1–4)

Likewise, it is the source of courage, audacity, violence, savageness, pugnacity, endurance, and the determination to conquer one's enemies:

Their spirit (*thumos*) craved war (*polemou*) even more than before, and they all stirred up a fight (*machēn*) that day. (Hesiod, *Th.* 665–7)

Son of greatest Zeus, you no longer possess a pious spirit (*thumon*) in your breast: restrain your arrogant violence (*bian*). (Bacchylides, *Ode* 17.20–3)

In a struggle (*ponōi*) he resembles the boldness (*tolmai*) of loudly roaring wild lions at heart (*thumon*). (Pindar, *Isth.* 4.45–7)

Yet [Tydeus] with his enduring (*karteron*) spirit (*thumon*) as always challenged the youths of the Cadmeans and easily defeated (*enika*) them in all things. (Homer, *Il.* 5.806–8)

And Achilles rushed on him, his spirit (*thumon*) full of savage might (*meneos agriou*). (Homer, *Il.* 22.312–13)

Thumos is associated, in other words, with a variety of aggressive traits and emotions that tend to characterize fierce fighters and heroic individuals.

---

[26] Aristotle corroborates this analysis of Achilles' psychology, citing this very passage, at *Rhet.* 1378b29–35.

[27] Conversely, soldiers who lack enthusiasm, confidence, or courage are often described as feeling "dispirited" (*athum-*) and in need of encouragement, as in Thucydides (e.g. *Hist.* 2.88.3.2, 7.60.5.3, 7.76.1.1) and Xenophon (e.g. *Anab.* 4.3.7.3, *Hell.* 7.5.23.5).

Despite the prominence of such connections, however, the emotional role of *thumos* is by no means limited to competitiveness and aggression. As we will see, it is also strongly associated with and the source of a rich range of other feelings and emotions. Shame is an especially important spirited emotion, and *thumos* is also responsible for feelings such as pity, grief, friendship, and love. As I will emphasize in Chapter 2, then, the epic and poetic *thumos* is responsible not only for the aggressive feelings that characterize strife and division between enemies, but also for the feelings of affection that characterize the bonds between friends and loved ones.

Third and finally, the term *thumos* can be used to refer to a specific *type* of emotion—namely, anger, passionate fury, or rage.²⁸ This is a usage we find, for example, in Euripides' *Medea*:

> Your husband tried to take away the young woman's angry mood (*orgas*) and wrath (*cholon*) and said, "You must not be unkind to your kin, but must cease from your anger (*thumou*) and turn your face toward us again."
>
> (1149–52)

In this passage *thumos* is no longer the distinct seat or subject of the person's emotional state; rather, it *is* the anger itself. Accordingly, in such contexts *thumos* is often used, as here in Euripides, synonymously with various other Greek terms for "wrath" or "anger" (such as *orgē*, *cholos*, and *mēnis*).²⁹

By contrast to *thumos*, the term *thumoeides* appears to have been a relative neologism in Plato's time. It was used primarily to describe human and animal character types or temperaments, as evident from its prominent use in two main fifth- and fourth-century sources. The first is the Hippocratic treatise *Airs Waters Places*, which is typically dated to the mid- or late fifth century, and which contains the earliest known usage of the term *thumoeides*.³⁰ In it the

---

²⁸ This usage is less prominent, or even absent, in Homer, who prefers other terms for occurrent anger (see Considine's [1966] survey), but it becomes increasingly prevalent in the poetic tradition leading up to the time of Plato. Cf. Cairns (2004: 21).

²⁹ Indeed, Plato himself sometimes uses the terms *orgē* and *thumos* synonymously, including at *Rep.* 440a5 in his argument for tripartition; cf. 440c2. It is worth noting, however, that because of the archaic connotations of *thumos*, the orators and sophists of Plato's time use it relatively rarely, showing a marked preference for the term *orgē* instead. See discussion in Allen (2002: Ch. 9 and 2004) and Desclos (2007).

³⁰ Jaeger (1946) discusses the Hippocratic origin of Plato's term; cf. Calabi (1998: 191–3 and n. 6). Socrates' description of different types of regional character at *Rep.* 435e–436a, which includes his claim that the Scythians, Thracians, and "those to our north" are thought to be distinguished by τὸ θυμοειδές, provides further evidence of the influence of Hippocratic ethnography on Plato's thinking. Cf. Renaut (2014: 261–4) and Vegetti (1998: 66, n. 89), who comments, "Il termine *thymoeides* applicato all psicologia sociale e non a quella animale deriva certamente a Platone dall'etnologia di Arie acque luoghi." I return to this Hippocratic influence in Ch. 9.

Hippocratic author provides an ethnological account of the different character types associated with various geographical regions and climates. Whereas the inhabitants of Asia, he explains, are characterized by a lack of spirit (*athumiēs*, 16.3)—literally "without *thumos*" —the people of Europe are distinguished by their "spiritedness":

> The same reasoning also applies to character. In such a climate [i.e. one subject to violent and sudden changes] arise savageness (*to agrion*), unsociability (*to ameikton*), and spiritedness (*to thumoeides*).[31] For the frequent shocks to the mind impart wildness (*agriotēta*), destroying tameness (*to hēmeron*) and mildness (*to ēpion*). For this reason, I think Europeans are also more stouthearted (*eupsuchoterous*) than Asiatics. For uniformity engenders slackness of spirit (*rhaithumiai*), while variation fosters endurance (*talaipōria*) in both body and soul; and cowardice (*deiliē*) grows out of idleness (*hēsuchiēs*) and slackness of spirit (*rhaithumiēs*), courage (*andreiai*) out of endurance (*talaipōriēs*) and labor (*ponōn*). That is why Europeans are more warlike (*machimōteroi*).   (23.19–31)

Here *thumoeides* describes a character type that reflects many of the distinctive traits of the Homeric and poetic warrior *thumos*: spirited people are courageous, savage, bellicose, and suited for endurance. Those who lack spiritedness, by contrast, are cowardly.

The second important source for the term *thumoeides* is Plato's contemporary Xenophon, who uses the language of spiritedness to describe the natures of dogs and horses in his manuals on hunting and equestrianism.[32] He repeatedly describes excitable or recalcitrant horses as "spirited" (*thumoeidēs*);[33] he says that hounds should show signs of *thumos* when they are closing in on a hare;[34] and he even likens the *thumos* of horses to human anger:

> First, then, it must be realized that spirit (*thumos*) in a horse is precisely what anger (*orgē*) is in a man. Therefore, just as you are least likely to make a man angry (*origzoi*) if you neither do nor say anything harsh (*chalepon*) to him, so

---

[31] Cf. occurrences of θυμοειδές in the text at 12.41 and 16.11.

[32] Harrison (1953) discusses the use of the term *thumoeides* in hunting language and proposes that Plato consciously borrowed the term from hunting talk.

[33] Xenophon uses the term *thumoeides* (along with comparative and superlative forms of it) especially frequently in *Eq.* 9, e.g. at 9.4.1 and 9.5.3. See also its use at 1.8.8 and 10.17.3, and at *Symp.* 2.10.6, *Mem.* 4.1.3.5, and *Anab.* 4.5.36.3; and cf. *Eq.* 3.12.7 (ὑπέρθυμοι) and 11.12.2 (εὐθυμότατοι).

[34] *Cyn.* 4.4.

he who abstains from harshness toward a spirited (*thumoeidē*) horse is least likely to rouse his anger (*exorgizoi*).   (*Eq.* 9.2)

Xenophon readily describes dogs and horses as *thumoeidēs* and attributes spirit to them in prose contexts, which suggests that, by Plato's time, the language of *thumos* has become standard in describing canine and equine temperaments in aristocratic parlance.[35] The type of temperament it describes, moreover, is one that Xenophon associates with animals that are stubborn or orgulous, exceptionally eager for victory (*philonikotatoi, Eq.* 9.8.4), or prone to anger. The temperament Xenophon has in mind, therefore, clearly bears some resemblance to the ethnological type described as "spirited" in the Hippocratic school, despite the fact that Xenophon is describing horses and dogs rather than human beings. Both in Xenophon and in *Airs Waters Places*, the term *thumoeides* is used to describe natures or temperaments distinguished by qualities that are prominently associated with *thumos* in earlier literature.

Plato's account of the spirited part of the soul and spirited motivation, we will see, owes much to these uses and connotations of *thumos* and *thumoeides*. Like the epic and poetic *thumos*, his spirited part of the soul is strongly associated at the physiological level with the heart and blood; it is (in its very essence, I will suggest) a psychic source of volition and emotion; and *thumos* in the sense of the occurrent emotion of anger or rage is one of the spirited part's most distinctive expressions. Likewise, in line with contemporary uses of *thumoeides*, Plato uses the language of spiritedness to distinguish different political and social character types, and he plays on its associations with horses and dogs by liberally employing equine and canine metaphors and analogies in characterizing the spirited part of the soul. Over the course of this book I will expand on some of these connections in more detail, as well as additional ways in which Plato's views on psychology are influenced and illuminated by other early Greek literature. Important aspects of Plato's account of the spirited part and spirited motivation in general, and their role in human social and political life in particular, can be better appreciated by recognizing their place in the history of early Greek thought. I hope to bring some of that relevant context to light in the course of making my arguments.

---

[35] The (ps.-)Platonic *On Virtue* also includes discussion of "spirited" (θυμοειδεῖς) and "spiritless" (ἄθυμοι) horses and hunting dogs (378d). Cf. also Sophocles, *Electra* 25–7: "A noble horse, even if he is old, does not lose his spirit (θυμόν) in a time of danger"; and fr. 661, where *thumos* is said to be εὐνηθείς, a Greek term that in the passive means "to be lulled to sleep" and is applied to dogs in the sense of "to lie kenneled." The later Platonist Plotinus also describes horses as μάχωνται, φιλονεικῶσι, and ζήλῳ θυμῶνται (*Enn.* 3.3.1.14–15), and he likens the spirited part of the soul itself to a dog (*Enn.* 4.3.28.14–16).

* * *

This book is divided into four parts. Part I establishes the background assumptions and interpretive resources that I will take for granted and apply in the rest of the book. In Chapter 1, I address the theory of tripartition itself, beginning with a brief defense of a methodological assumption I make in this book: that Plato is serious when he advocates tripartite theory and is earnestly and even deeply committed to it. This constitutes a response to skeptical commentators who suggest his investment in tripartite psychology, and especially in a *spirited* part of that psychology, is unserious, tentative, or fleeting. I then outline what precisely I take Plato to mean in speaking of a spirited "part" of the soul. I suggest that each of the three parts of the soul should be understood as a distinct source of psychological states and activities, including especially the ones that constitute *motivations*—the various qualities, dispositions, desires, emotions, and other affective states that explain or cause human behavior.

In Chapter 2, I turn to the question of which motivations have their source in the spirited part of the soul, and which hence count as "spirited" by the lights of tripartition. I begin by providing an overview of motivations that are already widely attributed to the Platonic *thumos* by "traditional" interpretations, which typically focus on spirit's aggressive, competitive, and ambitious expressions—for example, love of honor or victory—and which explain its various motivations in terms of them. I argue that this traditional interpretation represents only half of the picture. In addition to its competitive side, Plato also recognizes a second, cooperative or gentle side of spirit that is responsible for feelings of familial affection, friendship, and political fellowship, as well as related emotions like admiration and shame. I argue that a complete understanding of spirited motivation must account for both aspects of *thumos*, and that the most primitive expressions of spirit's two sides are the impulses or qualities attributed to noble dogs in *Republic* 2: hostility to what is foreign (*allotrion*) and gentleness toward what is familiar (*oikeion*). This two-sided analysis of spirited motivation informs my interpretation in the rest of the book.

In Chapter 3, I develop the idea that spirit is the distinctively *social* or *political* part of the soul. For Plato, it is what makes us capable of cooperating together in united social and political groups and protecting those groups against outsiders, and it is the source of the desires, emotions, and sensitivities by which we absorb the influence of others through social and cultural means. I also identify two key challenges that arise out of these aspects of spirit's nature. Plato's critical assessment of Athenian education and politics in the *Republic* shows that the social aspects of *thumos* give rise to two pressing political problems in corrupt cities, and both problems involve spirit's subordination to acquisitive or "pleonectic"—from the Greek term *pleonexia*, which typically refers to the greedy or unjust pursuit of more than one's fair share of wealth, property, and other worldly resources—desires and values that Plato associates with the appetitive part of the soul. The first is the problem of moral education. In places like Athens, citizens and cultural authorities transmit and absorb vicious pleonectic values to and from one another socially by way of their spirited motivations. This, in turn, contributes to a second problem related to civic unity. In cities where people value the finite pleonectic goods of the material world, citizens inevitably come to view one another as rivals or competitors for those goods, which gives rise to hostility, mutual faction, and ultimately civic strife and instability instead of friendship and political solidarity. The rest of the book examines Plato's preoccupation with these two social and political problems—both how they arise and how to resolve them—and with the role that spirited motivation and the *thumoeides* play in them throughout his career.

Parts II, III, and IV of the book apply the resources of Part I to three "stages" of Plato's career: "early" dialogues (in the sense of dialogues that are often assumed to predate the introduction of tripartition in the *Republic*); dialogues in which tripartite theory appears explicitly, focusing on *Republic* and *Timaeus*; and Plato's later works *Statesman* and *Laws*.

Part II draws attention to ways in which Plato's early works anticipate many of the ideas about spirited motivation, and its role in social education and politics, that form the heart of Plato's conception of the spirited part of the soul. Chapter 3 focuses on the *Protagoras*. My main argument will be that the "Great Speech" delivered by the dialogue's namesake presents spirited motivation as the *sine qua non* of human communities. According to Protagoras' myth, human society was impossible until the gods granted the "art of politics" to human beings. I argue that both sides of spiritedness are represented in this "art of politics," which includes both a capacity for war as well as a sense of shame and justice. The myth shows that human beings cannot defend their communities against outsiders without spirit's bellicosity, and that they cannot cooperate and form stable communities in the first place, nor influence and educate one another within those communities, without the shame, self-restraint, and friendly regard for others supplied by its gentle side. On my interpretation, when Zeus grants "the art of politics" to human beings, he turns them into spirited creatures with distinctively spirited feelings and

sensitivities. I conclude by identifying ways in which the dialogue also anticipates Plato's critical assessment of Athens: the text subtly suggests that
Athenian citizens *fail* to use their spirited emotional dispositions to instill
virtuous values in one another and to maintain genuine political fellowship in
the ways made possible by Zeus' allotment.

Chapter 5 continues this case through a survey of several other "early"
dialogues that depict the centrality of spirited motivation in social and political
life, while also showing that the presence of spirit by no means guarantees civic
unity or virtue among citizens. Early dialogues dramatize the problems of civic
strife and improper moral education in ways that both anticipate the
Republic's critique of contemporary Athenian culture, as well as set the stage
for its constructive political proposals for the Kallipolis. I conclude with a
discussion of how the continuity surveyed in Chapters 4 and 5 bears on the
issue of developmentalism in Plato's thought. While I do not insist that Plato
already had the tripartite soul in mind when he wrote his early works, I do
respond to one important obstacle to that conclusion. Many commentators
have been inclined to take spirit to be the "dark horse" or "third" part of the
soul in Plato's theory. I argue, on the contrary, that *reason* is the part of Plato's
tripartite soul that requires the most defense. The reason we find so much
emphasis on the role of reasoning in human desire and action in the early
dialogues, therefore, is not because Plato does not *yet* accept the existence of
non-rational forms of motivation, but rather because those are the forms he
can *already* take for granted.

Part III turns to Plato's positive account of *thumos* in the *Republic* and
Timaeus. In Chapters 6 and 7, I focus on the *Republic*'s constructive solutions
to the challenges of civic strife and moral education that Socrates develops
through his proposals for the Kallipolis. In Chapter 6, I examine musical and
gymnastic training and consider their various effects on the three elements of
psychology. I argue that music and gymnastics focus largely on training the
spirited part of the soul, but that they also have important effects on reason
and appetite. In Chapter 7, I consider the psychology of virtue that moral
education is supposed to produce, as well as Socrates' proposals for producing
political unity in the Kallipolis. In both cases, I argue, Plato's policies on
education and politics are designed to exploit the two sides of spirit's nature.
Moral education aims to make *thumos* a friend to reason by making rationality
oikeion or familiar to it, and to make spirit hostile to harmful appetite by
making the latter *allotrion* or alien to it. If moral education is successful, spirit
will obey reason and serve as its protective ally in the "war" against vicious
appetitive desires. Likewise, the economic and social institutions of the

Kallipolis, which seek to eliminate the "private" as much as possible in favor of the "common" and are designed to avoid civic strife and promote unity instead, work largely by exploiting the two sides of spirited motivation and making citizens familiar or *oikeioi* to one another.

Chapter 8 provides the cognitive underpinnings of this account of education and engages with the controversial question of the extent to which each of the three parts of the soul is "agent-like." On this issue my interpretation will be a minimalist or deflationary one: although spirit is a distinct source or subject of motivation in the soul, it is not necessarily a distinct subject of any of the soul's cognitive capacities. Focusing on the *Timaeus*, I defend an "imagistic" account of spirited (and appetitive) cognition, according to which the various activities of the spirited part—its role in motivating human behavior, its education through music and gymnastics, its responsiveness to reason, and its opposition to appetite—can all be explained at the cognitive level by appealing only to the shared psychic resources of sense-perception, memory, and imagination. I conclude by suggesting how this account might be projected backward onto the *Republic*'s theory of early education.

Finally, Part IV examines two of Plato's "late" political dialogues, the *Statesman* and the *Laws*. Although neither explicitly endorses or presents tripartite theory, I argue that both works make significant use of spirited motivations in their political philosophies in general, and in their accounts of civic unity and moral education in particular. First, in Chapter 9 I focus on the *Statesman*'s conception of politics as the "weaving" together of courageous and moderate citizens. I argue that these two civic temperaments are best understood in terms of the two sides of *thumos*, a reading that is informed by dichotomous political psychologies found in fifth-century authors like Hippocrates and Thucydides. On this interpretation, "courageous" individuals are those who incline toward behavior associated with the aggressive side of spirit, while the "moderate" ones are those who incline toward behavior associated with its gentle side. The defining task of the politician, on this view, requires attention to the spirited aspects of human nature. This idea is anticipated earlier in the dialogue, moreover, through the Myth of Cronus, where the Eleatic Visitor depicts a race of human-like people who are entirely devoid of spirited motivation and who, accordingly, have no families or cities. The myth illustrates that politicians in the present age must be concerned first and foremost with the spirited motivations that make human beings social creatures.

Chapter 10, finally, argues that the *Laws* remains committed to the centrality of spirited motivation in resolving problems of civic unity and moral education. To begin with, the policies the Athenian Visitor advocates with a view to promoting civic harmony draw heavily on Plato's two-sided account of spiritedness. Most significantly, many of his political proposals are designed to foster the feelings of friendship among citizens that are essential to the city's stability. Although he does not propose the *Republic*'s extreme policies of de-privatization, moreover, he nonetheless attempts to approximate those policies and their psychological effects to the extent possible in the "second best" circumstances of Magnesia, the potential city he and his interlocutors imagine. Likewise, the Athenian's account of musical and gymnastic education echoes the theories of the *Republic* and *Timaeus*, while also developing spirit's educational role in a novel way through the institution of wine-drinking parties. Regulated symposia are designed to test and mold citizens' sense of shame throughout their lives in accordance with the laws, and the psychological theory to which the Athenian appeals throughout his defense of this practice draws unmistakably on Platonic ideas about *thumos*. The *Laws*, then, shows that Plato's thinking about spirited motivation continues to inform his reflections on social and political philosophy all the way to the end of his career.

PART I

1

Tripartition and the Spirited "Part" of the Soul

Throughout this book I will use a variety of terms to refer to the spirited part of the soul, including "spirit," "the spirited part," the *thumoeides*, and (following a practice that is common among commentators) also simply *thumos*. In the present chapter I have two main objectives. First, I will offer some brief remarks intended to clarify and defend the project of this book, which grants to tripartition, and to Plato's account of spirit in particular, a privileged place in his reflections on human psychology. My approach assumes that when he presents the theory in the *Republic*, *Timaeus*, and *Phaedrus*, he is serious about it, and I argue that his views on social and political philosophy can be illuminated by the theory even in some dialogues that do not explicitly feature it. Some commentators, however, question whether and to what extent Plato was ever genuinely committed to tripartition—especially to the existence of a spirited part of the soul—in the first place. Others claim that his commitment to it, however weak or strong, was only temporary and limited to the works that present it, such that attempts to discern the theory's influence in other dialogues are dubious or fundamentally misguided. In order to prepare the way for my arguments, then, I will begin in Section 1 by defending Plato's commitment to tripartite theory against skeptical arguments and by clarifying some of my objectives in the book. My second aim, in Sections 2 and 3, is to sketch the interpretation of tripartition—of what exactly Plato means in claiming that the soul consists of three "parts," and hence what he means in positing a spirited "part" of it—that I will take for granted in the rest of this book. My suggestion, which draws on Plato's conception of the soul as a source of self-motion, will be that each of the three parts is a distinct source of the psychic motions and motivations that cause and explain human action.

The Political Soul: Plato on Thumos, *Spirited Motivation, and the City*. Josh Wilburn, Oxford University Press.
© Josh Wilburn 2021. DOI: 10.1093/oso/9780198861867.003.0001

1. The Place of Tripartition in Plato's Thought

Commentators have advanced three main lines of skepticism about Plato's commitment to tripartition that are worth considering. First, many point to conspicuous reservations Plato expresses about tripartite psychology in the works that actually present it. In the *Republic*, shortly following Socrates' argument for the three-part soul, he says that the truly just person "harmonizes the three parts of himself" and "binds together those parts *and any others there may be in between*" (443c–e). Socrates' comment is often, and reasonably, taken an indication that Plato is open to the possibility that the soul does not necessarily have exactly three parts after all.[1] A later passage in the dialogue seems to confirm this point. Socrates suggests that their account of the soul reflects its condition "while it is maimed by its association with the body and other evils," which attach to it like detritus to the sea god Glaucus. In order to discover the real nature of the soul, however, it would be necessary to look to its love of wisdom. "Then," Socrates claims, "we'd see what its true nature is and be able to determine whether it has many parts or just one (*eite polueidēs eite monoeidēs*) and whether or in what manner it is put together" (611b–612a). We find similarly cautionary remarks in both the *Phaedrus* and the *Timaeus*, immediately preceding the myth of the charioteer and his horses in the former, and immediately following Timaeus' introduction of the three anatomically located parts of the soul in the latter:

> Now here is what we must say about [the soul's] structure. To describe what the soul actually *is* would require a very long account, altogether a task for a god in every way; but to say what it is *like* is humanly possible and takes less time. So let us do the second in our speech.   (*Phdr.* 246a3–6)

> So, as for our questions concerning the soul—to what extent it is mortal and to what extent divine; where its parts are situated, with what organs they are associated, and why they are situated apart from one another—that the truth has been told is something we could affirm only if we had divine confirmation.   (*Tim.* 72d4–7)

---

[1] See, for example, Grube (1980: 134–5), Murphy (1951: 29–30), Smith (1999: 44), Robinson (1970: 42), and esp. Whiting (2012: 176–9). Ferrari (2007: 189–90) responds to this line of argument with an alternative interpretation of 443c–e.

In all three dialogues that present tripartition, then, Plato also expressly declines to endorse the theory confidently and unequivocally as a true account of the soul. Some commentators take this to show that he was not deeply or genuinely invested in the account after all.[2]

Second, commentators draw attention to apparent fallacies or infelicities in Socrates' argument for the three-part soul in *Republic* 4.[3] It is the only *argument* Plato ever offers for tripartite psychology in the whole of his works, so its conspicuous failure or inadequacy is taken to show that Plato may never have meant for the argument to succeed to begin with. Rather, it is a half-hearted attempt to defend a view he held at most half-heartedly, if at all. Some criticism to this effect, furthermore, especially concerns the spirited part of the soul. Several commentators claim that whereas Socrates' argument for dividing the appetitive and reasoning parts of the soul seems careful and fastidious, his arguments for distinguishing between the spirited part and the other two are comparatively quick and less rigorous.[4] Indeed, those arguments have been called "singularly few and weak,"[5] and on the ultimate question whether spirit is distinct from both reason and appetite, Hardie concludes:

> No adequate reasons are given by the discussion in the *Republic* for thinking that this is so, or for modifying the opinion, so strongly supported both by plain men and philosophers, that the fundamental division here is into two and not three.[6]

Often this line of argument has been coupled with doubts about the plausibility and coherence of Plato's account of the spirited part itself. As we will see in the next chapter, *thumos* is responsible for a rich variety of desires and emotions, and their range and apparent diversity has given rise to doubts

---

[2] See, for example, Robinson (1970: 119–20), as well as Taylor (1928: 516), commenting on *Tim.* 72d.

[3] Nussbaum (2009: 152, 157, 159), for example, takes Plato's argument to be "pretty weak," "puzzling and unsatisfactory," or even "hideously bad" and she concludes, "Plato has no good argument for his tripartite view." Bobonich (1994: 15; cf. 2002: 248–54) claims that Plato's argument cannot plausibly generate *exactly* three parts of the soul. See various other lines of criticism in Murphy (1951: 29), Shields (2001), Smith (1999), and Williams (1973; cf. 1993: 42–4). For responses to Williams' influential critique, see Blössner (2007), Ferrari (2005), Lear (1992), and Tianyue (2009).

[4] Robinson (1970: Ch. 3) assails Plato's arguments for tripartition in general and his commitment to spirit in particular, and Penner (1971: 111–13), presents a series of arguments designed to show that Plato neither presents nor has any good argument for the spirited part. Several commentators criticize Plato's argument itself but suggest he provides other resources beyond it for establishing the separate existence of *thumos*; see Annas (1981: 140–1), Gerson (2003a: 102, n. 6), Kamtekar (2017: 137–8), and Wilson (1995: 64–8).

[5] Penner (1971: 113).   [6] 1936: 142.

about whether it is possible to identify any unifying principle among them, or whether they represent merely an awkward motley collection.[7] Hence Plato's account of spirit has been described as "notoriously underdeveloped and obscure,"[8] "cryptic,"[9] and "elusive and tricky";[10] thumos has been called "the bastard child"[11] and "the dark horse of the psychic parts";[12] and commentators have suggested that Plato's introduction of the thumoeides is motivated more by the rhetorical aims or dialectical needs of the Republic than by careful or serious philosophical reflection.[13] As T. M. Robinson states, "The ambiguous status of the spirited element allows it to be fitted with some show of plausibility into a scheme of tripartition invented as an imposing analogue to the tripartite state. It serves a purpose in a context, and should not be pressed."[14] According to many interpreters, then, Plato either never took soul-division seriously at all, or, if he did, was primarily interested only in a bipartite psychology consisting of reason and appetite.[15] In either case, the spirited part of the soul finds itself without a secure place in Plato's thought.

Finally, although Plato wrote over two dozen dialogues, he presents tripartition of the soul only in the Republic, Timaeus, and Phaedrus, which are generally considered to be concentrated roughly around the late "middle" of Plato's career. Even many commentators inclined to take him seriously in those dialogues, therefore, nonetheless think that his commitment to the theory was relatively short-lived, and that in other preceding or succeeding dialogues Plato held alternative psychological views that are incompatible with tripartition.[16] Developmentalist views of this sort cast doubt on the power of the three-part soul to illuminate dialogues other than those in which it explicitly appears.

---

[7] Several interpreters worry, for instance, that Plato's account vacillates between portraying spirit as something bestial or irrational on the one hand and as something relatively sophisticated or rational on the other. See esp. Cornford (1912: 264), Hardie (1936: 142–3), and Penner (1971: 112). Gosling (1973: 47) and Annas (1981: 127) also raise this problem, but both suggest it is soluble. Other commentators who discuss the issue of spirit's apparent diversity include Fussi (2008: 238–9), Gill (1985: 8–9), Hobbs (2000: 3–4), Klosko (2006: 73–4), Reeve (1988: 136–8), and Williams (1973: 204–6).

[8] Nussbaum (2001: 130).   [9] Nussbaum (1986: 272, note; cf. 456, n. 5).

[10] Tarnapolsky (2015: 244).

[11] Weinstein (2018: 13) uses this term to describe skeptics' characterization of the spirited part but does not endorse it.

[12] Reeve (1988: 136).

[13] Cornford (1912: 258–64), for instance, explicitly claims that Plato "invented" the thumoeides in order to meet the demands of the city-soul analogy, and Williams (1993: 42–4) claims that tripartition was "designed from the beginning with political ends in view" and criticizes its coherence. For replies to such criticism, see Lorenz (2006a: 18–20) and Miller (1999: 98–9).

[14] 1970: 46.

[15] I will address the question of whether bipartition and tripartition are in any genuine competition with one another in Plato in Ch. 10.1.

[16] For references, see Ch. 5, n. 23 and Ch. 10, n. 2.

If skeptical commentators are right and Plato never, or only for a fleeting time and tentatively, really believed in tripartition of the soul in the first place, then at least some of the central ambitions of this book are likely to seem less promising. There are, however, compelling responses to all three of the above concerns.

To begin with, I think the fact that Plato expresses a lack of certainty about tripartition of the soul tells us very little about his degree of commitment to the theory. Rather, it much more plausibly reflects Plato's sensitivity to the limits of human knowledge, and the fact that he takes the true nature of the soul to be one of the most important and difficult things to know.[17] His humility about what we can know, and how easily we can know it, is one of the best things about Plato. The fact that he expresses conscientious skepticism about tripartition, however, is perfectly compatible with his also taking it to be the most credible and attractive theory available to us—*given* the limits of our knowledge—of the nature of the embodied human soul. The word "embodied" here is also important. If we examine Socrates' apparent reservations about the theory in *Republic* 10 more closely, we find that he distinguishes the nature of the human soul during its embodiment from its true and immortal *disembodied* nature. His doubts are directed at tripartition as an account of the latter, but not necessarily as an account of the former.[18] Socrates stresses that an inquiry into the real nature of the soul would require examining it when it is dissociated from the body, but he also emphasizes that "what we've said about the soul is true of it as it appears at present" (611c6–7), and that "we've given a fair account, I think, of what its condition is and what parts it has when it is immersed in human life" (612a5–6).[19] Plato leaves it open whether the immortal human soul consists of "parts," but he seems much more confident that incarnate human souls do.[20] Moreover, he may also have thought—and as I will argue throughout this book, did think—that, regardless of whether we

---

[17] Cf. Ferrari (1987: 119–23) and Guthrie (1971a: 230).

[18] I take it this uncertainty is why he seems to explore different possibilities regarding the immortality of appetite and spirit in *Phaedrus*, *Republic*, and *Timaeus*. I see no reason to think his theory of the *embodied* soul varies in those dialogues, however. For discussion of this issue, see Bett (1986), Gerson (1987), Hackett (1952: 75–7), and Robin (1908: 144).

[19] Similarly, following Timaeus' claim that only "divine confirmation" could assure them of the truth of his account of the soul, he adds, "But that our account is certainly at least a *likely* one is a claim we must risk…Let that be our claim, then" (72d7–e1). In context, moreover, his uncertainty actually appears to be directed more at the anatomical locations and functions attributed to the three parts of the soul, rather than at their existence itself.

[20] Brennan (2012: 103) and Woolf (2012) offer similar interpretations of Book 10, and see relevant remarks in Hall (1963: 69, n. 1 and 72–3), Taylor (1927: 281), and Wilamowitz-Moellendorff (1920: 467). Whiting (2012), however, defends a thesis she calls "radical psychic contingency," according to which it is contingent in the *Republic* how many genuine parts belong to any given individual human soul. She argues that a soul in which psychic conflicts did not arise would be a soul that is no longer

can have precise knowledge of the soul's structure, prominent problems in ethics and politics are diagnosed and resolved most effectively given the hypothesis of tripartition. He may, in other words, have found that as an account of embodied human psychology the theory is both philosophically probable (though not certain) and ethically useful. I think that is more or less Plato's view of tripartition, and that he takes the theory very seriously precisely because that is his view of it.[21]

Skeptical arguments based on perceived weaknesses *either* of Plato's *Republic* 4 argument *or* of his account of the spirited part of the soul also fail, in my view. For now I will set aside criticism of the latter, which I address briefly in Chapter 5.3, and which I hope to disarm with the arguments of this book by showing the coherence, plausibility, and power of Plato's account of spirit within his philosophical framework. Regarding the former, however, I find the inference from alleged shortcomings of Plato's argument for tripartition to the conclusion that Plato did not believe the theory itself to be misguided. I should first of all say that, in my judgment at least, a lot of the objections to Plato's argument are not actually successful. Many of them are based on what seem to me to be misinterpretations of the text or anachronistic assumptions, and they lose their force once we account for the actual context and aims of Book 4.[22] That is to say, I think Plato's argument for tripartition is actually a pretty good one.[23] Even granting that the argument has its flaws,

---

partitioned in a meaningful sense. She imagines, for example, an ideal Stoic-like sage who "*always and only* became angry *to the extent and only the extent*" judged appropriate by reason, and claims that "*Republic* IV's famous argument... is no argument for assigning to *her* soul a spirited part distinct from reason" (p. 182). I am skeptical of this view, for a few reasons. (1) In the *Phaedrus*, the "good horse" is ideally responsive to the "charioteer" but is nonetheless distinct from him and provides an important source of additional resistance to the "bad horse." (2) The *Timaeus* suggests there is teleological value in, say, having the task of hunger delegated by our divine creators to a separate appetitive part, *even if* appetite were never the source of hunger that conflicts with reason's judgments. (3) Even the soul of the ideal philosopher of *Republic* 9 is characterized in terms of parthood, e.g. at 586e–587a. (4) As I argue in this book, Plato takes spirit to play an *ineliminably* crucial role in social life and (especially early) moral education. All of that said, however, Whiting allows that Plato might still think the souls of *most* people have three parts; she insists only that alternatives are "in principle possible." Even if she were right, then, the claims of this book would apply to most people most of the time. Cf. Wilburn (2014a: 65–6, n. 18).

[21] Cf. Shorey (1903: 42–3) and Weinstein (2018: 25) on tripartition's political usefulness.

[22] Jacquette (2003) provides a useful example. He argues that Socrates' defense of tripartite theory in Book 4 fails because it leaves open *logically possible* alternatives to tripartition: "The counterargument need only show that there is another way of interpreting Socrates' evidence... If the alternative interpretation is at least logically possible, then Socrates' examples by Socrates' own Principle of Opposites do not prove the existence of distinct parts of the soul" (p. 60). I think Jacquette is right that the argument does not decisively foreclose all other logical possibilities, but wrong to think it therefore fails. *That* would follow only if Plato took the argument to establish a logically necessary conclusion in the first place, and for reasons just mentioned in the main text, that seems plainly false. For another line of argument not unlike Jacquette's, cf. Shields (2001: 147–8).

[23] Cf. Weinstein (2018: Chs. 1–3), who offers an extended defense of Plato's argument on different grounds.

however (what argument doesn't?) *and* that Plato was aware of some of them (which seems not at all unlikely), I still see no reason to take his sensitivity to that imperfection as evidence that he did not take the argument or its conclusion seriously. For one thing, for the reasons just stated, Plato likely found many views probable while also believing that establishing them with definitive *proof* may be elusive for human beings. Furthermore, it is not even clear that in Plato's mind, there *are* such things as "perfect" arguments— especially *written* ones—that establish important truths with the authority of incontrovertible necessity. Whatever else we may know about him, we know that Plato valued rigorous and *ongoing* debate and discussion. His commit-ment to untiring dialectical investigation seems to assume that no argument is final: there are always complexities to be examined, weaknesses to be addressed, caveats to be understood. In that sense, we might say, Plato took *all* arguments to be "flawed," in the sense that they are all incomplete and open to further questioning. This point becomes even more compelling, I think, when we recognize that the argument we find in Book 4 of the *Republic* is, like all arguments in his dialogues, a mere literary *imitation* of the kind of dialectical back-and-forth that constitutes authentic philosophical work in Plato's eyes. Even if he took Socrates' argument for tripartition to be the *best possible one* that he could write in the space allotted to it, that does not, I think, do very much to recommend it as his final say on the matter.[24] On the contrary, nothing in the whole of Plato's works should encourage us to think that he took the truth of tripartition—or any other important philo-sophical claim, for that matter—to hinge on the success of any argument that could be rehearsed in a few pages of a written text. Plato does not present his dialogues to the world as stone tablets to a Moses: they are designed not to compel us to believe but to invite us to inquire.

Finally, I have two lines of response to skeptical developmentalist worries. The first is a methodological point, which is that the *assumptions* employed by the arguments of this book are, for the most part, actually compatible with developmentalism about Plato's views on human psychology. None of my arguments will require the strong claim that Plato accepted tripartite theory, either in all of its details or even in outline, as he wrote every single one of his dialogues. Indeed, my arguments will not, in general, require even the much weaker claim that Plato accepted tripartite theory when he wrote *any* dialogue

---

[24] *Phdr.* 274c–278b suggests furthermore that Plato does not want to leave his readers with the impression that they *know* a given view is true simply because they can recite an argument in its favor. The practice of encouraging people to believe they understand what they have memorized is, from Plato's point of view, distinctive of sophists and antithetical to genuine education.

other than the *Republic, Timaeus,* and *Phaedrus.* When I discuss works in which tripartition does not explicitly appear, I will prefer to speak not of the spirited part of the soul but of spirited *motivations*—by which I will have in mind *motivations that are attributed to the spirited part of the soul under tripartite theory*—and I will use terms like "spirit" and *thumos* more loosely and neutrally to refer to *the propensity to experience such motivations,* or to *whatever it is about psychology that makes creatures experience them.* These stipulations will allow me the freedom in later chapters to talk about "spirited motivations" even in works that do not explicitly feature tripartition, without committing myself to the claim that Plato accepted that theory when he wrote those works. Many skeptics and developmentalist interpreters doubt that Plato believed in a spirited part of the soul when he wrote, for example, the *Protagoras* or the *Laws*; none could deny that he discusses anger in both of them, however, or that anger is a paradigmatically spirited emotion by the lights of tripartition. One of the central aims of this book will be to show that when we do examine Plato's treatments of spirited motivation in many of these other dialogues, we find much more continuity with his accounts of tripartition than traditional developmentalist accounts assume. I will make my own suggestions about how best to interpret that continuity, but it is important to note that my arguments self-consciously leave space for drawing different conclusions. Most readers, therefore, whatever their commitments, should be able to accept much of the substance of this book.

Second, although I will not respond to specific developmentalist arguments here,[25] I have a few general remarks in defense of prioritizing a theory that does not appear in the majority of Platonic texts. To begin with, most of the dramatic and dialectical aims and contexts of Plato's works do not demand explicit discussion of the structure of the embodied soul, and it would have been both artistically and philosophically cumbersome for him to defend tripartition anyway in every dialogue to which it has some relevance. The fact that Plato does present tripartite theory *repeatedly,* in three different dialogues and from three different perspectives, probably tells us much more about his degree of investment in the theory than his omission of it from all the rest of his works. It is also important that one of the dialogues in which tripartition appears is the *Republic,* which represents by far Plato's most concerted attempt in his whole career to provide a worked out account of

---

[25] I will respond to some of them later in this book, however: see discussion in Ch. 5.3, the introduction to Ch. 9, and Ch. 10.1. For some forceful general arguments against developmentalist approaches to Plato, see Shorey (1903), Annas (1999), and Kahn (1996).

the embodied human soul. He defends, develops, and explores the explanatory power of tripartite theory in extraordinary detail over the course of the dialogue, and it clearly holds a special place in Plato's reflections on human psychology.

This last point receives further support from the fact that his successors in the philosophical tradition overwhelmingly take it for granted that tripartition is *the* Platonic view of the embodied soul: it is attested by Aristotle and Peripatetic authors;[26] it appears in several later handbooks of Platonism and doxographical reports;[27] and it is assumed, employed, or referred to by various Platonist, neo-Platonist, and Platonically influenced commentators and philosophers throughout the ancient world.[28] If it is a mistake to grant to tripartition a privileged status among Plato's commitments, it is one in which the better part of the ancient philosophical community is complicit. Better, I think, to conclude that it is not a mistake: that Plato's interest in the tripartite soul is serious; that inasmuch as he held relatively settled and lasting views, we are justified in counting tripartition among them; and that it is reasonable to expect that some of the ideas and arguments we find in other dialogues will be illuminated if we consider them in relation to Plato's theory of the three-part soul. This is precisely the project I undertake in this book, with an emphasis on the spirited part of the soul and the motivations associated with it, and it is one I believe yields rich insights into important components of Platonic philosophy.[29] As a final response to skepticism about Plato's investment in tripartition, therefore, I point ahead to the fruitfulness of taking Plato's commitment to it seriously.

---

[26] Aristotle criticizes the tripartite theory of the soul at *DA* 432a19–b8 and *MM* 1185a15–25 and refers to the τριμερής soul twice at *Top.* 133a30–3. The same term appears in the Peripatetic text *On Virtues and Vices*, where tripartition is explicitly ascribed to Plato (1249a31). Aristotle also himself divides up the genus of desire—what he calls ὄρεξις—into appetite, *thumos*, and rational wish in a way that is obviously indebted to tripartite theory, e.g. at *DM* 700b22 and 701a36–b1, *MM* 1187b36–7, and *EE* 1223a26–7.

[27] See, for example, the doxographical report of Diogenes Laertius (*Lives* 3.67, 3.90), or Alcinoos' description of the τριμερής soul (*Handbook* 176.35–41; cf. 182.15–27 and comments in Dillon [1993: 149]). Apuleius provides a similar characterization (*Plat.* 1.13) of what Beaujeu (1973: 275, n. 3), glosses as "cette fameuse tripartition de l'âme et son implantation dans le corps." Annas (1999: Ch. 6) provides an excellent discussion of the prominence of tripartition among the Middle Platonists.

[28] Plotinus, for instance, freely uses the vocabulary of tripartition to talk about the embodied soul throughout the *Enneads*, e.g. at 1.1.7, where he refers to the "lion-like" part of the soul, the "various beast," and "the rational soul"; cf. 1.2.1 and 4.2.28. The same is true of the work of Plutarch (e.g. *Virt.* 441f–442b); Cicero (e.g. *Tusc.* 1.10.20); Galen (e.g. *PHP* 5.2.37–8), who also attests to Chrysippus' attribution of tripartition to Plato (e.g. *PHP* 3.1.14); Posidonius (e.g. F142 and F143 in Kidd [1972 and 1999]); and Proclus (e.g. *Alc.* 139.2–10). It is also significant that Platonists freely draw on tripartite theory in their interpretations of other Platonic dialogues like the *Alcibiades*. See, for examples, Proclus, *Alc.* 159.22–160.6 and 43.7–18; and Olympiodorus, *Alc.* 4.4–14. For discussion of the use of tripartition in Olympiodorus and other neo-Platonists, see Griffin (2016: 4–17).

[29] Cf. Renaut (2014: 18).

2. The Language of Tripartition

In order to understand what Plato himself means when he speaks of a spirited "part" of psychology, it is necessary to examine his tripartite theory of the soul more generally. Indeed, one of the central debates in scholarship on tripartition concerns what exactly Plato means in identifying three "parts" of the embodied human soul. The controversy is due in part to the rich variety of language and imagery with which Plato characterizes the divided soul. To begin with, he often describes the soul's "parts" in terms that implicitly or explicitly liken them to people or animals: the reasoning "part" is depicted as a "human being" within us; the appetitive "part" is compared to an unruly horse and on several other occasions to a "wild beast"; and the spirited "part" is likened to a variety of animals, including dogs, wolves, horses, and lions. Plato frequently characterizes the relations among these parts, moreover, using personifying language. For example, reason issues "commands" and "announcements" to the other parts, which they in turn can "obey" or "disobey"; spirit is the "ally" or "auxiliary" of reason; and the parts of the soul "fight," "enslave," and "rule" one another. Interpretive controversies have emerged out of such discussions concerning whether, how, to what extent, and in which respects we are to take Plato's metaphors and his use of personification literally, or more generally what they can or cannot tell us about his views on the soul.[30]

A second source of controversy is that, as previous commentators have noted, Plato does not describe the "parts" of the soul with any consistent technical terminology throughout his accounts of tripartition.[31] Indeed, although Plato uses forms of the term *meros*—the closest Greek equivalent to our "part"—to refer to the elements of the soul on several occasions, he more commonly uses the Greek words for "form," *eidos* (or plural *eidē*), and "class" or "type," *genos* (or plural *genē*).[32] Most often, however, Plato avoids

---

[30] Kamtekar (2006) offers an illuminating discussion of Plato's use of personification.

[31] See Andersson (1971: 107), Annas (1981: 124), Cross and Woozley (1964: 127–8), Kamtekar (2017: 131), Klosko (2006: 72), Lorenz (2006a: 35–6), Renaut (2014: 152–7), White (1979: 125), and Woolf (2012: 155 and n. 11).

[32] He applies *eidos* or *eidē* to the soul's elements at least six times in the *Republic* (437d3, 439e2, 440e8, 440e9, 572a6, and 580d3), four times in the *Timaeus* (69c7, 77b4, 89e4, and 90a3), and twice in the *Phaedrus* (both at 253c8); and he applies *genos* or *genē* to them six times in the *Republic* (441a1, 441c6, 441d9, 442b2, 443d3, and 444b5) and four times in the *Timaeus* (69d5, 69e4, 70a6, and 73c4). By contrast, he uses *meros* or *merē* in this way six times in the *Republic* (442b11, 442c5, 444b3, 577d4, 581a6, and 583a1) and only once in the *Timaeus* (91e6), along with one use of the related term *moira* (71d2).

commitment to any such terminology by using a variety of substantive phrases to refer to the parts of the soul. In the *Republic* the three expressions he prefers for this purpose are, translated literally, "that which reasons" (*to logistikon*), "that which is appetitive" (*to epithumētikon*), and "that which is spirited" (*to thumoeides*).[33] He also uses a rich variety of other such expressions throughout his accounts, however, as shown in Table 1.[34] Although the various expressions he employs are often quite naturally translated using the language of parthood—for example, "the spirited *part*" or "the *part* that engages in deliberation"—the Greek itself is neutral on the issue of what exactly "that which is spirited" or "that which engages in deliberation in us" actually *is*. Certainly any insistence on referring to the three constituents of the soul as "parts" is our own, not Plato's.[35]

In response to this controversy, some commentators reject or downplay the notion of parthood or soul division entirely. It has been argued, for example, that Plato's theory amounts to no more than a classification of three kinds or species of human *desire*. On such a view, what Plato is "dividing" in tripartite theory is not really the soul itself at all, but rather the genus of human motivation.[36] At the other extreme, commentators have argued that tripartition is a division of the soul into three separate agent-like entities, each of which has its own desires, cognitive abilities, and beliefs, and the three of which literally interact and communicate with one another in ways that are analogous to the interactions of human beings themselves.[37] There are, naturally, various versions of both the deflationary and literalist lines of thought, as well as a range of views in between.[38] My goal in the next section, however, is

---

[33] Less frequently, Plato also refers to reason simply as *logos* (*Rep.* e.g. 440b3, 440b5, 440d3; Tim. 70b3, 70d5) and spirit as *thumos* (e.g. *Rep.* 440b4, 440c5; Tim. 70b3, 70c2, 70d4, 70d5). Cf. plural uses of *epithumiai* (*Rep.* 440a6, 440b4; Tim. 70b5).

[34] This table is representative but not exhaustive. Notably, it does not include expressions that refer to more than one part of the soul, or ones whose referent is controversial. It excludes, for example, references to τὸ θνητόν in the *Timaeus* (e.g. 69d5, 69e1), which includes both appetite and spirit, as well as many of the expressions that appear in Book 10 of the *Republic* (e.g. τὸ παρὰ τὰ μέτρα δοξάζον, 603a1; τῷ ἀνοήτῳ, 605b9), where the issue of whether and how tripartite psychology maps onto the distinctions made there is controversial. See Ch. 10, n. 15 for further discussion.

[35] It is worth noting, however, that it is a trend that is already present in Aristotle (e.g. at *DA* 432a23–31).

[36] This is famously the view of Cornford (1929: 215).

[37] Bobonich (2002: 219–23) and Moline (1978) both advocate especially promiscuous versions of this sort of view.

[38] The dichotomy of deflationism and literalism oversimplifies the variety and complexity of positions and is intended only as a rough basis for classification. Within this framework, however, commentators who fall somewhere on the more literalist side of the spectrum include Annas (1981: 131), Carone (2001: 124–5), Dorter (2006: 117–18), Ferrari (1987: 200–1), Gill (1996: 251–3), Kahn (1987: 85–6), Reeve (1988: 139–40), and Zabarowski (2018). Barney (2016) also outlines a literalist (what she calls "analytical") interpretation that she appears to favor at least tentatively. Commentators

Table 1. Plato's Language of Psychic Parthood

"Part"	Literal Translation	Greek	Citation
Reason	that which reasons	τὸ λογιστικόν	Rep. 440e5–6, 441a3, 441a5, 441e4, 442c11, 550b1, 553d1, 571d7, 602e1, 605b4–5
	that which forbids [them from drinking]	τὸ κωλῦον	Rep. 439c6, 439c9
	that with which [the soul] reasons	τὸ ᾧ λογίζεται	Rep. 439d5
	that which has calculated about better and worse	τὸ ἀναλογισάμενον περὶ τοῦ βελτίονός τε καὶ χείρονος	Rep. 441c1–2
	that which is ruling	τὸ ἄρχον	Rep. 442c1
	the third thing in which thinking happens	τὸ τρίτον ἐν ᾧ το φρονεῖν ἐγγίγνεται	Rep. 572a6
	that with which a human being learns	ᾧ μανθάνει ἄνθρωπος	Rep. 580d10
	that with which we learn	ᾧ μανθάνομεν	Rep. 581b5
	that which is divine	τὸ θεῖον	Rep. 589d1; Tim. 69d6, 90a8, 90c4, 90c7–8
	that which is most divine	τοῦ θειοτάτου	Tim. 73a7
	that which is best	τὸ βέλτιστον	Rep. 572a1, 590e4; Tim. 70b9
	that which engages in deliberation	τοῦ βουλευομένου	Tim. 70e6–7
	that which is masterful	τὸ κράτιστον	Tim. 71a1
	that which understands	τὸ κατανοοῦν	Tim. 90d4
Appetite	that which is appetitive	τὸ ἐπιθυμητικόν	Rep. 439e5, 441a6, 442a5, 550b2, 571e1
	that which thirsts and draws like a beast toward drinking	τοῦ διψῶντος καὶ ἄγοντος ὥσπερ θηρίον ἐπὶ τὸ πιεῖν	Rep. 439b4–5
	that which urges [them to drink]	τὸ κελεῦον	Rep. 439c5, 439c7
	that with which it feels erotic desire, hunger, and thirst, and is agitated by the other appetites	τὸ ᾧ ἐρᾷ τε καὶ πεινῇ καὶ διψῇ καὶ περὶ τὰς ἄλλας ἐπιθυμίας ἐπτόηται	Rep. 439d6–7

who reject literalist readings or fall somewhere on the more deflationary side of the spectrum include Anagnostopoulos (2006: 176–9), Gerson (2003a: 100–24), Hardie (1936: 138–41), Murphy (1951: 36–40), Price (2009), Renaut (2014: 135–7), Stalley (2007), and Stocks (1915). My own view falls, like most, somewhere between the two extremes, although for what it's worth I certainly spend more time in my published work, including this book, criticizing literalist views than I do deflationary ones. See esp. Ch. 8 for relevant discussion and notes.

	that in him which is using force	τῷ βιαζομένῳ ἐν αὑτῷ	*Rep.* 440b2
	that which is appetitive and money-loving	τὸ ἐπιθυμητικόν τε καὶ φιλοχρήματον	*Rep.* 553c5
	that which is beast-like	τὸ θηριῶδες	*Rep.* 571c5
	that in the soul which has appetites for foods and drinks and whatever else it needs on account of the nature of the body	τὸ σίτων τε καὶ ποτῶν ἐπιθυμητικὸν τῆς ψυχῆς καὶ ὅσων ἔνδειαν διὰ τὴν τοῦ σώματος ἴσχει φύσιν	*Tim.* 70d7–8
	that which is base	τὸ φαῦλον	*Tim.* 71d4
Spirit	that which is spirited	τὸ θυμοειδές	*Rep.* 440e2–3, 441a2, 441e5–6, 442c1, 550b3, 553d1, 572a4, 581a9, 586c7, 590b7
	that which contains spirit and by which we become spirited	τὸ τοῦ θυμοῦ καὶ ᾧ θυμούμεθα	*Rep.* 439e3
	that which is irrationally spirited	τῷ ἀλογίστως θυμουμένῳ	*Rep.* 441c2
	that which is in the middle and loves victory and is spirited	ᾧ μέσῳ τε καὶ φιλονίκῳ καὶ θυμοειδεῖ	*Rep.* 550b6
	that by which [a person] becomes spirited	τὸ ᾧ θυμοῦται	*Rep.* 580d10
	that which is lion-like and snake-like	τὸ λεοντῶδές καὶ ὀφεῶδες	*Rep.* 590a9
	that which shares in courage and spirit in the soul	τὸ μετέχον τῆς ψυχῆς ἀνδρείας καὶ θυμοῦ	*Tim.* 70a2–3

neither to survey and refute competing interpretations, nor even to offer a complete defense of my own positive view. Rather, it is simply to stipulate and clarify the account of tripartition—and hence of the spirited "part" of the soul—that I will be taking for granted in the rest of this book. To that end, I will briefly state my interpretation and sketch some of the evidence in its favor.

3. Psychic Parthood

According to the account I will be adopting, what it means for something to be a "part" of the soul, on Plato's view, is that it is a discrete source of psychological states and activities, including especially the *motivations* that explain and cause human action and behavior. What it means for there to be three "parts" of the human soul, then, is that there are three *distinct* sources of motivation, each of which is capable of prompting or inhibiting action independently of the others based on the characteristic sorts of objects to which each part is attracted or averse.[39] The "spirited part," accordingly, is a distinct source of motivation, and "spirited motivations" refer to motivations that originate in the spirited part of the tripartite soul.

Several considerations support this line of interpretation. First, Plato provides the theoretical basis for it with two interrelated views that are central to his understanding of the soul and that he expresses throughout, and even beyond, his accounts of tripartition. The first is that the soul is a subject of motion: it is something that itself (essentially) moves. This point is especially clear in both the *Phaedrus* and *Timaeus*. In the former, Socrates defends the immortality of the soul by appealing to the idea that soul is, by its nature, self-moving. "All soul is immortal,"[40] he argues, "for whatever is always in motion is immortal . . . Only what moves itself never desists from motion, since it never stops being itself," and "nothing else other than soul moves itself" (245c–246a). Similarly, in the *Timaeus*, Plato consistently characterizes psychological phenomena and the condition of the soul, including both cosmic soul and the embodied human soul, in terms of motion: the proper reasoning that constitutes knowledge or true belief, for example, is identified with circular motions of the soul (37a–c), and the irrationality of infants is attributed to the overwhelming effect that the chaotic motions involved in bodily processes and sense-perception have on the soul's orbits when it is first incarnated (43a–44c). The disruption caused by such motions, moreover, evidently prompts the gods' creation of the "mortal form" of soul that consists of the spirited and appetitive elements. We are told that the mortal soul will "contain" the "necessary disturbances" associated with the body and will ideally keep such motions from interfering with the "divine" or reasoning element of the soul as

---

[39] This interpretation of psychic parthood is not original. Versions of it have been defended or suggested by a number of earlier commentators, e.g. Taylor (1927: 281), Carone (2005a: 50), Crombie (1962: 344–5), and Woods (1987: 25). The accounts of Gerson (2003a: 100–5) and Kamtekar (2009) are also somewhat similar to my own. Gerson argues that psychic parthood consists in being an *archē* of action, which he identifies as "the first moving cause" or the "terminal or ultimate explanation for an action," and Kamtekar characterizes the soul parts as distinct capacities or "powers" to do and experience certain kinds of things. Cf. Schiefsky (2012: 333–6), who suggests that on Galen's interpretation of tripartition, the parts of the soul are three "powers," and that "as powers, the three elements of the soul are viewed primarily as sources of motivation" (p. 335).

[40] There is controversy over whether to read the ψυχὴ πᾶσα at 245c5 in the collective sense as "*all* soul" (as I translate it) or in the distributive sense as "*every* soul"; see Allen (1981: 100–3), de Vries (1969: 121), Ferrari (1987: 124), Hackforth (1952: 64–5), and Nicholson (1999: 156–8). Nothing in what follows turns on this interpretive issue, however.

much as possible (69c–e).[41] Finally, Timaeus' account culminates in an unambiguous statement of the idea that the soul engages in motion: "There are, as
we have said many times now, three distinct forms of soul that reside within
us, each with its own motions (*kinēseis*)" (89e3–5). Significantly, he not only
attributes motion to the soul here, but also seems to distinguish or define the
three parts of the soul in terms of their distinct motions.[42] He apparently takes
this claim to be fundamental to the psychological picture he has been developing throughout his whole speech, moreover, since he expresses it as the
reiteration of a point he has already made "many times."

The second view is that the soul's motion is a source or cause of the motion
of *bodies*. In the *Phaedrus*, Socrates explains that what moves itself, the soul, "is
also the source and spring of motion in everything else that moves" (245c7–8),
and he goes on to distinguish two ways in which soul produces bodily motion:
from outside the body in the cases of soulless objects, and from inside the body
in the case of ensouled living things (245e). In the myth that follows, Socrates
provides a vivid example of the latter kind of motion through his account of
the experiences and behavior of a lover and his beloved when they are
together. Importantly, whether the lover approaches the young boy or not,
and whether the two of them indulge in intimate sexual behavior or not, is
determined by the interactions and struggles that take place within each of
them among the three elements of their souls, represented in the myth by the
charioteer and his horses. That is to say, the activity and movements of the
soul's parts are the source and cause of the person's actual bodily movements
involved in approaching the boy or engaging in sexual activity.

The idea that the soul's motions are the cause of bodily movement is also
implicit throughout Timaeus' account. The circular motion of the heavenly
bodies, for example, is explained by their ensoulment (38e–39b), and human
actions originate in emotions and other motivations within the soul (70b).
A similar picture is found in the *Laws*, where the Athenian Visitor defines the
soul as "the motion capable of moving itself" and identifies it as "the cause of
all change and motion in all things" (896a–b).[43] He further identifies the soul's
motions with various kinds of psychological activities and motivations:

---

[41] Johansen (2004: 140–52) argues that the disruptive necessary motions lead to the creation of the
tripartite soul, and he also advocates a literal reading of the circular motions that constitute (at least the
world-soul's) rationality.

[42] A similar idea appears to be at work in *Republic* 9: Socrates argues that each of the three soul parts
has its own kind of pleasure (581c) and goes on to say that "the coming to be of either the pleasant or
the painful in the soul is a sort of motion (κίνησίς τις)" (583e9–10).

[43] For discussion of the soul as a source of self-motion in *Laws* 10, see Halper (2003) and Parry
(2003).

Soul then drives (*agei*) all things in heaven, on earth, and in the sea through its motions (*kinēsesin*)—which are named wishing, investigating, supervising, deliberating, opining correctly and falsely, rejoicing, being pained, being bold, being fearful, hating, and desiring—and through all the motions (*kinēseis*) that are akin to these or primary; these take over the secondary motions (*kinēseis*) of bodies and drive (*agousi*) all things to growth and decay, separation and coalescence, and to the qualities that accompany them.

(896e8–897b1)

Although the *Laws* contains no explicit endorsement of tripartite theory, this account speaks to the consistency with which Plato, throughout his mature reflections on psychology, took the soul to be defined both by its own motion and by its capacity to produce bodily motion. All of this points to my preferred understanding of tripartition. If the soul is essentially and primarily a source of motion, then it stands to reason that Plato's division of the soul into three "parts" amounts to a division into *three distinct* sources of motion. Simply put: the embodied human soul consists of three independent sources of the psychic motions that constitute motivations, and those motivations in turn cause the bodily motions that constitute human action and behavior.[44]

Additional support can be found in Socrates' introduction and defense of the tripartite soul in Book 4 of the *Republic*. The very question that frames his discussion is illuminating: Socrates wants to investigate whether we learn, become angry, or desire the pleasures of food, drink, and sex with the *whole* soul on each occasion, or whether we engage in each of these activities with three different things within the soul (436a–b). What is at stake from the beginning of his argument, in other words, concerns motivations, psychological activities, and—by clear implication—the behavior associated with them.[45] At this initial point in his discussion, Socrates does not specify what it means for us to engage in a psychic activity or have a motivation "with" the soul ("with" translates a relatively noncommittal Greek dative), but the rest of his argument makes it clear that the soul is not merely a passive tool we use. We do not get angry "with" the soul in the way we hit a nail "with" a hammer;

---

[44] Note also an historical case for this way of understanding Plato's account: it makes his approach to psychology continuous with that of his predecessors in the pre-Socratic tradition. As Aristotle recounts in Book 1 of *De Anima*, early philosophers widely took *motion* to be an essential feature of the soul. Democritus, for example, identified the soul with fiery or fire-like atoms, because fire is an especially dynamic and mobile element (403b31–404b9). Moreover, Aristotle explicitly counts Plato among those who take the soul to move the body in virtue of its own motion (406b26–407b6). Cf. Reeve (2017: 81–2, n. 34).

[45] Cf. Calabi (1998: 189).

rather, the soul itself has an importantly active role in motivation. I will not attempt to dissect the precise logic of Socrates' subsequent argument, which previous commentators have examined in great detail.[46] I would, however, like to draw attention to two passages from his discussion that bear on the soul's relationship to motivations and actions. The first is his characterization of motivation in terms of opposite activities. Socrates' argument for the tripartite soul crucially relies on two main premises: the so-called "Principle of Opposites," which states that "the same thing will not be willing to do or experience opposites in the same respect, in relation to the same thing, at the same time" (436b8–c1; cf. 436e8–437a2); and the premise that motivations are the sort of thing that can be "opposite" to one another in the relevant way.[47] In particular, motivational states such as appetites and wishes are forms of, or pertinently analogous to, members of the opposite pairs that are assent and dissent, wanting to have something and rejecting it, or taking something and pushing it away. In his defense of this second premise, Socrates asks:

> Wouldn't you say that the soul of someone who has an appetite (*tou epithu-mountos*) longs (*ephiesthai*) for the object of his appetite, or that it draws toward (*prosagesthai*) what he wishes (*bouleta*i) to have; or again, that insofar as he wishes (*ethelei*) for something be provided to him, his soul nods assent (*epineuein*) to itself as if in answer to a question and stretches out (*eporegomenēn*) toward the fulfillment of his wish?...And what about not willing (*aboulein*), not wishing (*mē ethelein*), and not having an appetite (*mēd' epithumein*)? Aren't these among the very opposites—cases in which the soul pushes (*apōthein*) and drives (*apelaunein*) things away?   (437c1–10)

Here Socrates characterizes the soul as the source of motivations in a strong sense. When we as embodied human beings are motivated to do something, our soul is *itself* doing something that constitutes our being motivated: it is "drawing toward" something, "nodding assent," "stretching out," or alternatively, "pushing" or "driving" something away. This language clearly implies that motivations are or involve some sort of activity of the soul.

---

[46] See, for example, Bobonich (2002: 223–35), Brown (2012: 56–62), Irwin (1995a: Ch. 13), Lorenz (2004a and 2006a: Ch. 2), Robinson (1971), and Woods (1987).

[47] A close analysis of the argument would also need to account for the role of Socrates' point that "thirst itself is by nature only for drink itself." Because that issue is not of immediate relevance here, I leave it aside.

This point is further illustrated by the second passage, in which Socrates presents his first psychic division between (what he goes on to identify as) the reasoning and appetitive parts of the soul:

s. The soul of the thirsty person (*tou dipsōntos*), insofar as he's thirsty, wishes (*bouletai*) for nothing else other than to drink, and reaches out (*oregetai*) for this and rushes off (*hormai*) toward it.

GL. Plainly.

s. Therefore, if something drags (*anthelkei*) it back when it is thirsting, wouldn't that be something different in it from whatever thirsts and drives (*agontos*) it like a beast to drink? It can't be, we say, that the same thing, with the same part of itself, in relation to the same, at the same time, does opposite things.

GL. No, it can't.

s. In the same way, I suppose, it's wrong to say of the archer that his hands at the same time push (*apōthountai*) the bow away and draw (*proselkontai*) it toward him. We ought to say that one hand pushes (*apōthousai*) it away and the other draws (*prosagomenē*) it toward him.

GL. Absolutely.

s. Now, would we assert that sometimes there are thirsty people who are not willing (*ouk ethelein*) to drink?

GL. Certainly, it happens often to many different people.

s. What, then, should one say about them? Isn't it that there is something in their soul, urging (*keleuon*) them to drink, and something different, preventing (*kōluon*) them from doing so, which masters the thing that urges (*tou keleuontos*)?

GL. I think so. (439a9–c8)[48]

Once again motivations involve psychic activities: the soul "wishes," "reaches out," "rushes off," "drags," "thirsts," "drives," "urges," and "prevents." This second passage goes further, however: it shows that the question of whether the soul is divided *is* the question of whether there is only one or more than one source or subject of the psychic activities that constitute motivations. Socrates' argument is designed to show that what is doing the urging and striving in the soul when a person is motivated to drink is distinct

---

[48] For ease of reading, here and elsewhere I indicate which character speaks each line. Note, however, that the whole conversation of the *Republic* is reported by Socrates using phrases like "I said" and "he said," which I omit.

from what is doing the preventing and drawing away when the thirsty person refrains from drinking. His conclusion, in other words, is that the opposed motivations originate in two distinct sources of activity in the soul—namely, the reasoning and appetitive parts. When Socrates goes on to argue for further distinctions between the appetitive and spirited parts and between the spirited and reasoning, therefore, the ultimate conclusion he reaches—that the soul consists of three "parts," "classes," or "forms"—is plausibly understood as the conclusion that there are three distinct sources or subjects of the psychic activities that constitute motivations.

The particular language Plato uses to characterize the activities of the soul and its parts in the passages above is also significant. He employs a variety of terms that collectively emphasize the soul's responsibility for motivations and the actions that result from them, in at least three ways. First, Plato uses a number of terms that indicate movement toward or away from something—rushing off, reaching for, pushing away, and so on. This matters because such terminology describes the most basic and obvious physical actions in which people or animals actually engage when motivated to do or avoid something: when we want something (say, a drink), we approach it, reach for it, or bring it toward us; when we are averse to something, we move away from it or push it away from us.[49] Plato's choice of language, then, suggests that when we perform actions associated with desiring or being averse to something, it is because one or more parts of our soul is engaging in internal psychic versions of those actions.[50] We reach out for something because a part our soul is, in a sense, "reaching out" for it within us. The application of physical language to the soul in this way must be partly metaphorical—the soul does not literally have hands with which to reach or push, for instance—but by characterizing the soul's activities as pursuit-like and avoidance-like, such language suggests

---

[49] This parallel is further highlighted by Plato's use of the same terminology to describe the motion of an archer's hands when he draws his bow: one hand "pushes" the bow away and the other "draws" or "drags" it toward him. Notably, in Aristotle's own account of animal motion, he claims the "activities" (ἔργα) of movement consist in "pushing" (ὦσις) and "pulling" (ἕλξις) (DM 703a19–20), and his preferred generic term for "desire" is ὄρεξις, literally "a reaching out." Furthermore, although Aristotle rejects Plato's tripartite soul as a basis for soul-division in general, he accepts that desire or orexis comes in the three forms Plato identifies—rational, appetitive, and spirited (DM 700b22, EE 1223a26–7); he identifies desire by its role in causing animal movement (DA 433a22–b1, DM 700b35–701a1); and he implies that Plato's theory errs in part by "dividing up" this motive faculty of desire (DA 432b5–7). All of this suggests that Aristotle takes Plato's three parts of the soul to be three sources of action.

[50] Cf. Lorenz (2006a: 26 and n. 17), who suggests that opposed motivations might either "involve" or be "relatively like" movements of the soul in opposite directions. Miller (1999) similarly argues that the Republic advances a "kinetic theory of motivation" that conceives of desires and aversions as motions of some kind.

that those activities are the antecedent causes of *our* actual pursuit or avoidance of things.

This point is emphasized in a second, somewhat different way by Plato's use of the language of "driving" and "dragging." Significantly, the two Greek terms involved—*agō* (to "lead," "drive," or "draw") and *helkō* (to "drag" or "draw")—along with their cognates and synonyms, appear prevalently in Plato's discussions of the soul and are among his favorite ways of characterizing psychic states and motivations. They appear throughout the *Republic*, and in the myth of the *Phaedrus* the inner struggle of the lover is depicted as involving "driving" (*agomenō*, 254b2) and "dragging" (*helkusai*, 254c1; cf. 254d4, 254d7), along with "pulling against" (*antiteineton*, 254a7; cf. 254c3) and "jerking" (*spasas*, 254e3). Such language is also especially prominent in the *Laws*, where the Athenian Visitor presents a vivid image of the human being as a kind of "divine puppet" containing various "cords" (*neura*), "drags" (*helxeis*), "strings" (*smērinthoi*), and "pulls" (*agogē*) that "jerk" (*spōsin*) and "draw away" (*anthelkousin*, 644e3) toward different actions (644d–645b; cf. 659d–e). Terminology of this kind, like "reaching," "stretching," or "rushing" above, once again expresses physical movement toward or away from something, but with additional connotations of passivity that capture something about the experience of having (at least some of) our motivations. When we want something, we feel "drawn" to it. Sometimes—especially when we have *conflicting* motivations about the object or action—we feel "dragged" or "pulled" toward it, with all the associations of force that those terms can bear. Indeed, Plato often characterizes the soul's parts simply as "forcing" one another or the person to do something (e.g. at *Rep.* 440a–b), and he sometimes couples the language of "drawing" and "dragging" with this language of violence. Such terminology raises questions about the precise nature of the relationships the parts of the soul bear to one another and to the person, some of which will be addressed in later chapters.[51] For now, the important point is that when *we* feel drawn or pulled toward something, it is the parts of our souls that are doing the drawing and pulling.[52] Once again, in other words, Plato's language emphasizes that the parts of our soul are sources of the motivations that lead to our behavior.

---

[51] See esp. Ch. 7.1.

[52] Whiting (2012: 187–8, n. 15) claims that it is not actually the parts of the soul that drag the agent at *Rep.* 439c–d, but rather the agent's individual desires and (Whiting thinks) beliefs. I think this is at least misleading: if there is any sense in which the desire itself is doing the dragging, it is that the desire *is* the dragging.

Third, Plato uses terms that express desire or motivation themselves in significant ways. The first passage above (437c1–10) contains a notable ambiguity: the subject of several of the verbs of motivation could be either the person or the soul itself. Grammar allows, that is, the following alternative to the translation provided above: "Wouldn't you say that the soul of someone who has an appetite longs for the object of *its* appetite, or that it draws toward what *it* wishes to have; or again, that insofar as *it* wishes for something be provided to it, his soul nods assent to itself as if in answer to a question and stretches out toward the fulfillment of *its* wish?"[53] On this reading of the sentence, Socrates is suggesting that when a *person* has a desire, it is not simply because his soul is engaging in *some* activity (e.g. "drawing toward" or "nodding assent") in virtue of which we can attribute a desire to the person, as my original translation suggests. Rather, when a person has a desire, his soul is doing the actual desiring *itself*. The second passage (439a9–c8) in fact presents exactly this idea but without any ambiguity. Initially it is the *person* who is thirsty, but in the Socrates' next lines it is the *soul* itself that is thirsty and "wishes" for drink. This reflects a broader practice that we find throughout Plato's accounts of the tripartite soul: he often alternates seamlessly between attributing psychic activities and states to the embodied person and attributing them directly to the soul or one of its parts. This is evident, for example, in the phrases he uses to refer to the parts of the soul. The reasoning part, for instance, is called both "that which has calculated about better and worse" and "that with which *a human being* learns," and the spirited part is called "that by which *we* become spirited" and, later in the same passage, "that which *is* irrationally spirited."

This looseness has given rise to controversy among commentators about whether, properly speaking, it is the human being or one or the other part of their soul that is the subject of motivations and other psychological states and activities.[54] I have two lines of response to that debate. First, I think the issue ultimately turns on how Plato identifies motivations. On the one hand, the soul clearly engages in motion (as the passages from the *Phaedrus*, *Timaeus*, and *Laws* indicate) and is thus the *subject* of psychic motion. If, therefore, motivations are nothing *more* than certain kinds of psychic motion, then it makes sense to say that the soul is indeed the proper subject of those

---

[53] This reading of the sentence is reflected in the translation of Bloom (1968).

[54] Lorenz (2006a: 27–8) distinguishes between proper and derivative subjecthood and argues that the soul's parts are the *proper* subjects of desires and aversions in the *Republic*, while the person and the soul as a whole are only *derivative* subjects of them. Cf. Bobonich (2002: 226–7 and 528–9, n. 14) and Burnyeat (1976: 33). Price (2009) rejects this idea and argues that the soul parts are not (and cannot be) psychic subjects. Cf. Stalley (2007: 73) and Woods (1987). Cairns (2014: paras. 57–63) offers what I take to be the most convincing treatment of the issue.

motivations themselves. On the other hand, the *Timaeus* and remarks scattered throughout Plato's discussions suggest that many of our motivations and psychological states involve not only psychic motion, but also concomitant physiological conditions.[55] If many or all motivations are, speaking precisely, constituted by a combination of psychic motion *and* physiological condition, then arguably it must be the embodied person, not the soul itself, that is the proper subject of those motivations. Nonetheless, even if Plato accepts the latter view, we can still account for his willingness to attribute motivations directly to the soul by the fact that psychic motions are, from his point of view, the defining or most important constituent of motivation.

My second line of response is to note that this issue seems to be one that obsesses modern scholars much more than it ever did Plato. It is clear, in any event, that Plato himself was entirely comfortable ascribing a variety of activities and motivations both to the embodied human being and to their soul or one of its parts. And for my own purposes, that is all that matters. The interpretation of parthood I have advocated requires only that the soul's parts are the immediate *sources* of the motivations that lead to human action. The fact that Plato often speaks as if the soul is also the *subject* of the motivations to which it gives rise—whether or not it actually is the subject in the strictest sense—only serves to emphasize the soul's role in human motivation. The kind of responsibility the soul's parts bear for a person's various desires and wishes is so robust, in Plato's mind, that it is sometimes appropriate to speak as if they are the parts' *own* desires and wishes. This again strongly suggests that one of the defining features—if not *the* defining feature—of psychic parthood for Plato is being a source of the psychological activities and motivations that lead to human action.[56]

Finally, my preferred understanding of parthood is supported by Plato's actual *use* of the theory of tripartition in his works. In Book 4 of the *Republic*, the theory provides the resources to explain the specific actions that human beings do or refrain from doing in the cases Socrates examines: whether thirsty people drink or not, and whether (in cases I discuss in the next chapter)

---

[55] For example, in the *Republic*, Socrates claims that appetites come into being διὰ παθημάτων τε καὶ νοσημάτων (439d1–2), and he later characterizes "hunger, thirst, and the like" as κενώσεις τινές εἰσιν τῆς περὶ τὸ σῶμα ἕξεως (585a8–b1).

[56] My understanding of psychic parthood and the spirited part of the soul is thus at odds with the one offered by Renaut (2014: 163–4) in his study of Platonic *thumos*. On his view, each of the three parts is defined by *exactly one* unique capacity or function: "La raison *ne* fait *que* calculer, la fonction désirante *ne* fait *que* porter l'individu vers l'objet désiré, et la fonction intermédiaire *ne* fait *que* rendre sensible l'individu à un certain nombre de valeurs." Although I admire much in Renaut's book, I find this account of tripartition implausible, given the strong reasons for thinking all three parts have (or are) motivational capacities.

Leontius looks at the corpses or Odysseus immediately slaughters his adversaries, are all explained in terms of the soul's three parts. Plato's interest in tripartition extends further than the etiology of specific actions, however. He is also, and arguably more, interested in understanding why people live the *lives* that they do.[57] This is demonstrated, perhaps most obviously, by Plato's use of tripartite theory in his extensive analysis of different types of psychic "constitutions" in *Republic* 8 and 9. It is also reflected in the connections he explores between tripartite psychology and the so-called "doctrine of three lives," the idea that there are essentially three main types of human beings and corresponding lifestyles: the lives of the wisdom-lover, the honor-lover, and the money-lover.[58] This idea appears like a refrain, in various guises, in works that span his entire career.[59] It is significant, then, that when he invokes the doctrine in the context of tripartite theory, he explicitly links the three parts of the soul to the three lives. In Book 9 of the *Republic*, for example, Socrates explains that the reason there are three main types of people is that there are three parts of the embodied soul: what kind of person someone becomes depends on whether the reasoning, spirited, or appetitive part "rules" their soul (580d–581c).[60]

As I will also attempt to show in subsequent chapters, Plato uses the insights into human behavior and the philosophical resources provided by tripartite theory to develop educational and political proposals designed to foster virtue and stability in individuals and the cities they inhabit. The fact that Plato's actual application of tripartition throughout his works is overwhelmingly focused on the goal of understanding human behavior and promoting virtuous living adds further support to the idea that the parts of the embodied soul are, first and foremost, three sources of motivation. On this understanding, what is important to Plato about the tripartite soul is its role in human action: there are three distinct and often (but not necessarily) competing sources of desire

---

[57] This idea informs Rist's (1992) interpretation of tripartition. Cf. Annas (1981: 125).

[58] Scholars have debated whether the doctrine of three lives is originally Platonic or has an earlier Pythagorean provenance. The ancient evidence for the latter view derives largely from a story about Pythagoras ascribed to the fourth-century Academic Heraclides, recounted in Iamblichus (*Pyth.* 12.58–9), Cicero (*Tusc.* 5.3.8–9), and Diogenes Laertius (*Lives* 8.8). Festugière (1971) and Jaeger (1948: 431–3 and 432, n. 1), however, argue (rather persuasively) against a Pythagorean origin of the doctrine. Ultimately, though, I think the doxographical issue has little bearing on how to understand Plato's theory of the soul. As Grube (1980: 133 and n. 1) rightly notes, even if Plato was inspired by a preceding Pythagorean doctrine, his theory goes well beyond that doctrine.

[59] E.g. at *Apol.* 29d–e, *Phaedo* 82b–c, *Symp.* 205d, and *Laws* 632c–d.

[60] Likewise, in the *Timaeus*, Plato applies the idea that each of the three parts of the soul engages in distinctive kinds of motion directly to the doctrine of three lives: as a result of "exercising" the motions of one or another part of their soul, an individual ends up living a life devoted to "appetites," "love of victory," or "love of learning" and "wisdom" (89e–90d). Cf. *Phdr.* 250e–251a and 256b–c.

in our psychology that dictate how we act and live our lives, and for that reason, both our individual ethical destinies and our collective political ones ultimately depend on the soul's parts and how they relate to one another. The parts of the soul directly cause us embodied human beings to do the things that determine whether we become virtuous or vicious, and *that* represents Plato's primary interest in tripartite psychology.

Here one final point of clarification about my interpretation is apposite, which is that although this account of psychic parthood is the one I will assume in the rest of this book, the arguments and conclusions I will be presenting should be of interest even to those who understand the parts of the soul differently. For one thing, my understanding of the soul's parts is relatively minimalist. To be sure, it is not entirely deflationary. It does not dismiss Plato's talk of parthood or attempt to reduce tripartite theory to a mere taxonomical tool for classifying human desires. Nonetheless, its claims are modest in comparison to many of its competitors. It does not, for example, attribute a discrete psychological life or consciousness to each part of the soul and does not take the parts to be robustly agent-like. This modesty means that it should be inoffensive to commentators who resist or reject the literalist end of the interpretive spectrum. At the same time, its modesty also means that the view admits of amplification or inflation. My own view is that the account of parthood I have offered represents the *minimum* one that is both entailed by Plato's discussions of the tripartite soul and required by the full philosophical use he makes of it. Commentators who take Plato's theory of tripartition to be more extravagant than I do, and hence to require stronger assumptions about psychic parthood, will naturally want to make additions to my interpretation, but they need not reject the basic idea that the soul's parts are discrete sources of psychological activity and motivation. The minimalist account, then, should be tolerable to commentators who favor a wide range of interpretations.

Furthermore, and most importantly, this book is as much—indeed, arguably more—about spirited *motivations* as it is about the spirited part of the soul. Many of the insights I hope to offer into Plato's thinking about spirited psychology and its relation to ethics, education, and politics will stand (or, for that matter, fall) regardless of the particular views about psychic parthood and tripartite theory that one accepts. Even commentators who think the three parts of the soul are nothing more than three species of human desire and emotion, for example, will, I hope, find that I have valuable things to say about the spirited species of motivation. It is to that topic that I now turn.

2

Spirited Motivation and the Two Faces of *Thumos*

When I refer to "spirited" motivations in this book, I will have in mind motivations that are attributed to the spirited part of the soul under tripartite theory. For the sake of economy, I will be using the term "motivations" in a relatively elastic way. The term will serve as a "catch-all" that refers not only to desires, emotions, and impulses (like the emotion of anger or desire for honor), but also to psychological qualities and states that we might be more inclined to classify variously as tendencies, dispositions, or sensitivities (such as irascibility, understood as the tendency to feel the emotion of anger with relatively little provocation). That is to say, "motivations" will cover not only the psychic motions or activities that immediately cause or motivate human behavior (roughly, what Aristotle classifies as *pathē*) but also the underlying dispositions or habits a soul part has to engage in the motions that cause or motivate human behavior in those ways (roughly, what Aristotle classifies as *hexeis*).[1] What they have in common for Plato is that they all play a role in the process of motivating or inhibiting, and hence ultimately in causing and explaining, human action and behavior.

In this chapter I have two main aims. The first is to establish which sorts of motivations count as "spirited" for Plato in works that feature tripartition, and the second is to provide a new interpretative framework for understanding those motivations. In Section 1, I begin with a traditional survey of motivations whose status as "spirited" in Platonic psychology requires relatively little defense, because previous commentators have already widely and standardly attributed them to the *thumoeides*. I accept this "traditional" catalogue of spirited motivations as well but think it is incomplete. In Section 2, I argue that the traditional picture should be expanded in order to account for the full range of spirited desires and emotions. My argument will be grounded in a close analysis of *Republic* 375a–376c, the crucial passage from Book 2 in which Plato first introduces his conception of "spiritedness" in the dialogue through

---

[1] For Aristotle's distinction between *pathos and hexis*, see *NE* 1105b19–1106a14.

The Political Soul: Plato on Thumos, Spirited Motivation, and the City. Josh Wilburn, Oxford University Press.

an analogy to noble dogs. I will argue that Plato understands spirit in that passage as the source of *both* aggression toward what is "unfamiliar" or "foreign" (*allotrion*) *and* gentleness toward what is "familiar" or "one's own" (*oikeion*). According to this interpretation, the spirited part of the soul is responsible not only for feelings associated with anger and hostility, but also for feelings of friendship and affection for others. Finally, in Section 3, I offer a new interpretation of spirited motivation that is informed by this expanded view. According to my account, the dual aspects of spiritedness presented in Book 2 represent primitive expressions of two interconnected and complementary sides of spirited motivation as Plato understands it—an aggressive or competitive side, on the one hand, and a gentle or affectionate side on the other. The seemingly diverse range of spirited desires and emotions can be understood in terms of these two faces of spiritedness.

1. Traditional Survey of Spirited Motivations

The motivations I survey in this first section are all ones that have been commonly identified as spirited.[2] Although I offer brief explanation and textual evidence in support of attributing them to the *thumoeides*, their place in Plato's understanding of spirited psychology should be fairly uncontroversial. My survey in this section focuses on the *Republic*, which provides by far the richest and most informative passages on *thumos* and spirited motivation, though I also draw on the *Phaedrus* and *Timaeus*. Following the lead of previous authors, I organize my discussion below according to the three main sections of the *Republic* that explicitly discuss spiritedness: Socrates' introduction of the ideal warrior nature (Book 2), his argument for tripartition (Book 4), and his analysis of psychic constitutions and final defense of the just life (Books 8–9).

Plato's treatment of spirited motivation begins in *Republic* 2, in an important passage to which I will return in the next section, when Socrates and Glaucon seek to identify which qualities the warriors of their just city must possess. Socrates heuristically proposes that with respect to being an effective "guardian," the nature of a young man should be just like that of a well-bred dog. In both cases guardianship requires, to begin with, certain physical

---

[2] Commentators who identify motivations surveyed in this section as spirited include Cairns (1993: 381–92), Cooper (1984: 12–17), Cross and Woozley (1964: 120–3), Gosling (1973: Ch. 3), Hobbs (2000: 9–31), Lear (2006), Lyons (2011: 359–60), Moss (2005), Renaut (2014: 15–16), and Singpurwalla (2010: 883–4).

attributes such as sharp senses, speed, and strength. It also requires certain *psychological* characteristics, Socrates explains:

> Each must, furthermore, be courageous (*andreion*), if it is to fight (*macheitai*) well... And will any living thing, whether it is a horse or dog or anything else, ever willingly be courageous (*andreios*) if it is not spirited (*thumoeidēs*)? Or haven't you noticed how unbeatable (*amachon*) and invincible (*anikēton*) spirit (*thumos*) is, so that its presence makes every soul fearless (*aphobos*) and unconquerable (*aēttētos*) in the face of everything?... The physical qualities of the guardian, then, are obvious... And also those of his soul—namely, that he must be spirited (*thumoeidē*).   (375a9–b7)

With these remarks the terms *thumos* ("spirit") and *thumoeidēs* ("spirited") appear for the first time in the *Republic*. Note, however, that at this point in the dialogue, Plato has not yet introduced either tripartition or the spirited part of the soul, and in this passage *thumos* cannot be equated with what he goes on in Book 4 to identify as the spirited psychic part.[3] Indeed, although commentators often use the term *thumos*, as I do in this book, to refer to the part of the soul, Plato himself more often uses *thumos* to refer to the spirited *emotion* of anger or martial passion, and that is the usage we find here.[4] (For the soul part itself he occasionally uses *thumos* but generally prefers one of the expressions surveyed in Chapter 1.) Although Socrates is not yet talking about the spirited part of the soul explicitly, however, he is nonetheless drawing attention to what Plato ultimately considers an important class of spirited *motivations*. The spirited part of our nature, on his view, is the source of the emotion of *thumos* and other qualities or impulses associated with aggression and combat. Here Socrates initially mentions, in particular, fearlessness, courage, and indomitability. This last quality is especially emphatic. Socrates describes *thumos* with three different Greek terms that indicate, literally, the difficulty or impossibility of defeating something in battle, of being victorious over it, and of

---

[3] Arguably it is not until Plato first uses the substantive expression τὸ θυμοειδές (410d6) in Book 3 that he finally offers a proleptic reference to the spirited part of the soul. Cf. discussion in Hobbs (2000: 6–7).

[4] Accordingly, when Socrates says that their warriors must be "spirited" and that the presence of *thumos* makes a person or animal fearless, he does not mean that the spirited *part* must be present in their souls, nor that the mere presence of that part makes a creature brave and fearless. For Plato's theory attributes a spirited part to human souls *in general*, yet he clearly thinks many people would not make good soldiers, and that people and creatures with spirited parts often experience fear. Likewise, when Socrates comments in Book 5 that some women are θυμοειδής and others ἄθυμος (456a), he does not mean that some possess a spirited part of their souls while others do not. Rather, he means that some women have the spirited temperament that befits an auxiliary, while others do not. Even in Homer, there is no question that even cowards possess *thumos* (e.g. *Il.* 5.643, 13.279–83).

overcoming or besting it. Throughout the subsequent discussion of early education we find the list of aggressive and martial motivations expanded: spiritedness is responsible for making individuals and animals savage (*agrioi*, 375b9, 410d1, 410d4, 410d6, 411e1), harsh (*chalepoi*, 375c2, 376a5, 410d8), and prone to the use of violence (*biai*, 411d8), particularly toward those who are "foreign" or "unfamiliar" (*allotrioi*). We can also add boldness or rashness, along with anger, strength, daring, and endurance, to this group of spirited qualities and states that tend to promote hostile behavior and vigorous fighting.

The fact that Socrates introduces spirited motivations through a comparison to noble puppies, and that he attributes spiritedness and associated qualities and impulses to dogs, horses, and other animals, is also significant. It confirms, first of all, that on Plato's view not just human beings, but also other animals, possess spirited psychology. In this respect he follows the lead of his predecessors and contemporaries. We have seen in Xenophon that *thumos* and spiritedness were increasingly associated in the fifth and fourth centuries with the two animals used in aristocratic hunting: dogs and horses.[5] In early epic and poetic literature, moreover, spirit is attributed or compared to a number of different animals, including not just dogs and horses but also leopards, bulls, lambs, hares, birds, boars, wolves, and lions.[6] The association of *thumos* with lions has especially deep roots. "Lion-spirited" (*thumoleōn*) is a common epithet throughout the early tradition,[7] and a number of authors compare the *thumos* of courageous individuals to that of a lion:

... with a tawny lion's spirit (*thumon*) in his breast.   (Tyrtaeus, fr. 13)[8]

---

[5] Notably, Socrates later identifies "love of hunting" itself as characteristic of spirited individuals (549a), and he identifies Glaucon as an avid hunter (459a–b), while Adeimantus attributes spirited "love of victory" to his brother (548d). Indeed, talk of hunting is prominent throughout the *Republic*, particularly as a metaphor for philosophical inquiry (e.g. 432b–c), and Glaucon often serves as Socrates' enthusiastic supporter in his "hunt," thereby seeming to parallel the role of the spirited auxiliaries in relation to the philosopher-rulers of the ideal city. Cf. Xenophon, *Mem.* 3.6.1–18. Commentators who discuss Glaucon's "spiritedness" include Barney (2002: 214), Bloom (1968: 337–44), Craig (1994: 44–5), Gallagher (2004), Hammond (2005), Peterson (2011: 150–1), and Strauss (1964: 90–1, 112). For a different analysis, see Ferrari (2005: 21–5). It is at least fair to say that Plato flags Glaucon as possessing some qualities he identifies as spirited.

[6] For examples, see Homer, *Il.* 10.491–2 and 16.467–9 (horses), 16.352–5 (lambs), 22.263–4 (lambs and wolves), 17.21–2 (boars), and *Od.* 3.449–55 (bulls); and Hesiod, *Shield* 386–91 (boars). Frère (2004: 154–62) provides a useful overview of the various animals with which *thumos* is associated in early Greek literature and Plato.

[7] E.g. Homer, *Od.* 4.724 and 4.814; Hesiod, *Th.* 1007; and Aristophanes, *Frogs* 1041.

[8] Cf. Bacchylides, *Ode* 1.140–4.

Also relevant is the fact poetic writers often compare spirited humans to spirited animals when they want to emphasize the savageness or brutality of individuals or their actions:

> Like a savage-minded (ōmophrōn) wolf, the spirit (thumos) we have acquired from our mother cannot be soothed.   (Aeschylus, Lib. 421–2)[9]

Plato's association of thumos with "savageness" (to agrion) in Republic 2, therefore, is well-grounded in earlier usage.

Plato's attribution of thumos to animals in Book 2 also suggests that he takes a number of central spirited motivations to be relatively primitive: they are brute impulses and qualities that both humans and animals possess, or can possess, by nature. This point is confirmed throughout Plato's depictions of the tripartite soul. Most obviously, perhaps, in Book 4 Glaucon endorses the distinction between the spirited element of the soul and the reasoning, remarking, "Even in small children, one can see that they are full of thumos right from birth," whereas they initially lack capacities for rational calculation, to which Socrates responds, "That's very well put. And in animals too one can see that what you say is true" (441a7–b3). Infant humans and animals alike, then, possess spirit and express it in their behavior from the time they are born.[10] Plato also, as noted in Chapter 1, often likens the spirited part of the soul and spirited human beings to certain kinds of animals. In the Republic he repeatedly draws on the comparison of warriors to dogs (416a, 422d, 440d, 451d, 466c–d); he likens unduly vicious spirited individuals to wolves (416a); he uses metaphors to depict the spirited part of the soul itself as both a dog (440d) and a lion (588d, 590a–b); he describes spirit as "ape-like" and "snake-like" (590a–b);[11] and in the Phaedrus he represents spirit as a noble and

---

[9] See also Homer, Il. 24.41–3, "[Achilles] is set on savageness (ἄγρια), like a lion that at the urging of his great power (βίη) and mighty spirit (θυμῷ) goes out against the flocks of men to win himself a feast"; and Euripides, Her. 1210–13 and Medea 1342–3.

[10] For a study of Greek attributions of spirited anger to infants, see Hanson (2004).

[11] Jaeger (1946: 124–6) suggests that the term ὀφεῶδες ("snake-like") must be a corruption of ὀργῶδες ("capable of anger"), because "the snake has no resemblance whatever with the θυμοειδές and its qualities." However, two points tell against this. First, snakes do have at least one important trait in common with thumos, on Plato's view: both can be "calmed" or "charmed." Glaucon earlier likens the spirited character Thrasymachus to a "snake (ὄφις) that has been charmed (κηληθῆναι)" (358b2–3), and at 411b2 a person can "charm" (κηλῇ) their thumos with music. (See Wilson [1995] for attention to Thrasymachus' spiritedness.) Second, the ancients did, in fact, view snakes as prone to anger. In his De Ira (1.1.6), for example, Seneca lists the snake alongside other beasts who display their anger in visibly horrifying ways: inflantur irritatis colla serpentibus. Cf. Posidonius F169.12–18 in Kidd (1972 and 1999). These considerations undermine the motivation for Jaeger's emendation, and given that ὀργῶδες would be a hapax legomenon ("a lost word of the Greek language," Jaeger calls it), such motivation would need to be quite strong in order to justify the correction. Arruzza (2018: 52 and n. 14) also

obedient horse (246b, 253d). On Plato's view, then, some animals share distinctive features of our spirited psychology, and the spirit within our own souls can itself be understood (at least in some metaphorical sense) as beast- or animal-like.

Plato's next major discussion of *thumos* in the *Republic* appears in Book 4, where Socrates defends the tripartite theory of the soul and finally identifies the *thumoeides* as a discrete psychic part. After he has argued for a division between reason and appetite, Socrates asks whether "the part that contains spirit and by which we become spirited" is a third part of the soul, or whether it has the "same nature" as one of the other two. When Glaucon suggests that it might be identical with the appetitive part, Socrates invokes the infamous case of Leontius. According to the story Socrates has heard—and Glaucon, too, evidently (440a4)—Leontius was walking home from the Piraeus when he noticed some corpses lying by the Long Wall near the public executioner. Leontius wanted—literally, "had an appetite" (*epithumoi*)—to look at them, but he was also disgusted (*duscherainoi*) and turned away. He struggled (*machoito*) with himself and covered his face, but ultimately, "overcome by his appetite (*kratoumenos...hupo tēs epithumias*)," he opened up his eyes, ran toward the corpses, and exclaimed: "Look for yourselves, you evil wretches, take your fill of the beautiful (*kalou*) sight!" Socrates explains, "This story certainly shows that anger (*tēn orgēn*) sometimes wages war (*polemein*) against the appetites as if it were something different" (439e6–440a6).[12]

In the remarks that follow, Socrates and Glaucon elaborate further on spirit's relationships with appetite on the one hand and reason on the other:

s. Don't we often notice in other cases as well that when appetite is forcing someone contrary to reasoning, he reproaches (*loidorounta*) himself and becomes spirited (*thumoumenon*) against what's doing the forcing in him, so that of the two factions that are fighting a civil war, so to speak, spirit (*thumos*) becomes the ally of reason (*summachon tōi logōi*)? But I don't

---

defends the legitimacy of ὀφεῶδες. Reeve (2013a: 156) wrongly takes the term to refer to appetite, but that is implausible on grammatical and contextual grounds, both for the reasons just stated and others discussed in Adam (1902, ii: 365–6).

[12] There is some controversy over the precise nature of Leontius' appetite. Most commentators, e.g. Reeve (1988: 129, 137), take Leontius' appetitive desire to be sexual in nature. Ferrari (2007: 180–2), following Allen (2002: Ch. 10), rejects the sexual reading and proposes instead that what Leontius wants to look at is "the sight of justice wrought on criminals." While I have no special attachment to the sexual reading, clearly Leontius' desire needs to be distinctively appetitive for Socrates' argument to make any sense. I find Ferrari's reading unsatisfying in this respect, because it is unclear why we should think Plato would attribute a desire to gaze upon the work of justice to *appetite*. On the contrary, appetite seems characteristically insensitive to considerations of justice (e.g. at *Tim.* 70b). For additional discussion, see Tarnapolsky (2010a: 10–13) and Liebert (2013).

think you can say that you've ever seen spirit, either in yourself or anyone else, ally itself with an appetite to do what reason has decided must not be done.

GL. No, by god, I haven't.

S. And what happens when a person thinks he has done something unjust (*adikein*)? Isn't it true that the nobler he is, the less he gets angry (*orgizesthai*) if he suffers hunger, cold, or the like at the hands of someone whom he believes to be inflicting this on him justly (*dikaiōs*), and won't his spirit (*thumos*), as I say, refuse to be roused (*egeiresthai*) against that man?

GL. That's true.

S. But what happens if, instead, he believes that someone has been unjust (*adikeisthai*) to *him*? Doesn't the spirit within him boil (*zei*) and become harsh (*chalepainei*), fighting for what he believes to be just (*summachei tōi doukounti dikaiōi*)? Won't it suffer hunger, cold, and the like, and stand its ground (*hupomenōn*) until it is victorious (*nikai*), not ceasing from noble actions until it either succeeds, dies, or calms down (*praünthēi*), having been called to heel by the reason within him, like a dog by a shepherd?

GL. Spirit is certainly like that. And, of course, we made the auxiliaries in our city like dogs obedient (*hupēkoous*) to the rulers, who are themselves like shepherds of a city. (440a8–d6)

Socrates takes this to show that the spirited part is not appetitive after all. Rather, "in the civil war within the soul it sets its arms far more on the side of the rational part" (440e4–6), and it is "by nature the auxiliary of the rational part" (441a2–3). Socrates is so successful in establishing the closeness of spirit and reason, in fact, that his final task is to show that spirit is not simply "some form" of the rational part itself. For that he invokes the well-known case of Odysseus. When the rightful king of Ithaca finally finds his way home after many years away, he discovers that a throng of insolent suitors has been aggressively courting his faithful wife Penelope. Odysseus plots revenge on the suitors, but his plan is jeopardized when, hearing maidservants sneak off at night to assignations with the suitors, he becomes enraged and wants to exact hasty vengeance by killing them all right away. However, he checks his spirited anger by, as Socrates quotes, "rebuking his heart (*kradiēn*) with word

---

[13] *Od.* 20.17. Note that Socrates' conclusion rightly assumes the synonymity of "heart" and *thumos* in the Homeric passage. Cairns (2014: para. 46) comments, "Without citing any of the lines that actually contain the word, Plato is able to rely upon his readers' ability to make the link between Odysseus' address to his κραδίη and the Homeric θυμός."

(*muthōi*)."[13] Socrates concludes from the passage, "Here Homer clearly represents the part that has calculated about better and worse and does the chastising as different from the part that is spirited without calculation (*tōi alogistōs thumoumenōi*)" (441b7–c2).

In this discussion we find characteristics of spirited motivation that were already central in Book 2. Most notably, the spirited part of the soul is strongly connected with fighting and is the source of "harshness" and the emotion of anger.[14] Here in Book 4 Plato also considerably expands his conception of spirited motivation, however. One of the most important additions is that spirit is characterized as having both a cooperative relationship with the reasoning part and an antagonist relationship with appetite. The *thumoeides* is the "auxiliary" (*epikouros*) or "ally" (*summachos*)—literally, "fellow fighter"—of reason in the soul, and the reasoning part is able to "calm" spirit down or keep it in check simply by "rebuking" it. In subsequent remarks we also find that spirit is capable of being "obedient" to reason (*hupēkoōi*, 441e6), "following" it (*hepomenon*, 442b8), "carrying out [its] decisions" (*epiteloun ta bouleuthenta*, 442b8–9), and "preserving" its announcements (*diasōizēi*, 442c1). By contrast, we find that spirit "wages war" against and gets "angry" with appetite, and that together with reason it "fights" against recalcitrant appetitive desires. Similar characterizations also appear in both the *Phaedrus* and *Timaeus*. In the former, the spirited good horse is "obedient" (*eupeithēs*) to the "command" (*keleusmati*) of the charioteer who represents reason, and together they resist the pulling of the appetitive bad horse (253c–254e).[15] In the *Timaeus* the spirited part of the soul is supposed to "listen (*hupēkoon*) to reason and together with it restrain the part consisting of appetites by force" whenever necessary (70a5–7). Plato, then, consistently presents spirited motivations as both naturally supportive of rational motivations and often in tension with appetitive ones.[16]

---

[14] Thus Plato describes spirit's activity in the soul using a martial metaphor throughout the passage; the two cases used to distinguish spirit from the other parts of the soul both involve anger; and *orgē* is even used as a synonym for *thumos* at 440a5.

[15] Some commentators, by contrast, perceive a shift in the role of *thumos* in Plato's theory in the *Phaedrus*. Weinstein (2018: 35, n. 6), for example, claims that in the *Phaedrus*, "a critical aspect of the *Republic*'s view is absent: *thumos* plays no special role in assisting reason in its interaction with the appetites." Cf. Gerson (2003a: 134, n. 156). This reading is puzzling. The good horse is responsive to the charioteer's commands and strains against the bad horse, just as in the *Republic* the spirited part listens to reason and acts as its ally in resisting appetite. In both texts, moreover, the spirited element is associated with love of honor, shame, and sensitivity to accusations of cowardice. The myth does not provide nearly as many details about the good horse as the *Republic* does about the *thumoeides*, but the ones it does provide do not suggest any change in spirit's nature or psychic function.

[16] In Chapter 3.2, however, I also address ways in which spirit can and often does come to support and serve appetite and its desires. Their relationship is complicated.

Next, Book 4 also shows that the spirited part of the soul is sensitive to considerations about justice and injustice, and that this sensitivity is explicitly connected to the emotion of anger. When a person believes he is the victim of injustice, he becomes angry and fights against it; when he believes he is being subjected to physical pain or discomfort justly, by contrast, he does not get angry about it (at least, insofar as he is noble). This seems to represent a more complex or sophisticated expression of anger than the sort suggested in Book 2, where the aggression in question was directed not against perceived injustice, but simply against the "unfamiliar" (*allotrion*) or "unknown." The main difference is that in Book 4, Socrates highlights spirit's sensitivity to justice and injustice partly in order to demonstrate its close relationship with *reason*. In other words, what distinguishes the hostility of Book 2 (the sort shared with other animals) from the anger of Book 4 is that the latter occurs when spirit is in the psychic company of a rational part. This connection is even clearer in the *Timaeus*, where we are told that "spirit's might" will "boil over at a report from reason that some unjust action involving these members [of the body] is taking place—something being done to them from outside, or even something originating from the appetites within" (70b3–5). A similar phenomenon can also be observed in Socrates' account of courage later in *Republic* 4: he claims that a person is courageous "when the spirited part preserves through pleasures and pains the announcements of reason about what is and is not fearful" (442b9–c3). In Book 2 courage was characterized as a primal spirited quality found even in irrational wild animals; now, however, courage evidently requires both the presence of reason and spirit's cooperation with it. These discussions indicate that spirit's role as the "ally of reason" involves its responsiveness to certain kinds of rational judgments, prominently including judgments about what is just and unjust, fearful or not fearful. I return to and fill in the details of this relationship in Chapters 7 and 8.

Book 4 also points to another important class of spirited motivations: the *thumoeides* is the source of a twofold concern with, and reaction to, what the agent perceives as either admirable (*kalon*) or its opposite shameful (*aischron*). On the one hand, spirited motivations include an attraction to what is admirable; feelings of admiration and awe toward, and a desire to praise, what appears admirable in others and their actions; and the emotion of pride in response to perceived admirability in oneself.[17] On the other hand,

---

[17] For examples of spirited attraction to the *kalon* outside of Plato, see Bacchylides, fr. 20b.19–20; and Theognis, *Eleg.* 1.695–6: "My heart (θυμέ)...endure: you're not the only one to have a passion for noble things (τῶν καλῶν)"; and cf. the association of love of the *kalon* with the (spirited) desires for

they also include a complementary aversion to what appears shameful; feelings of blame, disgust, and disdain toward what appears shameful in others and their actions; and the emotion of shame, *aischunē* or *aidōs*.[18] On the Platonic and Greek understanding, spirited shame includes both retrospective feelings of shame when agents take themselves to have done something disreputable, as well as a forward-looking sense of shame, typically rooted in respect for others, that inhibits individuals from acting in ways they take to be ignominious, especially in front of those whose opinions they value.[19] Book 4 hints at this class of motivations through Leontius' spirited opposition to his appetites: he feels "disgusted" by the thought of looking at the corpses; he covers his head, a paradigmatic way of expressing shame in Greek culture; and he angrily tells his eyes to behold the "admirable" sight, a sarcastic description of something he actually considers extremely "shameful" or "ugly" (hence his disgust).[20] Spirited concern for what is shameful and admirable is also taken for granted throughout the discussion of early education in Books 2 and 3 (as I discuss more in Chapter 6), and the connection between *thumos* and shame is especially emphatic in the *Phaedrus*. The spirited horse of the myth is "a lover of honor along with moderation and shame," it is "controlled always by shame," it "drenches the whole soul with sweat out of shame and astonishment," and it resists the pull of its yokemate "with shame" (253d–254e).

Book 4 also draws attention to spirit's role as a psychic source of endurance. This is suggested first of all by Socrates' use of the Homeric passage in which Odysseus "speaks" to his *thumos*. The very next line of the poem, which records Odysseus' actual words to himself, states, "Endure (*tetlathi*), heart, you have endured (*etlēs*) worse before."[21] This next line would have been

---

revenge and honor in Herodotus (*Hist.* 7.11.16–18) and Xenophon (*Cyrop.* 1.3.3.4–5), respectively. For especially insightful discussion of the connection between *thumos* and the *kalon* in Plato, see Lear (2004: 137–45 and 2006). For an example of a "proud" (ὑψηλόφρων) *thumos*, see Euripides, *Iph.* 919.

[18] The association of *thumos* with shame is especially prominent in Homer and throughout Greek literature, e.g. Homer, *Il.* 6.523–5, 15.561, 15.661; and Pindar, *Nem.* 9.26–7. For an example of spirited disdain (ὑπερφρονεῖν), see ps.-Anacreon, *Anac.* 58.13–14.

[19] Plato does not, like some Greek authors, consistently distinguish between *aischunē* and *aidōs* in his usage, and in fact often uses them interchangeably—e.g. at *Laws* 646e–647b, where he straightforwardly identifies them. Konstan (2006: 93–9) and Tarnapolsky (2010b: 11–13) both discuss the distinction between *aischunē* and *aidōs* in Greek literature, and Tarnapolsky also concludes that Plato typically uses the two terms synonymously. For more on shame in Plato and Greek ethics and psychology, see Cairns (1993), Hamblet (2011: Ch. 3), Militello (2020), Tarnapolsky (2010b), Williams (1993: Ch. 4), and Woodruff (2000: 143–6).

[20] Some commentators also emphasize the presence of other people when Leontius looks at the corpses—at least the executioner, and possibly other witnesses too, since the story becomes well-known. See Hobbs (2000: 17), Ferrari (2007: 181), and Bieda (2012: 147–8).

[21] *Od.* 20.18 Ferrari (2007: 186) notes that a literal translation of Odysseus' rebuke is: "You have endured 'more dog' (*kunteron*) than this." Hence the canine metaphor does some additional subtle work in Socrates' allusion.

familiar to Plato's readers, and as Socrates reminds Glaucon, he has actually already quoted *both* lines of the passage earlier as an illustration of admirable fortitude (390d4–5). The repetition of the passage in Book 4, then, brings with it the attribution of endurance to the "heart" that was explicit earlier in their conversation.[22] Book 4 also elucidates the connection between *thumos* and endurance in another way. As noted above, Socrates explains that noble individuals will not become angry when they "suffer through" justly inflicted bodily pain or hardship. Conversely, a victim of perceived injustice will "stand their ground" and put up a spirited fight for justice, despite "suffering" bodily pain or discomfort, even if that persistence ultimately leads to his demise. The language of "standing one's ground" and "suffering through" is, for the Greeks, the language of soldierly endurance.[23] This passage further illuminates Socrates' earlier characterization of *thumos* as fearless and indomitable. Those motivated by strong *thumos* are willing to sustain bodily discomfort, injury, or even death in order to achieve their spirited aims, and their fearless imperviousness to concerns about bodily well-being makes them especially ebullient and formidable warriors.[24]

Finally, two key discussions in *Republic* 8 and 9 offer informative and overlapping portraits of spirit and spirited motivation. First, in Book 8 Socrates discusses four main types of non-virtuous individuals and the political regimes that correspond to them. The first character and regime he analyzes are the "timocratic" man, who is "ruled" by his spirited element, and the analogous "timocratic" or "timarchic" constitution. Socrates' description of both provides insight into the motivations and behavior that are prominent in individuals and cities dominated by spiritedness. Second, in the course of defending the supreme happiness of the just life in Book 9, Socrates offers further details about the spirited part of the soul and spirited lives and individuals. The most notable development in these two discussions is that both of them emphasize the centrality of the desires for honor, victory,

---

[22] The association between *thumos* and "endurance," especially of suffering, pain, risk, or hardship, is also strong in Homer and the poetic tradition. For example: "If again some god shall smite me on the wine-dark sea, I will endure (τλήσομαι) it, having in my breast a spirit (θυμόν) that endures affliction (ταλαπενθέα)" (*Od.* 5.222; cf. *Il.* 10.232). Cf. Tyrtaeus, fr. 5.4–6; Theognis, *Eleg.* 1.825–6; and Hesiod, *WD* 147. Plato could, therefore, fully expect his audience to recognize or assume this connection.

[23] Note also Socrates' examples of what a person animated by *thumos* will "suffer through": twice he mentions hunger, cold, and "everything else of the sort." Significantly, Socrates has just identified hunger and other impulses related to bodily affections as expressions of appetite. Hunger and thirst are, in fact, the "clearest" (ἐναργεστάτας) forms of appetitive desire (437d3–4). What a person with endurance must often "endure," then, are bodily conditions to which appetite is constitutionally averse.

[24] In this respect Plato's description of *thumos* as "unbeatable" (ἄμαχόν) is reminiscent of Heraclitus, DK B85. Cf. Democritus, DK B236.

power, and reputation in spirited psychology. In Book 9 Socrates asks, "What about the spirited part? Don't we say it is always wholly eager to pursue power and victory and good reputation? ... So wouldn't it be appropriate for us to call it 'victory-loving' (*philonikon*) and 'honor-loving' (*philotimon*)?" (581a9–b3). Likewise, we learn that "due to the dominance of spiritedness" in the timocratic city, "one thing alone is most distinctive in it: love of victories and love of honors" (548c5–7). The timocratic individual himself, moreover, is identified as loving victory, ruling, and honor, having turned over control of his soul to "the part that loves victory and is spirited" (549a, 550a–b). Outside of the *Republic*, the spirited part of the soul is described as "victory-loving" in the *Timaeus* (70a3), and the spirited horse of the *Phaedrus* is "a passionate lover of honor" (*timēs erastēs*, 253d6). Throughout Plato's accounts of tripartition, then, spirit and spirited individuals are distinguished by competitiveness, ambition, and (like their Homeric predecessors) a concern with status and reputation—traits that express the desire for *timē* and sensitivity to the economy of honor.

Books 8 and 9 also offer assorted details about spirited souls and individuals that are related to or expand on what we have already seen. In Book 8 we find that the timocratic individual is "stubborn" (*authadesteron*); he is a lover of music and speeches, though skilled in neither; he is "savage" (*agrios*) with slaves but "obedient" (*hupēkoos*) to rulers; he places high importance on "warlike deeds and everything related to war"; he loves gymnastics and hunting; and he is "disdainful" (*kataphronoi*) and "proud" or "high-minded" (*hupsēlophrōn*) (548e–549b, 550b). In Book 9 we also learn more about some of the psychological flaws associated with spiritedness. Love of honor can lead to envy (*phthonōi*) and love of victory to violence (*biai*); spirited individuals can be characterized by "bad temper" (*duskolia*) and irrational anger; and the spirited part of the soul can acquire "cowardice" (*deilian*) instead of courage or become excessively "strained" through stubbornness (*authadeia*) and bad temper (586c–d, 590a–b).

2. Spirit and the *Oikeion*

The traditional catalogue of motivations just surveyed is crucial to understanding Plato's account of the spirited part of the soul. It is, however, incomplete. In particular, it fails to fully recognize an important class of spirited motivations that involve gentleness and feelings of affection for others. In order to make my case for this expanded conception of *thumos*, I return now for a closer examination of the extended passage at *Republic* 375a–376c, where, as we saw above, Plato first introduces spiritedness into the text. Immediately after Socrates determines that the guardians must be "spirited" in order to be courageous and effective warriors, he notices a problem. Spirited individuals, he suggests, are likely to be "savage" (*agrioi*) and "harsh" (*chalepoi*) not only to enemies (*polemious*), but also to their fellow citizens (*politais*). Yet if they are going to be good guardians, they must be "gentle" (*praious*) to those within their city—those who are "familiar" (*oikeious*) to them; otherwise, they will destroy the city themselves before outside aggressors have a chance. The problem, then, is that their warriors must be both "gentle" (*praion*) and "great-spirited" (*megalothumon*), but gentle nature and spirited nature are opposites of one another and seem impossible to combine. Socrates and Glaucon are at a loss until Socrates recalls the comparison with which they began their discussion:

s.   We overlooked the fact that there *are* natures of the sort we thought impossible, natures in which these opposites are indeed combined... You can see them in other animals, too, but especially in the one to which we compared the guardian, for you know, of course, that a well-bred dog has a character of this sort by nature—he is as gentle (*praiotatous*) as can be to those he's accustomed to and knows (*tous sunētheis te kai gnōrimous*), but the opposite to those he doesn't know (*tous agnōtas*).

GL. I do know that.

s.   So the combination we want is possible after all, and our search for the good guardian is not contrary to nature.

GL. Apparently not.

s.   Then do you know that our future guardian, besides having spiritedness (*toi thumoeidei*), must also be by nature philosophical (*philosophos*)?

GL. How do you mean? I don't understand.

s.   It's something else you see in dogs, and it makes you wonder at the animal.

GL. What?

s.   When a dog sees someone it doesn't know (*agnōta*), it gets angry (*chalepainei*) before anything bad happens to it. But with someone it knows (*gnōrimon*), it warmly welcomes (*aspazesthai*) him, even if it has never received anything good from him. Haven't you ever wondered at that?

GL. I've never paid any attention to it, but obviously that is the way a dog behaves.

s.   Surely this is a refined quality in its nature and one that is truly philosophical.

GL. In what way philosophical?

s. Because it distinguishes anything it sees as either a friend (*philēn*) or enemy (*echthran*) on no other basis than that it knows (*katamathein*) the one and doesn't know (*agnoēsai*) the other. And how could it be anything besides a lover of learning (*philomathes*), if it defines what is familiar (*oikeion*) and what is foreign (*allotrion*) to it in terms of knowledge (*sunesei*) and ignorance (*agnoiai*)?

GL. It couldn't.

s. But surely the love of learning (*to philomathes*) is the same thing as philosophy or love of wisdom (*philosophon*)?

GL. It is.

s. Then, may we confidently assume in the case of a human being, too, that if he is to be gentle (*praios*) toward his own (*tous oikeious*) and those he knows (*gnōrimous*), he must be a lover of learning and philosophical?

GL. We may.

s. Then anyone who is to be a fine and good guardian of our city must have a nature that is philosophical (*philosophos*), spirited (*thumoeidēs*), fast, and strong. (375b9–376c5)

The key to resolving Socrates' initial puzzle lies in the distinction between two kinds of social groups: the *allotrion* and the *oikeion*. The term *allotrion* literally means "other" and comes to have the meaning "foreign," "strange," or "unfamiliar," often with connotations of hostility; hence in the above it includes those who are "unknown" or "enemies." The term *oikeion* literally means "belonging to the household" and comes to have the meaning "familiar," "one's own," "part of one's family," "kin," or simply "friendly"; in the above it includes those who are "known," along with one's fellow citizens and friends. Based on this distinction, Socrates makes a point derived from readily observable canine behavior: dogs are harsh and aggressive toward strangers, but gentle and affectionate toward those they recognize. This shows that spiritedness and gentleness not only *can* be combined after all, but already *are* combined, by nature, in the temperament of many dogs.

The Greek word Socrates uses to characterize a dog's response to people it knows, *aspazesthai*, is significant. The term means, in the first instance, "to welcome or greet warmly or with kindness," and it can also refer both to actions that express warm greeting, such as embracing, kissing, or (as in the case of dogs) fawning, as well as to the feelings that motivate such action, such as cherishing or feeling kindness, warmth, love, or affection toward someone.

Hence in the passage from Book 2 at hand, we find that dogs "warmly welcome" those they consider "friendly" (*philēn*), and in Plato's *Lysis*—a dialogue about what it means to be a "friend"—the terms *philein* ("to love, feel friendship") and *aspazesthai* are at one point used interchangeably (217b). Likewise, in a telling passage from the *Symposium*, Aristophanes explains that young men who enjoy intimacy with and befriend (*philousi*) older men do so because they are masculine and courageous and "tend to cherish (*aspazome-noi*) what is similar (*homoion*) to themselves"; they grow up to be men who love boys because, again, they "cherish (*aspazomenos*) what is related (*sun-genes*) to them"; and when such a man meets a young boy who is his "other half," he is "struck by friendship (*philiai*) and a sense of familiarity (*oikeiotēti*)" (191e–192c).[25] Here, as in Book 2, *aspazesthai* and feelings of friendship are synonymous: both are the natural and spontaneous responses to what is familiar or related to oneself. And in the Book 2 discussion, Socrates evidently takes the friendly relationships that should exist among citizens to be the same in kind as "warm embracing" and love or friendship between individuals. All of this matters because it shows that the primitive displays of gentleness and warmth that a dog exhibits toward its master are on a single continuum of affectionate emotions that extends all the way to the feelings of kindness, love, and respect associated with familial relationships, friendship, and ultimately political fellowship. Just like well-bred dogs, the spirited guardians of the city must possess not only savageness toward enemies, but also the gentleness appropriate to family, friends, and fellow citizens.

The central interpretive question for my purposes is whether the quality of "gentleness" and feelings of affection experienced by dogs and humans toward the *oikeion* are *spirited* qualities and feelings. Do they have their origin, that is, in the spirited part of the soul, or rather in one of the other two parts? Surprisingly few commentators address this issue, despite the evident impor-tance of the Book 2 passage to the psychological picture Plato develops in the text. Most commentators who do say something about it, however, assume that *reason*, rather than spirit, is the source of human gentleness and affec-tion.[26] At least three considerations initially seem to support this reading. First, Socrates clearly identifies gentleness as the "opposite" of spiritedness, which

---

[25] Cf. also *Parm.* 128a, where *philia* is characterized as a way of being *oikeion*.
[26] Nettleship (1935: 14–17), for example, takes gentleness to be "almost equivalent to" love of wisdom, and similar views are explicit or implied in Bloom (1968: 364), Nichols (1988: 53), North (1966: 170–1), Popper (1962: 53), and Renaut (2014: 256–61). Two important exceptions are Tarnapolsky (2007: 299, 309–12; cf. 2010a: 2), who explicitly attributes both harshness and gentleness to *thumos*, and Brennan (2012), who offers an especially insightful discussion of spirit's attachment to the *oikeion*.

makes it difficult to see how gentleness could *itself* be a "spirited" quality. Second, the passage is explicit that gentleness requires being "philosophic," and the "philosophic" aspect of human nature that is discussed throughout Books 2 and 3 is eventually identified with—or at least, identified as a nascent form of—the reasoning part of the soul. This might in turn might suggest that gentleness and affection are themselves rational motivations. Third, a later passage in Book 3 seems to confirm this reading. Having earlier assumed that musical and gymnastic education were for the soul and the body, respectively, Socrates now begins to revise his position. He notices that excessive attention either to gymnastics at the expense of music, or to music at the expense of gymnastics, has noticeable effects on the *soul*. When Glaucon asks what effects he has in mind, Socrates explains:

S.   Savagery (*agriotētos*) and hardness (*sklērotētos*) in the one case, and softness (*malakias*) and tameness (*hēmerotētos*) in the other.

GL. I get the point. You mean that those who devote themselves exclusively to physical training turn out to be more savage (*agriōteroi*) than they should, while those who devote themselves to music and poetry turn out to be softer (*malakoteron*) than is admirable for them?

S.   And surely the spirited part of their nature (*to thumoeides tēs phusēs*) provides the savageness (*to agrion*). If rightly nurtured, it would be courageous (*andreion*), but if it is strained (*epitathen*) more tightly than it should be, it would likely become hard (*sklēron*) and harsh (*chalepon*).

GL. That is my opinion.

S.   And what about this? Wouldn't the philosophic nature (*hē philosophos phusis*) hold the tameness (*to hēmeron*)? And if it is relaxed (*anethentos*) somewhat more, it would be softer (*malakoteron*) than it should be, while if it is finely nurtured, it would be tame (*hēmeron*) and orderly (*kosmion*)? (410d1–e3)

Here "tameness" is clearly parallel to its synonym "gentleness" in the earlier passage: both are opposed to the "savageness" and "harshness" that are attributed to spiritedness or the spirited aspect of the soul. Jointly, then, the passages identify two opposed groups of qualities: on one side are savageness, harshness, hardness, and the aggression associated with them; and on the other are gentleness, tameness, softness, and the affection associated with them. For the sake of simplicity, call the first "aggressive" motivations and the second "gentle" ones. In the Book 3 passage, Socrates states that "the philosophic nature" is what "has" or "holds" (*echoi*) tameness in the soul, which suggests that reason (or the immature form of it in children or adolescents) is the source of gentleness, tameness, and motivations associated with them. If that is right, then feelings of affection toward the familiar are not ultimately spirited, but rather *rational*.

Despite the prima facie case for attributing gentle motivations to the reasoning part, however, there are compelling reasons for rejecting it. To begin with, the arguments in its favor are weaker than they initially appear, for two reasons. First, although Plato identifies spiritedness as the opposite of gentleness in the Book 2 passage, note that he has just used the term "spirited" to describe the psychology of dogs, horses, and human beings who fight fearlessly and tenaciously as a result of feeling or possessing strong and aggressive *thumos*. It carries with it connotations of animals that are wild and pugnacious, as well as its connection to the invigoration of *thumos* that is distinctive of impassioned and violent Homeric warriors. It is true, then, that "spiritedness" in this sense is the opposite of the gentleness and affection displayed toward loved ones, but "spiritedness" in this sense is not intended to cover any and all motivations that Plato eventually wants to attribute to the spirited part of the soul.[27] The passage does not show, therefore, that all "spirited" motivations are fundamentally opposed to gentleness. Significantly, perhaps, in the second, Book 3 passage, Plato no longer opposes gentleness to "spiritedness" itself, but instead to "savageness," "hardness," and "harshness."

Next, the Book 3 passage (410d1–e3), which initially seems to support this reading, is itself rather vexed upon closer examination of the Greek. Socrates first says that the spirited aspect of nature provides savageness and explains that depending on how "it"—that is, *to thumoeides tēs phuseōs*—is nurtured, it can become either courageous or unduly harsh. That much is straightforward enough. A difficulty arises in the case of tameness, however. Socrates says that the philosophic nature "holds" tameness, and that depending on how "it" is nurtured, it can become either tame or unduly soft. To preserve the parallel here, we would expect the "it" to refer to "the philosophic nature"—that is, *hē philosophos phusis*. As James Adam points out in his commentary, however, this is a grammatical impossibility. The adjectives used are neuter, and therefore can only refer to "tameness" (*to hēmeron*), not the feminine "philosophical nature." This means that it is tameness, not philosophic nature, that is

---

[27] As a general rule, when Plato uses the adjective *thumoeidēs*, he applies it more restrictively to animals or people who exhibit the savage or aggressive side of *thumos* (in keeping with its contemporary usage). He attributes both aggressive *and* gentle motivations to the spirited part of the soul, however, which he refers to using the noun expression *to thumoeides*.

"relaxed" or "nurtured," and that as a result becomes either excessively "soft" or appropriately "orderly" and "tame." This is not exactly a felicitous result (Adam calls it "hardly tolerable"). On this reading Socrates is making the odd claim that when "tameness" is properly nurtured, it becomes "tame." I submit, speculatively, that the grammatical infelicity may reflect the fact that (as I argue in what follows) Plato clearly takes the relevant softness and tameness to be attributes of the spirited part of the soul, not the reasoning, and hence resists language that might suggest otherwise. More importantly, given the textual issues, we should not rest the case on this passage alone, especially in the face of strong countervailing evidence.

There is a more substantial argument against attributing gentle motivations to reason, however, which we can see by considering how the "philosophic" aspect of the soul is introduced through Plato's canine analogy. According to Socrates, dogs must be "philosophical" or "wisdom-loving" by nature, since they distinguish who is an enemy and who is a friend through "learning" or "knowing" the latter but not the former. If they were not "philosophical" in this way, they would not be gentle to their *oikeioi*. It is on this basis that Socrates concludes that the guardians must also be "philosophical" in order to be gentle to their friends and fellow citizens. The problem that immediately arises if we attribute gentle motivations to the reasoning part of the guardians' souls, however, is that well-bred dogs exhibit that same class of motivations, yet canine souls do not, on Plato's view, contain an active reasoning part.[28] For Plato, non-human animal souls consist only (or at most) of appetitive and spirited parts. This is, in fact, a point that Socrates himself makes in the course of defending the distinction between spirit and reason. Recall that when Glaucon observes that infants are full of spiritedness but lack reasoning, Socrates adds that the same is true of animals.[29] If we insist on attributing gentle motivations to the rational part of the *human* soul, therefore, we face a dilemma: either Plato thinks dogs are also rational animals after all, or gentle motivations originate in one part of the soul in animals but another part in human beings. Both claims are dubious. The superior alternative is that gentle

---

[28] I say "active" because Plato sometimes appears to leave it open that animal souls possess some latent or inoperative form of reason. In the *Timaeus*, for example, animal souls are reincarnated souls of humans. Plausibly, those souls possess some form of reason, or rather what used to be reason in its former incarnation, but cannot *use* it given animal physiology. See Sorabji (1993: 9–12) for discussion of this issue; cf. Broadie (2012: 91).

[29] For additional evidence of Plato's view that animals lack reasoning, see *Tim.* 91d–92c; *Laws* 653e–654a, 963e; *Lach.* 196e–197c; and the etymology offered for ἄνθρωπος at *Crat.* 399c1–3: "Other animals do not investigate (ἐπισκοπεῖ) or reason (ἀναλογίζεται) about anything they see, nor do they observe anything closely." Cf. *Epin.* 977b–c. Outside of Plato, see Xenophon, *Oec.* 13.6–8; Aristotle, *DA* 429a5–8, *EE* 1225b26–30; and Theophrastus, *Sens.* 44, on Diogenes of Apollonia.

motivations originate in the same part of the soul in dogs and human alike: *thumos*.

This interpretation raises a question of its own, however. If Plato denies rationality to dogs, then why does he credit them with being (and make their gentleness dependent on their being) "philosophic"? The first point to make in response is that Plato is, if not outright joking, at least being playful in his characterization of dogs.[30] The very fact that the term "philosophical" is one Plato usually applies only to a sublimely elite class of *human beings* should already alert us that something less than literal is going on. Some commentators have seen in Plato's characterization a sideways reference to the Cynics, which does not seem implausible and may be part of what is going on.[31] I think there is a further explanation, however. Later in the *Republic*, Socrates refers to "an ancient quarrel between philosophy and poetry," in which the poets evidently liken philosophy to "a dog yelping at its master" (607b3–c3). Plato also draws attention to a similar line of jocular criticism in the *Laws*. In the course of explaining how philosophers have acquired a reputation for atheism and other blasphemy, the Athenian Visitor comments, "Indeed, the poets took to reviling them, and likening those who philosophize to dogs barking in vain, and other such senseless slanders" (967c5–d1).[32] In the Book 2 passage, then, Plato seems to be turning a familiar joke on its head: the poets and comedians suggest there is something dog-like about philosophers, and Plato in turn suggests there is something philosophical about dogs. If we take the passage's whimsical nature into account, therefore, we can avoid the conclusion that it seriously advocates ideas that conflict with Plato's sober views on psychology. Dogs are not literally "philosophical," and they do not literally possess a reasoning part of the soul like the one found in human beings.[33]

---

[30] One sign of the passage's lightheartedness is that it begins with a play on the Greek words for "puppy" and "guardian"—*skulax* and *phulax*, respectively—as noted by Adam (1902, i: 106) and Andersson (1971: 86).

[31] See Diogenes Laertius, *Lives* 6.60–1 on Diogenes the Cynic's association with dogs, and Themistius, *On Virtue* 44 for an interpretation of that association that explicitly draws on the *Republic*.

[32] Commentators on the *Laws* often draw a connection between this remark and the one in the *Republic*. See, for example, Pangle (1980: 537, n. 29), Jowett (1892: 295, n. 3), and Diès (2007: 86, n. 2). England (1976, ii: 633) even suggests that the *Republic* supplies one of the very passages to which the *Laws* is alluding. Some interpreters, however, e.g. Murray (1997: 18) and Nightingale (1995: 60–7), suggest Plato invents or embellishes the "ancient quarrel." See Most (2011) for a thorough treatment of the controversy; and cf. Adam (1902, ii: 417–18) and Ober (1998: 225, n. 125). Even if Plato exaggerates either the quarrel itself or its ancientness, however, the joint testimony of the *Republic* and *Laws* provides strong reason for thinking at least that the poets' use of some canine line of teasing was real and not merely a Platonic fiction.

[33] Note also that the first use of the term ἀρετή in the dialogue (335b8) occurs in Socrates' argument that when dogs or horses are harmed, they are harmed with respect to distinctly canine and equine virtue, respectively. Plato, then, introduces three terms that are crucial in the text—"virtue," "spirited," and "philosophical"—by way of dogs and horses.

Despite this important point, however, I do think Plato employs his playful analogy in order to hint at something serious—namely, the idea that spirited impulses must be informed by *knowledge* of some kind in order to be reliably useful.[34] A fiercely spirited animal that did not recognize or "know" anyone would treat everyone, including its own kin, as "unknown" strangers and enemies. As a hunter like Glaucon would know, a dog or horse like that would be of no value to its owner. To be sure, the kind of learning or "knowledge" that dogs achieve in order to recognize their kin is not knowledge in the Platonic sense. Presumably, it is based entirely on some combination of sense-perception and memory.[35] Nonetheless, by pointing out that even the primitive spirited instincts of dogs cannot effectively serve any salutary purpose in the absence of "knowledge," Plato is able to introduce a crucial idea that he develops over the course of the *Republic*: spirited impulses are not beneficial unless they are subordinated to reason and informed by the intelligence and knowledge that only reason can provide. Spirit must be the faithful "auxiliary" of the reasoning part within the soul, and the spirited warriors of the just city must be auxiliaries of the wise and knowledgeable philosopher rulers. Despite the fact that dogs are not literally "philosophical," therefore, Socrates' tongue-in-cheek suggestion that they are serves a dialectical purpose.[36]

In addition to these reasons for rejecting the alternative interpretation, there are decisive positive considerations *in favor* of the view that gentle motivations should be attributed to the spirited part of the soul instead. First, several passages throughout the *Republic* are unequivocal in doing just that. Perhaps most tellingly, following the vexed passage discussed above, in which Socrates initially seems to attribute tameness and softness to "the philosophic" aspect of the soul, he immediately elaborates and makes it unmistakably clear that he instead attributes those qualities to spirit. When a person begins listening to the "soft" (*malakas*) and plaintive sounds of flute-playing, Socrates explains, his previously "useless and hard (*sklērou*)" spiritedness (*thumoeides*) is

---

[34] Cf. Brennan (2012: 108). Others who discuss the "joke" and its import include Annas (1981:80–2), Bloom (1968: 350–1), Jaeger (1944a: 209), Tarnapolsky (2015: 254–5), and Weinstein (2018: 166–8).

[35] Cf. Weinstein (2018: 171).

[36] Dogs provide an especially fitting illustration of Plato's point because they are known for being exceptionally good at *recognizing* people. Odysseus' dog Argos, for example, famously identified him (and "wagged his tail") immediately, and with greater ease than Odysseus' own family and friends (*Od.* 17.300–4). The Greeks were also aware of both dogs' hostility toward strangers and their affectionate response to their kin. E.g. Heraclitus: "Dogs too bark at anyone they do not know (γινώσκωσι)" (DK B97); and Aristotle classifies dogs as animals that are τὰ δὲ θυμικὰ καὶ φιλητικὰ καὶ θωπευτικά (*HA* 488b21–2). Cf. Xenophanes DK B7, who mockingly recounts a story in which Pythagoras takes pity on an abused puppy, having "recognized" (ἔγνων) it as a "friend" (φίλου).

initially "softened like iron" (*hōsper sidēron emalaxen*) and made "useful." However, if he continues to indulge in such music, his *thumos* is "melted" and "dissolved" and finally "melts away completely" (*tēkei kai leibei, heōs an ektēxēi*) until at last he becomes a "soft" or "weak" (*malthakon*) warrior. Here it is explicit and emphatic that *thumos* is the aspect of the soul that is "relaxed" and made "soft" and "tame" by music (411a5–b4).[37] By contrast, music and poetic speech actually have exactly the *opposite* effect on the philosophical component of a person's nature: instead of calming it, they "invigorate" it or "stir it up" (*egeiromenon*, 411d4).

A second passage that follows the formal introduction of the tripartite soul corroborates this point. After stressing his idea that spirit should be reason's obedient ally, Socrates reiterates that a balanced combination of musical and gymnastic training makes the two parts harmonious "by straining (*epiteinousa*) and nurturing the one with admirable speeches and learning, while relaxing (*anieisa*) the other by soothing (*paramuthoumenē*) it, and making it tame (*hēmerousa*) by means of harmony and rhythm." (441e8–442a2).[38] This passage is important, firstly, because it functions as an indication by Plato that the philosophic and spirited aspects of nature that were discussed earlier in the dialogue (prior to the introduction of tripartition) are now being identified with the reasoning and spirited parts of the soul.[39] It is also important because it confirms the earlier picture. Musical education has the effect of "relaxing," "soothing," or "taming" the *thumoeides*, and once again, it affects the rational part of the soul in exactly the opposite way: it does not relax it, but rather "stretches" or "strains" it. Other remarks throughout the text support attributing the relevant set of qualities to spirit: it can be "made gentle" (*praünthēi*) by reason (440d3); the moderate man, before sleeping, "makes his spirited part gentle (*praünas*) and does not fall asleep with his spirit stirred up out of anger" (572a2–5); and "softness" (*malthakia*) is the blameworthy condition of an overly "slackened" (*chalasei*) or "relaxed" (*anesei*) spirited part (590b3–4).[40]

---

[37] Cf. discussion in Wersinger (2001: 172–9) and Brancacci (2005: 102–6).

[38] I analyze this extended passage in more detail in Ch. 6.

[39] See also Vegetti (1998: 136, n. 132), but cf. Irwin (1977: 330–1, n. 28) and Bobonich (1995: 319, n. 18), who doubt the correspondence between the reasoning and spirited parts of Book 4 and the philosophic and spirited elements of Books 2–3.

[40] Note also that it would be odd if the spirited part could be characterized as savage but not tame, or as hard but not soft. Aristotle actually makes a version of exactly this point, using spirit as an example: contraries belong to the same faculty, he argues; if hatred is found ἐν τῷ θυμοειδεῖ, therefore, then *philia* should be there too (*Top.* 113a33–b3).

We also find confirmation of this line of interpretation in Aristotle's *Politics*. In the course of examining which sorts of natural qualities politicians should possess, Aristotle comments:

> Some say guardians should have precisely this quality: they must be friendly (*philētikous*) to those they know (*gnōrimōn*) and fierce (*agrious*) to those they do not (*tous agnōtas*), and that spirit is what makes them be friendly (*ho thumos estin ho poiōn to philētikon*). For spirit is the capacity of the soul by which we feel friendship (*hēi philoumen*). (1327b38–1328a1)

Although Aristotle does not mention Plato by name, he is clearly referring to the passage from *Republic* 2.[41] His remarks are significant for two reasons. First, most obviously, he takes Plato's position to be that spirit is responsible not only for savageness and aggression, but also gentleness and affection.[42] My interpretation of the passage, in other words, is also Aristotle's. Second, Aristotle emphasizes feelings associated with friendship, *philia*. Although he otherwise adopts Plato's own vocabulary, Aristotle replaces the term "gentle" (*praioi*) with the term "friendly" (*philētikoi*). This shows that he identifies the "gentleness" that guardians are supposed to show toward family, friends, and fellow citizens in Plato's passage with "friendliness" or "friendship." Not only does Aristotle think spirit is responsible for gentleness, therefore, but he also takes it for granted that gentleness, on Plato's view, is identical with, or on the same continuum as, feelings of love and friendship toward others. Indeed, Aristotle is marvelously explicit that *thumos* is the part of the soul responsible for friendship. On this point, too, Aristotle's interpretation confirms my own.

Finally, this interpretation makes Plato's view of *thumos* continuous with that of the epic and poetic tradition, in two important ways. The first is that early Greek literature provides abundant precedent for attributing feelings related to friendship and affection for others to spirit. In Homeric and poetic literature *thumos* is associated not only with anger and martial passion, but also with a diverse range of emotional states that in various ways express love, care, compassion, and goodwill toward others. Of immediate relevance to the Book 2 passage, *thumos* is sometimes identified as the source of the desire to "embrace," *aspazesthai*, someone or something.[43] Beyond that, variations of

---

[41] Cf. Reeve (1998: 202, n. 32).

[42] The Peripatetic *On Virtues and Vices* also explicitly locates πραότης in the spirited aspect of the soul (1249b26–8, 1250a4–6); cf. *Rhet.* 1380a5–9.

[43] See e.g. the comic use in Aristophanes' *Peace*: on behalf of the farmers who have just been promised a return to their land, the Chorus Leader declares, "After many long seasons, my spirit

the epithets "dear (*kecharismene*) to my spirit (*thumōi*)"[44] and "beloved (*philos*) of my spirit (*thumōi*)"[45] are common in Homer, and throughout Homeric and poetic literature more generally *thumos* is the psychological site of emotions such as grief,[46] pity,[47] longing for those from whom one is separated by distance,[48] the joy of reuniting with loved ones,[49] and love and friendship themselves.[50] Achilles himself strongly endorses one form of spirited care and affection:

> From me alone of the Achaeans he has taken and keeps my wife, the darling of my heart (*thumarea*) ... Whoever is a true man, and sound of mind, loves (*phileei*) and cherishes (*kēdetai*) his own (*tēn autou*), just as I too loved (*phileon*) her with my spirit (*thumou*). (*Il*. 9.335–43)

Here Achilles not only attributes feelings of love and "cherishing" to *thumos*, but also emphasizes the manly duty of loving "one's own"—language that anticipates Plato's own talk of gentleness toward one's *oikeioi* in Book 2.

A second important point of continuity that my interpretation preserves is that Homeric and poetic literature frequently characterizes spirit using the

---

(θυμός) wants to embrace (ἀσπάσασθαι) the fig trees I planted when I was a young man" (558–9). Cf. *Euripides*, fr. 362.33–4, where excessive "embracing" (ἀσπάζομαι) is due to a "womanly *thumos*" (γυναικόφρων θυμός).

[44] E.g. at *Il*. 5.243, 5.826, 10.234, 11.608; *Od*. 4.71, 6.23.

[45] E.g. τοι φίλος ἔπλετο θυμῷ (*Il*. 23.548); ἐμῷ θυμῷ πάντων πολὺ φίλτατε παίδων (*Il*. 24.748); and ἐμῷ θυμῷ δαέρων πολὺ φίλτατε πάντων (*Il*. 24.762).

[46] For example, at the death of Patroclus, Menelaus comments: "I should be minded to stand by Patroclus' side and protect him; for his death has touched my *thumos*" (*Il*. 17.563–4). Cf. descriptions of grief and suffering at *Od*. 4.812–14, 5.81–3, and 5.156–8. *Thumos* is also the site of "worries" (μελεδήματα), e.g. *Il*. 23.62, *Od*. 4.650 and 20.56.

[47] E.g. *Od*. 19.209–10; cf. *Od*. 5.190–1, 11.55, 11.87, and 11.395. Likewise, *thumos* is affected by hearing about the sufferings of others: "Eumaeus, truly you have deeply stirred the spirit in my breast in telling all these tales of the sorrows you have had to endure" (*Od*. 15.486–7); cf. *Od*. 14.361–2.

[48] At *Od*. 11.202–8, Odysseus' mother tells him that longing (πόθος) for him ultimately wasted away her *thumos*, and in response Odysseus' *thumos* drives him to reach out and try to embrace her. Cf. *Il*. 3.139–40.

[49] When the swineherd Eumaeus is reunited with his master Telemachus, for example, he says, "Come, enter, dear child, that I may delight my *thumos* with looking at you here in my house" (*Od*. 16.25–26).

[50] In Homer *thumos* is the site of "loving" and "caring." E.g. Eumaeus speaks of his former master Odysseus with *aidōs*, "for greatly did he love (ἐφίλει) me and care (κήδετο) for me in his *thumos*" (*Od*. 14.146); cf. *Il*. 1.196, 1.209 and *Od*. 3.223. Homer also describes *thumos* as "congenial" or "likeminded" (ὁμόφρονα, *Il*. 22.263; cf. Theognis, *Eleg*. 1.81) and associates it with "friendliness" (φιλοφροσύνη, *Il*. 9.255–6), "friendship" (φιλότης, *Od*. 5.126), and "kindly affection" (φίλα φρονέῃσ', lit. "thinking friendly thoughts," *Od*. 6.313, 7.41–2, 7.75). Cairns (1993: 89–95) and Hooker (1987: 124) discuss the close connections between spirited *aidōs* and *philotēs* in Homeric literature. For select examples from the poets: Bacchylides speaks of a "friendly" (εὐμενής) *thumos* (fr. 21.3), Pindar of putting a "love-charm" (φίλτρον) into *thumos* (*Pyth*. 3.63–4), Alcaeus of a "friendly" ([εὐνόω]ι) *thumos* (fr. 34.3), Theognis of a *thumos* troubled over friendship (φιλότης, *Eleg*. 1.1091–4), and Euripides of a *thumos* "smitten with love" (ἔρωτι)" (*Medea* 6).

language of both "hardness" and "softness."[51] On the one hand, *thumos* can be described as "obdurate" (*allēkton*),[52] "tough as oak" (*prinōdē*),[53] "tough" or "stout" (*alkimon*),[54] "cold" (*psuchros*),[55] "steel-hearted" (*sidērophrōn*),[56] "hard-hearted" (*tetlēoti*),[57] "hard" or "unyielding" (*apēnea*),[58] or "swollen" (*sphigōnta*) like a tumor,[59] and it can be made of "iron" (*sidēreos*),[60] "stone" (*lithoio*),[61] "adamant" (*adamantos*),[62] or even "seven-ply oxhide" (*heptabeoious*).[63] But it can also be "warmed" or "melted" (*ianthē*),[64] "loosened" (*luōn*),[65] or "softened" (*malthassēi*),[66] and "softness" (*malakia*) is itself a synonym for cowardice (*deilia, anandria*)— which early Greek literature widely identifies as a flawed condition of *thumos*.[67] The epic and poetic use of such language, moreover, precisely parallels Plato's own: a hard, stiff, dense, or taut *thumos* is one that is vicious, aggressive, or unfeeling; and a soft, elastic, loose, or slack *thumos* is merciful, gentle, or loving. It is worth emphasizing here that neither the attribution of gentle motivations to *thumos*, nor the characterization of it in terms of the language of softness or plasticity, is in any way rare or exceptional in early Greek literature. Quite to the contrary, both are pervasive and consistent throughout the centuries of epic and poetic treatment of *thumos* leading up to the time of Plato. Previous commentators have often emphasized the indebtedness of Plato's account of spirit to the emotional role of *thumos* in Homeric and poetic literature. What they have not typically recognized in that context, and the point I am making here, is that in those early Greek depictions, the emotional role of *thumos* ineliminably involves *both* aggression *and* gentleness, hardness *and* softness. In combination

---

[51] Cf. Wersinger (2001: 172–3).   [52] *Il.* 9.636–7.   [53] Aristophanes, *Wasps* 383.

[54] Tyrtaeus, fr. 10.17, 10.24; Callinus, fr. 1.1 (and cf. 1.10, applied to ἦτορ).

[55] Sappho, fr. 42.1.   [56] Aeschylus, *Seven* 52.

[57] *Od.* 23.100, 23.168; cf. Euripides, *Medea* 865.   [58] *Od.* 23.97.

[59] Aeschylus, *Prom.* 382. Sommerstein (2008: 485, n. 45) comments: "The angry spirit is compared to a tumour, which the doctor should not attempt to reduce until it has ripened and begun to soften of itself."

[60] *Il.* 22.357, *Od.* 5.591 (cf. *Il.* 24.521 and *Od.* 4.293, applied to ἦτορ and κραδίη, respectively).

[61] *Od.* 23.103, applied to κραδίη, which is synonymous with the *thumos* of lines 97, 100, and 105.

[62] Hesiod, *Th.* 239, *WD* 147. Cf. *WD* 358–9, where theft has the effect of "congealing" (ἐπάχνωσεν) the thief's "heart" (ἦτορ), used synonymously with *thumos* of line 357.

[63] Aristophanes, *Frogs* 1017.

[64] *Il.* 24.321, 24.119; *Od.* 4.548–9, 6.155–6, 23.47; Bacchylides, *Ode* 13.220; Pindar, *Ol.* 7.42–3; Theognis, *Eleg.* 1.1122. Cf. Archilochus, fr. 25.2: [κα]ρδίην ἰαίνεται; and Bacchylides, fr. 20b.7, where *thumos* is "softened by heat" ([θάλπη]σι). Clarke (1999: 97, n. 90) notes, "ἰαίνω in non-psychological contexts refers at once to heating and to melting or softening," as in the case of "bronze, water, or wax"; Clarke also emphasizes (pp. 97–100) that *thumos* alternately "softens and coagulates" in Homer.

[65] E.g. *Il.* 23.62, *Od.* 20.56 and 23.343.

[66] Aeschylus, *Prom.* 381: applied to κέαρ, which is used synonymously with θυμόν in the next line. Cf. Aristophanes, *Wasps* 644: πεπᾶναι ("to soften by ripening") is applied to τὴν ἐμὴν ὀργήν, used synonymously with τὸν ἐμὸν θυμόν of line 648; and Euripides, *Alc.* 770: ὀργὰς μαλάσσουσ'.

[67] E.g. *Il.* 13.275–87.

with the above arguments, then, this provides further support for my interpretation. Plato does not cleave one half of spirit's emotional endowment away from its historical precedents, thereby reducing it entirely to competitiveness and aggression alone; rather, he follows the deep tradition established by his predecessors of attributing "soft" motivations to *thumos* as well.

3. A New Account of Spirited Motivation

The previous section showed that Platonic *thumos* is responsible for an even richer variety of desires and emotions than typically thought. In this section I offer a new framework for understanding the nature of spirited motivations and how they cohere with one another. In order to appreciate what is distinctive about that framework, it will be useful first to orient it in relation to other influential or historically significant attempts to account for the unity of spirited motivation, especially those from the past few decades. Although recent interpretations differ in their details, they also tend to overlap with one another on key points that can be considered well-established or "traditional." In particular, they all emphasize one or more of the following interrelated expressions of spiritedness: the desire for victory and honor; the pursuit of recognition, esteem, and pride; and the attraction to what is admirable or *kalon*. Rachel Singpurwalla provides a representative example:

> Socrates seems to think that spirit's fundamental aims are victory and honor. Thus, the spirited element wants to assert itself against an opponent and triumph, and, equally if not more importantly, it wants to be recognized and admired for this. We might say, then, that the spirited element is the source of an assertive desire to be seen both by oneself and others in a positive light, or, more specifically as being an honorable person or achieving an honorable aim.[68]

Commentators similarly argue that love of honor is at "the essence" of spirited desire,[69] or that *thumos* is "the part of us that loves to win" and is distinguished by "a competitive desire to be seen as the best" that is prominently manifested in the love and pursuit of the *kalon*.[70] Others suggest that spirited desire is rooted in "competitiveness and the desire for self-esteem and . . . esteem by

---

[68] 2010: 884. Cf. Singpurwalla (2013: 56).   [69] Brennan (2012: 109). Cf. Moline (1978: 10).
[70] Lear (2006: 118; cf. 2004: 139).

others," in "an aspiration to distinguish oneself," or in "the need to believe that one counts for something and...[the] tendency to form an ideal image of oneself in accordance with one's conception of the fine and noble."[71]

I find the similarities among these various suggestions more pronounced than their differences, and I think they all gesture in more or less the same general direction. I also think they all get something importantly *right* about spirited motivation, and my aim is to supplement rather than supplant them. To see why these traditional interpretations *need* to be supplemented, however, consider two general observations in light of the conclusions of the previous section. First, most traditional accounts (though not all) focus on relatively mature expressions of spirited motivation found in human beings, such as love of honor, making it more difficult to account for primitive expressions of *thumos* shared with non-rational animals, like the horses and dogs by way of which Plato introduces spiritedness in the first place.[72] Second, and most relevant to my own interpretation, traditional accounts focus primarily or exclusively on the aggressive and competitive aspects of spirited motivation at the expense of its gentle and affectionate ones.[73] They do not make it obvious or explicit, for example, whether or how they can accommodate something like friendship or love of one's family.[74] And although most traditionalist interpreters attribute at least *some* motivations that I am calling

---

[71] Cooper (1984: 14–15), Lorenz (2006b: 151), and Hobbs (2000: 30), respectively. Along similar lines, Cross and Woozley (1964: 118) characterize spirited motivations as "desires of ambition and self-assertion," and Calabi (1998: 199) writes, "Il tratto più caratteristico è il ruolo che vi gioca lo *thymoeides*, origine di rivalita è di ambizioni." Craig (1994: Ch. 4) argues (unconvincingly, I think) that spirit itself has two distinct *sub*-parts: one that loves honor and another that loves victory. For additional characterizations of spirited motivation in the traditionalist line of thought, see Annas (1981: 126), Arruzza (2018: 49–51), Fussi (2008: 238), Gill (1985: 8–9), Gosling (1973: Ch. 3), Nettleship (1935: 13), Purviance (2008: 2–4), and Reeve (2013a: 158–63).

[72] This emphasis is reflected in Klosko (2006: 74), who suggests that what all spirited motivations have in common is the concern "with someone's image of himself and his desire that others share that image." He acknowledges, however, that the spiritedness of animals and children is not motivated by self-image and comments, "Aside from these two exceptions, Plato's position is consistent and generally clear." Thus Klosko sees the primitive forms of spirited motivation not as the foundation of more complex expressions, but rather as *outliers* to an otherwise unified picture.

[73] Purviance (2008: 2–4), for example, characterizes *thumos* as a disruptive force in political life that operates through honor-seeking and indignation. She comments, "This is not to say that spiritedness is permanently at odds with the social world; rather it acts out when its normal course of legitimate self-seeking is blocked" (p. 4). The idea seems to be that *thumos* is *either* active and disruptive to the *polis*, or inactive and not disruptive. There is no clear place in this account for an active emotional role of *thumos* in social cooperation and peaceful political life.

[74] There are noteworthy exceptions, however. Brennan (2012: 115–18) comes closest to my presentation. He recognizes that the spirited part cares about the *oikeion* and comments, "Unlike appetite, spirit can be motivated to act for the benefit of others" or "to achieve something for the group" (p. 115). I examine his view in Ch. 3.2 further and note some important differences in our interpretations, however. Cf. remarks in Arruzza (2018: 52–4), Bloom (1968: 355), Ludwig (2007: 223), and Mansfield (2006: 207). The work of Burnyeat (2006: 9–10) and Balot (2014: 173–6) is also relevant. Finally, Tarnapolsky (2007; cf. 2010a: 12) defends a novel account of the "bipolar" nature of *thumos* that

"gentle" to the spirited part (such as shame), they nonetheless tend to reduce those motivations to, and explain them entirely in terms of, spirit's aggressive side.[75]

To some extent, it might be interjected, both points of emphasis are justified by the fact that in *Republic* 8 and 9, Socrates himself identifies the spirited part of the soul as victory- and honor-loving and as seeking good reputation—all expressions of spirited desire that reflect competitiveness and ambition, and all ones that tend to fall on the more sophisticated end of the spectrum. However, it is important to note that while Socrates' characterization certainly provides insight into Plato's conception of *thumos*, it is *not* intended either as a *definition* of spirited motivation or as an account of what all such motivations have in common. Consider Socrates' parallel description of appetite in Book 9:

> If we said that its pleasure and its love are for profit, wouldn't that best settle it under a single heading for the purposes of our argument and insure that we are clear about what we mean when we speak of this part of the soul, and wouldn't we be right to call it money-loving and profit-loving?   (581a3–7)

Two points stand out. First, Socrates' aim is rather modest: he wants to fix terminology for the sake of clarity and discussion. He is not providing a definition of the essence of appetitive desire, but simply offering a rough-and-ready characterization of it designed to facilitate the conversation at hand. Second, the terms on which he settles manifestly do not, and are not supposed to, identify what is common to all appetitive desires or what they are all rooted in. On the contrary, Socrates himself clarifies that love of money and profit are actually themselves grounded in something *else*—namely, the desire for bodily pleasure. They arise because appetites for things like food, drink, and sex "are most easily satisfied by means of money" (580e2–581a1). Love of money is a decidedly mature expression of appetitive desire, and it would be patently misleading and implausible to suggest that all appetites, including those found in non-human beasts, are at bottom derived from or constituted by it.[76] The reason Socrates characterizes the appetitive part as a lover of money and profit is rather that, as he has already established in Book 8, those are the things

---

accommodates its gentleness and concern for others. She develops her view differently, however, in that she takes *philonikia* and *philotimia* to be the distinctive expressions of the two opposite sides of spirited desire: the former of its harshness, the latter of its gentleness.

[75] Gosling (1973: 45–6), for example, characterizes shame simply as a frustrated desire to win or gain honor.

[76] Cf. Burnyeat (2006: 16–17).

around which human beings ruled by their appetites tend to organize their lives. Likewise, he characterizes spirit as a lover of victory and honor because those are the things around which people ruled by their *spirited* desires organize their lives. That is not to say in either case that those are the only appetites or spirited motivations there are, only that they are desires that conspicuously feature in the behavior and life pursuits of appetitive and spirited human beings.[77] Just as our account of appetitive motivations would be deficient if we took love of money to be the unifying principle or underlying foundation of all appetites, therefore, our account of *thumos* is similarly incomplete if we assume that the desires for victory and honor are at the heart of all other spirited motivations as well. While my own account builds on and is largely compatible with previous traditional interpretations, therefore, it also addresses what I take to be some of their limitations.

The central claim of my positive proposal is that Plato recognizes *two* faces of spiritedness, the most primitive expressions of which are the ones found in *Republic* 2: savageness and aggression toward the foreign or *allotrion* on the one hand, and gentleness and affection toward the familiar or *oikeion* on the other. The remaining spirited motivations surveyed in this chapter all emerge out of these primitive impulses and collectively constitute the two faces of spiritedness, as presented in Table 2 below. On one side are hostile and competitive motivations such as anger, envy, and love of victory. They all have in common the fact that they express, or are rooted in, aggression and the desire to distinguish oneself from, or assert oneself against, a perceived *other*.[78] This is the face of *thumos* on which previous commentators have focused, and my characterization here is in line with much of what they have to say. The crucial difference is that what they present as accounts of spirited motivation *in general* I am presenting as an account only of its aggressive side. The innovation of my approach is that it *also* recognizes the full range of, and explains, the second, "gentle" face of spiritedness as well, which includes motivations such as friendship, shame, and obedience to rulers. Gentle motivations have in common the fact that they express, or are rooted in, affection, friendship, and protective care toward "one's own," as well as the inhibitory impulses of care, consideration, respect, and restraint that often accompany such feelings. Hence those who feel respectful shame toward their superiors, for example, will hesitate to strike them, and fellow citizens who feel friendship for one another will refrain from internecine violence.

---

[77] Cf. 581c3–4, where Socrates explicitly ties this discussion to the doctrine of three lives.
[78] Cf. Annas (1981: 127), Nettleship (1935: 13), and Cooper (1984: 15–16).

Table 2. The Two Sides of Spirited Motivation

	Motivation	Transliteration of Greek Term(s) Corresponding to Bold[79]
Aggressive, competitive, assertive	(Aggression toward the) **unfamiliar**	*allotrion*
	Savageness	*agriotēs* (adj. *agrion*)
	Harshness	*chalepotēs* (v. *chalepein*)
	Hardness	*sklerotēs*
	Anger	*thumos* (v. *thumesthai*) or *orgē*
	Envy	*phthonos*
	Jealousy, rivalrous emulation	*zēlos*
	(Tendency to use) **violence**	*bia*
	(Attraction to) **war** and **battle**	*polemos; machē*
	(Sensitivity and resistance to perceived) **injustice**	*adikia*
	(Desire) **to exact revenge**	*timōrein*
	(Desire for) **fame, glory, praise, and honor**	*doxa; kleos; epainos; timē*
	(Desire) **to have a good reputation**	*eudokimein*
	(Desire to be) **admirable**	*kalos*
	Love of honor, ambition	*philotimia*
	Love of victory, competitiveness	*philonikia*
	Love of power, love of ruling	*philarchia*
	(Desire) **to control**	*kratein*
	Love of gymnastics	*philogumnastia*
	Love of hunting	*philothēria*
	Pride	*megalopsuchia* or *phronēma*
	(Being) **high-minded**	*hupsēlophrōn*
	Stubbornness	*authadeia*
	Endurance	*karteria*
	Hate	*misos*
	Boldness	*tolmē*
	Shamelessness	*anaideia*
	Rashness	*thrasutēs*
	Fearlessness	*aphobia*
	Courage	*andreia*
	Zeal, enthusiasm	*prothumia*
	(Disposition or inclination) **to blame, dishonor,** or **reproach** (inferior or shameful others)	*psegein* or *memphesthai; atimazein; loidorein;*
	Feeling disdain	*huperphronein* or *kataphronein*
	Feeling disgusted	*duscherainein* or *bdeluttesthai*

Continued

---

[79] The terms here transliterate the nominative forms of Greek nouns, neuter or masculine singular forms of adjectives, and the infinitive forms verbs, but transliterations of their other grammatical forms appear throughout this book as well when I provide them for quoted Greek, depending on how the terms are declined or conjugated in the original text.

Table 2. *Continued*

	Motivation	Transliteration of Greek Term(s) Corresponding to Bold[79]
Gentle, cooperative, affectionate	(Affection for the) **familiar**	*oikeion*
	(Inclination) **to warmly welcome**	*aspazesthai*
	Tameness	*hēmerotēs* (adj. *hēmeron*)
	Gentleness	*praotēs* (adj. *praion*)
	Orderliness	*kosmiotēs* (adj. *kosmion*)
	Softness	*malakia*
	Softness of spirit	*rhaithumia*
	(Feeling or sense of) **shame**	*aischunē* or *aidōs*
	Moderation	*sōphrosunē*
	(Desire to avoid) **blame** or **dishonor**	*psegos* or *mempsis*; *atimia*
	(Aversion to being) **shameful**	*aischros*
	Friendship	*philia*
	(Tendency to be) **obedient** (to rulers or superiors)	*hupēkoon*
	(Disposition or inclination) **to praise, honor,** or **admire** (admirable others)	*epainein*; *timan*; *thaumazein*
	(Sensitivity to and willingness to submit to perceived) **justice**	*dikē* or *dikaiosunē*
	Fear	*phobia* or *deos*
	Cowardice	*anandria* or *deilia*
	Pity	*eleos*
	Grief, longing	*kēdos*
	To love, cherish; to care for	*stergein*; *kēdesthai*

This two-sided framework for understanding spirited motivations requires several points of clarification and elaboration. To begin with, I should be clear that in identifying all of the above qualities and states as "spirited," I do not mean to endorse the strong claim that every time any of the relevant terms appears in Plato's works, it necessarily or exclusively refers to a spirited quality or state. In some cases strong claims are probably justified. For example, I think Plato consistently portrays *philotimia* and *philonikia* as spirited motivations in the *Republic*. In at least some cases, however, things are not so simple, for a number of reasons. First, Plato uses some terms more loosely than others. In Book 9 of the *Republic*, for instance, he applies the terms "savage" and "tame" to the different heads of the polycephalous beast within us (588c, 589a–b). The beast represents the appetitive part of the soul, and the "heads," presumably, different appetites or types of appetite. Clearly in that context "savageness" and "tameness" describe appetite, therefore, not *thumos*. Second, some spirited motivations involve Greek or Platonic concepts that are rich and multifaceted, and that as a result may in some contexts concern a part of the soul *other* than spirit, or at least concern other parts of the soul *in addition* to spirit. Fear, for example, is an emotion that presumably involves, perhaps sometimes more saliently than anything else, the *appetitive* part of the soul with its characteristic aversion to bodily pain. Likewise, the Greek notion of *sōphrosunē* is notoriously complex. Some of its connotations, like "self-knowledge," make the role of rationality especially salient (no doubt informed by its literal meaning, "sound-mindedness"), while others, such as the understanding of *sōphrosunē* as "self-control," emphasize mastery over one's appetites. And on the view Plato presents in the *Republic*, *sōphrosunē* essentially involves *all three* parts of the soul. Even courage—one of the most distinctively spirited virtues in Greek tradition—requires the activities of both spirit *and* reason on Socrates' analysis in Book 4. Finally, because the spirited part, as the "ally of reason," shares or converges in some of its concerns with the rational part, some of the tendencies we find in spirit also have a parallel in reason. Most notably, because the reasoning part seeks and loves knowledge, it is a lover of the Forms of Justice and the *Kalon*. Not only spirit, then, but also (and arguably more directly and truly) reason is attracted to what is just and admirable, and conversely averse to what is unjust and shameful. For all of these reasons, then, not all of the motivations listed above are always or purely spirited ones. What I do mean in identifying all of the above as spirited motivations, however, is that there are recognizable and prominent versions of all of them, on Plato's account, that primarily or exclusively originate in or involve the spirited part of the soul.[80]

Next, it is important to address how the two faces of *thumos* are related to one another. The first and most obvious observation to make about them is that they are contraries or opposites. At the general level, impulses of self-assertion and aggression are contrary to impulses of self-restraint and friendliness, and at the specific level, many of the motivations on the two sides constitute pairs of opposites: savageness and tameness, pride and shame, courage and cowardice, admiration and disgust, and so on. This means that in one sense the two sides of *thumos* tend to exclude one another: it is impossible to experience, for example, both admiration and disgust, or both pride and shame, toward the same object or person (at least, at the same time

---

[80] Note that I classify pity and grief as spirited emotions in this sense, whereas some interpreters might prefer to count them as appetitive instead. While I do think the preponderance of evidence suggests that Plato follows his literary predecessors in attributing both emotions to *thumos* in most cases (cf. Destrée [2011]), however, neither emotion features prominently in the rest of this book, so I do not insist upon the point.

and in the same respect).[81] Note, however, that although aggressive and friendly motivations are contraries, they are not entirely incompatible. It may be true that we cannot feel both admiration and disgust toward a single individual at the same time, but nothing prevents us from feeling admiration toward one person and disgust toward another. Indeed, as Socrates' treatment of savageness and gentleness in *Republic* 2 shows, the two faces of *thumos* can be reconciled because the opposite motivations in question are experienced with respect to different and opposite objects or individuals—aggressive impulses toward an *allotrion* group of people on the one hand, and friendly ones toward an *oikeion* group on the other.[82] Aristotle actually explores a version of exactly this issue in the *Topics*. He explains that "doing good to friends is contrary to the doing of evil to friends," but that "the doing of good to friends is not contrary (*enantion*) to the doing of evil to enemies, for both are choiceworthy *and part of the same disposition* (*tou hautou ēthous*)" (113a2–10). Indeed, the popular Greek characterization of justice as "helping friends and harming enemies," which Aristotle is invoking, itself illustrates the same general point, and in the next chapter I explore connections between that formulation of justice and the two faces of *thumos*.

The two sides of spiritedness are not merely compatible, however, but actually *complementary* to one another. For comparison, consider two primitive *appetitive* motivations: desire for bodily pleasure and aversion to bodily pain. Although desire and aversion are opposites, the appetitive desire and aversion in question are experienced with respect to two *opposite* things—pleasure and pain. The two impulses are not in conflict with one another, therefore, but actually two sides of the same coin.[83] The same is true in the case of spirited motivation: aggression toward outsiders complements affection toward insiders; the desire to earn praise complements the desire to avoid blame; the desire to rule one's inferiors complements the willingness to be ruled by one's superiors; and so on. Key passages in early Greek literature illustrate the complexity and interconnectedness in this relationship between

---

[81] Indeed, we find in early literature various versions of the idea that we cannot feel toward someone, simultaneously, two contrary spirited emotions: anger (*thumos* or *cholos*) is incompatible with fear or shame (Aristotle, *Rhet.* 1380a32–4), with friendship (Homer, *Il.* 14.206–7, 14.305–6), or with pity (Aeschylus, *Ag.* 1069); harshness (*chalepanein*) is incompatible with pity (*Rep.* 336e10–337a2), gentleness (*Rep.* 354a11–12), or shame (*Rep.* 501c4–502a2); and daring or boldness (*tolmē, tharsos*) are incompatible with shame (*Phdr.* 241a6–7; Hesiod, *WD* 317–19).

[82] Hence simultaneously feeling affectionate toward one's family and hostile to one's enemy is no violation of Socrates' Principle of Opposites.

[83] See Most (2003) on the interconnectedness of pity and anger in particular in Homer.

the two sides of spirit. Consider, for example, the following lines from the *Odyssey*:

> And as a dog stands over her tender pups growling, when she sees someone she does not know (*agnoiēsas'*), and is eager to fight (*machesthai*), so his heart growled within him in his wrath.   (20.14–16)

We know Plato's thinking about spiritedness was informed by this very passage. These lines appear in the crucial Odysseus scene that Plato approvingly cites twice in the *Republic*, first as an example of spirited endurance and second to illustrate the distinctness of the *thumoeides* from reason.[84] Indeed, these lines immediately precede the words Plato quotes on both occasions: "But he struck his breast and reproached his heart with word."[85] Furthermore, the passage depicts exactly the canine behavior to which Plato draws attention when he first describes spiritedness in Book 2. Plato even echoes the language of the original passage: dogs are aggressive toward those they "do not know" (*tous agnōtas*, 375e4; cf. 376a5, 376b4–5). The Homeric lines reveal something else about the nature of spirited aggression that is typically unremarked, however. The hostility the mother dog displays toward strangers is implicitly due, at least in part, to the fact that she is guarding over her weak young pups.[86] Her desire to protect her offspring, which is presumably rooted in motherly affection, motivates her to "fight" someone she perceives as a threat to them. In other words, love for one's *oikeioi* can motivate or intensify aggression toward *allotrioi*.

A similar phenomenon can be observed in another Homeric scene. When the Achaean soldiers find themselves backed up against their own ships by the Trojans, Nestor offers the following words of encouragement:

> My friends (*philoi*), act like men (*aneres*) and take into your hearts (*thumōi*) shame (*aidō*) before your fellow human beings, and remember, each one of you, your children and wife, your possessions and your parents, whether they

---

[84] Note that Odysseus is identified as a lover of honor in the myth of Er (620c), which suggests that (from the *Republic*'s perspective) he was ruled by the spirited part of his soul. Cf. Reeve (2013b: 51).

[85] Plato also quotes this line at *Phaedo* 94d7–e1. The passage is clearly a popular and familiar one. Cairns (2014: para. 42) comments, "The passage is so well known that Plato needs to quote only a single line, but knowledge of the whole passage is clearly assumed."

[86] This complementary two-sidedness of spirit may also be reflected in Plato's choice of the language of guardianship. Tarnapolsky (2015: 249) notes, "The Greek noun and verb used to describe the nature of this guardianship (*phulassein* and *phulax*, respectively) cover instances of guarding against others, but also protecting, observing, and cherishing others."

be living or be dead. For the sake of those who are not here with us I implore you to stand now with endurance (*krateros*), and not to take flight in panic.

(*Iliad* 15.661–6)

As before we find that the two sides of *thumos* are closely tied to one another.[87] In order to motivate the soldiers to fight with "manly" courage and endurance, Nestor exhorts them to feel shame and think of their loved ones. His advice presupposes that the two kinds of motivation inform and influence one another, and that they can wax and wane together. The soldiers become fierce and aggressive fighters not by suppressing or expelling their "soft" emotions, but rather by stimulating and dwelling on them. And we are told that his speech is ultimately successful: it has the effect of "rousing the strength and spirit of every man."[88]

Another question that might be asked of my account is whether one side of spirited motivation—the aggressive or the gentle—is more fundamental than, or the foundation of, the other. In one sense the question is misguided: it is a bit like asking which side of a coin *is* the coin. Aggression and gentleness are both basic expressions of spiritedness, and neither is reducible to the other. However, there is another sense in which aggressive impulses at least *appear* prior to gentle ones. As Socrates' discussion in Book 2 shows, gentleness is conditional on certain kinds of experience or "knowledge" in a way that aggression is not. It is true that a spirited creature is equally born with the disposition *both* to be savage toward what is alien *and* to be affectionate toward what is familiar. But acquiring familiarity requires experience, and it takes time to learn who and what is *oikeion*. One way to think of this process is as a circle of familiarity that expands outward from the animal. The most primitive and "wild" animals recognize nothing as *oikeion* other their own bodies. Their aggressive instincts toward others serve the interest of protecting and preserving *themselves*. For them, we might say, the only gentleness or affection they experience takes the form of *self*-love or *-philia*. All other animals are beyond the self, and thus treated as threatening and hostile agents. More sophisticated, social animals, however, recognize animals other than themselves as *oikeion*—their offspring, say, or members of their pride or pack.

---

[87] For other Homeric examples of correlation between concern for others and vigorous martial exertion, see *Il.* 3.8–9, 14.487–9, and 15.561–4. See also Callinus, fr. 1.1–8, which encourages young men to cultivate a sense of shame and a tough *thumos*, "For it is a splendid honor for a man to fight on behalf of his land, children, and wedded wife against the foe"; and Euripides, *Supp.* 907–17.

[88] See Cairns (1993: 69–70) for an interpretation of *Il.* 15.661–6 in line with my reading. Balot (2014: 199–201) discusses the role of shame as a battle cry and exhortation among Iliadic warriors, as well as the intensive shaming practices of Homeric heroes.

And in human beings, the *oikeioi* can come to include not just family, but friends and fellow citizens. According to this picture, then, it will often be the case, as a matter of empirical fact, that animals conspicuously display primitive forms of aggression before exhibiting primitive forms of gentleness (toward anyone but themselves, at least).[89] In at least this sense, therefore, we might say that the aggressive side of *thumos* enjoys a sort of observable priority or anteriority to the gentle side.[90]

Finally, my account takes the *thumoeides* to be the distinctively *social* and *political* part of the soul, for Plato. I develop this interpretation in more detail in the next chapter, but note that we already have preliminary resources in support of this idea. We have seen that spirit is the part of the soul uniquely sensitive to an animal's or person's relationship to others: its aggressive side is a response to the perception that someone else is an *other*, a competitor, rival, or threat of some kind; and its gentle side is a response to the perception that someone else is in some sense the person's own, a friend, loved one, or respected superior. For *thumos* the world is divided up into the *allotrion* and the *oikeion*, and the desires and emotions for which it is responsible are dictated by an agent's sense of their position and role in the world of human or animal interaction. Plato's use of the term *oikeion* to characterize spirited motivation amplifies this point. As Aristotle teaches, for the Greeks the household or *oikos* is the basic political unit out of which larger communities and ultimately cities are composed,[91] and the term *oikeion*, as noted, most literally means "belonging to one's household" or family. Hence the most primal expression of spiritedness, on Plato's view, calls to mind its social orientation. As Plato's introduction of spirit in Book 2 also shows, both sides of spirited motivation play an important role in the maintenance and preservation of political communities. In order for their just city to survive, its

---

[89] Some animals, moreover, are not naturally equipped or inclined *ever* to acquire the relevant "familiarity" with others, and as a result display *only* wild and savage behavior. The Peripatetic text *Problems* raises precisely this issue, noting that while all ἥμερα animals are also found in ἄγρια forms, the converse does not hold (895b24–33).

[90] To be sure, *both* aspects of spirit admit of maturation and sophistication. The competitive pursuit of honor, for example, presupposes an individual has learned and internalized a complex system for distributing marks of social acclaim, and the idea that both sides of human *thumos* can be trained is central to Plato's account of moral education (see Chapters 6 and 7). Nonetheless, aggressive instincts can thrive and determine an animal's behavior from a state of relative ignorance and inexperience, whereas most expressions of affection and gentleness, even relatively primitive ones, require some amount of experience and acquired "learning."

[91] See *Pol.* 1252a24–1253a7, *EE* 1242a19–b1, and *NE* 1162a15–29, and cf. comments by Nagle (2006: 31) and Roy (1999: 1). For discussion of Aristotle's view of the household and its relation to the city, see Ambler (1985), Booth (1981), and Nagle (2006).

warriors must display both aggressive *and* gentle forms of spirit: without the former the city would be destroyed by outsiders, and without the latter they would destroy the city themselves from the inside. I turn now to elaborating on this line of interpretation, and to how spirit's nature influences and determines key aspects of our moral, social, and political lives.

3

The Social and Political Nature of Spirit

In this chapter I develop the idea the *thumoeides* is the social or political part of the soul in two important senses. First, spirited motivations are what make it possible for human beings to live together in and protect their communities, and second, a person's spirited desires and emotions are the ones directly and primarily shaped by social and political influences—that is, by the other people and institutions *in* their communities. These facts about spirit, in turn, give rise to important challenges related to moral education and civic unity that make it a determinate factor in the moral fate of political communities and their citizens. The success or failure of moral education depends first and foremost on the kinds of values young people absorb and internalize from their peers and fellow citizens in the form of spirited feelings, emotions, and desires. The success or failure of the city itself, meanwhile, largely depends on how citizens *feel* toward one another—whether they are united by bonds of spirited friendship and fellowship, or whether they view one another as rivals, competitors, or even enemies. These two issues are related and mutually reinforcing, moreover. Most obviously, the kinds of values citizens socially absorb directly affect the relationships they have with one another and hence whether the city itself is stable and unified or volatile and full of division. The problems of moral education and civic strife, then, are inextricably connected, and the common psychic source of that connection is spirited motivation.

My goal in this chapter is to establish this interpretation by focusing on what happens with spirited motivations when things go *wrong*—when moral education fails and cities are unstable—in corrupt places like Athens. On Plato's view, I argue, popular Greek education and politics fail because they reflect a pleonectic value system that is informed primarily by desires rooted in the appetitive part of the soul and that consequently prioritizes bodily, external, and material goods. Moral education fails because these corrupt values are absorbed by way of spirited desires and emotions, which in turn leads to civic discord as citizens' aggressive and competitive spiritedness becomes directed against *one another*. This chapter provides background for the rest of this book, then, by identifying the central role of *thumos* and spirited motivation in Plato's problematization of the twin challenges of moral education and civic

The Political Soul: Plato on Thumos, *Spirited Motivation, and the City*. Josh Wilburn, Oxford University Press.
© Josh Wilburn 2021. DOI: 10.1093/oso/9780198861867.003.0003

unity. As we will see in Parts II, III, and IV of this book, these two issues preoccupy Plato throughout his career, and he consistently addresses them in ways that anticipate, reflect, or make explicit their connection to spirited motivation.

In order to provide some historical context for Plato's account, I begin in Section 1 with a brief survey of early epic and poetic literature, which anticipates Plato in depicting both the aggressive and the gentle faces of *thumos* as playing a decisive role in the preservation or collapse of social groups and political communities. In the rest of the chapter, I turn to Plato's critical account of popular Greek ethics and politics, focusing on the following sections of the *Republic*: Book 1, where Socrates engages directly with various conventional views of justice; Glaucon's and Adeimantus' speeches at the beginning of Book 2, which, respectively, articulate popular ideas about justice and describe traditional educational practices; Book 6, where Socrates explains how those with philosophical natures are treated in cities like Athens; and Books 8–9, where Socrates describes various corrupt political regimes and individuals. What these sections of the *Republic* have in common is that they prominently draw attention to and—implicitly or explicitly—*diagnose* what Plato takes to be flaws of conventional Greek ideas and practices. I will refer to these, therefore, as "diagnostic" sections of the *Republic*, by contrast with what I will call the "constructive" sections, which focus less on actual contemporary ideas and practices and more on developing and defending positive proposals for Socrates' just city.[1] If the former diagnose the ethical, social, and political ills that afflict contemporary Greek society, the constructive sections that I will examine in Chapters 6 and 7 present the sanative measures necessary for resolving or averting them.

In Section 2, I clarify some key points about spirit's relationship to appetite that are relevant to understanding the account of popular ethics and politics that Glaucon and Adeimantus articulate in their speeches, to which I turn in Section 3. In Sections 4 and 5, I then outline Plato's understanding of the problems of moral education and civic strife, respectively, in more detail.

---

[1] I intend the distinction between "diagnostic" and "constructive" to be rough only, meant for the purposes of discussion. The complexity of the *Republic* defies a neat division, since there is often a bit of both diagnosis and construction happening alongside one another.

1. *Thumos* and Community in Early Greek Literature

Early Greek epic and poetic literature provides generous precedent for the idea that motivations attributed to *thumos* are essential for the preservation of communities. Most obviously, early authors identify spiritedness as key to defending or protecting communities. As we saw in Achilles' response to the loss of his "wife" Briseis in the last chapter, in Homer the successful protection of one's family, one's "own," or one's *oikos* depends on, and is closely connected with, fighting with strong *thumos*.[2] In later authors this idea is expanded to the political level:

> This is a common benefit for the state and all the people (*xunon d' esthlon touto polēi te panti de dēmōi*), whenever a man stands firm with those on the front lines of battle, gives no thought to shameful (*aischrēs*) flight, risking his life and displaying an enduring spirit (*thumon tlēmona*), and speaks emboldening words to the man next to him. This man is good in war…Let everyone strive with all his *thumos* to reach the pinnacle of this virtue, with no slackening in war.   (Tyrtaeus, fr. 12.15–20, 44–5)

In this passage, Tyrtaeus explicitly links the shared good of fellow citizens with their willingness to fight together courageously against external enemies.

Early authors also illustrate the converse idea, however: that the soft or gentle side of *thumos* is necessary for preserving the *internal* bonds of families and cities. This point is clearest through the many examples in early Greek literature of what happens, and how characters react, when the affection and sympathy appropriate to friends and family are missing. Consider, for instance, Penelope's initially cold reception of her husband Odysseus, who has finally returned home after twenty years. She is skeptical, she says, because she has always worried that an imposter might trick her by claiming to be her long-lost husband. Her son Telemachus rebukes her for her apparent indifference, however:

> My mother, cruel mother, whose spirit (*thumon*) is unyielding (*apēnea*), why do you stand aloof from my father, and not sit by his side and question and

---

[2] For further discussion of autonomous households or *oikoi* in the organization of Homeric society, and the relation between the head of household's protection of the *oikos* and honor or virtue, see Adkins (1960: 34–6 and 1970: 28–32).

find out about him? No other woman would harden (*tetlēoti*) her spirit (*thumōi*) as you do...but your heart (*kradiē*) is always harder (*stereōterē*) than stone (*lithoio*).   (*Od.* 23.97–103)

Odysseus, likewise, tells her she has a "heart that cannot be softened" (*kēr ateramnon*), that she has "hardened" (*tetlēoti*) her *thumos*, and that she has "a heart of iron in her breast" (*sidēreon en phresi ētor*) (23.166–72). In military contexts, or for the purposes of enduring grief or hardship, a firm and inflexible *thumos* is a virtue; in the context of personal relationships, by contrast, it stands in the way of due affection or intimacy and is grounds for reproach. This is especially true, it should be noted, for *women*, of whom Greek norms expect and demand an especially soft and yielding *thumos*, along with corresponding feelings of love and affection. Although men and women alike can be criticized for an excessively "hard" spirit (see discussion of Achilles below), there is nonetheless a masculine/feminine dichotomy at work in Greek views of psychology and *thumos* that makes "hard-heartedness" in women especially subject to disapproval and censure (and, conversely, cowardly "softness" in *men* especially subject to reproach).[3] Accordingly, Penelope's own emotional reunion with her husband takes place only after Odysseus proves his identity and Penelope's spirit is finally "softened": her *thumos* is "persuaded" and her "knees loosened where she sat and her heart melted" (23.205, 230).

A similar case, but with a far more macabre outcome, is that of Euripides' Medea.[4] Throughout the drama, Medea's plot to kill her children as revenge against her faithless husband Jason is attributed to her wrathful *thumos*. Her children are warned early on of Medea's anger (*cholos*), her "savage" (*agrion*) nature, her "hateful (*stugeran*) and stubborn (*authadous*)" mind, and her "growing *thumos*" (98–108), and Medea herself famously laments that *thumos* is the "master of her deliberations" (1079). Likewise, when Medea reveals her plan, the Chorus implores her not to break "the laws of mortals" (811–13) and says she must be "a stone or a piece of iron" (*petros ē sidaros*, 1280)[5] to plot the

---

[3] For relevant discussion of how this masculine/feminine dichotomy relates to Greek conceptions of virtue and related qualities, see Hobbs (2000: 68–74).

[4] One of the play's central themes is the misfortune that follows dissolution of familial bonds. Because Jason has abandoned his marriage, for instance, "all is enmity (ἐχθρα), and the closest ties of love (τὰ φίλτατα) are diseased" (16). See also 520–1, where ὀργή and ἔρις destroy bonds of *philia*; and 469–73.

[5] Cf. Nurse's comments on Medea: "She is as deaf to the advice of her friends (φίλων) as a stone (πέτρος) or a wave of the sea (θαλάσσιος)" (28–9).

act of filicide. Surely, they argue, she will not be ruthless enough to go through with it:

> How will you summon up the boldness (*thrasos*) or the resolve in hand and heart (*kardiai*) to dare (*tolman*) this dreadful deed?...When your children fall as suppliants at your feet, you will not drench your hands in their blood out of hard-hearted spirit (*tlamoni thumōi*).   (856–65)

The chorus makes it clear that killing her own children will require a callous and unflinching spirit that admits none of the soft and affectionate feelings normally due to loved ones. Medea herself tragically acknowledges this very point as she steels herself for the deed:

> Come, put on your armor (*hoplizou*), my heart (*kardia*)!...Do not play the coward (*kakistheis*), do not remember your children, how much you love (*philtath'*) them, how you gave them life. Instead, for this brief day forget them.   (1242–8)

Medea understands that allowing herself feelings of maternal love and concern would prevent her from exacting her revenge—an omission that, in her mind, would involve the contemptible kind of softness associated with cowardice. What her *thumos* needs, she understands, is hard-hearted indifference to her own children. Finally, when her husband Jason finds out what she has done, he condemns her inhuman act, which "no Greek woman would have dared (ἔτλη) to do":

> Hateful creature, utter enemy (*echthistē*) to the gods, to me, and to the whole human race, you dared (*etlēs*) to take the sword to your own children!...You are a she-lion (*leainan*), not a woman, with a nature more savage (*agriōteran*) than Scylla the Tuscan monster!   (1323–43)

The tragedy of Medea, then, is presented as the story of a breakdown in the spirited feelings of affection that constitute the bonds of domestic relationships. Medea's *thumos* is hard, savage, and vengeful even against those to whom it should be soft, gentle, and kind; the outcome is the complete destruction of her family.

The case of Medea also illustrates a further point: that those who do not share in the gentleness and affection due to family and friends are unfit for human society. Medea violates the "laws of mortals" and is an "enemy" of the whole human race; she does what no Greek woman would have done and is a beast or monster. In other words, Medea is uncivilized and barbarous: her egregious savagery alienates her from the relationships and communities that characterize a social human life. Appropriately, the drama ends with Medea's flight from Corinth; she literally and figuratively withdraws from civilization.

A similar phenomenon, in a very different context, can be observed in the *Iliad*. After Achilles is dishonored by Agamemnon, his unyielding anger leads him to abandon his fellow soldiers. Even when an embassy of his desperate friends implores him to return, he is deaf to their entreaties:

> Achilles has set the proud spirit (*megalētora thumon*) in his breast on savageness (*agriou*), unrelenting (*schetlios*) man, and he has no regard for the friendship of his comrades (*philotētos hetairōn*), with which we honored him among the ships above all else—pitiless (*nēlēs*) one!...As for you [Achilles], the gods have put in your breast a spirit (*thumon*) that is obdurate (*allēkton*) and evil because of a single girl; but now we offer you seven, far the best that there are, and many other gifts besides; so make your spirit (*thumon*) gracious (*hilaon*), and respect (*aidessai*) your house: for under your roof we have come from the mass of the Danaans, and we are eager to be the most cherished (*kēdistoi*) and dear (*philtatoi*) to you beyond all the other Achaeans.   (9.628–42)

As this speech by Ajax makes clear, the source of Achilles' alienation from his fellow soldiers is his hard and implacable spirit.[6] He lacks the kindness and respect due to friends and spends much of the *Iliad* outside of the army camp, estranged from the community of his comrades. It is only later, when Achilles "relents from his wrath," mourns the loss of comrades who died in his absence, and softens his stubborn *thumos* (19.61–8), that he is finally able to make peace with his friends and rejoin the Greek army. Once again, then, spirited tenderness, warmth, or flexibility is the necessary psychological condition of social cohesion.

A final illustration of the role of *thumos* in human social life is found in Hesiod's *Works and Days*. Throughout the text human conflict and the downfall of civilizations are explained by and associated with conditions of *thumos* and spirited emotion. In particular, Hesiod establishes a dichotomy between conflict and violence on the one hand, which are destructive of human life and society, and justice and shame on the other, which foster

---

[6] Hainsworth (1993: 143) paraphrases: "I never thought you would treat your friends like this."

peace and community. In the very opening of the text, the author introduces two kinds of "strife," *eris*, which are "thoroughly opposed in spirit (*thumon*)." While one kind of strife gives rise to productive ambition and competition, the other kind "fosters evil war and conflict (*polemon te kakon te dērin*)—unrelenting (*schetlios*)—no mortal loves that one" (11–26). Hesiod applies these ideas in his account of the different ages of humankind. Zeus destroyed the race of silver because they refused to honor the gods and could not restrain themselves from violence against one another (134–9). The "terrible and strong" race of bronze, meanwhile, "cared only for the painful deeds of Ares and for acts of violence (*hubreis*). They were "unbending" (*aplastoi*), as they possessed "hard-hearted spirit (*kraterophrona thumon*) of adamant," and ultimately, because of their violent nature "they went down nameless into the dank house of chilly Hades, overpowered by one another's hands" (145–54). The wicked kind of strife, likewise, is what destroyed the generation of heroic demigods through "evil war and dread battle" (161–2). Hesiod's warning about what will happen to the current iron age of humankind is most telling, however. Eventually, he explains, "shame (*aidōs*) will no longer exist" among mortals, because Shame and Indignation will abandon the earth and "leave human beings behind." Hesiod's description of the social and political conditions associated with the departure of shame are illuminating: fathers and sons, and comrade and comrade, will no longer be like-minded (*homoiios*); brother will no longer be "dear" or "friend" (*philos*) to brother; people will dishonor (*atimēsousi*) their parents unrelentingly; they will destroy one another's cities; they will honor (*timēsousi*) the wicked and the violent instead of the just and virtuous; bad men will harm their superiors; people will take justice (*dikē*) into their own hands; and, finally, "Envy (*zēlos*) will accompany all human beings" (180–200). Hesiod urges his brother Perses to prefer justice to violence, for when men obey justice, "their city blooms and the people in it flower," and they enjoy peace instead of war. By contrast, Zeus exacts vengeance on those who scorn his daughter Justice (*Dikē*), and "often a whole city suffers" because of those who are violent and cruel (213–41). The poet concludes, "Give heed to Justice, and put violence entirely out of your mind. This is the law that Cronus' son has established for humankind: that fish and beasts and winged birds eat one another, since Justice is not among them; but to human beings he has given Justice" (275–80). In Hesiod, a hard and violent *thumos* produces "strife" that has devastating effects on family bonds and human society, while shame and justice keep them intact.[7]

2. Spirit, Appetite, and the Social Interpretation

My analysis of the diagnostic sections of the *Republic* will rely on two ideas about appetite, and spirit's relationship to it, that are worth highlighting and clarifying before I begin. First, my interpretation will assume that human desires for bodily pleasures, and for the wealth, property, and other material goods that facilitate their satisfaction, are ultimately rooted in the appetitive part of the soul. Plato says as much at *Republic* 580e–581a, as noted in the previous chapter: it is called the "appetitive" part "due to the intensity of its appetites for food, drink, sex, and all the things associated with them," and, because such desires are "most easily satisfied by means of money," it is also called "money-loving" and "profit-loving." This is not an especially controversial interpretation of appetite, but I flag it here as a background premise of my arguments going forward.

The second is the idea that the spirited part of the soul can become "subordinated" to appetite, in the sense of motivating the person to pursue the characteristic objects of appetitive desire just identified, when spirited desires for honor, feelings of admiration, and so on become oriented toward attaining and protecting appetitive goods. I will say more in Chapter 7 relevant to understanding the intrapsychic dynamics of this phenomenon, but for now it is worth noting how this complicates the picture presented in the last chapter, where we saw that Plato often characterizes spirit's relationship to appetite as *antagonistic* rather than subordinate or obsequious. Tad Brennan provides useful resources for illuminating this complication. According to his account, spirit's role in the soul is defined by its relation to appetite on both the internal and external levels. *Thumos* is necessary not only for the purpose of opposing and resisting appetitive desires from within the agent's own soul, however, but also for contending against other appetitive people and animals who are competing for limited resources in the world. To give a primitive but

---

[7] Cf. Renaut (2014: 28–36), who also draws attention to Thucydides' similar characterization of *thumos* and *orgē* as dangerous sources of *stasis* or faction in the city. Also relevant is Euripides' Jocasta, who warns of the destructive effects of the "unjust goddess" Love of Honor (*Philotimia*) on communities: "Often she goes in and out of prosperous cities and houses and ruins those who have dealings with her!...Far finer, my son, to honor Equality (*Isotēs*), which binds friends to friends, cities to cities, and allies to allies" (*Phoen.* 531–8).

ubiquitous example, animals must fight to protect themselves against preda-tors motivated by hunger.[8] In the human case, as we have seen, individuals and cities must fight to keep themselves safe against attacks from others seeking appetitive gain in the form of wealth and resources. Note, however, that spirit's relation to appetite is not *merely* defensive: the spirited aggression of hungry animals or greedy cities is itself prompted by appetitive bodily needs or desires. Animals fight not only *against* the appetitive urges of others, but also *for* their own. In other words, *thumos* is psychologically necessary both because we must fight and compete to satisfy our own appetites and because we must protect and defend ourselves against other agents doing the same in a world with finite resources. This account, then, highlights an important fact about our psychic economy: although spirit makes it possible for agents to *resist* their own appetitive desires, it can also, and often *does*, serve the interest of the agent's own appetites as well. Or to put the point differently, *thumos* is the psychological source of aggressive and competitive motivations, and often the things for which animals and humans are fighting and competing are objects of appetitive desire.[9]

Here a clarification is in order, however, that will help bring into focus my understanding of spirit's role in social and political life. On the view Brennan develops, *all* of spirit's psychological functions "involve responding to and relating to appetitive souls."[10] According to him, Plato dramatizes this idea by introducing the warrior class in the *Republic* only *after* the "healthy" or simple city of Book 2 has become a "feverish" one. The former, which Socrates outlines following the speeches by Glaucon and Adeimantus examined below, consists only of the farmers and craftspeople required for providing necessities like food, clothing, shelter, and the like. The inhabitants of the simple city, Brennan argues, possess necessary, and *only* necessary, appetites, but they lack spirited desires. From Plato's perspective, however, this is an impossible fiction.[11] Left to their own devices, appetites do not remain mod-erate and contained; their tendency, on the contrary, is to grow without principled limit, and they need spirit to keep them in check. That is why Plato has Glaucon prompt Socrates to turn the healthy city into a "feverish" one filled with unhealthy and unnecessary appetites for luxuries, which in turn prompts the need for warriors who will fight both to protect the city's

---

[8] Cf. Cooper (1996: 250–1).   [9] Cf. Brennan (2012: 114).   [10] 2012: 103.
[11] 2012: 103–5. Other commentators who take the healthy city to be impossible or unrealistic on various grounds include Barney (2002: 219–20), Bloom (1968: 346), Reeve (1988: 171), and Strauss (1964: 95).

resources and to seize the resources of other cities.[12] Ultimately the feverish city is "purged," and the productive class of the Kallipolis will ideally be one with moderate appetites that looks not unlike the original simple city of farmers, craftspeople, and merchants. According to Brennan, however, Plato needs the "detour" through the feverish city in order to illustrate spirit's function. He explains, "A fully accurate picture of spirit requires you to see it exactly as a response to the dangers and excesses inherent in appetite. If one never saw appetite get out of hand, one would never understand why spirit is needed in the city."[13] Plato illustrates that spirit's purpose is to fight against appetite, Brennan concludes, by showing appetites getting out of hand in the city and then introducing a spirited army that restores order to it.[14]

While I agree with Brennan that the transition from the healthy city to the feverish one is likely designed, at least in part, to illustrate the need for a spirited element in both the city and the soul, I disagree that that need can be explained entirely in terms of opposition to appetite. The problem is that for Brennan, spirit's relation to appetite *exhausts* its purpose, and all of its motivations—as well as their value to us as human beings—can be reduced to, or understood in terms of, that relationship. "Spirit's value is relational," he comments, "and lies solely in opposing appetite."[15] Hence although Brennan himself recognizes, and even emphasizes, spirit's attachment to the *oikeion*, he takes that attachment to be teleologically parasitic on its relation to appetite and love of honor, which he identifies as spirit's most characteristic desire. On his picture, the pursuit of honor is useful for defending against or resisting appetites (because it can motivate us to withstand pain or forego pleasure for the sake of reputation), and it is useful for honor-loving creatures to distinguish between *oikeion* and *allotrion* groups for the purposes of determining

---

[12] On this point Brennan (2012: 105, n. 7) explicitly dissents from Barney (2002: 214), who suggests that Glaucon's indignant objection to the healthy city "is the voice less of appetite than of *thumos*." She notes that couches and tables, which are among Glaucon's demands, are the furnishings of a symposium and hence symbols of civilized Athenian society; Glaucon, therefore, is reacting spiritedly to the perceived indignity of their absence. Cf. Balasopoulos (2013: 15–16), Burnyeat (1999: 231, 244–5), and Ludwig (2007: 225–6). Other commentators who, like Brennan, attribute Glaucon's objection to appetitive desires or concerns include Tarnapolsky (2015: 248) and Weinstein (2018: 135–8).

[13] 2012: 104.

[14] For further discussion and a range of interpretations of the healthy city, see Annas (1981: 73–9), Balasopoulos (2013) Barney (2002), Cross and Woozley (1964: Ch. 4), Reeve (1988: 176–8), and Strauss (1964: 93–7). Weinstein (2018: Chs. 6–9) offers an especially detailed analysis of its role in the dialogue. Like Brennan, he argues that the need for *thumos* arises out of the insatiability of appetitive desire.

[15] 2012: 112.

what kinds of honors to seek and from whom one seeks to receive them.[16] From the perspective of my account, however, this represents a failure (at least as a matter of emphasis) to fully account for the *distinct* role and value of spirited gentleness or friendship in making communities and all their moral and political benefits possible. Brennan is certainly right that the ability to fight against appetites in the pursuit of honor is *one* thing that helps preserve communities. Cities must be capable of defending themselves against greedy outside aggressors, and the desire for honor or glory can motivate citizens to fight. Citizens must also, of course, be capable of resisting appetitive desires to harm *one another* for material gain, and the aversion to dishonor can serve as an important deterrent to such behavior. As we will see in this chapter, however, if members of a community have desires to mistreat one another in the first place, or abstain from them *only* to avoid dishonor or disreputability, then their community is an unhealthy and unstable one at best (if it is truly one at all, on Plato's view). What is missing in such cases are the genuine feelings of love, friendship, and affection in virtue of which members of communities no longer view one another as competitors for perceived material goods.[17] Such feelings, importantly, are irreducible to antagonism between *thumos* and appetite. To give another primitive example, it is not that loving parents—human or otherwise—want to withhold or steal food from their children but suppress that desire in order to avoid dishonor in the eyes of their offspring or peers, but rather that, because of the spirited love they feel for them, they never have such desires in the first place. Likewise, as we will see in later chapters, the success of moral education requires not only opposition to appetite, but also support for or "friendship" with reason that fundamentally affects the soul's inner dynamics.[18] Hence, although Brennan is right that

---

[16] He comments: "The entire world of status, reputation, and sensitivity to honor [is] a system for distributing appetitive goods to the members of a social group in accordance with their merit, where merit in turn is originally based on the ability to acquire and defend these same appetitive goods" (2012: 105). In a sense, what Brennan here characterizes as *essential* to spirit (i.e. its orientation to the attainment of appetitive goods), I will be characterizing as its condition in *non*-virtuous souls in which it is subordinated to appetitive or pleonectic values. It does not apply in ideal cases (like the Kallipolis) in which love of honor is oriented toward (non-appetitive) aretaic goods.

[17] Note, moreover, that moral education ultimately provides the foundation for the distinct and supreme good of the philosopher's achievement of wisdom.

[18] Brennan himself raises an important objection to social interpretations of *thumos*. Because spirited motivations are often directed against appetites *within the person's own soul*, he argues, references to society and other people are often superfluous or misleading. Weinstein (2018: 19–21) rejects social interpretations using similar logic, arguing that the *Republic* defines spirit's psychological function not in terms of sociality, but rather in terms of its relation to reason in the virtue of courage. (In response to Weinstein's specific point: it is important to distinguish the unifying feature of spirited motivations from their *function* in a virtuous soul. The fact that spirit's proper function involves its relationship with reason does not necessarily tell us that all spirited motivations, especially those of non-human animals, are themselves *defined* by or reducible to something involving that relationship.)

thumos is needed as a febrifuge to temper the excesses of the luxurious city, its effectiveness in doing so requires not only aggression or honor-seeking ambition, but also, and even *primarily*, its gentleness.[19] That is why Socrates himself is quick to introduce and emphasize the need for both faces of spiritedness, and its gentleness is what is required for *internal* cohesion in the city. In line with the early Greek literature surveyed above, in Plato friendship and affection provide crucial psychological foundations that make the individual and collective goods of civic unity and moral education possible. They will prove to be essential, that is, in Plato's proposed *solutions* to the social and political problems I outline in the rest of this chapter.

3. Popular Culture and the Corruption of Spirit: Preliminary Sketch

The preliminary sketch of Plato's critique of popular education and politics goes like this. First, because most people and cultural influences have mistaken values, conventional education instills a misguided conception of the good in citizens in large part by exploiting and perverting their spirited psychology. In particular, it makes them value appetitive goods such as bodily pleasure and wealth, resulting in an uncomfortable tension: on the one hand, it makes

Both objections have a similar structure: they call attention to *intra*psychic expressions of spirit—in relation to appetite and reason, respectively—and suggest it would be a mischaracterization to describe those as "social," presumably because they do not immediately involve outside agents. I have two responses. (1) I do not find it obvious that spirit's relations to appetite and reason cannot be cashed out in terms of social instincts. For one thing, Plato himself is keen to characterize its relationships with appetite and reason in social terms, using the same language of friends and enemies, loving and hating, *oikeion* and *allotrion* (a point I develop in Ch. 7). Even if one rejects the idea, as I do, that Plato thinks of the soul parts as agent-like, one might still think that these "relationships" reflect and involve spirit's primitive social instincts in some way. Furthermore, when spirit opposes an appetite or supports a rational judgment, what that ultimately means, plausibly, is that spirit motivates the person to refrain from or pursue courses of action that play out in the social worlds of living things (a point I develop in Ch. 8). (2) I would like to distinguish between "weak" and "strong" versions of the social interpretation. On the weak version, spirit is the source of all distinctively social/political motivations, and *many or most* spirited motivations are distinctively social/political. On the strong version, spirit is the source of all distinctively social/political motivations, and *all* spirited motivations are distinctively social/political. Although I accept the strong version myself, the main claims of this book—namely, that spirited motivation is a necessary condition of political life, and that spirit is the element of our psychology primarily shaped by social and cultural influences—require only the weak one. At the heart of my account is the conception of spirit's dual reactions toward the *oikeion* and *allotrion*. If commentators want to insist that when the *oikeion* or *allotrion* in question is appetite or reason, spirit's relation to it cannot count as social, that does not affect my main ideas or arguments. For a different criticism of social interpretations of *thumos*, see Kraugerud (2009).

[19] Cf. Cross and Woozley (1964: 79), who remark that people in the healthy city join together "not because they have any need of each other in social terms, for friendship or company, but because they have needs of economic goods such as food, housing and clothes." Cf. Futter (2017: 28–9) and Weinstein (2018: 117).

people ashamed to engage in greedy and unjust *pleonexia*; on the other hand, it also teaches them that the sorts of goods obtained through *pleonexia* are of the highest value for living a happy life. The corrupting effect of conventional education, moreover, has its most destructive effects on the talented and ambitious—who, though by nature superior to the majority in their cities, must ultimately conform themselves to popular values in order to achieve the success they crave. Second, the problem of civic strife, on Plato's analysis, is closely connected with the ethics of helping friends and harming enemies that emerges out of spirit's primitive affection for the familiar and hostility to the alien. The issue is that people develop more intense affection for, and loyalty to, those they consider "their own"—their private lovers, friends, and family—than they do for fellow citizens who fall outside of their *oikeion*-groups. This becomes especially problematic when coupled with the pleonectic conception of value instilled by popular education. When people place ultimate value on the finite appetitive goods of the material world, they end up holding misguided views about what it means to "help" their *oikeioi*, and they come to view many of their fellow citizens as competitors. As a result, they come to think that acting justly means exclusively benefiting *others* by sacrificing appetitive goods that they perceive as beneficial to themselves and their friends. They come to think, that is, that justice is as Thrasymachus describes it in Book 1 of the *Republic*: "the good of another (*allotrion*)". When that happens, *thumos* is no longer a reliable psychological restraint against excessive appetites, but rather the source of a competitive motivation to engage in pleonectic behavior and pursue the honor associated with appetitive goods.[20]

My starting point for filling in the details of this sketch is the speeches of Glaucon and Adeimantus in *Republic* 2, which famously pose a challenge to Socrates' view that justice is valuable for its own sake and that the just life is happier than the unjust one. According to Glaucon's argument, which he takes over from Thrasymachus, Socrates' position is in conflict with what everyone else actually thinks. No one *willingly* acts justly, he claims. People establish

---

[20] The dramatic context of the *Republic*—which is carefully designed to call to mind the doomed, *pleonexia*-driven Athenian politics of the Peloponnesian War, as well as the civil strife throughout that period that culminated in the violent reign of the Thirty Tyrants—amplifies the critique of traditional ethics and politics outlined in this chapter. Indeed, while Plato's critique takes aim at much that is common throughout the Greek world and tradition, he clearly takes late fifth-century Athens to be an especially vivid representation of popular Greek values and the evils that can result from them. I am in complete disagreement, then, with Annas (1999: 77), who claims, "Athenian politics of the fifth and fourth century do not actually shed any light on the *Republic*. Seldom can a work have owed less to its political context." Ferrari (2005) responds to Annas, commenting, "[Plato] is certainly at pains to lay the shadow of the Thirty and of its bloody failure over the *Republic*'s opening pages" (p. 11). Leroux (2005) also examines Annas' interpretation at length, and see also Howland's (2014) speculative historical proposal.

laws and agree to be just only because they are incapable of committing injustice with impunity. Human nature, however, inherently (*pephuken*) pursues *pleonexia* as good, and anyone, if given the opportunity to seize more than their fair share without suffering the penalties of injustice, would do so. Not only that, but they would be *right* to do so: the life of the unjust person with a reputation for justice is far superior to that of the just individual who is believed to be unjust. The latter suffers all of the punitive consequences of injustice without any of the benefits, while the former enjoys all of the benefits of injustice—all of the "honors and rewards" (*timai kai dōreai*)—with none of the consequences (358e–362a):

> He rules his city because of his reputation for justice; he marries into any family he wishes; he gives his children in marriage to anyone he wishes; he makes contracts and associates (*koinōnein*) with anyone he wants; and besides benefiting himself in all these ways, he makes a profit because he feels no disgust (*duscherainein*) at doing injustice. In any contest, public or private, he's the winner and gets more (*pleonektein*) than his enemies. And by getting (*pleonektounta*) more than them, he becomes wealthy, benefiting his friends and harming his enemies (*tous te philous eu poiein kai tous echthrous blaptein*). He makes substantial sacrifices to the gods and sets up extravagant offerings to them. He takes better care of the gods, therefore— and, indeed, of any human beings he wishes—than a just person does. Hence it's likely that he, in turn, will be more beloved by the gods than the just person.   (362b2–c6)

If Glaucon articulates the popular view of justice, Adeimantus' complementary speech shows that the popular view is supported by traditional moral education. Not only citizens themselves, but also the poets who provide the foundational works of Greek ethics and education, fail to praise justice for its own sake.[21] Rather, their praise emphasizes only the ordinary consequences of having a *reputation* for justice. Being thought just normally leads not only to the benefits cited by Glaucon, but also to the favor of the gods. Those who act justly are rewarded in the afterlife, while the unjust are punished. On the other

---

[21] Jaeger (1944a: 214–15) comments, "We cannot understand Plato's criticisms of poetry unless we remember that the Greeks thought it was the epitome of all knowledge and culture, and that the poet's utterance was a standard for all men to admire." Cf. Nussbaum (1986: 12–13), and for general discussion of Plato's critique of poetry, see Ferrari (1989), Janaway (1995), and especially Hobbs (2000: Ch. 7), who focuses on Plato's thinking about *thumos* in relation to the heroic ideal of Achilles.

hand, however, citizens and the poets also suggest in various ways that the life of injustice is *in itself* happier and better than the just life. They claim that justice and moderation are difficult and laborious, while injustice and licentiousness (*akolasia*) "are shameful only according to reputation and law"; that injustice is generally more profitable than justice at both the private and public levels; that many unjust individuals are nonetheless happy, while many just ones miserable; and that the unjust can even gain the favor of the gods and absolve their misdeeds simply by making sufficiently generous sacrifices to them. The clear message of their accounts is that the best life for a human being consists in committing injustice in secret while *pretending* to be just. Adeimantus concludes by asking Socrates to show that, contrary to what traditional education implies, the life of justice is better than the unjust life regardless of whether an individual has a reputation for justice or not (362e–367e).

4. The Problem of Moral Education

Glaucon's and Adeimantus' speeches draw attention to two social and political problems that end up being programmatic for the *Republic*. The first concerns moral education. To begin with, note that Adeimantus' description of traditional education emphasizes the role of spirited motivation. The social and cultural methods by which popular values are transmitted in the city are ones that prominently engage the individual's sense of shame and spirited sensitivity to practices related to honor.[22] The focus of Adeimantus' account is on what citizens and poets praise (*epaintountes*, 363a2; cf. 363e3, 366c3, 366e1), blame (*psegei*, 366d2; cf. 363e4), honor (*timan*, 364a7; cf. 365a6, 366c1, 366e4), dishonor (*atimazein*, 364a8), exhort (*parakeleuontai*, 362e5), criticize (*loidorountōn*, 367d7), and glorify (*enkōmiazousin*, 363d5; cf. 367d7), and the overall effect of traditional education is to affirm the value of a *good reputation* (*eudokimēseis*, 363a2; cf. 363a6, 366e4, 367d4) for justice, while instilling fear of a *bad* reputation (363e1). This focus also informs the way Glaucon and Adeimantus articulate their challenge to Socrates. They want to hear a contrast to conventional praising and blaming practices, asking Socrates to "praise"

---

[22] Cf. Gosling (1973: 76–7), who notes that Socrates' criticism of popular culture and poetry in Books 2 and 3 suggests that traditional education influences and shapes *thumos*. Gosling, however, concludes that Plato does not recognize this fact *until* the *Republic*, a line of thought I assess in Ch. 5.3.

justice and "blame" injustice *themselves* (358a7, 358d4, 358d5, 359b8, 367d3, 366e3), rather than their reputations and ordinary consequences.

Glaucon's and Adeimantus' speeches also establish that the many have a *pleonectic* conception of value, according to which they identify the happy life with the attainment of bodily and external goods. I take it that these include objects of both appetitive and spirited desire, but that the many are especially preoccupied with the former: they place the highest value on physical pleasure and wealth, and they value spirited goods like honor, reputation, and power largely as means to those appetitive ends. The pleonectic worldview is most obvious in Glaucon's explicit assertion that human beings *by nature* seek *pleonexia*, or getting more than one's rightful share. It is also confirmed by the sorts of "benefits" that Glaucon's popular account takes to accrue to undiscovered and unpunished injustice: stolen property, sexual pleasure, favorable contracts and marriages, and money and profit. Importantly, these are the sorts of things, he claims, that *anyone* would pursue through injustice if given the opportunity, and they are what the many value in the life of injustice. Conversely, the "evils" Glaucon assigns to the just person with a reputation for injustice all involve physical punishment and bodily pain. Adeimantus, for his part, identifies similarly appetitive and pleonectic values in traditional poetry. The gods reward the just with bountiful crops, fertile livestock, and many children and descendants, and in Hades they "make them spend all their time drinking—as if they thought drunkenness was the finest wage of virtue" (363a–d). The poets claim that *akolasia*, licentiousness or lack of restraint, is "sweet and easy to acquire," and they honor the rich and dishonor the poor (364a–b). Perhaps worst of all, poetry suggests that even the gods are venal and share pleonectic values, since they can be bribed and appeased with riches and lavish sacrifices.

In addition to the above, Plato associates the many with appetite and its desires in various other ways throughout the *Republic*. The largest, "money-making" class of the just city, for example, corresponds to the appetitive part of the soul in Plato's analogy between the city and person, and the democratic constitution of Book 8 is likened to a soul marked by the influence of multifarious appetites (559d–561e). The many think wealth makes it easy to bear misfortune (329e); they admire those who profit from everything and hoard their money (554a–b); and most people spend their whole lives like cattle trying to satisfy their desires to "feed, fatten, and fornicate" (585e–586b). Finally, Socrates is especially clear in identifying the appetitive bent of popular ethics in Book 6. When the question of the nature of the good arises, he tells Adeimantus, "You certainly know that the many believe that *pleasure* is the good" (505b). For Plato, then, the majority of citizens in places like Athens hold a false, pleonectic conception of value that prioritizes appetitive pleasure and wealth, and that conception is instilled in people during their upbringing by their fellow citizens and poetic influences. As the previous point shows, moreover, those false values are instilled through the spirited sensitivities, emotions, and desires in each person's soul.

There is a further point to make, however, which Plato develops in Book 6 of the *Republic*: popular education has its most deleterious effects on the most promising and ambitious young people in a city. Socrates presents this idea in the course of explaining how those who are by nature *philosophic*—that is, born with the exceptional natural qualities required to become philosophers— become vicious. According to Socrates, their corruption is due in part to the very qualities that make them fit for philosophy. In general, the best natures fare worse than ordinary ones when they are unsuitably nurtured, and the same is true of souls: "Those with the best natures become outstandingly bad when they receive a bad upbringing" (491d–492a). Socrates dissents from the popular view that promising young people are corrupted by sophists and paid private teachers, however.[23] Rather, it is the many *themselves* who corrupt them:

> When many of them are sitting together in assemblies, courts, theaters, or army camps, or in some other public gathering of the crowd, they loudly blame (*psegōsi*) some of the things that are said or done, and praise (*epainōsin*) others in the same way, shouting and clapping, so that the very rocks and surroundings echo the din of their praise (*epainou*) or blame (*psogou*) and double it. In circumstances like that, what is the effect, as they say, on a young person's heart (*kardian*)? What private training can hold out and not be swept away by that kind of praise and blame and be carried by the flood wherever it goes, so that he'll say the same things are admirable (*kala*) and shameful (*aischra*) as the crowd does, follow the same way of life as they do, and be the same sort of person?   (492b5–c8)

Indeed, Socrates says, not only are sophists *not* the ultimate source of corruption of the young, but sophists themselves teach nothing other than the many's own convictions. Socrates likens sophists to someone who raises a wild beast and learns its "feelings of anger (*orgas*) and appetites (*epithumias*)," along with what makes it harsh or tame and how to make it gentle or wild. Having raised

---

[23] Cf. Irwin (1995b: 578).

the beast in this way, the trainer claims he has "wisdom" about the beast that he can sell to others. However, he knows nothing about what is truly admirable and shameful or just and unjust; those are merely names he gives to what pleases or angers the beast (493a–c). Socrates asks:

> Does this person seem any different from the one who believes that it is wisdom to understand the anger (*orgēn*) and pleasures (*hēdonas*) of the multifarious many, whether they concern painting, music, or, for that matter, politics? If anyone approaches the many to display his poetry or some other piece of craftsmanship or his service to the city and gives them power over him to any degree beyond what's necessary, he'll be under Diomedean compulsion, as it's called, to do the sort of thing which they praise (*epainōsin*).   (493c10–d7)

The many are incapable of valuing philosophy; therefore, sophists and anyone else whose success depends on pleasing the crowd inevitably "casts blame" on philosophy as well (493d–494a).

In such circumstances, Socrates explains, the naturally philosophic have little chance of realizing their potential. On the contrary, their exceptional nature itself makes it almost impossible. Because the young man will naturally display the outstanding qualities that make him well-suited for philosophy as he grows up, his "family (*oikeioi*) and fellow citizens (*politai*)" will want to use him for their own affairs. They will flatter and honor (*timōntes*) him in anticipation of the power (*dunamin*) they expect him to achieve, with the result that he becomes full of pride and ambition and will "think himself capable of leading (*hēgoumenon*) the affairs, not only of the Greeks, but of the barbarians as well." Even if someone *were* to approach the young man in this condition and attempt to attract him to the philosophical life, and even if the young man felt drawn to it because of his nature, his companions would make sure he did not pursue it and would punish the person trying to take him away from them. This, Socrates concludes, is how the best, philosophic natures are destroyed and corrupted, "and it is among these men that we find the ones who do the greatest evils to cities and individuals" (494b–495b).[24]

---

[24] Socrates' analysis in Book 6 has striking parallels to Alcibiades' autobiographical speech in the *Symposium*, as well as to the *First Alcibiades* itself. As commentators have noted, the discussion seems designed to bring to mind Socrates' failed effort to save Alcibiades from the city's influence. See Wilburn (2015a: 26–7), as well as Adam (1902, ii: 25–7), Arruzza (2016: 49–53), Destrée (2012: 204), Dušanić (1995: 339), Gribble (1999: 219–20, 240–1), Reeve (2006: 131, n. 12), Taylor (1976: 64), and

This section of the *Republic* is, I think, especially important for understanding some of Plato's most urgent anxieties about moral education. First, we should note that the passage confirms and reiterates, from a somewhat different perspective, the twin ideas about education that emerge from Glaucon's and Adeimantus' speeches: that the many have misguided, pleonectic values, and that they instill those values in one another, especially in the young, by way of the spirited element of psychology. Their influences takes place primarily through their expressions of praise and blame, and the effects are registered on the young person's "heart" or *kardia*—the very word Plato uses synonymously with *thumos* in his Book 4 argument for tripartition. The passage also shows that the values of the many are informed by appetitive and spirited concerns. They necessarily "cast blame" on love of wisdom, because their tempers, pleasures, and appetites dictate what they judge to be good and bad, and it would be "absolutely ridiculous," Socrates says, to argue that the things they value are truly good.

The passage's immediate objective, though, is to show that the harmful effects of popular education are *most* pronounced on the promising and ambitious, and Socrates' discussion reveals two additional ways in which that special harm also involves spirited motivation. The first is that the many use *honor* to gain the favor of an exceptional young man. They praise and celebrate him with undeserved honors, and as a result he becomes overly confident, ambitious, and power-seeking. He comes to believe, quite literally, that he is capable of ruling the whole world. The arrogant self-assessment inculcated in him by his flatterers, moreover, means that he will not recognize his own ignorance and hence will not seek the education he lacks. In other words, his friends and fellow citizens gratify the young man's spirited desire for honor, and that in turn feeds his thumoeidic sense of pride and desire for power and glory.

Second, young men who desire honor and glory in democratic cities are forced to conform to the tastes of the many. This is true not only of sophists and orators, Socrates says, but also, notably, of poets and *politicians*. In order to achieve acclaim, they necessarily have to produce poetic works or perform political deeds that satisfy the "appetites" and "pleasures" of the crowd and thus earn its "praise." The result is morally nocuous for the ambitious: they come to believe that "wisdom" consists in understanding how to please the

---

Waterfield (2012: 16). I take no stand on the authenticity of the *First Alcibiades*, although I tend to find arguments for its spuriousness unconvincing or inconclusive. In defense of Platonic authorship, see Benitez (2014); for doubts, see Kurihara (2014), Smith (2004), and Tarrant and Roberts (2014).

crowd; they "have no other account to give" of what is admirable or shameful, good or bad, or just or unjust, other than what pleases or angers it; and, like the crowd they serve, they inevitably disapprove of love of wisdom. The psychological fact that spirited young men desire fame and glory, combined with the social fact that they can satisfy those desires in their cities only by pleasing the many, has the effect that they assimilate not only their works and actions, but also their own *values*, to popular tastes and opinions. Those who are ambitious in corrupt cities are at the mercy of the corrupt crowd by whom success is granted.[25] Once again, then, spirited motivation exerts additional psychological pressure on the ambitious to internalize the pleonectic values of the many.

5. The Problem of Civic Strife

The second social and political worry that emerges out of the brothers' speeches is the problem of civic strife, which is itself closely connected to moral education. As we saw above, traditional education creates a troubling tension. On the one hand, it encourages people to act justly and conform to the laws of their city. On the other hand, by affirming the supreme value of bodily and external goods, it also promotes the idea that the happy life is achieved through *pleonexia*—that is, through the *unjust* attainment of more than one's share. The ultimate effect is that people come to distinguish their own private good from the good of their fellow citizens and city, which has a destabilizing and divisive effect on the *polis*. In particular, popular education results in the subordination of spirited motivations to appetitive ends in two interrelated ways that threaten civic unity.

The first concerns the ethical imperative to help one's friends and harm one's enemies, which is ubiquitous in early Greek literature, politics, and popular thought, and which Plato evidently felt a strong philosophical need to confront, as it appears in various iterations throughout his works and plays a major part in the *Republic* itself.[26] From Plato's perspective this imperative is

---

[25] Cf. Euripides *Iph.* 525–7, which characterizes *philotimia* as a form of base servility or allegiance to the "crowd" or *ochlos*.

[26] See discussion of Plato in Ch. 5.2 and 7.4. In Greek literature, Pindar, for example, writes, "Let me be a friend to a friend, but against an enemy, I shall, as his enemy, run him down as a wolf does" (*Pyth.* 2.82–4), and the defendant in a speech by Lysias admits to being only moderately annoyed by the spurious case brought against him by his adversaries, "since I consider it ordained as a rule to treat one's friends well and one's enemies badly" (Lysias 9.20). For additional examples, see Hesiod, *WD* 342–55; Homer, *Od.* 4.687–92; Theognis, *Eleg.* 1.337–9; Archilochus, fr. 23.11–16; Aeschylus, *Eumen.* 858–66; Euripides, *Medea* 656–62, *Androm.* 985–6, *Her.* 275–8, and *Phoen.* 374–5; *Dissoi Logoi* 3.2–6; Gorgias, *Palamedes* 25; Xenophon, *Agesilaus* 9.9 and *Mem.* 2.1.28, 4.5.10; and (ps.-)Plato, *On Justice*

rooted unmistakably in the spirited part of the soul. *Thumos* is what makes people protective of their loved ones and hostile toward outsiders. Confronting the ethics of helping friends and harming enemies, therefore, requires attention to the spirited motivations at its heart. The problem is that, given the pleonectic orientation of traditional education, the spirited instinct to "help friends and harm enemies" becomes directed toward attaining a greater share of pleonectic goods for oneself and one's household, family, friends, and political allies. Citizens come to view one another not as civic friends to be treated as *oikeioi*, but rather as *allotrioi* or competitors for limited appetitive and spirited resources. Glaucon actually makes the pleonectic orientation of the spirited impulse to help friends and harm enemies explicit in his speech. The unjust "get more" (*pleonektein*) than their enemies, and by "getting more" (*pleonektounta*) they become wealthy and are able to benefit their friends and harm their enemies. On the popular view, what it means to help or harm is to promote or damage a person's material interests: help and harm are made possible by money and means, and they consist in the sorts of things money can buy. The desire to help one's friends, therefore, manifests itself as the desire to help one's friends attain more than their share as well— that is, get away with and profit from injustice. Indeed, Glaucon explains that one of the benefits of injustice is "getting to release from prison" whomever one wants (360b–c). When an unjust man's actions are discovered and he needs to use force to protect himself, moreover, he will be able to use "the substantial wealth and friends with which he has provided himself" (361b). To that thought Adeimantus adds that the unjust will form "secret societies and political clubs" to help keep their acts of injustice hidden (365d). Spirited affection for, and desire to protect, friends and *oikeioi* remain salient features of human psychology and behavior even in unjust cities, therefore; it is just that they are directed toward those private subsets of the city—family members, friends, or political confederates—that each person considers allies in his own pursuit of pleonectic goods.[27]

The same point is illuminated in the discussions of the two formulations of justice that receive the most consideration in Book 1. First, Polemarchus

---

374c–d, *Eryx.* 393e, and *Theages* 122b. For secondary literature on the ethics of helping friends and harming enemies in Greek and Athenian culture, see Blundell (1989, esp. Ch. 2), Foxhall (1998), Mitchell and Rhodes (1996), and Rhodes (1998).

[27] For illuminating discussion of this issue, see Shaw (2015: 175–81), who refers to social groups (families, friends, cities, and so on) that cooperate in the pursuit of pleonectic goods as "pleonectic alliances." He usefully notes that some such alliances are subsets of other ones, that alliances can overlap in complex ways, and that this complexity "can cause tension and conflict between and among groups" (p. 179).

endorses the view that justice is "to treat friends well and enemies badly." When questioned by Socrates, he claims that the just man benefits his friends and harms his enemies most obviously during war, but that during times of peace, he helps his friends—and, by implication, harms his enemies—through "contracts and shared enterprises." In particular, he does so in shared enterprises related to "money matters" when wealth must be "guarded." Since clever guardians must also be clever thieves, however, the just person must also be clever at *stealing* money, which results in the view that "justice seems to be some sort of craft of stealing, one that benefits friends and harms enemies." The appetitive orientation of this popular understanding of justice is clear: friends help friends by helping them make a profit, and people harm their enemies through deceit and theft in financial and material matters. Polemarchus, naturally enough, finds this conclusion unseemly, but he cannot explain why it does not follow from his account of justice, nor is he yet willing to give up that account (332a–334b).

There are further problems with his view, however. One is that the many are *mistaken* in their judgments about who is good and who is bad for them, with the result that they have morally bad friends and morally good enemies.[28] This point anticipates Plato's depiction of the spirited instincts of dogs in *Republic* 2: they are affectionate to their *oikeioi* whether or not they have ever received anything good from them, and are hostile to *allotrioi* despite never having suffered any harm from them. Indeed, the fact that what is good can come apart from what is *oikeion* or a friend is, in a sense, at the very core of why spirit is corruptible. The immediate implication for Polemarchus' argument is that, for those who are mistaken about their friends and enemies, justice will consist in benefiting the bad people who are their friends and harming the good people who are their enemies. Polemarchus rejects this idea and insists that justice must mean helping only *good* people who are one's friends and *bad* people who are one's enemies. However, Socrates suggests, to harm someone is to make them *worse* with respect to human virtue—which means making them more *unjust*—and justice itself can never be the cause of *injustice*. Therefore, it is never actually just to harm *anyone*, even one's enemies (334b–335e). Socrates' use of this argument draws further attention to the pleonectic assumptions that underlie Polemarchus' account of justice. The

---

[28] This is no mere theoretical point for Plato's readers. Foxhall (1998) discusses the volatility and uncertainty of friendships in the Greek world, remarking that "the ethic of *philia* in which friends return good for good ... seems to have been honoured more in the breach than in the observance" (p. 56). For anxiety about the stability of friendship in the Platonic tradition, see *Eryx.* 396a–e and especially *Demod.* 385c–386c.

argument succeeds precisely because it replaces the pleonectic conception of benefit and harm with an aretaic one.[29] The popular view of justice as helping friends and harming enemies is animated and justified by the assumption that help and harm consist in promoting or diminishing external and appetitive "goods" or "evils." When that assumption is withdrawn and supplanted by the view that help and harm consist in promoting or diminishing *virtue*, the popular account collapses. Socrates concludes that the popular conception of justice probably originated with "Periander, or Perdiccas, or Xerxes, or Ismenias of Corinth, or some other wealthy man who believed himself to have great power" (336a).

The pleonectic orientation of spirited motivation is also inherent in Thrasymachus' view of justice, according to which "justice is the advantage of the stronger" (338c). Those who are powerful, he claims, always seek "their own good" (*agathon to hautōn*) and what will "benefit themselves,"[30] and justice, he says, is "the good of *another* (*allotrion*)." He explains that an unjust man always "gets more" (*pleonektein*) than a just one: he takes advantage of the virtuous in contracts and shared enterprises, and he pays less in taxes to the city and profits more when public funds are distributed than do the just (343b–e). Thrasymachus adds:

When each of them holds a ruling position in some public office, a just person, even if he isn't penalized in other ways, finds that his own (*oikeia*) affairs deteriorate because he has to neglect them, that he gains no advantage from the public purse because of his justice, and that he's hated by his relatives (*tois oikeiois*) and those he knows (*tois gnorimois*) when he's unwilling to do them an unjust favor. The opposite is true of an unjust man in every respect. (343e1–7)

This passage reflects the Greek distinction between "public" and "private," *koinon* or *idia*, and the popular idea that the public good of the city often conflicts with the private good of the individual and the household, which is the central site and symbol of private life and gain.[31] To the extent that one devotes oneself to benefiting the city through justice, one thereby neglects one's household and family. The unjust, by contrast, profit in their private

---

[29] Cf. Reeve (1988: 7–8).

[30] Cf. 338e1–2 and 341a1–2: rulers seek τὸ αὐτῇ συμφέρον and τὸ αὐτῷ βέλτιστον, respectively.

[31] See Natali (2005), who highlights "la morale d'acquisition" (p. 220) that characterizes the Greek *oikos* and discusses its relation to Plato's views on families and the household in the *Republic* and *Laws*. For an example of the antagonism between private and public, see Thucydides, *Hist.* 6.12.2.

lives. The pitch of this kind of beneficial injustice, Thrasymachus says, is "to appropriate the property of others (*ta allotria*) through stealth or force" (344a). This passage is once again striking for its anticipation of the language used in Book 2 to introduce spiritedness. Thrasymachus contrasts people and material goods that are "one's own" or "known" with ones that are "foreign" or "other." In light of the later discussion, Thrasymachus' account suggests that the spirited impulse to love and protect the *oikeion* is directed largely toward increasing one's own wealth and property, along with that of the select people to whom one feels some attachment or loyalty. On this picture, what is "one's own" prominently includes one's private material possessions, and spirited affection for the *oikeion* is directed toward maximizing and protecting those possessions.[32] Conversely, spirited aggression toward the *allotrion* is directed against those who fall outside of one's private associations and aims at appropriating their wealth and property. In other words, people view their own fellow citizens as "other" and compete with them for pleonectic goods. As we saw above, this is precisely the idea that emerges from Glaucon's and Adeimantus' speeches. And indeed, the latter concludes by warning Socrates that unless he is able to praise justice and blame injustice in themselves and not for the reputations they bring, "we'll say that you agree with Thrasymachus that justice is the good of another (*allotrion*)" (367c2–3).[33]

Popular moral education also results in the subordination of spirited motivations to appetite in a second, related way: the willingness and ability to take more than one's fair share comes to be identified—especially among the powerful—with the virtue of courage and manliness, while the just and moderate contentment with one's share, and the unwillingness or inability to take more, is conceived as foolish cowardice. This idea is implicit in Thrasymachus' account of justice as the advantage of the "stronger," and it is confirmed by Glaucon and Adeimantus:

People value justice not as a good but because they cannot get away with injustice themselves due to their weakness (*arrōstiai*). Someone who has the power (*ton dunamenon*) to do this, however, and is a true man (*alēthōs*

---

[32] Hence Lear (2006: 120) not inappropriately characterizes Thrasymachus, who clearly displays some spirited traits, as dominated by a *thumos* that has been corrupted by appetite.

[33] Cf. Reeve (2013b: 68), who notes that Thrasymachus' man of "great power (*ton megala dunamenon*) who gets more (*pleonektein*)" is clearly the prototype for Glaucon's "man who has the power (*ton dunamenon*) to do injustice with impunity." Strauss (1964: 86), meanwhile, recognizes that Thrasymachus' view is not unique, but rather the view of "the many."

andra), wouldn't make an agreement with anyone not to do injustice in order not to suffer it. For him that would be madness.   (359a8–b4)

Given all that has been said, Socrates, how is it possible for anyone of any power (*dunamis*)—whether of soul, wealth, body, or noble birth—to willingly honor justice and not laugh aloud when he hears it praised?... Through cowardice (*anandrias*) or old age or some other weakness (*astheneias*), people do indeed blame injustice. But it's obvious that they do so only because they lack the power (*adunatōn*) to do injustice.   (366b7–d3)[34]

According to the popular view defended by the brothers, it is a mark of masculine courage to use one's power and resources in the service of injustice, and a mark of cowardice or weakness to live a life of virtue. This point is, in fact, a corollary of the pleonectic orientation of spirited impulses with respect to the *oikeion* and the *allotrion*. Defense of one's own, as we will see, is a characteristic expression of *thumos*: it is cowardice to *fail* to protect one's own or help one's friends, and courage to fight for them even in the face of risks. Once "one's own" comes to be identified with material goods and members of one's exclusive private circles, and "helping one's friends" with promoting their material interests, it is unsurprising that those unwilling to seize pleonectic opportunities for the sake of their *oikeioi* would be considered timid and weak, while the willing would be lauded as bold and brave.

Two noteworthy passages from Book 8 reinforce this idea. The first is from Socrates' description of how a good-natured young man becomes honor-loving and timocratic. Socrates explains that the youth's father is a good man who avoids honors, ruling positions, and every kind of "meddling in other people's affairs," and who is even willing to put up with "getting less of a share" (*ellatousthai*, the contrary of *pleonexia*) than others (549c). The problem, however, is that the young man is raised in a badly governed city, and his mother, other members of his household, and his fellow citizens denigrate his father's lifestyle:

He listens to his mother complaining that her husband isn't one of the rulers and that she gets less (*ellatoumenēs*) than other women as a result. Then she sees that he's not very concerned about money and doesn't fight back (*machomenon*) when he's insulted, whether in private or in public in the

---

[34] See also 360e–361b, where the completely unjust person must possess courage and strength and be capable of both speaking persuasively and using force; and 365a–c, where it is the "clever" young people who choose the life of covert injustice.

courts, but is soft-spirited (*rhaithumōs*) in the face of everything of that sort
... Angered by all this, she tells her son that his father is unmanly (*anandros*)
and too yielding (*aneimenos*) ... And the servants of men like that—the
ones who are thought to be kindly disposed to the family—say similar things
to the son in private. When they see the father failing to prosecute someone
who owes him money or has done him injustice in some other way, they urge
the son to take revenge (*timōrēsetai*) on all such people when he grows up
and to be more of a man (*anēr mallon*) than his father. The boy hears and
sees the same kind of things when he goes out: those in the city who do their
own work are called fools and considered insignificant, while those who
meddle in other people's affairs are honored and praised (*timōmenous te kai
epainoumenous*).   (549c8–550a4)

I take it that this passage describes the circumstances of a virtuous or philosophical man and his son in a place like Athens.[35] Like the democratic many,
the citizens of this corrupt city have an appetitive conception of value that
prioritizes money and wealth. Their esteem for a man depends on the extent to
which he participates successfully in the culture of *pleonexia*—whether he
"gets more" or "gets less" than his fair share. Those who fail to defend their
own wealth and property against the unjust, and who refuse to compete for
material goods for the sake of their families, are not considered "real men."
Rather, they are described as "soft-spirited" and overly "yielding"—both terms
that refer to an inappropriately gentle, weak, or acquiescent *thumos*.
Conversely, those who compete effectively for pleonectic goods receive the
admiration and honor of the crowd. Once again, popular ethics subordinates
spirited motivation to appetitive ends: the unjust pursuit of material goods
is identified with courage and manliness, while toleration of a lesser share
is characteristic of a weak *thumos*.[36]

The second passage is from Socrates' discussion of the origin of the democratic youth, who is the son of an oligarchic man. Socrates explains that his
father is ruled by the appetitive part of his soul, which means that he organizes
his life around the pursuit of wealth. As a result, he is thrifty—not wanting to
waste money on extravagances—and attempts to instill frugality in his son as
well. He encourages his son to exert self-control and resist the sorts of
"unnecessary" appetites that deplete wealth, and inasmuch as he is successful

---

[35] Note that Adeimantus considers the behavior of the timocratic youth's mother familiar and
typical (549e2).
[36] Significantly, of course, the ultimate effect of their influence is that the young man becomes a
lover of honor ruled by the spirited part of his soul (550b5–7).

he instills a kind of "shame" in his son's soul. The democratic youth, however, also associates with dangerous criminal types who exhort him to a flagitious life: they encourage him to indulge in unnecessary appetites and "every variety of multicolored pleasure in every way," and they denigrate his father's values (559d–560d). As a result, "false and boastful" beliefs take over the youth's soul. Socrates explains:

> Don't they call a sense of shame (aidō) "foolishness" and banish it out with dishonor (atimōs), and call moderation (sōphrosunēn) "cowardice" (ana-ndrian) and cast it out? . . . And they return insolence, anarchy, profligacy, and shamelessness (anaideian) from exile in a blaze of torchlight . . . They praise the returning exiles and give them fine names, calling insolence "proper education," anarchy "freedom," profligacy "magnificence," and shamelessness (anaideian) "courage" (andreian).   (560d2–561a1)[37]

The details of the young man's transition are complex, but of special note for present purposes is the way Socrates characterizes the relationship between the two faces of thumos. On the one hand, moderation and the sense of shame, which are typically understood as gentle virtues, are reconceived as foolish forms of cowardice—that is, as contemptible deficiencies of appropriate competitive motivation. Conversely, shamelessness, which typically constitutes an abhorrent lack of proper respectful restraint, is reconceived as the virtue of courage. This inversion of values, moreover, is closely connected to appetitive desire: cowardice is the abstemious unwillingness to indulge one's appetites, while courage is the indiscriminate pursuit of every pleasure. In encouraging this way of thinking, the criminal influences give voice not to the explicit values of democratic education, but rather to the implicit pleonectic ones that traditional culture signals to those capable of getting away with injustice.

Plato does not merely draw attention to the fact that citizens compete with one another for greater shares of pleonectic goods, however; he also identifies that fact as the cause of civic discord and disunity. This is hinted at, to begin with, in the duplicity that characterizes citizens' relationships with one another. We have already seen that according to Glaucon and Adeimantus, the many ultimately want to have a reputation for justice while actually being unjust. In other words, they want to mislead their fellow citizens into believing

---

[37] As many commentators have noted, e.g. North (1966: 176), this passage closely parallels Thucydides' description of the effects of civil war in Corcyra—which, notably, he attributes to a combination of pleonexia, philotimia, philonikia, and prothumia (Hist. 3.82.1-8).

they are trustworthy, while surreptitiously getting away with injustice whenever they can. Glaucon makes the deceit inherent in their relationships explicit when he considers how people would react if someone had the opportunity to seize other people's property with impunity but did not take it. *Everyone*, he says, would think a man like that is "wretched and stupid." However, he adds, "Of course they'd praise him in public, deceiving each other for fear of suffering injustice" (360d). In order to discourage others from *pleonexia* while also promoting their own reputation for virtue, citizens advocate justice publicly while secretly wishing to commit injustice against one another.[38] The suspicion and duplicity that mark their relationships with one another betray a tenuousness in the bonds of civic fellowship.[39]

Other passages are more explicit. First, in response to Thrasymachus' claim that the best cities will commit injustice against other cities, Socrates argues that no city or community can achieve anything, even injustice, in the complete absence of justice. Rather, if a city or "any other group with a common unjust purpose" wants to achieve its goal, its citizens or members must at least treat *one another* with justice in the process. The reason, Socrates explains, is that "injustice causes factions (*staseis*), hatred (*misē*), and fighting (*machas*) among themselves, while justice brings friendship (*homonoian*) and likemindedness (*philian*)." As a result, "Injustice has the power to make whatever it arises in—whether a city, a family, an army, or anything else, incapable of achieving anything together, because of the factions and disagreements it creates" (351c–352a). Here Socrates draws a clear connection between civic disunity and the kind of behavior applauded by Thrasymachus. To the extent that citizens do one another injustice in the pursuit of appetitive and spirited goods, they *weaken* the city and make it ineffective. The culture of helping friends and harming enemies is politically destructive when coupled with the pleonectic conception of value that encourages people to count only *subsets* of the city as their friends and to make enemies of their fellow citizens. Any city in which people treat one another in the ways encouraged by Thrasymachus, in other words, will be marked by discord and instability.[40]

---

[38] Cf. 365c, where Adeimantus suggests that traditional education encourages an exterior "shadow-painting" of virtue with a devious *interior*. Similar criticism of popular morality is evident in other early or contemporary sources as well, e.g. Democritus, DK B181.

[39] Socrates highlights the danger of deceit, in particular of citizens toward their rulers, at 389b–c: it is "subversive" and "destructive" to a city.

[40] Cf. Xenophon, *Mem.* 2.61.21, where Socrates describes the socially destructive effects of the "hostile" (πολεμικά) elements of human nature that lead people to "fight" (μάχονται) with one another for pleonectic goods: "Strife (ἔρις) and anger (ὀργή) lead to hostility (πολεμικόν), love of getting more (πλεονεκτεῖν ἔρως) to enmity (δυσμενές), envy (φθόνος) to hatred (μισητόν)."

Another passage confirms that, on Plato's view, most actual cities, including *Athens*, are marked by precisely the discord and instability against which Socrates warns. In Book 4, Adeimantus raises a worry about how their just city would fare in war against an exceptionally wealthy and powerful one (422a). Socrates, however, objects to the notion that any other city but the just one is properly called a city at all. Rather, he says:

> Each of them is a great many cities, not *a* city... At any rate, each of them consists of two cities at war with one another, that of the rich and that of the poor, and each of these contains a great many. If you approach them as one city, you'll be making a big mistake. But if you approach them as many and offer to give to the one city the money, power, and indeed the very inhabitants of the other, you'll always find many allies and few enemies.
>
> (422e8–423a5)

According to this passage, *all* other cities lack the civic unity of the just city.[41] Instead, they are unstable collections of smaller "cities" or communities that view one another as enemies and competitors. In addition to the opposed cities of "rich" and "poor," Socrates presumably has in mind groups like households, villages, and political clubs and factions. These various private communities compete with one another for greater shares of wealth, power, and resources, and that gives rise to mutual enmity in place of the feelings of friendship that bind cities together. *Pleonexia*, and the corresponding subordination of spirit to appetitive and pleonectic ends, is the cause of civil strife and instability.[42]

In the rest of this book we will see how, throughout his career, Plato dramatizes, examines, and offers solutions to the twin problems of corrupt education and civic strife that arise out of (and can be resolved only through attention to) human spirited psychology.

---

[41] Socrates claims that no other city "among either Greeks or barbarians" is as great as their truly unified one (423a9–b1).

[42] Book 8 confirms the volatility of disunified cities. Socrates claims that oligarchy is "sick" with antagonism between rich and poor and needs only the slightest provocation to fall into civil war (556e). In doing so Plato is appealing to empirical observations that are familiar to his audience and have a special bite given Athens' recent history of civil strife, war, and regime change between oligarchic and democratic factions in the late fifth century.

PART II

4

Political Psychology in the Great Speech
of the *Protagoras*

In this chapter and the next, I examine several "early" dialogues—understood loosely to include works that predate, or that commentators have commonly taken to predate, the *Republic*—in order to draw attention to ways in which they anticipate Plato's account of the spirited part of the soul and the social and political nature of its motivations. Plato's early works highlight the crucial role of spirited motivations, first, in making it possible for people to form and defend communities together and in determining whether they are unified or divided within those communities; and, second, in allowing people to be molded and educated by one another through social influences, for better or worse. In this chapter I focus on the *Protagoras*, before turning to several other early dialogues in Chapter 5. Nothing in these two chapters will assume or entail that Plato accepted tripartite psychology and the existence of a spirited part of the soul when he wrote his earlier dialogues. My arguments *will* show, however, that Plato recognized a circumscribed class of motivations characterized by their social or political nature—ones that had, moreover, *already* been strongly associated with *thumos* in the early Greek tradition, and that Plato himself would eventually attribute to the spirited part of the soul.[1]

In the current chapter I focus on the Great Speech of the *Protagoras*, and my main aim is to show that Plato characterizes spirited motivation there as the *sine qua non* of human social and political life. I begin in Section 1 with an overview of the Great Speech itself, in which the dialogue's namesake describes the conditions of early pre-political and political human life. According to

---

[1] Historically, developmentalist commentators have often take *Protagoras* to provide the strongest evidence of a shift in Plato's views on psychology between early dialogues and the *Republic*. Non-developmentalists, meanwhile, typically argue only that the theories of the two dialogues are compatible or that the earlier dialogue hints at the views of the later, rather than that the *Protagoras* positively advocates or assumes tripartition of the soul. Hobbs (2000: Ch. 4), Shaw (2015: Ch. 2), and Renaut (2014: Ch. 2) all identify precursors to the *Republic*'s spirited part of the soul in the *Protagoras*. Morris (2006: 225–9) argues that it is "not unreasonable to suppose that Plato held the *Republic* view [of psychology], or something like it" when he wrote the *Protagoras*. Cf. also Bentley (2003, esp. 95–6, n. 20) and McCoy (2008: 78–9), who freely use the language of tripartition in their interpretations of the dialogue. I return to the issue of developmentalism in Ch. 5.3.

The Political Soul: Plato on Thumos, Spirited Motivation, and the City. Josh Wilburn, Oxford University Press.
© Josh Wilburn 2021. DOI: 10.1093/oso/9780198861867.003.0004

Protagoras, human beings were incapable of living together in cities until the gods granted them "the art of politics." In Sections 2 and 3, I argue that this "art" consists in capacities for spirited motivation. Both the aggressive and gentle sides of *thumos* are necessary psychological conditions of human civilization, without which political life is impossible. Part of their contribution, moreover, consists in making moral education possible. Protagoras depicts spirited motivations as both the instrument and target of the education transmitted through culture and socialization. This is, in fact, a corollary of spirit's role in making human communities possible in the first place: *thumos* makes people sensitive to the judgments and actions of other people in their communities, and that sensitivity makes it possible for them to be educated in accordance with, and live together with their fellow citizens in conformity to, the shared values, customs, and laws of their communities. In Section 3, I conclude by noting ways in which Protagoras also hints at the problems of moral education and civic strife, as surveyed in the last chapter, that arise in corrupt or non-ideal political conditions.

1. The "Art" of Politics

The central action of Plato's *Protagoras* begins when Socrates' young friend Hippocrates knocks on his door early in the morning to announce that the celebrity-sophist Protagoras has arrived in town. Hippocrates is eager to visit Protagoras and become one of his students in order to obtain some of the sophist's "wisdom," and he wants Socrates' help. The cautious Socrates, however, recommends they first find out more about precisely what it is that Protagoras teaches. When they finally meet the sophist and ask him to state how he benefits his students, Protagoras answers:

> What I teach is sound deliberation (*euboulia*), both in domestic affairs (*tōn oikeiōn*)—how best to manage one's household (*oikian*)—and in the affairs of the city (*tōn tēs poleōs*)—how to become as powerful (*dunatōtatos*) as possible in action and speech that concerns the city (*ta tēs poleōs*).
>
> (318e5–319a2)

Socrates wants to make sure he understands Protagoras' claim: "You appear to be talking about the art of politics (*tēn politikēn technēn*)," he says, "and to be promising to make men good citizens (*politas*)." Protagoras confirms: that is *exactly* what he teaches. Socrates is skeptical, however. He suspects the art of politics itself is not actually teachable, for two reasons. First, when an art *is* teachable, only recognized experts in that field—those to whom the art has been taught—are permitted to speak in the Athenian assembly on technical matters. Only builders, for example, are taken seriously as the city's advisors on building projects. By contrast, the Athenians permit *any* citizen to speak up on political issues and "management of the city" (*tōn tēs poleōs dioikēseōs*). That suggests *no one* is considered an expert in politics, which in turn suggests that politics is not a teachable expertise. Second, Socrates notes that the most accomplished Athenian politicians, such as Pericles, regularly fail to make their own sons good citizens. If it were possible to teach the art of politics, however, then surely those who possess it would impart it to their own children through moral education (319a–320c).

It is in response to Socrates' concerns that Protagoras delivers his Great Speech in defense of the teachability of the "art of politics."[2] Roughly speaking, he divides his speech into two main parts, beginning with a myth designed to show that all human beings *by nature* have some share in political art. According to Protagoras, when the gods created the mortal animals on earth, they assigned to Epimetheus the task of equipping each species with appropriate "powers" or "capacities" (*dunameis*). These "powers" included various features designed to promote survival—for example, speed, strength, wings for flying, or thick pelts for keeping warm. Unfortunately, however, the short-sighted Epimetheus used up all the "powers" on the "unreasoning" (*aloga*) animals but left humans entirely unequipped for survival (*sōteria*). When the far-sighted Prometheus noticed what had happened, he stole the art of fire from Hephaestus and wisdom in practical arts from Athena and gave them to the human race. As a result, humans were able to use language and to develop the skills of farming food and constructing shelter and clothing. Protagoras emphasizes, however, that the "wisdom" they possessed at that time was sufficient only for staying alive; they did not yet possess "political" wisdom, which was guarded by Zeus (320c–322a). He describes the conditions of these pre-political humans in an important passage:

> Human beings at first lived in scattered isolation; there were no cities (*poleis de ouk ēsan*). They were being destroyed by wild beasts because they were weaker in every way, and although their technology was adequate to obtain

---

[2] For general discussion of the Great Speech from various perspectives, see Cairns (1993: 354–60), Guthrie (1971b: 63–7), Jarratt (1991: 50–3), McCoy (1998 and 2008, Ch. 3), Nussbaum (1986: 100–6), and Weiss (2006: 31–8).

food, it was deficient when it came to war (*polemon*) against the wild animals. This was because they did not yet possess the art of politics, of which the art of war is a part (*poltikēn gar technēn oupō eichon, hēs meros polemikē*). They did indeed try to join together and keep safe by establishing cities (*hathroizesthai kai sōizesthai ktizontes poleis*). The outcome when they did so was that they committed injustice (*ēdikoun*), since they did not yet possess the art of politics (*tēn politikēn technēn*), and so they would scatter again and be destroyed. Zeus was afraid that our whole race might be wiped out, so he sent Hermes to bring shame (*aidō*) and justice (*dikēn*) to humans, so that there would be order within cities and bonds of friendship to unite them (*poleōn kosmoi te kai desmoi philias sunagōgoi*). Hermes asked Zeus how he should distribute shame and justice to humans. "Should I distribute them as the other arts were? This is how the others were distributed: one person practicing the art of medicine suffices for many ordinary people; and so forth with the other practitioners. Should I establish justice and shame among humans in this way, or distribute it to all?" "To all," said Zeus, "and let all have a share. For cities would never come to be (*ou gar an genointo poleis*) if only a few possessed these, as in the case of the other arts. And establish this law as coming from me: Death to him who cannot partake of shame and justice, for he is a disease to the city (*ton mē dunamenon aidous kai dikēs metechein kteinein hōs noson poleōs*)."   (322a9–d5)

Protagoras draws from the myth a conclusion that answers to Socrates' first argument against the teachability of politics: the reason Athenians allow anyone to contribute to debate about "political virtue (*politikēs aretēs*), which must proceed entirely from justice (*dikaiosunēs*) and moderation (*sōphrosunēs*)," is not that they think *no one* is an expert in political art, but rather that *all* human beings "have a share in justice and the rest of political virtue (*metechein dikaiosunēs te kai tēs allēs politikēs aretēs*)"; otherwise, "no cities would exist (*mē einai poleis*)" in the first place (322e2–323a7).[3]

---

[3] Commentators debate whether, and to what extent, the Great Speech is based on actual source material from the historical Protagoras. At one extreme, Guthrie (1971b: 63–4 and 64, n. 1) assumes the speech reproduces the substance of the historical figure's own views, but most interpreters are more cautious or agnostic. Likewise, I take the speech to be Plato's own literary and philosophical creation, but one that may attempt to explore the implications of at least some historically Protagorean ideas as Plato understood them. For my purposes, however, what matters most is Plato's use of the ideas presented in the speech, not their ultimate intellectual provenance. For discussion of Plato's familiarity with Protagorean views and the historicity of the Great Speech, see Barney (2006: 86, n. 16), Cairns (1993: 355–6 and n. 37), Maguire (1977), Prior (2002: 318–19), Schiller (1908), Stalley (1995: 3–7), and Taylor (1976: 83–4).

The first thing to note about this passage is its unmistakable emphasis on the idea that Zeus' allotment to human beings—for the moment, call it simply "the art of politics" —is the necessary condition of human community: there were no cities before human beings possessed it; when humans tried to form cities without it, they invariably failed; cities could never come into existence in its absence; and unless *all* people had some share in it, there would be no cities at all. Protagoras' message is resounding: whatever happens when Zeus grants the art of politics—literally, "the art related to cities" —is what makes it possible for human beings to join together and live in groups. It is the *sine qua non* of human community and civilization.

The central claim I want to defend about the myth is that the art of politics allotted by Zeus consists in capacities for experiencing spirited motivations. The interpretation goes like this. Protagoras identifies two main obstacles to human survival during pre-political times: they cannot wage war and defend themselves against beasts of prey, and they cannot maintain order and treat one another justly when they attempt to form communities. Each problem is due to a deficiency with respect to the two sides of *thumos*. Before humans receive the art of politics, spirited impulses and emotions are either absent from their nature entirely, or they at least play no detectable or meaningful role in their lives. To use the language of *Republic* 2, early humans were incapable of being sufficiently savage to their bestial enemies, and they were incapable of being sufficiently gentle to one another. The art of politics, which is constituted by "the art of war" on the one hand and "shame and justice" on the other, remedies this natural deficiency. The art of war represents, or develops out of, the capacity to experience feelings of spirited anger and aggression that are conducive to effective fighting, and shame and justice represent (or prominently include) capacities for experiencing spirited emotions and desires conducive to friendship, cooperation, and the stability of communities. Shame and justice endow human beings with sensitivities they did not previously possess. Because of those sensitivities, people care about and respect fellow members of their communities, and they are responsive to others' behavior toward, and opinions about, them. The motivations associated with the art of war and shame and justice, moreover, make it possible for citizens to acquire civic virtue and become law-abiding through moral education. According to this line of interpretation, the art of politics makes communities and cities possible by making human beings into spirited animals.[4]

---

[4] Cf. Nussbaum (1986: 102). McCoy (1998; cf. 2008, Ch. 3), however, explicitly argues *against* Nussbaum's view that Zeus' intervention changes human nature by making it political. Rather, she

Now, there is an immediate worry to raise about this account: the art of politics is a *technē* that is compared to other branches of teachable technical knowledge like medicine and shoemaking; it is called a form of "wisdom," *sophia*; and Protagoras evidently identifies it in some way with *euboulia*, the ability to offer sound deliberation. All of this suggests that what human beings gain when they receive the art of politics is not spiritedness, but rather something *rational*—a specialized kind of knowledge. Simply put: *technē*, *sophia*, and *euboulia* certainly sound like things Plato would want to assign to the reasoning part of the soul, rather than the spirited, in his later works.

I have two lines of response to this worry. First, we should note that the language of "art" or *technē* is not actually Protagoras' preferred vocabulary. In fact, he uses the phrase "the art of politics" —which is originally introduced by Socrates—only twice in his entire speech (322b5, 322b8), and he uses the related expressions "political wisdom" (321d4–5) and "the art of war" (322b5) only once each. His four total uses of these expressions, moreover, all occur early in the myth, *prior* to his account of Zeus' intervention. Once Zeus and Hermes begin discussing the additional allotment to human beings, Protagoras pivots in his terminology: he never again uses the phrase "the art of politics" or characterizes politics as a *technē*.[5] Instead, from this point on he speaks not of political *art*, but of political *virtue*: Zeus grants to human beings "justice and shame," which are soon equated with the virtues of "justice and moderation," and Protagoras uses the term for virtue, *aretē*, twenty-one times in the rest of his speech, including in four occurrences of the phrase "*political* virtue."

The contrast between the language of technical knowledge prior to Zeus' intervention and the language of virtue following it is striking, and it is clearly deliberate on Plato's part. It also matters in the present context, for whereas the terms *technē* and *sophia* have strong connotations of knowledge and

claims, both before and after humans receive *aidōs* and *dikē*, they are non-social creatures who value primarily survival and bodily goods. Her arguments emphasize several places in the Great Speech which suggest that "justice and shame are naturally weaker than self-centered human tendencies," and that "when claims of self-interest and communal interest conflict . . . self-interest will triumph" (p. 127). I actually accept these points—and even emphasize similar ones in Section 4 below—but I reject the inference to her conclusion. Rather, I take one of the subtle lessons of the Great Speech to be that although (spirited) social desires, emotions, and sensitivities make it possible for humans to become virtuous and live in unified communities together, they do not (as we saw in Ch. 3) guarantee that outcome. From the perspective of my interpretation, the Great Speech highlights the centrality of spirited motivation in education and politics, while also hinting at the dangers of subjecting our spiritedness to the wrong cultural influences. McCoy and I agree that Plato is drawing attention to flaws of Protagorean and democratic values (and I admire McCoy's treatment of this issue), but where she takes those deficiencies to show the *lack* of social nature, I take them to show the *corruption* and *subordination* of social nature to self-interested or appetitive ends.

[5] He uses the term *technē* only twice in the whole rest of his speech, and both times it refers to ordinary, *non*-political crafts.

rationality for any Greek speaker in Plato's time, that is not necessarily true of the terms for shame, justice, moderation, or virtue in general. Indeed, although Protagoras casually equates political *technē* with virtue in his speech itself, in an exchange with Socrates that immediately follows that speech, it quickly becomes clear that not even Protagoras *himself* takes the political virtues to be forms of knowledge, despite what his loose language might have suggested. When Socrates questions him about the relation between knowledge and the rest of the virtues, Protagoras insists that each virtue, including knowledge, is distinct and different from all the others, and that "they are not like each other in function in any way" (329e–330b). To be sure, this view does not represent Plato's own final say on the issue. One of the guiding puzzles of the *Protagoras*—and, for that matter, Plato's philosophy more generally—is the question of precisely how to characterize the relationship between knowledge and virtue. Over the course of the dialogue, Socrates presents a series of arguments designed to establish similarity or identity between wisdom and the rest of the virtues, and his arguments have the effect of eroding Protagoras' commitment to his initial position. It is also fair to say that Plato's own settled view is that *genuine* virtue, at least, either is or requires knowledge. However, we can distinguish what Plato considers true virtue from the sort of virtue described by Protagoras in his speech. While Plato may very well think the former is or requires knowledge, he may also think (and, I will argue below, does think) that the latter primarily involves the development and inculcation of habits related to spirited motivation. In this regard the fact that not even Protagoras himself concludes from the Great Speech that political virtue is a form of, *or even similar to*, knowledge, is significant. Talk of the "art of politics" early in the myth, therefore, does not show that Zeus grants to human beings something rational rather than spirited.

The second line of response is a concession of sorts. My main thesis is that Zeus' intervention makes human beings spirited animals, and that their spiritedness makes it possible for them to be educated in civic virtue. However, it should not be denied that citizens who have acquired political art or virtue in Protagoras' sense will also express their virtue in ways that are distinctively *rational*. Virtuous citizens will, for example, engage in deliberation about what is just and good for them and their cities, present arguments to one another in support of their views, and in general *reason* about how they should act and live in private and public life. All of these are activities Plato would clearly want to attribute to the reasoning part of the soul by the lights of tripartition. I do not, however, take this to be a problem for my interpretation. As we have already seen, Plato takes the spirited and reasoning parts of the soul to have a close relationship with one another. Part of their closeness—to anticipate some of my arguments from Chapters 6 and 7—consists in the fact that a person's mature rational judgments and values are largely influenced by the spirited emotions the individual develops during youth. In other words, people tend to make rational judgments about things like justice or goodness that express and accord with the values they have internalized through social and political processes that constitute moral education. That does not mean, however, that reason is what makes it possible for people to be educated through those social and political processes in the first place. Rather, it supplies reasoning that supports and reflects the outcome of that education. The point is this: of *course* adult human beings express the political virtue outlined by Protagoras in ways that involve their reasoning—they are, after all, *rational* creatures—but that does not mean the capacity for political virtue, or the psychological mechanisms by which that virtue is initially acquired, are themselves rational capacities and mechanisms.

2. Political "Virtue" and Spirited Nature

The first main reason for thinking that Zeus' intervention involves the addition of spirit to human nature is that Protagoras characterizes Zeus' allotment using language that anticipates the account of spirited motivation in the *Republic*. Human beings receive "justice" and "shame" or "moderation," which make it possible for them to form "bonds of friendship" and maintain "orderly" (*kosmioi*) cities, and they also acquire the capacity to fight their external enemies through "war" (*polemos*). As we saw in Chapter 2, Plato's introduction of the spirited part of the soul in *Republic* 4 emphasizes its sensitivity to considerations about justice and injustice; shame is a characteristically spirited emotion; spirit is the part of the soul responsible for orderliness, friendship, and affection for the *oikeion*; and *thumos* is the psychic source of aggression in martial contexts.

It is worth pausing to remark on the inclusion of moderation, or *sōphrosunē*, on this list of presumptively spirited kinds of motivation. After all (as noted in Chapter 2.3), when the word's literal meaning of "sound-mindedness" is at the fore, it is often translated as "prudence" or "discretion," which suggest a condition of reason, not *thumos*.[6] There are, however, other

---

[6] Indeed, later Socrates exploits this sense of the term by contrasting moderation with "foolishness" in an argument designed to equate moderation with wisdom (332a–b).

senses of the term in which spirited emotions and sensitivities are much more prominent. Three such uses are especially relevant in social and political contexts. First, *sōphrosunē* is strongly associated with the spirited emotion of shame. In the *Charmides*, for instance, the dialogue's namesake proposes that *sōphrosunē* just *is* shame: "Moderation seems to me to make people feel ashamed (*aischuneshtai*) and bashful (*aischuntēlon*), so I think shame (*aidōs*) is precisely what moderation really is" (160e3–5).[7] Second, and closely related to the first, *sōphrosunē* is a virtue that involves awareness of, and respect for, one's place in relation to other people—*especially* one's superiors.[8] For that reason, it is often characterized as the virtue of women and children, whom Greek social norms expected to be deferential to their husbands and elders.[9] Likewise, in the *Republic* a city is considered moderate when its worse citizens willingly submit to the rule of its better ones (431b–e). Given that spirit is the part of the tripartite soul preeminently concerned with a person's relation to others, this sense of moderation is one that naturally invokes Platonic *thumos*. Third, *sōphrosunē* can refer to the virtue of self-control, understood as mastery or control over one's appetites, especially those that motivate shameful or unjust behavior. Spirit, of course, often plays a key role in restraining the appetites, and accordingly, Plato takes spirited motivations like shame and friendship to be importantly related to this kind of moderation.[10]

We have good reasons for thinking that these spirit-forward senses of *sōphrosunē* are the ones primarily at work in the Great Speech. First, Protagoras himself uses *sōphrosunē* synonymously with the term *aidōs*: after the mythical portion of his speech he replaces the latter with the former. Second, as noted above, after his speech Protagoras himself actually rejects the idea that *sōphrosunē* is *in any way* similar to knowledge. And finally, as we will see below, Protagoras describes the cultivation of *sōphrosunē* through moral education in ways that emphasize spiritedness and shame-related emotions and sensitivities.

---

[7] For the close connection between moderation and shame, see Sophocles, *Ajax* 1069–83.

[8] North (1966: 155–8), Kahn (1996: 187–8), and Renaut (2014: 70–3) all note that the character of young Charmides displays an instinctive sense of shame and obedience to his elders in the dialogue that has more in common with non-rational (spirited) moral emotions than with an intellectualist or philosophical form of virtue.

[9] See e.g. Xenophon, *Oec.* 7.14; Euripides, *Alc.* 615–16; Aeschylus, fr. 168.23; and Aristophanes, *Lysis.* 471–5, 506–8.

[10] These three senses are interconnected, moreover: those who recognize others as peers or superiors feel respect or shame before them, and therefore they will suppress appetitive impulses to commit disrespectful, shameless, or unjust acts in front of or against them.

If all of this is right, then Protagoras' myth strongly suggests Zeus turns human beings into spirited creatures, and that spirited motivation is the necessary condition of social and civic life.

A second main argument complements this first one. Prior to Zeus' intervention, Protagoras does not describe *pre*-political human beings using any language suggestive of spirited psychology or behavior. By contrast, Protagoras makes it clear that early humans already share in both appetitive and rational nature. We know they have appetites, because their lives are devoted largely to satisfying bodily needs: they harvest "food from the earth"; they make clothing and shelter to protect their bodies against the weather; and they evidently possess the art of medicine for curing their bodies of painful diseases. They also clearly possess sophisticated forms of reasoning: they are contrasted with the "irrational" (*aloga*) animals; they possess "wisdom in the practical arts" and technology; they have religion and worship the gods; and they use speech to communicate with one another. Thus Protagoras provides resources for an argument by elimination: prior to Zeus' intervention, human beings already possess psychological and behavioral characteristics that Plato considers distinctively appetitive and rational by the lights of tripartition, yet humans are incapable of living in communities.[11] This suggests that appetite and reason are not by themselves sufficient for social and political life, which adds support to the case for thinking that spirit is what is missing from pre-political life.

These twin arguments find their precedents in the two sources of the Prometheus myth that predate Plato: Hesiod and Aeschylus. Because Hesiod's original versions of the story (*Theog.* 507–616, *WD* 42–105) provide the foundation for later adaptations, Plato's myth already naturally invokes Hesiodic themes. Plato seems especially eager to remind the reader of this connection, moreover: his use of the archaic pairing "shame and justice," *aidōs* and *dikē*, recalls the prominent use of those terms in Hesiod's description of civic unrest and the ultimate downfall of the iron race.[12] As we saw in Chapter 3.1, Hesiod's account of the different metallic races emphasizes *thumos* itself and associated emotions and behavior. Hard-hearted *thumos*, envy, and shamelessness bring destructive violence and injustice, while

---

[11] Importantly, pre-political humans are evidently capable of calculating the strategic benefits of banding together in groups (hence they at least *try* to do so), but that reasoning does not yet make them capable of successfully participating in and maintaining such groups.

[12] Cf. Taylor (1976: 85–6). For discussion of *aidōs* and *dikē* in Hesiod, see Cairns (1993: 148–56) and Renaut (2014: 31–3). Jarratt (1991: 69) and McCoy (1998: 23–4) also comment on the relation of Protagoras' myth to its Hesiodic or Aeschylean antecedents.

friendship, shame, and honor for one's family are accompanied by justice and make cities flourish. Hence Hesiod anticipates the central role of spirited motivation in determining the moral fate of a community. The Aeschylean version of the Prometheus myth, meanwhile, adds support to the idea that Prometheus' gift to humankind consisted of rational skills. According to Aeschylus' Prometheus, before he made human beings "intelligent (*ennous*) and endowed with understanding (*phrenōn*)," they were "infants" (*nēpious*) who lived in caves and did everything "without planning" (*eikēi*) and without "judgment" (*gnōmēs*). But Prometheus taught them astronomy, arithmetic, writing, domestication of animals, architecture, ship-building, medicine, the mantic arts, and the extraction of precious metals from the earth—in short, "every technical expertise" (*pasai technai*) humans possess (442–506). In specifying a variety of practical and rational "skills (*technas*) and devices (*porous*)" that Prometheus provides to humankind, Aeschylus supplements the Hesiodic version of the myth, where Prometheus steals only fire and there is no indication of other teachings. One way of understanding Plato's version is that he is adding a friendly amendment to the Aeschylean account. All the advancements of reason made possible by Prometheus would ultimately be for naught, Plato shows, if humans lacked the dispositions necessary to be social and form political communities.

3. Democratic Moral Education

A further line of argument concerns the relation between the myth and what follows in the rest of Protagoras' speech, and it requires first clarifying a point of ambiguity in the Great Speech. As we have seen, Protagoras initially claims that Zeus allots shame and justice to all human beings, and he quickly identifies shame and justice with the *virtues* of moderation and justice. This implies that as a result of Zeus' intervention, all human beings *naturally* possess, or are *born with*, political virtue. However, this is clearly not what Protagoras has in mind. As previous commentators have noted, Protagoras is not always careful to distinguish in the Great Speech between the natural *capacity* to acquire political virtue on the one hand, and the *actual* political virtue possessed by those who have learned or acquired it on the other. When he says that everyone is fit to give advice on matters of politics because everyone has a share of political virtue, he must be referring to actual, acquired virtue. When he describes Zeus' allotment of shame and justice to human beings, however, Protagoras must have in mind the capacity, not acquired virtue itself. Protagoras is not making the unlikely claim that all human beings are *born* virtuous; instead he is making the much more plausible claim that all human beings are naturally *capable* of acquiring virtue. Although he is not initially clear on this point, he quickly makes it explicit: political virtue is not something that is possessed "by nature" (*phusei*) or attained "automatically" (*apo tou automatoui*); rather, it is "developed through teaching" (*didakton*) as the result of "diligent care" (*epimeleias*) by those who acquire it (323c5–7). Indeed, Protagoras' main aim is to counter Socrates' suggestion that the art of politics is *not* the sort of thing that can be taught, and the rest of the Great Speech is concerned with arguing *that*, and explaining *how*, political virtue is in fact "teachable" (*didakton*, 324c4), "acquired by practice" (*paraskeuaston*, 324c5), and "gained through education" (*paideutēn*, 324b6).

The relation between the myth and the second part of Protagoras' speech, then, is this: the myth establishes that all human beings have the capacity for political virtue, and the rest of the speech explains how people develop that capacity and interact with one another because of it.[13] Or, to put the point slightly differently: Zeus grants to human beings the inborn nature that makes moral education possible, and the rest of Protagoras' speech describes the training and practices that constitute and reflect moral education. This relationship is significant, because Protagoras' account of how political virtue is acquired emphasizes the management and cultivation of desires, emotions, and attitudes that are distinctively spirited. The idea that Zeus grants spiritedness to human beings, therefore, is confirmed by the fact that the processes of nurturing the nature he grants are processes of training and expressing spirited forms of motivation.

The role of spiritedness in Protagoras' account of democratic education is evident in three main ways, much of which importantly anticipates Adeimantus' description of education in *Republic* 2. First, it is evident in the *modes* of teaching virtue. According to Protagoras, moral education begins early. From the time children are very young, their nurses, tutors, mothers, and fathers encourage them to become virtuous by telling and showing them how they should and should not act. In particular, they indicate which actions are just (*dikaion*) or unjust (*adikon*) and which ones are admirable (*kalon*) or shameful (*aischron*) (325c6–d5). Later, children are sent to school, where they

---

[13] Cairns (1993: 356–9 and n. 40), by contrast, downplays Zeus' allotment, allowing that it may consist in some kind of innate capacity, but arguing that Protagoras' speech suggests the "inculcation, rather than the exploitation, of a sense of *aidōs*." On my view, education inculcates a *correct* sense of shame, but that inculcation is possible only because the sensitivity to shame and shaming practices is already innate.

read and memorize works of poetry that "contain numerous exhortations, and many passages that praise (*epainoi*) and glorify (*enkōmia*) the good men of old, so that the child imitates (*mimetai*) them and strives to become like them out of jealous emulation (*zēlōn*)" (325d7–326a4). They also receive musical and gymnastic training, and, finally, the laws themselves provide a model for just behavior (326a–e). These methods of imparting virtue assume that from the time they are young, citizens are naturally sensitive to matters of justice and admirable or shameful action, and that they care what their family members and peers think about such things. These modes of education also, crucially, exploit citizens' concern for what their family members and peers think of *them*. Young people want to become like the praiseworthy heroes who are lionized in stories. They want, in other words, to be admired and earn a good reputation among their fellow citizens.

Second, the emphasis on spiritedness is evident in Protagoras' account of the psychological *effects* of socialization and education in virtue. Through moral education, children acquire "orderliness" (*eukosmia*, 325e1); because of their musical training, they gain moderation (*sōphrosunē*, 326a4), and because of their physical training, they do not succumb to cowardice (*apodeilian*, 326c1); they become "gentler" (*hēmerōteroi*) as their souls "become familiar" (*oikeiousthai*) with rhythm and harmony (326b2–3); and just and gentle citizens are contrasted with the uncivilized "savages" (*agrioi*) who grow up outside of human society (327d3). The terms used here strikingly anticipate Plato's account of spirited motivation in the *Republic*, and in particular (as I explore more in Chapters 6 and 7) Socrates' description of the effects of early education on the spirited element of the soul. Protagoras indicates that the laws, meanwhile, teach citizens how "to both rule and be ruled" (*kai archein kai archesthai*, 326d7), just as in the *Republic* the spirited part of the soul is a "lover of ruling," and timocratic individuals not only love to rule but are also willing to be ruled by superiors.

Finally, Protagoras draws attention to spirited motivations in his description of the ways citizens treat one another concerning the acquisition of virtue. On the one hand, they are eager to help one another cultivate civic virtue. Throughout their lives all citizens "enthusiastically" (*prothumōs*, 327b3; cf. *prothumian*, 327b4) teach one another what is just,[14] and they do not "enviously begrudge" (*phthonei*, 327a8) their own facility in matters of justice, but rather share it with "unenvious generosity" (*aphthonian*, 327b5). The terms

---

[14] Protagoras also uses martial language to characterize this zeal: parents and teachers "go to battle" or "fight" (διαμάχονται, 325d1) to make children virtuous.

used here are significant. In the *Republic* envy, *phthonos*, is the emotional result of a *thumoeides* ruined by love of honor; it is a competitive spirited motivation with divisive social effects. Likewise, earlier in the *Protagoras* itself, the sophist explains that foreigners like himself, who visit great cities and encourage promising young men to abandon their relatives (*oikeioi*) and associate with themselves instead, are met with "feelings of envy (*phthonoi*) and hostility (*dusmeneiai*)" (316c5–d3; cf. 316e4–5). In this context, then, *phthonos* is aggressive malice directed at outsiders or those one considers to be in competition with the interests of oneself and one's *oikeioi* or community. The lack of envy with which citizens share their understanding of virtue, by contrast, is an emotional response appropriate to those one considers friends: it suggests a gentle *thumos* kindly disposed to one's fellow citizens. The fact that Protagoras describes this positive generosity using a cognate of *thumos*, "enthusiasm" or *prothumia*, intensifies this effect.

On the other hand, the affectionate generosity with which citizens encourage one another to *become* virtuous has an aggressive counterpart in their emotional response when fellow citizens *fail* to acquire virtue. Protagoras explains that when people are afflicted with evils as a result of nature or bad luck, no one "becomes angry" (*thumoutai*, 323d1) with them. When they are evil due to a perceived lack of learning and practice, however, they are met with "feelings of anger" (*thumoi*), admonishment, and punishment (323e2–3). Such is the case with political virtue: when people act immoderately or commit acts of injustice, their fellow citizens "become harsh" (*chalepainousin*, 323b1), "get angry" (*thumoutai*, 324a2), and "admonish" them. Here Protagoras clearly illustrates the role of spiritedness in the social practices associated with moral education. In doing so he also provides especially strong support for the idea that Zeus' original allotment consisted of distinctively spirited sensitivities: Zeus granted human beings a sense of shame and justice, and evidently one of the effects of that intervention is that humans respond with spirited anger—the emotion of *thumos* itself—to perceived displays of shamelessness or injustice.[15]

The significance of Protagoras' use of *thumos*-terminology in the Great Speech is amplified by the way spirited anger is characterized throughout the dialogue. Here it is worth noting that the noun *thumos* and the verb *thumeomai* are relatively rare in dialogues generally considered "early" or "Socratic." Combined, the two terms occur only seven times total in those

---

[15] Cf. Renaut (2014: 59–74), who also takes the emotion of *thumos* to be closely connected with *aidōs* and *dikē* in the speech.

works, and *six* of those seven occurrences are in the *Protagoras* itself.[16] The *Protagoras*, therefore, is in a privileged position to offer a glimpse into Plato's early conception of the namesake for his spirited part of the soul.[17] With that in mind, four additional comments in the text—three on *thumos*, and one on its synonym *orgē*—all suggest a view remarkably continuous with Plato's presentation of *thumos* in the *Republic*. First, Protagoras goes on in his speech to claim that, by contrast to those who punish with a view to teaching better behavior, those who angrily seek only revenge for a past injustice are exercising "the irrational vengefulness of a wild beast" (*thērion alogistōs timōreitai*, 324a6–b1).[18] Second, Socrates himself later characterizes anger as an impediment to friendship and affection for one's *oikeioi*. When good men become angry (*orgisthōsin*) with their parents or their city for committing injustice, he explains, they "calm themselves down" (*paramutheisthai*) and force themselves to "feel friendship for their own" (*philein tous heautōn*) and to praise (*epainein*) them. By contrast, bad men in the same situation cast blame (*psegein*) on their family or country and produce further feelings of hatred or hostility (*echthras*) (345e6–346b5). Third, Protagoras later identifies *thumos* as a source of both power (*dunamis*) and boldness (*tharsos*) (351a1–b2). And finally, Socrates includes *thumos*—along with erotic desire, fear, pleasure, and pain—among the passions of the soul that in some sense compete with or oppose knowledge (352b5–c2).[19] In these passages we find much that anticipates Plato's account of the *thumoeides*.[20] Especially relevant to the present argument is that Socrates characterizes anger and its contrary calmness as

---

[16] The seventh occurs in the *Euthyphro*; see Ch. 5.2.   [17] Cf. Renaut (2014: 50).

[18] Protagoras' remark anticipates Socrates' reference to the spirited part of the soul as "that which is irrationally (ἀλογίστως) angry" in the *Republic* (441c2).

[19] Socrates, of course, ultimately denies that *thumos* and other passions are capable of overpowering knowledge in the soul, but he does not reject the basic idea that they can be in tension with knowledge in some sense or other. His objection is not to the view that things like *thumos* or *erōs* exist in the soul as distinct from knowledge, but rather that they can be *stronger* than it. See also Singpurwalla (2006: 248–9). Kahn (1996: 227–9) suggests that Plato actually has Euripides' *Medea* in mind when he speaks of *thumos* in this passage, and a number of later writers (e.g. Galen, *PHP* 3.3.13–17; Alcinous, *Handbook* 177.4–9) in the Platonic tradition take Medea's words at 1079–80 as a paradigmatic example of akratic action in which spirit prevails over reason. The interpretation of those lines is controversial, however. See discussion in Diller (1966: 274–5), Foley (1989), Gill (1983), Irwin (1983), Lloyd-Jones (1980), Rickert (1987), and Renaut (2014: 124–9).

[20] The *Protagoras* also hints at spirited psychology in its final discussion of the *kalon* and courage. Having elicited from Protagoras, as proxy for the many, the hedonistic identification of the good with pleasure, Socrates asks whether going to war is honorable and whether, being honorable, it must also be good and therefore pleasant (359e–360a). Although Protagoras agrees, the exchange points to a weakness in the popular account. On their view, an action that is painful in the short term can still be considered good if it yields greater pleasure in the long term. The problem is that fighting in war involves pain and risk of *death*. Those who die in battle, while perhaps achieving honor, never gain long-term pleasure. This suggests that the pleasant and the honorable are actually distinct from one another, and that when courageous individuals risk their lives fighting, they seek the latter rather than

being closely connected both with practices of praise and blame and with feelings of friendship or hostility—in other words, with the psychological and social phenomena at the heart of Protagoras' myth and account of education.

4. Plato's Skepticism

According to the Great Speech, all human beings are endowed with a spirited sense of justice and shame that makes it possible for them to live together harmoniously in cities and educate one another in civic virtue. This general conception of spirit's positive role in politics, social life, and moral education anticipates Plato's own considered view of political psychology as he presents it in works like the *Republic*.[21] Protagoras also makes a further claim in his speech, however, that Plato himself emphatically rejects—namely, that *Athens*, in particular, is a well-functioning city in which citizens *successfully* impart virtue to one another. The sophist's optimism on this point reflects the fact that, in the dialectical context, he is trying to defend democratic political ideas and practices against Socrates' objections. Although Plato does not *directly* confront Protagoras' endorsement of the Athenian system in the dialogue itself, he signals his skepticism in subtle hints throughout the dialogue, including in the Great Speech itself.[22] In doing so, he draws attention to precisely the worries sketched in Chapter 3: although spirited motivation makes civic unity and the cultivation of virtue possible, it by no means guarantees them.

To begin with, Protagoras tellingly compares the way Athenians collectively teach virtue to the way they collectively teach Greek. He mockingly says, "You're spoiled, Socrates, because *everyone* here is a teacher of virtue, to the best of his ability, yet you can't see a single one. You might as well look for a

---

the former. This in turn implies an aspect of our nature, prominent in displays of courage, that motivates us to pursue *honor* rather than bodily pleasure—i.e. it suggests something like the spirited part of the soul. Cf. discussion of the *Protagoras'* treatment of courage and the *kalon* in Denyer (2008: 185), Dimas (2008: 259–60), Duncan (1978: 222–3), Goldberg (1983: 313, n. 22), Klosko (1980: 321), Moss (2006: 509 and 2014a), Sesonske (1963: 79), Sullivan (1961: 20), Taylor (1976: 208–9), Wilburn (2015b), and Wolz (1967: 216–17).

[21] Commentators who note features of the Great Speech that anticipate Plato's educational proposals in the *Republic* include Hobbs (2000: 60–1), Kamtekar (2008: 341), Moss (2014a: 301), O'Brien (1967: 143–6 and n. 27), Prior (2002: 323), and Shorey (1903: 21). See also Nussbaum (1980), who discusses ways in which the description of education offered by the "Stronger Argument" in Aristophanes' *Clouds* (961–9) anticipates the *Republic*'s account, and who notes similarities between that account and the Great Speech.

[22] Other commentators who discuss implicit weaknesses of Protagoras' account of virtue and education in the Great Speech include Cairns (1993: 359–60), McCoy (1998: 27–33), and Shaw (2015: 85–8).

teacher of Greek; you wouldn't find a single one of those either!" (327e1–328a1). His comment subtly betrays the culturally variable, and hence fallible, nature of the educational system he defends. It is true that any city is equipped to teach a language to its young, but *which* language it teaches is a matter of convention that varies from one society to the next (a line of thought that was, moreover, familiar to Plato and his audience).[23] The obvious problem, from the Platonic perspective, is that what is admirable or just is not, unlike language on the popular view, relative to convention. Democratic education will be effective in establishing true virtue, therefore, only if Athens and its citizens uniformly promote the correct values.

Plato offers an important clue within the Great Speech itself that Athenians do *not* impart the correct values to one another, however. Protagoras observes that it is considered wildly irrational in places like Athens for any man to admit that he is unjust, even if he really is. Rather, people universally believe that "everyone ought to claim to be just, whether they are or not," and that "it is madness not to *pretend* to possess justice" (323b2–7). Assuming, plausibly, that this shared belief reflects the very values citizens acquire through their social education, the implication is that the democratic system encourages or produces the mere *appearance* of justice, rather than its reality. To the extent that Athenians impart values to their children and one another that prioritize falsely seeming, over truly being, just, those values are vicious and mistaken, on Plato's view. Moreover, such a value system is likely to strain civic harmony and stability, inasmuch as it permits, or even encourages, citizens' willingness to deceive one another and commit injustices against their fellow citizens in secret.

Plato reinforces these worries later in the dialogue when Socrates questions the sophist about the relationships among various virtues. In an important exchange, he asks Protagoras whether he thinks "being moderate" (*sōphronein*) is compatible with "committing injustice" (*adikein*), and Protagoras (perhaps disingenuously) responds that although he himself would be ashamed to make such a claim, it is in fact what "most people" think. He goes on to explain that, according to this majority view, "being moderate" means "thinking well" (*eu*

---

[23] A version of it appears in the *Dissoi Logoi*, which discusses the teachability of virtue using the same language analogy invoked by Protagoras but adds: "If one sent off a child to Persia as soon as he was born and the child was raised there without hearing the Greek language, he would speak Persian. If someone should bring a child here from there, he would speak Greek" (6.12). Taylor (1976: 78–9) and Versenyi (1962: 181 and n. 7) also note parallels between the Great Speech and the *Dissoi Logoi*. See also variants of the language analogy in *Alc.* 110d–112d and in Euripides, *Supp.* 913–17.

phronein) or "deliberating well" (*eu bouleuesthai*) in the execution of unjust acts, and ultimately "faring well" (*eu prattein*) and obtaining "good things" (*agatha*) as a result (333b–e).[24] Later, moreover, we learn precisely what sorts of "good things" the majority has in mind. In the dialogue's final argument, Protagoras once again acts as a spokesperson for "most people" and admits that they have no other conception of goodness than what is pleasant or causes pleasure (and no conception of badness other than what is painful or causes pain), where this is cashed out in terms of bodily feelings and material goods (353b–355a).[25] The importance of these passages is, I think, underappreciated, for they cast doubt on the whole system of democratic education that Protagoras was at such pains to defend in his Great Speech.[26] If the democratic "many" consider the two central civic virtues, moderation and justice, to be in tension with one another; if they believe that their own living well consists in cunning acts of injustice against others; and if they recognize no other good than bodily pleasure and its sources; then then they assuredly have not, from Plato's point of view, absorbed the right values from one another.[27]

In the *Protagoras*, then, Plato highlights the fact that spirited psychology is a necessary condition of fostering civic unity and virtue, but he also intimates the crucial idea he develops in the diagnostic sections of the *Republic*: that it is not a *sufficient* condition. In corrupt cities like Athens, the *Protagoras* implies, citizens teach each other to praise and blame, and to feel admiration for and be ashamed of, the wrong things. Consequently, the political harmony that arises in such cities, like the virtue on which it rests, is volatile and illusory. In the next chapter I examine how Plato develops this critique further in other early dialogues.

---

[24] Cf. Adam and Adam (1893: 138), who note that the argument's conclusion is ὠφέλιμα πράττειν = ἀδικεῖν, "a thesis which is it is the object of the *Republic*...to refute."

[25] This line of interpretation takes the final argument of the dialogue to reveal that the democratic many (along with Protagoras himself) are committed—perhaps without realizing it—to a hedonistic conception of the good. I defend this reading in Wilburn (2016), which provides references to secondary literature on this controversial issue (nn. 1–2). See also Shaw (2015) for an especially compelling and in-depth defense of this reading.

[26] Several commentators interpret the dialogue's final section as a critique of sophistic, Protagorean, or popular education and values, including Dyson (1976: 42–3), Ebert (2003: 17), Ferrari (1990), and Kamtekar (2008: 340–1), but most do not draw explicit connections between that critique and the Great Speech. McCoy (1998) is a notable exception.

[27] The dramatic setting of the *Protagoras*, which takes place around 432 on the eve of the Peloponnesian War, casts further doubt on the effectiveness of democratic education. The events of the coming decades were notoriously characterized by injustice, civic unrest, and infighting in Athens that, from Plato's perspective, unmistakably belied the supposed success of its citizens in making one another virtuous. Cf. Coby (1987: 23–5) and Nussbaum (1986: 91–2).

5

Spirited Motivation and the Novelty of Reason

Plato's Early Dialogues

In this chapter I examine several early works in which Plato characterizes spirited motivation in ways that overlap with Protagoras' depiction of them, while also anticipating, point by point, the *Republic*'s diagnostic critique of traditional education and politics. Throughout his "early" dialogues—loosely understood to include any works commonly assumed to predate the *Republic*—Plato consistently portrays spirited motivations as playing precisely the psychological role they do in the Great Speech: they make people fight their enemies and love their friends, and they make them absorb the values of their fellow citizens through emotions such as admiration, shame, and sensitivity to honor. At the same time, Plato also shows that, although these facts about spirit make it a potential source of virtue and political harmony, *in practice* they make it a cause of vice, injustice, and civil strife in actual cities like Athens. The same spirited motivations that make it possible for people to acquire the *right* values also make it possible for them to acquire the *wrong* ones when their peers and fellow citizens are corrupt. Spirited gentleness toward the *oikeion* and aggression toward the *allotrion*, likewise, give rise to strife and discord, rather than harmony, when citizens come to view one another as competitors and enemies. Having outlined these twin problems at length in Chapter 3, and having offered a detailed interpretation of the *Protagoras* in the last chapter, in this chapter I provide only a sketch of relevant passages and ideas from a representative selection of other early dialogues. My main aim in doing so is to highlight patterns in Plato's early thought that parallel and anticipate the *Republic* in their political characterization of spirited motivation. I will first consider Plato's early treatment of moral education and popular values in Section 1 and will turn to early characterizations of political unity, civic strife, and the ethics of helping friends and harming enemies in Section 2.

The Political Soul: Plato on Thumos, *Spirited Motivation, and the City*. Josh Wilburn, Oxford University Press.

In Section 3, I turn to my second aim in this chapter, which is to address the question of what conclusions we are justified in drawing on the basis of Plato's treatment of spirited motivation in his early works. In particular, I will confront the question of why Plato evidently focuses much more on *rational* motivation and intellectualist lines of thought in early dialogues. Many commentators have taken this as evidence that Plato did not yet recognize non-rational forms of motivation when he wrote those works. I will argue that, quite to the contrary, Plato focuses on rational motivations in them because he could already *take for granted* the existence of, and his readers' acceptance of the existence of, appetitive and (especially) spirited ones. The challenge for Plato, given his time and place in the history of Greek thought, was never to prove the existence of appetite or *thumos*, but rather to show that *reason*, as a source of distinct desires and aspirations of its own, is a genuine part of our human nature—and the most important one at that.

1. Education and *Pleonexia* in Early Dialogues

Several early dialogues draw attention to the transmission of social values through praise and blame, and to the prominence of shame, admiration, and the desire for honor in the absorption of those values, alongside criticism of or skepticism about popular ethics. Three examples are illuminating. First, in the *Crito*, when Socrates refuses his friend's offer to help him escape from prison, Crito assures him that it will not cost Socrates' friends much money to save him. Moreover, he worries, if Socrates is executed, his friends and associates will be held in ill-repute. The "many" will attribute their failure to save Socrates to their greed and pusillanimity, and, he says, "There can be no more disgraceful reputation (*doxa*) than to be thought to honor money more than one friends." Socrates is unmoved, however. Considerations about money and reputation belong to the many or majority, whose opinions should not concern them (44b–46a). In general, he explains, people should "honor" (*timan*) only the opinions of the wise, while disregarding those of the majority. An athlete, for example, should pay attention only to, the "praise and blame" of the doctor or physical trainer, which he should "warmly welcome" (*aspazesthai*); if he instead "dishonors" (*atimasas*) them and "honors" (*timēsas*) the "the many who have no knowledge," he will ultimately suffer bodily harm. The same is true in the case of what is "just and unjust, shameful and admirable, good and bad": we should "feel shame" (*aischunesthai*) only before those who are wise. If we instead fear the opinion of the majority, we will end up harming "that part of ourselves that is improved by just actions and destroyed by unjust ones" (47a–d). According to this discussion, people express their values through praise and blame and are sensitive to the praise and blame of others. In particular, they feel *shame* in response to the people and opinions they *honor*, and to those among whom they seek a good reputation. Most people have the wrong opinions and praise and blame the wrong things, however—things like money and reputation. Those who honor the many, therefore, and who think and act in accordance with the sense of shame inculcated by them, will do so to their own detriment. Signs of such corruption are apparent even in Crito, who is clearly moved by precisely the sorts of concerns Socrates relegates to the ignorant majority.[1] In this passage, then, Plato presents both the idea that the many have ignorant, pleonectic values, *and* that spirited attitudes and emotions play a central role in the social transmission of those values.

The role of spiritedness in education and social life is also evident in the *Symposium*.[2] First, Phaedrus emphasizes the morally edifying effects of love, *erōs, in* his encomium of Love:

There is a certain guidance each person needs for his whole life, if he is to live well; and nothing imparts this guidance—not noble birth, not public honor, not wealth—as well as Love. What guidance do I mean? I mean a sense of shame toward acting shamefully and a love of honor in acting admirably (*tēn epi men tois aischrois aischunēn, epi de tois kalois philotimian*). Without these, nothing admirable (*kala*) or great can be accomplished, either in public or in private. What I say is this: if a man in love is found doing something shameful (*aischron*), or tolerating such acts because he makes no defense out of cowardice (*anandrian*), then nothing would give him more pain than being seen by the boy he loves—not even being seen by his father or his comrades. We see the same thing also in the boy he loves, that he is especially ashamed (*aischunetai*) before his lover when he is caught doing something shameful (*aischron*). If only there were a way to start a city or an army made up of lovers and the boys they love! Theirs would be the best possible system of society, for they would hold back from all that is shameful

---

[1] For other commentators who note that Crito has internalized popular Athenian values, see Ahbel-Rappe (2010: 35), Shaw (2015: 139–40), and Harte (1999).

[2] Commentators who draw attention to hints, foreshadowing, or implicit use of tripartite theory in the *Symposium* include Destrée (2012: 203), Fussi (2008), Hobbs (2000: Ch. 9), Nehamas (2007a: 115–17 and 2007b: 6), Reid (2017), Reeve (2013b: 121), and Silva (2018). Cf. Kahn (1987) and Sheffield (2012: 216–17), who argue that tripartition is *compatible* with the psychology of the *Symposium*.

(*apechomenoi pantōn tōn aischrōn*) and seek honor (*philotimoumenoi*) in each other's eyes. (178c5–179a1)

Here Phaedrus is not describing conventional education as it occurs on the civic scale, but rather education as it occurs in private pederastic relationships. His characterization of the psychology that underlies moral education, however, suggests it is the same in kind as the education described in the *Protagoras* and *Republic* 2.[3] It centrally involves the individual's sense of shame and sensitivity to what others—or in this case, one *particular* other— find shameful or admirable.[4] The lover feels shame before his beloved, we are told, *even more* than he does before his own father and peers. The implication is that he also feels shame in their presence, but that erotic love is an especially intense bond that therefore gives rise to especially intense spirited sensitivities, feelings, and desires. The connection to *thumos* is also highlighted by the fact that Phaedrus characterizes the lover's positive desire to be admirable and pursue the *kalon* as "love of honor" or *philotimia*. Later, Aristophanes and Agathon reinforce this connection in their own speeches. For the former, love draws us toward the *oikeion* (193d1–2) and "strikes lovers out of their senses with friendship (*philiai*) and a sense of familiarity (*oikeiotēti*)" (192b7–c1); for the latter, love is compatible only with a "soft" (*malakon*) soul, not a "tough" or "hard" (*sklēron*) one (195e4–7), and its presence empties us of all "otherness" (*allotriotētos*) and "savagery" (*agriotēta*) and fills us instead with "familiarity" (*oikeiotētos*) and "tameness" (*praiotēta*) (197d1–4).

The *Symposium* disabuses the reader of Phaedrus' romantic optimism about the value of spirited shame and ambition, however, by dramatizing ways in which spirited psychology can facilitate moral *corruption*. The most vivid example is provided by Alcibiades.[5] In his drunken account of his complicated relationship with Socrates, he explains:

He always compels me to agree with him that, despite the fact that my own shortcomings cry out for attention, I neglect myself and waste my time on the affairs of the Athenians... Socrates is the only man in the world who has made me feel shame (*aischunesthai*). You didn't think I had it in me, did

---

[3] Cf. Renaut (2014: 55–8).

[4] On the role of spirited psychology in Phaedrus' account of education, see also Fussi (2008) and Reid (2017: 29–31).

[5] Another subtle example is Diotima's recognition that what is *oikeion* and what is good may come apart (205d–206a). When they do, she implies, then to the extent people "warmly welcome" (ἀσπάζονται, 205e6) the familiar over the good in such cases, it will be to their own detriment.

you? Yes, he made me feel ashamed (*aischunomai*): I know perfectly well that I can't prove he's wrong when he tells me what I should do; yet, the moment I leave his side, I go back to my old ways: I give in to the honor I receive from the crowd (*hēttēmenōi tēs timēs tēs hupo tōn pollōn*). My whole life has been one constant effort to escape from him and keep away, but when I see him, I feel ashamed (*aischunomai*) in light of what we had previously agreed upon.   (216a4–b6)

His remarks illustrate two important points. First, his friendship with Socrates exemplifies the kind of intense bond that Phaedrus earlier identified as a necessary force for moral improvement. Like the lovers Phaedrus described, Alcibiades feels spirited "shame" in Socrates' presence and consequently is motivated to become more virtuous in the eyes of the man he loves and admires. However, his speech also exposes the *limits* of morally salutary personal relationships. This relates to the second point, which is that Alcibiades' spirited love of honor actually draws him *away* from virtue.[6] In particular, his desire for esteem leads him to embrace a reprobate way of life in the presence of the many, who do not share Socrates' philosophical values and among whom Alcibiades seeks to achieve power and glory. The problem, then, is that not even the kind of love Alcibiades feels for an exemplar of virtue like Socrates can guarantee morally beneficial outcomes when such love arises in the context of a corrupt society. Both Socrates and the many influence Alcibiades' values by way of his spirited emotions and desires—the former through shame, the latter through his love of honor—and in the end, the sway of the crowd prevails, resulting ultimately in the licentious drunkard we find before us.[7] In characterizing the downfall of Alcibiades in this way, Plato adumbrates exactly the worries expresses in *Republic* 6: the harmful effects

---

[6] For Plato and his contemporaries and successors, Alcibiades epitomized an honor- and power-loving personality. Plato attests to his competitiveness at *Prot.* 336d–e, and Socrates describes his inexhaustible ambition at *Alc.* 105a–c. Among Plato's contemporaries, Xenophon claims that Alcibiades (along with Critias) was φύσει φιλοτιμοτάτω πάντων Ἀθηναίων (*Mem.* I.2.14; cf. I.2.16, I.2.39, I.2.47). See also Thucydides, *Hist.* 6.15.2–4; Isocrates, *Horses* 37–8; Plutarch, *Alc.* 6.3, 7.3, 11.1, 27.4, and 29.2; Proclus, *Alc.* 115, 138–9, 146–51; and Olympidorus, *Alc.* 24.1, 31.3, 33.6–11, 38.15, and 71.15–16. For other commentators who discuss Alcibiades' spiritedness, see Bury (1932: li), Destrée (2012: 203–4), Fussi (2008: 254), Hobbs (2000: Ch. 9), Parra (2010), Sheffield (2006: 202), and Wohl (1999: 366–9). On the significance of Alcibiades' in Plato's thinking about *thumos* and moral education, see Wilburn (2015a).

[7] Silva (2018) develops a reading of Alcibiades' speech not unlike my own and concludes, "Há a possibilidade de uma tematização da tripartição da alma já na fala da personagem Alcibíades" (p. 103).

of corrupt education do the most damage to promising young men who are driven by spirited ambition to seek their honor among the crowd.[8]

Finally, in the extended speech Callicles delivers in the *Gorgias*, he offers a critical characterization of traditional education:

> The people who institute our laws are the weak and the many. They do this, and they assign praise and blame (*tous epainous epainousin kai tous psogous psegousin*) with themselves and their own advantage in mind. They're afraid of the more powerful among men, the ones who are capable of having a greater share (*pleon exchein*), lest they take a greater share from them, and so they say that getting more than one's share (*to pleonektein*) is shameful (*aischron*) and unjust (*adikon*), and that doing what's unjust (*to adikein*) is a matter of trying to get more than one's share... We mold (*plattontes*) the best and most powerful among us, taking them while they're still young, like lion cubs... telling them that they must get only their fair share (*to ison*), and that that's what is admirable (*kalon*) and just (*dikaion*).   (483b4–484b2)

In addition to Callicles' focus on spirited motivations and concerns like praise, blame, justice, and shamefulness throughout his discussion, it is significant that he likens moral education to the taming of a lion—a paradigmatic Greek example of a spirited animal.[9] His speech is also noteworthy for its emphasis on *pleonexia*. The distinctive aim of traditional education, he claims, is to discourage pleonectic behavior. The democratic many establish laws that identify *pleonexia* with injustice, and they use praise and blame to make citizens *ashamed* to pursue more than their share and feel admiration for taking an equal or fair one.[10] In the discussion that follows, moreover, Callicles elaborates on this view and eventually identifies *pleonexia* with the unrestrained satisfaction of appetitive desires and the pursuit of material ends. What is *truly* admirable, he claims—not merely admirable by convention—is for a man "to allow his own appetites to get as large as possible and not to

---

[8] Cf. Destrée (2012: 200–1). For further discussion of Plato's depiction of Alcibiades as an indictment against Athens and Athenian modes of education, see Reeve (2013b: Ch. 2), Sharpe (2014: 143–4), Sheffield (2006: Ch. 6), and Wilburn (2015a).

[9] Moss (2005: 163–8; cf. 2007: 43–4) similarly argues that Callicles' speech anticipates both the *Republic*'s idea that *thumos* is malleable, as well as its program of early education designed to mold spirit's orientation toward the *kalon* and *aischron*. Other commentators who take the *Gorgias* to acknowledge or set the stage for non-rational motivations or a divided soul include Carone (2004), Cooper (1999), Hobbs (2000: Ch. 5), and Scott (1999).

[10] Shame plays an especially rich and important role in the *Gorgias* to which I cannot fully do justice here. For further discussion, see Futter (2009), Hamblet (2011: 83–101), Moss (2005), Tarnapolsky (2010b: Ch. 2), Renaut (2014: 105–16), and Shaw (2015: Ch. 4).

restrain them; and when they are as large as possible...to fill them with whatever he may have an appetite for at the time" (491e–492a).

If Callicles is to be believed, traditional education discourages the pleonectic pursuit of appetitive ends, and his own acquisitive values make him an opponent of popular ethics. Plato, however, discredits Callicles on both points. Socrates shows that, despite how it may appear on the surface, traditional morality is decidedly materialistic and appetitive in its ethical orientation. Indeed, the *Gorgias* is especially aggressive in its criticism of the Athenian "many" and their values. For example, Socrates concedes that "nearly every Athenian and foreigner" will agree with Polus' claim that absolute tyrannical power represents the highest pitch of happiness, even when—or rather, *especially* when—that power is obtained and used unjustly in the service of pleonectic ends (472a–b; cf. 466b–c). Later Socrates describes Athens to Callicles as a diseased city that is "swollen and festering," thanks to the willingness of earlier politicians to "feast them lavishly with whatever they had an appetite for" (518c–519a). This kind of blandishment, moreover, is *required* for political success in a place like Athens. As Socrates explains in his earlier exchange with Polus, those who aspire to political influence and honor among the many must employ rhetoric that appeals not to what is truly best, but to what the ignorant majority finds pleasing (464b–465d).[11] Because the only "services and benefits" the many recognize are *pleasures*, their most admired politicians, people like Pericles and Themistocles, necessarily achieve their status by making themselves like pastry chefs who "flatter" the appetites of the crowd (521e–522b).[12] In advocating an ethics of pleonectic hedonism, therefore, Callicles is not defying the values of traditional education, but rather serving as its consummate spokesperson. Despite his evident contempt for the crowd, Callicles himself has thoroughly absorbed their values and been corrupted by them.[13] Hence Socrates calls him a "lover of the Athenian *dēmos*" who "shifts back and forth" in his speeches in order to conform to the fickle whims of the majority (481d–482a). Over the course of the dialogue, then, Plato exposes the inconsistencies and contradictions of both democratic

---

[11] Socrates also identifies the crowds found in the law courts and assembly as "those who lack knowledge" (459a3–5; cf. 471e2–472a2), and he "disregards" the many and does not even bother to discuss things with them (474a5–b1).

[12] Socrates likewise tells the ambitious Callicles that if he wants to achieve political glory and become the city's "friend," he should "imitate" the crowd and become as much like it (ὁμοιότατον) as possible, "for each group of people takes delight in speeches given in its own character (τῷ αὐτῶν ἤθει), and is annoyed by those given in an alien (τῷ ἀλλοτρίῳ) manner" (513a1–c2). Cf. relevant discussion in Moss (2007: 241–3).

[13] On Callicles' assimilation to popular values, see Wilburn (2015a: 18–20 and n. 34), Shaw (2015: 132–7 and n. 25) and Kamtekar (2005: 334–8).

education and Callicles himself: the former fosters the desire to pursue appetitive ends even through unjust means, despite pretending to discourage it, and the latter epitomizes the materialistic morality of the many, despite superficially disdaining them.

2. Friends, Enemies, and Civic Strife in Early Dialogues

Characters in several early works give voice to the ethics of helping friends and harming enemies, often in ways that emphasize its popular connection to courage and competitive *pleonexia*. Courageous virtue is frequently identified with or taken to require benefiting, rescuing, or saving one's friends and *oikeioi*, on the one hand, and conquering or harming one's enemies, on the other, where the benefits and harms themselves are typically cashed out in pleonectic terms. To begin with, in the *Symposium*, immediately following the excerpt from his speech discussed above, Phaedrus explains why he thinks an army composed of lovers would be especially formidable:

> Even a few of them fighting (*machomenoi*) side by side, would conquer (*nikōien*) all the world, I'd say. For a man in love would never allow his loved one, of all people, to see him deserting ranks or abandoning (*apobalōn*) his weapons. He'd rather die a thousand deaths! And as for leaving the boy behind, or not rescuing (*boēthēsai*) him in danger—why, no one is so base that true Love could not inspire him with virtue, and make him as noble as if he'd been born a hero.   (179a1–b2)

Here Phaedrus associates courageous virtue with the willingness to fight and even face death in order to "rescue" a loved one, a point he illustrates with several examples. Alcestis' willingness to die for her husband, he explains, demonstrated her profound *philia* for him; by contrast, his own parents' unwillingness to die for him made them look like strangers (*allotrioi*) compared to her. Phaedrus contrasts her courage with the cowardice or "softness" (*malthakizesthai*) of Orpheus, who did not want to die himself for his beloved. Finally, Phaedrus cites the paragon of Greek *thumos*, Achilles, as an exemplar of this kind of courage, reflected in his spirited willingness to die in order to avenge the death of his beloved friend Patroclus (179b–180b).

The *Crito* and *Laches* echo similar ideas about helping loved ones but also point to the perceived tension between public and private benefit in popular thought. Crito elaborates on his worry that his friends will suffer dishonor if they permit Socrates' execution:

> I feel ashamed (*aischunomai*) on your behalf and on behalf of us, your friends (*epitēdeiōn*), lest all that has happened to you be thought due to cowardice (*anandriai*) on our part ... since we did not save (*esōsamen*) you, nor you save yourself, when it was possible and could be done if we had been the slightest use.   (45d9–46a3)

Crito evidently identifies cowardice with the failure to "save" oneself and one's friends. Hence he also criticizes Socrates for not being appropriately "enthusiastic" (*prothumoumenōn*, 44c5) about leaving prison, and for wrongly choosing the "most soft-spirited" (*rhaithumotata*, 44c6) path instead. Courage, by implication, consists in or requires a person's *successfully* keeping themselves and their friends safe. In this case, significantly, Crito's proposed means of "rescuing" Socrates involves breaking and subverting the city's laws, and Socrates frames his own refusal in terms of a commitment to justice and lawfulness (50a–51c). In the *Laches*, likewise, Lysimachus reports that his own father, as well as Melesias', achieved "many admirable things ... both in war and in peace in their management of the affairs both of their allies and of the city here." However, he also *blames* their fathers for neglecting their own children's education while they were preoccupied with public life and the affairs of "other people" (179c–d). Laches reiterates this point, explaining, "What he said applied very well to them and to us and to everyone engaged in civic affairs (*ta tōn poleōn*), because this is what generally happens to them: they neglect their private affairs (*ta idia*), children as well as everything else, and manage them carelessly" (180b1–7).[14]

Finally, both *Meno* and *Gorgias* also invoke the ethics of helping friends and harming enemies in contexts that suggest or make explicit a pleonectic construal of that ethical imperative. First, when Socrates asks Meno to state what he thinks virtue is, he responds:

> If you want the virtue of a man, it is easy to say that a man's virtue consists in being capable of managing the affairs of the city and in doing so to benefit his

---

[14] Cf. Critias' explanation of the view that moderation consists in "doing one's own" (τὸ τὰ ἑαυτοῦ πράττειν) in the *Charmides*: actions that promote one's own benefit are τὰ αὑτοῦ or οἰκεῖα, he claims, while actions harmful to oneself are ἀλλότρια (163b–e).

friends and harm his enemies (*prattonta tous men philous eu poiein, tous echthrous kakōs*) and to be careful that no harm comes to himself.

(71e2–5)

Meno identifies manly virtue as a whole with the ability to use political power to the advantage of one's friends and the disadvantage of one's enemies. Later, Socrates' questioning reveals that in speaking of benefits, Meno has in mind exclusively the same problematic goods of popular ethics: health and wealth, gold and silver, and honors and offices in the city (78c4–d1). This pleonectic interpretation of helping friends and harming enemies becomes emphatic in the *Gorgias*. The indiscriminate endorsement of appetitive ends, which is implicit in Polus' celebration of tyrannical power and which Callicles explicitly affirms, is a value system that encourages injustice in the pursuit of pleonectic goods for oneself and one's friends and family at the expense of one's enemies. On this view, moreover, the power to get away with unbridled *pleonexia*—a power to which the Gorgianic oratory under discussion contributes greatly— constitutes the virtue of *courage*. Those who "get more" and can defend themselves and their friends against prosecution, punishment, or retaliation are the "strong" and "brave," while the incapacity or unwillingness to commit injustice with impunity, or to defend or "rescue" oneself or one's loved ones against it, is a sign of weakness, cowardice, or "softness" (*malakia*). The man who is weak in this way can be "robbed of all his property by his enemies" and will end up living in an "empty house." The many, therefore, who share Callicles' pleonectic values but are powerless to satisfy their appetites through injustice, "blame such men out of a sense of shame" and claim that lack of restraint is "shameful." They praise moderation and justice only out of *cowardice*, "allotting no greater share to their friends than to their enemies" (485e–486d, 491a–492c).[15]

Plato's early works also anticipate the *Republic* in identifying spirited competitiveness, especially in the service of *pleonexia*, as a destructive social and political force. The first example is part of Socrates' rebuke to the Calliclean conception of value just surveyed:

---

[15] Socrates himself sketches a reinterpretation of the moral imperative to "rescue" or keep oneself and one's friends "safe" in the dialogue. He denies virtue consists in "preserving and being preserved" at all, if that means preserving a person's life or material property. Rather, what is truly shameful is to be incapable of rescuing oneself or one's family from the greatest evil, which is injustice. Hence he rejects the idea that one should use oratory to defend (rather than to *prosecute*) oneself or loved ones who have acted unjustly (480a–d, 511c–512e, 522c–e). Cf. my discussion of Plato's reimagination of courage in the *Republic* in Ch. 7.2–3.

A person who wants to be happy must practice moderation (*sōphrosunēn*).
Each of us must flee lack of restraint (*akolasian*) as quickly as his feet will
carry him...He should not allow his appetites (*epithumias*) to be unrestrained (*akolastous*) or undertake to fill them up—a never-ending evil—
and live the life of a criminal. Such a man could not be considered a friend
(*prosphilēs*) to another man or to a god, for he is incapable of sharing in
community (*koinōnein*), and where there is no community (*koinōnia*), there
is no friendship (*philia*). Wise men claim that community and friendship,
orderliness (*kosmiotēta*) and moderation (*sōphrosunēn*) and justice
(*dikaiotēta*), hold together heaven and earth, and gods and men...You've
failed to notice that geometrical equality (*isotēs*) has great power among both
gods and men, so you suppose that you ought to practice always getting more
(*pleonexian*).   (507c6–508a7)

In this passage Socrates expresses ideas that closely parallel those found in
Protagoras' Great Speech. Just as before, the virtues of justice and moderation
promote and are the necessary conditions of friendship and community. Those
who are immoderate and engage in unjust criminal behavior, by contrast, are
incapable of taking part in shared social life.[16] Socrates explicitly characterizes
moderation and justice, moreover, in terms of the appetitive and pleonectic
behavior championed by Callicles. According to Socrates' picture, moderation
is the virtue opposed to *akolasia*, understood as the unrestrained indulgence of
one's appetites, and justice is the virtue opposed to *pleonexia*, or the unlawful
pursuit of more than one's share out of the desire to satisfy one's appetites. The
sense of *sōphrosunē* or moderation that is at the fore, in other words, is its
meaning "self-control," or the tempering of one's appetites; and justice, in this
context, is the virtue of treating others in a way that reflects self-control—
respecting others' "shares" and desiring only one's due. Here it is worth noting
that the Greek word for "community," *koinonia*, derives from the word *koinon*,
or "[that which is] held in common" or "shared." People who engage in
uninhibited *pleonexia* are incapable of taking part in communities because
they are literally incapable of *koinonein*, of "sharing" or "holding things in
common." Given that Callicles holds the same basic values as, and has indeed
absorbed his values *from*, the people of Athens themselves, Plato is gesturing at
a damning feature of Athenian society. Later, Socrates reinforces this point. He

---

[16] Cf. *Phaedo* 81d–82b: those who possess the "political" virtues of justice and moderation are
reincarnated as "political" and "gentle" animals and eventually born as "orderly" men again, by contrast
to the unjust, who are reborn as savage animals like the wolf. Cf. *Cleit.* 409a–e and *Menex.* 237c–d.

attributes to Homer the view that the "just are gentle," yet he observes that the fifth-century politician Pericles made Athenians citizens "more savage and hence more unjust" through his influence, as did other supposedly great leaders of the past who immoderately flattered the appetites of the crowd (516c).

Likewise, other early dialogues draw attention to the politically toxic effects of spiritedness when its competitive and aggressive side is directed against one's fellow citizens. In the *Lysis*, for instance, friendship—which is itself suggestively characterized as a love of the *oikeion* (221e–222e)—is taken to be incompatible with injustice (214b–c), and it is contrasted with the spirited motivations of envy (*phthonos*), love of victory (*philonikia*), and hatred (*echthra*) (215d).[17] In the *Apology*, Socrates attributes his own trial to the ambition of his prosecutors and their ilk, and to the spite of the democratic masses. The former are honor-loving (*philotimoi*), violent (*sphodroi*) men who become angry (*orgizontai*) or annoyed (*achthomenos*) with Socrates for exposing their ignorance and retaliate by defaming him to others (23c–24b). "This will be my undoing," he concludes, "the slanders and malicious envy (*phthonos*) of the many. This has destroyed many other good men and will, I think, continue to do so" (28a7–b1). Socrates offers a similar diagnosis in the *Euthyphro*, where he explains, "The Athenians do not mind anyone they think clever, as long as he does not teach his own wisdom, but if they think he makes others like himself, they get spiritedly angry (*thumountai*), whether because of envy (*phthonos*) or for some other reason" (3c7–d2).[18] In these passages, Plato identifies the pursuit of honor, and the malice or *thumos* associated with it, as the explanation not only for Socrates' own trial and execution, but for the downfall of good or wise men in the city in general. When spirited ambition causes people to view their fellow citizens as agonistic rivals rather than civic partners, they often turn against the most admired and excellent of their peers, perceiving them as a threat to their own success. Hence competitiveness and envy have destabilizing and destructive effects on the city by making its best and brightest citizens the casualties of petty ambitions and rivalries.

The *Menexenus*, finally, offers a more panoptic view of spirit's potentially calamitous effects on civic unity through Socrates' survey of recent Athenian history in his *epitaphios logos*, or funeral oration, on behalf of Athens' fallen soldiers. His speech, which he claims to have learned from Aspasia, is notorious both for its infidelity to historical accuracy (a trait not uncommon for its genre), as well as for the evident sarcasm or irony with which it effusively

---

[17] For discussion of the *Lysis* and its relation to the *Republic*, see Nichols (2006).
[18] For general discussion of Plato's conception of *phthonos*, see Brisson (1996 and 2020).

praises Athens.[19] Whatever the intended effects of the speech or dialogue as a whole, Socrates' remarks draw attention to the role of spirited motivation in political preservation and destruction. Three comments on the period of the Peloponnesian War and its aftermath are especially noteworthy. First of all, he blames the war itself on the jealousy (*zēlos*), envy (*phthonos*), and competitiveness (*philonikia*) that other Greeks felt toward Athens, which consequently forced the city to wage war against them "unwillingly" (242a, 243b). Competitive spirited motivations, in other words, were responsible for causing the war that devastated Athens' resources, population, and empire. The conspicuous omission of the role Athenian acquisitiveness and imperial aggression played in instigating the conflict, along with the dubious denial of any positive motive for the war on Athens' part, superficially purport to exonerate Athens for its losses, but in fact hint caustically at its own destructive ambitions.

Second, Socrates recounts how the Athenians "behaved nobly in conquering (*nikēsantes*) their enemies and rescuing (*lusamenoi*) their friends" in the naval battle of Arginusae. Because of the courage of the men who fought there, Athens not only prevailed in the battle itself, but "won the rest of the war." Their actions led to the popular belief that the city could never be defeated in war (*katapolemēthēnai*), even if all of mankind united against it. "And that opinion was true," he comments. "We were conquered (*ekratēthēmen*) by our own quarrel (*diaphorai*), not by other men; we remain undefeated (*aēttētoi*) by them to this day. But we were victorious (*enikēsamen*) over ourselves and suffered loss (*hēttēthēmen*) at our own hands" (243c1–d7). Socrates' praise here is bitter, or bittersweet at best. For he undermines his ostensible praise of Athenian military might by highlighting how worthless such strength turned out to be given the city's internal strife. Athenians made enemies of one another and destroyed the city from within, for their internecine fighting debilitated Athens and made it incapable of successfully conquering external rivals and aggressors. The reference to their effectiveness in "rescuing" their friends at Arginusae is especially sarcastic, since in fact, thousands of shipwrecked sailors drowned precisely because storms prevented their rescue, and outrage over those losses led to civil unrest in Athens, and ultimately to the trial and execution of six of the generals in charge.[20] The glaring incongruity of

---

[19] For various interpretive perspectives on the *Menexenus* and its rhetorical features and aims, see Coventry (1989), Eucken (2010), Kahn (1963), Müller (1991), Pradeau (2002: 14–35), and Trivigno (2009). I concur with Kahn (1963: 220) and the majority of scholars from recent decades that we have no good reason to doubt the Platonic authenticity of the dialogue; cf. Loraux (1974: 172–3). For history of the controversy and a partially dissenting view, see Engels (2012).

[20] Notably, of course, this was the trial to which Socrates refers in the *Apology* as evidence of his commitment to justice: he considered it illegal and actively tried to stop it (32a–b).

the claim that Athens "won the rest of the war," finally, in light of the historical record, is a particularly stinging reminder of what could have been in the absence of political strife.

Finally, Socrates' account of the civil war of 404–403 is striking for its ironic celebration of the politically unifying qualities and emotions he ascribes to Athenians on both sides of the conflict:

> There was a civil war (*oikeios polemos*) among us, fought (*epolemēthē*) in such a way that, if people *had* to engage in faction (*stasiasai*), no one would pray for his city to be stricken in any other. So readily and affectionately (*oikeiōs*)... did the citizens from the Piraeus and those from the city deal with each other! So moderately (*metriōs*) did they bring the war against the men at Eleusis to a conclusion! And the sole cause for all that was their genuine kinship (*sungeneia*), which provided them, not in word but in deed, with firm friendship (*philian*) based on a common nature (*homophulon*)... They did not lay hands on each other through wickedness or hatred (*echthra*), but through bad luck. And we, the living, are witnesses of this ourselves, since we, who are of the same stock, have granted forgiveness (*sungnōmēn*) to one another for what we did and for what we suffered.
>
> (243e1–244b3)

Whatever else the civil war of that time was, it was no model of restraint and mutual affection. The brutal and indiscriminate violence of the oligarchic regime led by the Thirty Tyrants is legendary, and the resentments and hostilities that resulted from it had lasting effects on Athenian society long after the conflict was resolved, despite Socrates' cheerful assurance of mutual amnesty. His paradoxical claim that the civil war was merely a genteel dispute moderated by the friendship of fellow citizens who viewed one another as *oikeioi* and family, therefore, points a mocking finger at precisely the qualities that would have prevented the disastrous conflict in the first place.

3. The "Third" Part of the Soul: A Case against Developmentalism

Throughout his early dialogues, then, Plato presents spirited motivations in a variety of ways that anticipate the *Republic*'s account of *thumos* and the moral, social, and political challenges associated with it. What implications do these important stands of continuity have for the question of development in Plato's views on psychology? There are two main interpretive possibilities. The first—call it the "strong" conclusion—is that when he was writing his earlier works, Plato had already conceived his tripartite theory of the soul as we find it in later dialogues, or at least some early version of it, including a more or less worked out account of the *thumoeides*. According to this line of thought, the continuity we find in his presentations of spirited motivation is explained by the fact that, although he does not yet explicitly endorse tripartition in his early works, they are nonetheless already informed by his acceptance of that theory and its ascription of certain kinds of emotions and desires to a distinct, spirited source of motivation in the soul.[21] The second, "weak" conclusion is that Plato had *not* yet conceived tripartite theory in his early works, and that the continuity we find is due to his *later* recognition, and then theorizing, of relevant patterns that are discernible in his early dialogues. In other words, the early works depict (among other things) human psychology and sociology as Plato finds, observes, and critically assesses them in his Greek and Athenian environment; those depictions repeatedly feature certain motivations playing key roles in our moral and civic lives; and Plato eventually goes on to attribute those motivations to *thumos*, rather than appetite or reason, as a unified and distinctively "spirited" set of motivations. On this developmental view, tripartite theory and the spirited part of the soul are theoretical resources that Plato develops *later* to account for psychological and social phenomena that are problematized in earlier dialogues.

I do not think the textual evidence *entails* the strong conclusion, although my own considered judgment is that it is at least the more probable of the two explanations, given the preponderance of evidence.[22] While I will not insist on that conclusion, however, in what follows I do want to undermine one prevalent way of framing Plato's introduction of tripartition in the *Republic* that is likely to lead commentators astray on this question. Simply put, developmentalist interpreters commonly treat the non-rational appetitive

---

[21] Jaeger (1944a: 105) endorses a version of this strong conclusion: "As he wrote them, as he moved from the *Apology* to the *Gorgias* and from the *Gorgias* to *The Republic*, he must have had in mind the plan of taking his readers step by step upwards to the pinnacle from which they could look out to all the horizons of his thought."

[22] Gerson (2003a: 99) argues that there is no "non-question-begging answer" to the question of whether Plato accepts tripartition prior to the *Republic*, since he does not use the language of that theory or speak of soul "parts" or "principles of action" in earlier works. I certainly agree that no conclusion about the presence of tripartition in the early dialogues follows deductively or inevitably from the evidence. However, my aim in Chs. 4–5 is more modest. I want to draw attention to underappreciated points of continuity between early dialogues and the *Republic*, and thereby to relieve some of the pressure that drives commentators toward developmentalist conclusions about Plato's psychology. I aim only to make it seem *more plausible* (or less unlikely) that when Plato wrote the earlier works, he already had tripartite theory in mind.

and (especially) spirited parts of the soul as *additions* to an antecedent "intellectualist" —I use the term quite loosely here—theory that acknowledges only the role of rationality in human psychology. There are various interpretations of the details of this intellectualism, but roughly speaking, commentators often attribute some version of the following views to the Socrates of the early dialogues:[23] all motivations are rational in the sense that they are identified with rational judgments or desires, or at least, all *actions* result from such motivations; the ways people act and live are explicable entirely in terms of how they use reason to evaluate available actions and life choices; if they act virtuously or live well, therefore, it is because they have knowledge or true belief about what they should do, and whenever they act or live badly, it is due exclusively to false belief or ignorance; all moral education or reform, consequently, must consist in rational forms of teaching or persuasion.[24]

From this perspective, the pressing question about tripartition often becomes: What leads Plato to introduce appetite and spirit into his account of psychology? What theoretical and explanatory work do these "new" sources of motivation do for him that he could not accomplish with an intellectualist theory of the soul? Because, moreover, Plato introduces not one new part of the soul but *two*, and since appetitive motivations seem especially primitive

---

[23] Commentators who posit developmental shifts from some sort of Socratic or early Platonic "intellectualist" position (which interpreters define in different ways, not all of them as rigidly intellectualist as the position outlined above) to the views of the *Republic* and other later dialogues include: Bobonich (1994: 3; 2002: 216–18; and 2007: 41–2), Brickhouse and Smith (2007: 16–7 and 2010: 199–205), Cooper (1999: 74–5), Dorion (2007: 125–6; and 2012: 37–8, 48–50), Frede (1992: xxx), Gardner (2002: 200–3), Gerson (2003a: 99–100), Gill (1985: 2–6), Gosling (1973: 75–6 and 1990: 20–3), Gulley (1965), Irwin (1977: 191–5 and 1995a: 209–11), Klosko (2006: 60–1), Lesses (1987: 147–8 and 1990), Nussbaum (1986: 121 and 1980: 86–7), Penner (1971: 103–11; 1990: 49–61; 1992; and 2003), Price (1995: 8), Reeve (1988: 134–5), Rowe (2003 and 2007: 25–6), Scott (1999: 29–30), and Vlastos (1969; 1991; and 1994a). Commentators who challenge developmentalism or explicitly adopt unitarian or anti-developmentalist approaches to Plato's early and middle dialogues include: Annas (1999), Carone (2001), Ferrari (1990: 139 and 2007: 168–9), Kahn (1996, esp. 243–57), Morris (2006), O'Brien (1967: 136–8, n. 21), Renaut (2014), Shields (2001 and 2007), Singpurwalla (2006), Stalley (2007: 80–3), Weiss (2006), Whiting (2012: 175), and Wilburn (2014a, 2015a, and 2015b).

[24] Some developmentalists, e.g. Penner (2000: 164) and Rowe (2007: 24–5), argue that Plato accepts a "Socratic" intellectualist approach to moral reform in early dialogues, but later realizes its inadequacy, leading him to introduce the tripartite soul. This idea might have more weight if early dialogues regularly depicted Socrates *succeeding* at reform—confronting characters with rational argument alone, and changing their minds and lives for the better as a result. But that is not at all what typically happens. On the contrary, Plato often goes out of his way to shine a spotlight on Socrates' conspicuous *failures*. Several of Socrates' interlocutors are well-known political figures of the late fifth century, notorious for their flaws, failures, or even heinous crimes. To put Socrates in a conversation with Critias and Charmides set around 432 on the topic of *sophrōsunē*, for example, is a bit like writing a play set in the 1990s in which Bernie Madoff offers a lesson on professional ethics. The idea that *Plato the author* is committed to an intellectualist method of moral reform at the very moment he is dramatizing its spectacular failure defies plausibility. Alternatively, I have tried to show that in early dialogues, Plato draws attention to many of the social, political, and psychological obstacles that ultimately doomed Socrates' best efforts in a city like Athens. Cf. comments in Nehamas (1999: Ch. 2, e.g. at 37) and Kahn (1996: 186).

and recognizable as a generic class to modern readers, the question becomes even sharper in the case of spirit: Why is a simple division into rational and non-rational insufficient for his purposes? Why does Plato need *thumos* as a "third" part of the soul?[25]

There are two important problems with this approach. The first is that, although the early dialogues as a whole certainly emphasize the role of reason and rational judgment in human behavior and life, that does not necessarily mean non-rational motivations are excluded from them, as the rich array of spirited desires and emotions surveyed in this chapter and Chapter 4 suggests. However, according to the standard intellectualist line of interpretation, all the motivations I have identified as "spirited" in the early dialogues are ones that, in those works at least, Plato would ultimately identify in some way or other with rational beliefs or states of reason.[26] Again, I do not think that possibility can be ruled out incontrovertibly. However, at least two passages from the early works that call attention to *animal* psychology seem to tell against it. Their significance is that in both passages Plato attributes spirited desires and states to animals he considers *non*-rational, *and* he takes those desires and states to be the same in kind as, or on a continuum with, their human corollaries. The first example is from the *Symposium*. According to Diotima's account, love is the desire to possess the good forever, which consists in part in the desire to *live* forever. The closest approximation to immortality available to mortal creatures, however, is through reproduction, which is why all animals "terribly desire" to have intercourse with one another and reproduce. Once they have done so, moreover, they fight for the "nurture" (*trophēn*) of their offspring. "For their sake," Socrates explains, "the weakest animals stand ready to battle (*diamachesthai*) against the strongest and even to die for them, and they may be racked with famine (*limōi*) in order to feed (*ektrephein*) their young" (206e7–207b6). The impulse to fight to protect one's young is, of course, one of the most primitive and paradigmatic expressions of *thumos*. This connection is reinforced by the fact that in this case, what

---

[25] Hence Kamtekar (2017: 165), in a chapter titled "Why Is the Divided Soul *Tripartite*?" asks, "The *Republic* identifies the sources of rational and appetitive motivation as calculation or reasoning of some kind, and bodily conditions. But why are there three parts, and why is the third part spirited?" Likewise, Cornford (1912: 259) comments, "The new and peculiar feature of this psychology is the invention of the part called τὸ θυμοειδές, intermediate between Reason and Desire." Vander Waerdt (1985a: 373) concurs, and see similar remarks in Gosling (1973: 76), Mackenzie (1981: 168), Robinson (1970: 41), and Tarnapolsky (2010b: 37).

[26] Kamtekar (2017: 67 n. 38), for example, is skeptical of the evidence of non-rational desires in early dialogues provided by Brickhouse and Smith (2010; cf. 2015) and Devereaux (1995), on the grounds that any putatively non-rational motivations that appear in early dialogues can be reinterpreted in intellectualist terms. Cf. Robinson (1970: 40–1).

motivates animals to fight against one another for their offspring also motivates them to ignore or resist their *appetites*, just as in the *Republic* the spirited part is willing to fight through appetitive "hunger, cold, and everything of the sort" for what seems just.[27] The most important feature of Diotima's account for present purposes, however, is that she extends it to the human case and characterizes love of honor, *philotimia*, as a desire that *also* aims at immortality: people want to "become famous" and are prepared "to brave any danger (*kindunous kinduneuein*) for the sake of this, even more than they are for their own children; and they are prepared to spend money (*chrēmata*), labor through hard work (*ponous ponein*), or even die" for the sake of living on in memory through "glorious fame" (*doxēs eukleous*), which is a kind of "offspring" (208c2–e1). As in the animal case, humans are willing to frustrate their appetitive desires—by spending money, enduring painful toil, or even suffering bodily harm or death—for the sake of honor and fame, and the desire that motivates them to do so parallels the general desire animals have to protect their young. Diotima's speech, then, suggests that the aggressive and courageous behavior of human beings is one in kind with their bestial analogues. Given that Plato, presumably, does not want to reduce the latter to rational beliefs or states of reason, therefore, this account suggests that spirited motivations are similarly non-rational in the human case.

The second and even more telling discussion is from the *Laches*. In the course of the dialogue, Socrates and his interlocutors consider various characterizations of the virtue of courage that echo popular conceptions of it and anticipate spirit's role in opposing appetites in the *Republic*. To begin with, when Socrates asks what courage is, Laches suggests that the courageous (*andreios*) person is the one who, like a good hoplite soldier, is willing "to remain at his post and defend himself against his enemies without running away" (190e4–6). Socrates objects, however, that Laches' proposal is too narrow to account for the full range of cases in which people demonstrate courage:

I wanted to include not only those who are courageous in warfare but also those who are courageous in dangers at sea, and the ones who show courage in illness and poverty and in political affairs; and then again I wanted to include not only those who are brave in the face of pain and fear but also those who are skillful at fighting against appetites and pleasures (*pros epithumias ē hēdonas denoi machesthai*), whether by standing their ground

---

[27] Notably, Diotima explicitly denies reason or λογισμός to non-human beasts (207b6–c1).

or running away—because there are some men, aren't there, Laches, who are brave in matters like these?   (191c7–e2)

The virtue of courage, according to Socrates, involves not only fighting against external enemies, but also fighting against one's own appetitive desires. Moreover, he claims that courage is "the *same* power" in all these cases, and in response Laches suggests that courage must then be "some sort of endurance (*karteria*) of the soul" (192b5–c2). The task of opposing appetites, then, is here attributed to two states that Plato later attributes to the spirited part of the soul: courage and endurance. The most significant passage, however, appears in the exchange that follows Nicias' proposal that courage consists in "knowledge of the fearful and the encouraging in war and in every other situation" (194e11–195a1). Socrates notes that Nicias' view entails a dilemma in the case of non-human animals: either one must deny that wild beasts such as lions, leopards, or wild boars are courageous; or, if they are courageous, one must concede that they not only possess knowledge, but possess it automatically *by nature*. As his rival Laches is quick to point out, "everyone agrees" that these animals possess courage (196e–197a). And indeed, Socrates' list of beasts is informed by the Homeric and poetic tradition that attributes a fierce *thumos* to all of them. Nicias, however, rejects the popular view, embracing the first horn of the dilemma:

> By no means do I call wild beasts courageous, or anything else that does not fear what should be feared due to lack of understanding (*anoias*). Rather, I would call them fearless and stupid. Or do you really suppose that I call all children courageous, who fear nothing because they have no sense (*anoian*)? On the contrary, I think that fearlessness and courage are not the same thing. My view is that very few have a share of courage and foresight (*promēthias*), but that a great many, men and women and children and wild animals, share in boldness (*thrasutētos*) and daring (*tolmēs*) and fearlessness and lack of foresight. These cases, which you and most people call courageous (*andreia*), I call rash (*thrasea*).   (197a6–c1)

What is notable about this exchange is that, despite their disagreements, the characters all take for granted that animals possess non-rational forms of motivation that make them intrepid and willing to face danger. Their dispute is simply whether such motivations deserve to be called "courage," but none of them doubts *either* that the animals in question are motivated in these distinctively spirited ways *or* that the psychological source of that behavior is independent of reason and intelligence.[28] Not only that—and this is the critical point—but they also accept without argument that animal rashness and fearlessness are one in kind with *human* occurrences of these emotions that appear in children and ignorant adults. The *Laches*, then, seems to assume that at least some distinctive expressions of human *thumos* are non-rational in nature.[29] The *Symposium* and *Laches*, therefore, exert pressure against developmentalist interpreters and make room for the possibility that spirited motivations featured in early other dialogues can be cashed out in non-intellectualist terms as well.

The second and more fundamental problem with the intellectualist approach, however, is that by framing tripartition in terms of Plato's introduction of appetite and *thumos*, it gets things exactly backwards and ignores the historical context in which Plato develops his theory. When we account for his cultural and intellectual setting, it becomes evident that the *rational* part of the soul—not appetite or spirit—is the headlining Platonic innovation of the three-part soul. Appetitive and spirited motivations and ways of structuring lives already constituted a well-established and universally recognized core of folk psychology. Indeed, the very idea that spirit in particular is the "dark horse" of tripartite theory, the Platonic excess most in need of justification and defense, is implausible on its face. No other psychological concept is more richly developed in the Greek literary tradition, or more deeply entrenched in the cultural and popular consciousness of the times, than *thumos*.[30] To be sure, Plato refines the concept for his own purposes. Earlier poets and authors were not interested in providing anything like a philosophical *account* of spirit, and its treatment by different thinkers over the course of several centuries reflected the variation and diversity discussed in the Introduction. Plato, then, imposes theoretical structure on an elastic psychological concept, defining it and delineating its boundaries in ways that did not concern his predecessors. But the concept itself—with the emotions and desires he centrally attributes to it, and the characteristic behavior and life goals he explains in terms of it—required no introduction to his Greek readers.

---

[28] Cf. *Meno* 88a–d, where Socrates distinguishes between psychological states that are identified with or directed by thought (*phronēsis*) or mind (*nous*) and those that are not. Among the latter he mentions "courage, when it is not thought but like a kind of boldness (θάρρος)," and he recognizes a parallel form of moderation.

[29] Hobbs (2000: Ch. 3) discusses the *Laches'* account of courage and *thumos* at length. She argues that the dialogue shows both Plato's dissatisfaction with the rigidly intellectualist view put forth by Nicias, as well as the need for the *Republic*'s conception of spirit. See also Manuwald (2000) and Renaut (2014: 93–102).

[30] Gill (1996: 251, n. 36) rightly comments, "The distinction between spirited and appetitive elements has sometimes been seen as psychologically implausible, and as a product of the need to find a psychic equivalent to the auxiliaries in the *polis*. But the central role of the emotions linked by Plato with *thumos*, as distinct from *epithumia*, in the Greek poetic tradition should be enough to correct this view."

By contrast, the idea that human *reason* might have independent aims of its own like truth or wisdom, divorced from the materialistic and worldly aims of appetite and spirit, was a radical one. This is evident from several considerations. First, Plato himself makes it clear throughout his works that appetitive and spirited desires motivate most people and determine the goals they accept without controversy as sources of a happy life. This is already evident in our survey of Plato's early works: money and reputation are, as the *Crito* teaches us, the concerns of the "many," whereas the discrete goals of reason are foreign to most people.[31] More to the point, Plato introduces the tripartite soul in the *Republic* as an *alternative* to the problematic understanding of human psychology that underlies popular morality. According to Glaucon, as we saw in Chapter 3, what "every nature naturally pursues as good" is *pleonexia*, which he and Adeimantus cash out in unmistakably appetitive and spirited terms: everyone's desires "draw" (*axei*) them toward things like money, property, and power, and everybody knows that.[32] *That* is the view of human nature that motivates and validates the Thrasymachean conception of justice and the idea that "no one does justice willingly," and it is the psychology to which the theory of tripartition represents a critical response. What is different and new about the three-part soul, then, is *reason* and its desires. This point becomes even more acute when we consider Socrates' later analysis, beginning in Book 5 and continuing into Books 6 and 7, of the objects of knowledge and wisdom at which the rational part of the soul ultimately aims. He is at great pains to emphasize the profound strangeness and inaccessibility of the knowable realm to most people. The majority lack the capacity "to tolerate or believe in the reality" of intelligible objects that exist beyond the perceptible world. They "cannot be philosophical," therefore, and "inevitably cast blame on those who engage in philosophy" (493e–494a; cf. 479e). The distinctive objects of rational desire are, Plato thinks, literally *inconceivable* for most people.

---

[31] These are precisely the terms in which Plato's Socrates characterizes his own mission in the *Apology*. Socrates is determined to exhort his fellow citizens to virtue by asking, "Are you not ashamed of your eagerness to possess as much wealth, reputation, and honors as possible, while you neither care for nor even think about wisdom or truth, or the best possible state of your soul?" (29d2–e3). Kahn's (1998) study of pre-Platonic ethics similarly finds that early Greek literature and thought uphold bodily or external goods as the key to happy life, whereas "it will be the task of the philosophers to define and exalt the goods of the psyche" (p. 30).

[32] Kamtekar (2017: 131) offers an alternative understanding of Glaucon's folk psychology: "[His] challenge supposes that human nature is not many, but one, oriented toward having more—more than one has, and more than others." This psychological thesis, Kamtekar's suggests, is part of what gives salience to Socrates' framing of tripartition in Book 4 in terms of the question "whether we are 'one or many.'" While I diverge from Kamtekar in thinking that Plato likely understands the pleonectic conception of psychology in terms of the dual, messy desires of both spirit and (especially) appetite, rather than as a simple and unified motivational nature, our interpretations are like-minded in taking tripartition to be a response to the psychology posed by Glaucon and the pleonectic ethics it justifies. See also Reeve (1988: 15).

We can also see novelty of the reasoning part of the soul by comparing Plato's tripartite account with parallel characterizations of human psychology that appear in the works of some of his predecessors and contemporaries in the fifth and fourth centuries. Although none of them is quite concerned, as Plato is in Book 4 of the *Republic*, with developing a *theory* of the soul, several of them do offer inventories—some of which clearly purport to be exhaustive—of possible objects of human desire. Crucially, what we find in these authors is that while they enumerate a variety of appetitive and spirited ends and aspirations, they conspicuously omit anything that corresponds to the aims of the reasoning part of the soul of Plato's theory. Consider just three examples of many. In Gorgias of Leontini's *Defense of Palamedes*, the speech's namesake defends himself against the charge of treason in part by arguing that he could not possibly have *wanted* to commit the crime. Over the course of his argument, he addresses one by one the *possible* aims he could have had in acting treasonously and explains the implausibility of his having been motivated by any of them. The motives he considers are power, wealth and money, honor, security, helping friends or harming enemies, and, finally, escaping from danger out of fear (13–19). His defense works only if he has exhausted all possible human motives, yet he mentions only the material, worldly aims that Plato associates with appetite and spirit.[33] Isocrates, making use of a similar line of argument in his own fictionalized defense speech, provides an even more explicit example. He writes, "I maintain that everyone does everything he does for the sake of pleasure or profit or honor. For I observe that no desire springs up in men save for these objects. If this is so, it only remains to consider which of these objectives should be attained by corrupting the youth" (*Antidosis* 217–18).[34] Finally, in Thucydides, the historian himself regularly explains the motives of cities and individuals in terms of the twin aims of greed and ambition, *pleonexia* and *philotimia*.[35] Likewise, historical characters and political speakers justify their actions, issue praise or condemnation, or make

---

[33] Cf. Woodruff (1999: 299), Gagarin (2001: 287), and De Romilly (1992: 62), who notes that Gorgias aims to give "the impression of having exhausted every possibility." For discussion of Plato's familiarity with *Palamedes*, and of its possible influence on his own *Apology*, see Calogero (1957), Coulter (1964), and Morr (1929).

[34] Similarly, in *Letter* 6.12 the writer warns an aspiring potentate about ambitious peers who encourage him to pursue tyranny: "It is the powers, the profits, and the pleasures they see in royalty and expect to enjoy, whereas they fail to observe the disturbances, the fears, and the misfortunes that befall rulers and their friends." The writer neither condemns the pleonectic goods at which the man's allies aim nor proposes an alternative good; rather, he simply thinks they have failed to account for the worldly costs—the pleonectic "bads," we might say—that accompany them for a tyrant.

[35] The Athenians, for example, "were led by private ambition (φιλοτιμίας) and personal gain (κέρδη)" (2.65.7), and civil conflicts throughout the Greek world were due to "the [desire for] power (ἀρχή) due to greed (πλεονεξίαν) and ambition (φιλοτιμίαν), and the enthusiastic (πρόθυμον) pursuit of victory (φιλονικεῖν) that resulted from them" (3.82.8).

the case for their side of a debate, in terms of the same goals of profit and power. Hermocrates, for example, speaking to representatives of Sicilian cities, comments, "The Athenians can be forgiven for a policy of greed (*pleonektein*) and foresight; the people I blame are not those who want to rule (*archein*) but those who are too ready to submit (*hupachouein*). For it has always been human nature to rule (*archein*) those who submit and to guard oneself (*phulassesthai*) against attack" (4.61.5).[36] Similarly, the Athenians justify their inevitable domination of the vulnerable Melians by affirming, "Of the gods we believe, and of human beings we know, that it is a necessary law of their nature to rule whatever they can conquer" (*hupo phuseōs anankaias, hou an kratēi, archein*), and anyone else with the same "power" (*dunamis*) as the Athenians would act precisely as they are (5.105.2). In Pericles' funeral oration, meanwhile, the statesman insists, "It is only the love of honor (*philotimia*) that never grows old; and to be honored (*to timasthai*), not, as some would have it, to make a profit (*to kerdainein*), is what brings joy" (2.44.4). Here, in this famous encomium to Athenian culture and values, it is only the familiar goods of honor and wealth that compete for his audience's attention and between which Pericles feels the need to adjudicate.[37]

The point here is not to insist that Plato was the first Greek thinker ever to conceive of human desires and ends apart from appetitive or spirited ones, or to associate such ends with human reason.[38] Rather, the point is that whatever

[36] Cf. Diodotus' warning to the Athenians: "The things that drive men to take risks are poverty, which produces daring (τόλμαν) out of necessity; affluence, which fuels their greed (πλεονεξίαν) with arrogance and pride; and those other conditions of high emotion (ὀργῇ), when irresistible impulses overcome us" (3.45.4–5).

[37] In Xenophon, Isomachus draws a similar contrast between *philotimia* and the desire to be praised (*epaineisthai*), on the one hand, and *philokerdēs* or *pleonexia*, on the other (*Oec.* 14.7–10; cf. 13.9–10 and 21.9–10).

[38] The emphasis on *logos* was, of course, a key feature of the fifth-century sophistic movement, but that does not mean Plato's predecessors in the rationalist tradition understood reason in his terms. Gorgias' *Palamedes*, for example, is often taken to present a rationalist view of human psychology. As Segal (1962) argues, Palamedes seems to present the possible motives for his alleged crime as if they exhausted the *rational* motives he could have had for acting. However, as just noted, the goods he presents as possible objects of supposedly rational choice are all ones Plato takes to be set by appetitive and spirited interests. Hence Segal concludes that Gorgias' conception of reason "stands in the greatest contrast" to the one shared by Socrates and Plato (pp. 133–4). To generalize this point, I take it that one of Plato's goals in his reaction against the sophists—and against some of his contemporary philosophical rivals—is to show that even many so-called "philosophers" and intellectuals are imposters who do not really promote the true wisdom at which our rational nature aims, but instead peddle reason only as a means to the same pleonectic goods adored by the crowd. It is remarkable, for example, that in the final section of *Protagoras*, Socrates presents an argument which entails that the life-saving "knowledge" Protagoras himself advertises is reducible to a hedonic calculus, an "art of measurement" of pleasure and pain, and that Socrates' argument is received with glowing admiration from a room full of sophists and prominent Athenians alike (357b–358b). Part of Plato's goal in his dialogues, then, is not just to respond to popular ethics and psychology, but also to show that the "rationality" for sale from other contemporary thinkers is a sham version of it that caters to that same psychology and value system. For discussion of Plato's response to the intellectualist or sophistic tradition, see Dodds (1945), Nehamas (1990), Weiss (2006), and Woodruff (2000).

groundwork may have been laid by some of his predecessors for recognizing distinctively rational motivations, aims, values, and ways of life, the ones associated with appetite and spirit were by far *more* widely recognized by, and well-established in, the popular and even intellectual minds and practices of the times. The reasoning part of the soul, therefore, is the one with the least *prima facie* plausibility for Plato's audience, and the one that consequently requires the most defense and explanation. Reason, *not* spirit, is the dark horse of Plato's theory, the "third" part of the tripartite soul.

Consider now three implications of this insight. First, as discussed in Chapter 1, commentators who find fault with Socrates' defense of the tripartite soul in Book 4 often claim that his arguments for the *thumoeides*, especially his use of Odysseus's case to distinguish it from reason, seem weak, and some take this as grounds for skepticism about Plato's sincere commitment to spirit's presence in the soul.[39] The argument in question, however, does not strictly speaking defend the existence of the spirited part. Rather, it is an argument for the *separateness* of spirit from reason. Interpreters have tended almost invariably to assume that if the argument fails, spirit is the part of the soul left out of the theory. On logical grounds alone, however, it is just as possible to call into question the existence of the reasoning part, and given the centrality of *thumos* to Greek folk psychology, that would have been a much more likely conclusion for Plato's audience to draw. Indeed, *thumos* and its motivations have a long history of opposing and enduring bodily or appetitive feelings and desires. From the Greek perspective, therefore, there is nothing unnatural about thinking that anger, shame, or love of honor could be the source of both a person's resistance to the appetites and their pursuit of virtue or noble aims.[40]

Second, to return to the interpretive issue at hand, this suggests an alternative way of explaining the alleged intellectualism of Plato's early works, and Socrates' focus in them on the role of rationality in human motivation. Of course, I have already suggested that I find the contrast between the psychology of the early dialogues and that of later ones like *Republic* to be much less pronounced than commentators typically suppose: non-rational desires and emotions are more prevalent in the former, and (I argue in Chapters 6 and 7) rational ones more interconnected with non-rational ones in the latter, than

---

[39] Annas (1981: 140–1), for example, comments, "There is no application of the Principle of Conflict, and hence no satisfactory argument to show that spirit is really distinct from reason, and so a distinct part of the soul." For additional examples, see Ch. 1.1 and nn. 3–14 in that chapter. Ferrari (2007) is distinct in affirming the weakness of Socrates' argument but concluding that reason actually *is* (in a sense) the part left out.

[40] Cf. Ferrari (2007: 171–2). Note that in Homer *thumos* even shares in cognitive functions that Plato himself reserves for reason. Cf. Ch. 8.2 (and Ch. 8, n. 24) and Intro., n. 23.

most interpretations admit. Nonetheless, there is a least a difference in *emphasis* in the early dialogues. We need not explain that difference, however, by attributing to the earlier Plato an intellectualist view that excludes non-rational motivations from human psychology, and which he later repudiates with the introduction of tripartition. Such an interpretation requires that Plato radically rejects the familiar concepts of popular psychology in his early works and then "rediscovers" *thumos* and the rest of the non-rational soul in the *Republic*.[41] That is not impossible, of course, but neither is it especially attractive. The alternative gives due attention to context. The world of the early dialogues is populated with Greek and Athenian characters who, representative of their culture, take for granted both the existence of irrational desires and emotions as well as the ethical value of pursuing appetitive and spirited ends. Plato's challenge as a writer, and Socrates' challenge as a character, is to insist on and explore the unrecognized ways in which reason is interrelated with *all* our motivations, even seemingly non-rational ones, while also making unique contributions of its own to our psychology and human nature in such a way that the success of our actions and ultimately the happiness of our lives depends on it. Every reader of Plato's early dialogues is familiar with Socrates' determination to call into question the things his interlocutors are the surest they know, what they presuppose without reflection, the common sense ideas they have never bothered to doubt. Because Socrates engages with characters who already *assume* both that appetitive and spirited desires feature in our psychology and determine our values and life goals, therefore, *those* are the assumptions he must confront.[42] Socrates, consequently, focuses on and explores the role of reason in our psychology and behavior because that is what requires defense and elaboration.[43] It is a correction—perhaps, at times, a deliberate *over*correction—to his interlocutors' complacent acceptance of folk psychology and the ethics it supports.

Finally, we should note how drastically this perspective affects the framing of Plato's introduction of tripartition. Once we recognize that reason, not

---

[41] Nussbaum (1980: 87) evidently endorses a version of this idea: "His account of human nature in *Republic* IV opposes itself to Socratic intellectualism... Plato recognizes that this necessitates a return to much that Socrates had discarded."

[42] Note that on the two occasions in early dialogues when Socrates encounters characters who advocate intellectualist positions—Critias in the *Charmides* and Nicias in the *Laches*—Socrates undermines their commitments no less vigorously than anyone else's.

[43] See Reeve (2013b: 108–9) and Kahn (1996: 246–7), who comments: "The intellectualist texts in question... make no general claims about the psyche at all; and so they do not provide us with a moral psychology different from that of the *Republic*. What they offer instead is a sketch of rational choice theory: a blueprint for the *logistikon*, not for the psyche as a whole." Annas (1999: 121–2) shows that this is in line with how ancient Platonists understood the psychology of the early dialogues in relation to the *Republic*.

appetite or spirit, is the novel contribution of the three-part soul, the question becomes: What leads Plato to introduce *reason* into his account of psychology? What theoretical and explanatory work does this new source of motivation do for him that he could not accomplish with the resources of folk psychology alone? And of course, once we frame the *explanandum* this way, the mystery of tripartition's philosophical value to Plato vanishes. The reasoning part of the soul, and the distinctive desires and goals it contributes to our nature, provide the whole psychological basis for genuine human virtue, the life of philosophy, the just city, and the human and divine rewards both make possible.[44] Plato's innovation is not the introduction of appetite or spirit, but the subordination of both to the rule of reason for ethical and political ends.

---

[44] This insight, then, turns on its head the common argument that spirit is introduced in Book 4 only because, as Penner (1971: 113) puts it, "Plato had compelling political reasons for making *thumos* a part of the soul." The response: No, Plato had compelling political reasons for making *reason* a part of the soul.

PART III

6

Musical and Gymnastic Education
in the *Republic*

We have seen that in early dialogues and diagnostic sections of the *Republic*, Plato highlights two interrelated social and political problems that concern *thumos*: corrupt moral education and civic strife. In this chapter and the next, I examine the constructive solutions to these problems that Plato develops in his policy proposals for the Kallipolis. Roughly speaking, Socrates' approach is twofold. First, he aims to replace pleonectic values with genuinely virtuous ones through early moral education, thereby putting spirit in the service of reason and rational ends instead of appetite. And second, he attempts to make citizens view one another as friends and family through the Kallipolis' social, economic, and political policies, thereby using spirited motivations for the purpose of maintaining social bonds and civic unity. In the present chapter I focus on early moral education. My main goal is to establish that musical and gymnastic training in the *Republic* primarily aim at shaping the spirited part of the soul, although I will also address important ways in which they affect reason and appetite as well. In Section 1 I begin with a brief overview of Socrates' account of early education. I then focus on his musical program in Sections 2 and 3 and address gymnastic training in Section 4. In the next chapter I will explain the psychology of virtue—the intrapsychic dynamics and relationships that early education is designed to produce among the soul's parts—and I will also examine Plato's constructive response to the problem of civic strife.

1. Early Education in the Kallipolis

Socrates addresses the topic of early education immediately following his account of the natural qualities a good guardian must possess—that is, following the Book 2 passage in which he establishes that their warriors must be both aggressive to the city's enemies and gentle to their fellow citizens. It is the next logical step in their discussion: having determined what kind of *nature*

The Political Soul: Plato on Thumos, *Spirited Motivation, and the City*. Josh Wilburn, Oxford University Press.
© Josh Wilburn 2021. DOI: 10.1093/oso/9780198861867.003.0006

the young guardians must possess, they must now determine what kind of *nurture* they should receive.[1] Socrates suggests, and Adeimantus agrees, that "it is hard to find anything better than that which has developed over a long period: gymnastic training for bodies and music for the soul" (376e). They agree that music should precede gymnastics, beginning when children are very young (377a–b), and in the rest of Book 2 and much of Book 3 Socrates establishes a series of policies or "patterns" to guide musical education. His proposals cover the content of stories and poetry, along with the literary genres and styles in which they are written; they regulate the lyrics, harmonic modes, rhythms, and instruments used in music and song; and they extend, remarkably, even to seemingly mundane artifacts and products of craft, including the city's architecture, painting, embroidery, and furniture. Broadly speaking, his proposals are designed to expurgate traditional Greek poetry, music, and culture by removing morally ambivalent or corrupt material and influences and replacing them with, or leaving in place only, ones that promote virtue. When Socrates turns to the topic of gymnastic education, he establishes policies and guidelines for military exercises, physical training, diet, lifestyle, and medicine, and he indicates that the same models should be applied to dancing, hunting, athletic contests, and the use of dogs and horses (412b). His gymnastic program promotes an austere and simple lifestyle that conduces to bodily health and is meant to be "akin" to, and complement, his program of musical education (404b).

At the conclusion of his remarks on gymnastics, Socrates reconsiders their original assumption that musical and gymnastic education are for the soul and the body, respectively. On the contrary, he claims, their guardians will engage in gymnastic exercises and labors not primarily in order to acquire physical strength, as athletes commonly do, but rather with a view to stimulating (*egeirōn*) the spirited element of their nature (*to thumoeides tēs phuseōs*) (410b–c). This suggests that musical and gymnastic education are both primarily for the *soul*. In two important subsequent passages (which I label to

---

[1] My account does not require me to take a stand on the controversial issue of whether the lowest producer class receives any or all of the education outlined in Books 2–3. Commentators who deny they receive early moral training include Bobonich (2002: 48), Ferrari (2005: 46), Hourani (1949), Meyer (2005), Strauss (1964: 114), Wilberding (2009: 355–6), and Reeve (1988: 186–91). This reading is also supported by the testimony of Aristotle (*Pol.* 1264a29–35). Commentators who are more optimistic about the producers' education include Brown (2004: 285–6 and 298, n. 44), Jeon (2014: 186, n. 9), Klosko (2006: 126), Vasilou (2008: 232–4), and Vlastos (1973: 136–8). Mintz (2016) argues the text is deliberately ambiguous. My own inclination is to think that, because the guardians' education is characterized as a specialty training analogous to the crafts the producers learn, it is probably largely limited to the guardians, just as only the city's cobblers learn the skill of shoemaking. However, that leaves open the possibility that (as Vasilou suggests) the producers benefit by growing up in a cultural environment curated by the philosopher-kings.

facilitate discussion throughout this chapter and the next), Socrates supports
this idea by describing the psychological effects of music and gymnastics. First,
he immediately offers an extended commentary regarding their effects on the
spirited and philosophic aspects of human nature. We have already encountered the first part of this passage in Chapter 2: proper gymnastic training
makes people courageous, but in excess makes them savage, hard, and harsh;
and proper musical training makes people gentle, orderly, and moderate, but
in excess makes them inappropriately soft and cowardly. Socrates explains that
when someone begins listening to the soft sounds of the flute, initially his
thumos becomes "softened, just as iron is tempered, and having been hard and
useless before, it becomes useful"; but if he continues unremittingly, eventually
his spirit is "melted and dissolved" and he becomes "soft" (410c–411b). He
then continues:

T1

s.   And if he had a spiritless (*athumon*) nature from the beginning, this
     process is soon completed. But if he had a spirited (*thumoeidē*) nature,
     his spirit (*thumos*) becomes weak (*asthenē*) and unstable, flaring up at
     trifles and extinguished as easily. The result is that such people become
     quick-tempered (*akrakoloi*), prone to anger (*orgiloi*), and filled with dis-
     content (*duskolias*), rather than spirited (*thumoeidous*).

GL. That's certainly true.

s.   What about someone who works hard at gymnastic training and eats well
     but never touches music or philosophy? Isn't he in good physical condi-
     tion at first, full of pride (*phronēmatos*) and spirit (*thumou*)? And doesn't
     he become more courageous (*andreioteros*) than he was before?

GL. Certainly.

s.   But what happens if he does nothing else and never associates with the
     Muse? Doesn't whatever love of learning (*philomathes*) he might have had
     in his soul soon become weak, deaf, and blind, because he never tastes any
     learning (*mathēmatos*) or investigation (*zētēmatos*) or shares in speech
     (*logou*) or any of the rest of music, to nurture (*trephomenon*) and arouse
     (*egeiromenon*) it?

GL. It does seem to be that way.

s.   I believe that someone like that becomes a hater of reason (*misologos*) and
     unmusical (*amousos*). He no longer makes any use of persuasion through
     speech (*logōn*) but bulls his way through every situation by force (*biai*) and
     savagery (*agriotēti*) like a wild animal, living in ignorance and stupidity
     without either rhythm or grace.

GL. That's most certainly how he'll live.

S. It seems, then, that a god has given music and gymnastics to human beings not, except incidentally, for the body and the soul, but for the spirited (*to thumoeides*) and philosophic (*to philosophon*) aspects of the soul itself, in order that these might be in harmony with one another, each being stretched (*epiteinomenō*) and relaxed (*aniemenō*) to the appropriate degree.

GL. It seems so.

S. Then the person who achieves the most beautiful blend of music and gymnastics and impresses it on his soul in the most measured way is the one we'd most rightly call completely harmonious and trained in music, much more so than the one who merely harmonizes the strings of his instrument. (411b6–412a7)

The aim of early education, according to this picture, is to produce moderation and courage in the guardians by making sure the philosophic and spirited aspects of their nature are appropriately trained and have the right relationship to one another. He later identifies these aspects with the reasoning and spirited parts of their souls in the second key passage on the psychology of early education. Following his introduction of the tripartite soul in Book 4, Socrates recapitulates some of the main effects of music and gymnastics:

T2

S. Isn't appropriate for the rational part to rule (*archein*), since it is truly wise and exercises foresight on behalf of the whole soul, and for the spirited part to obey it (*hupēkooi*) and be its ally (*summachōi*)?

GL. It certainly is.

S. And isn't it, as we were saying, a mixture of music, on the one hand, and gymnastics, on the other, that makes the two parts harmonious, stretching and nurturing the one part with admirable speeches and learning, and relaxing the other part by soothing it, making it gentle by means of harmony and rhythm (*to men epiteinousa kai trephousa logois te kalois kai mathēsin, to de anieisa paramuthoumenē, hēmerousa harmoniai te kai rhuthmōi*)?

GL. That's precisely it.

S. And these two, having been nurtured in this way, and having truly learned their own roles and been educated in them, will govern the appetitive part, which is the largest part in each person's soul and is by nature most insatiable (*aplēstotaton*) for money. They'll watch over it to see that it isn't filled with the so-called pleasures of the body and that it doesn't become so big and strong (*polu kai ischuron*) that it no longer does its own work but attempts to enslave (*katadoulōsasthai*) and rule (*archein*) over the classes it isn't fit to rule, thereby overturning everyone's whole life.

GL. That's right.

s. Then, wouldn't these two parts also do the finest job of guarding the whole soul and body against external enemies—reason by planning (*bouleumenon*), spirit by fighting (*propolemoun*), following its leader, and carrying out (*epiteloun*) the ruler's decisions (*bouleuthenta*) through its courage (*andreiai*)?

GL. Yes, that's true.

s. And we call a single individual courageous (*andreion*), I suppose, because of the spirited part (*to thumoeides*), namely, when it preserves through pains and pleasures the declarations of reason about what is to be feared and what isn't (*diasōizei dia te lupōn kai hēdonōn to hupo tou logou parangelthen deinon kai mē*).[2]

GL. That's right.

s. And we'll call him wise because of that small part of himself that rules in him and makes those declarations and has within it the knowledge of what is advantageous for each part and for the whole soul, which is the community of all three parts.

GL. Absolutely.

s. And isn't he moderate because of the friendly and harmonious relations among these same parts—namely, when the ruler and the ruled share the belief that the rational part should rule and don't engage in civil war (*stasiazōsin*) against it? (441e4–442d1)

This passage sheds further light on what it means for the philosophic and spirited aspects of nature—now the reasoning and spirited parts of the soul—to be "harmonized." Their proper relationship consists in reason's being in control of the soul and spirit's serving as its obedient "ally," with both jointly guarding against the harmful influence of excessive appetite. At a coarse-grained level of analysis, then, we can say that early education ultimately aims at promoting proper psychic order among reason, spirit, and

---

[2] This text follows Adam (1902, i: 260) and Leroux (2002: 616, n. 105), who prefer ὑπὸ τοῦ λόγου to Burnet's (1902) ὑπὸ τῶν λόγων. Nothing in my interpretation depends on this philological issue, however.

appetite—psychic order which is, in turn, identified with the virtues of the individual.[3] The central interpretive questions concern its fine points, however: in precisely what manner musical and gymnastic training are supposed to accomplish this aim, and, in particular, what effects they are intended to have on each of the three parts of the soul.

2. Musical Education and *Thumos*

According to my interpretation, musical education *as a whole* largely (though not exclusively) aims at training the spirited part of the soul. Although this general idea is by no means new, the "as a whole" part of the claim is contentious. T1 and T2 are explicit that musical training has at least *some* effect on spirit: excess or deficiency of music make it cowardly or savage, respectively, and harmony and rhythm "soothe" *thumos* and make it gentle. Commentators are, therefore, widely agreed that musical training affects the spirited part of the soul in some way or other.[4] The question is *how* and *how much*. Recent controversy focuses, in particular, on what we might call the *axiological* effects of music, or its effects on the young person's "values" (understood very loosely here): what they find, believe, judge, perceive, or respond to as admirable or shameful, just or unjust, honorable or dishonorable, fearful or not fearful, or good or bad. Again, commentators widely agree that music has such effects. The question is whether it has them on the spirited part of the soul or rather, as some commentators argue, primarily or exclusively on the *reasoning* part. Historically speaking, the former is the more predominant view. Music, according to this line of thought, trains spirit at a time when reason is underdeveloped, and in doing so prepares spirit to have a harmonious relationship with reason when the child matures into a rational

---

[3] Note that my interpretation requires only that the auxiliaries who receive musical and gymnastic education in the Kallipolis thereby acquire the psychic harmony that constitutes the virtue outlined at the end of Book 4. However, it leaves open the possibility (and I myself believe) that such psychic harmony falls short of the genuine or perfect virtue of philosophers, and that reason does not "rule" in the auxiliaries' souls in exactly the same way it does in the souls of the rulers. For commentators who discuss these issues, see Annas (1981: 135–6), Bobonich (2002: Ch. 1), Cooper (1977: 152–3 and 1984: 14), Jeon (2014), Kahn (2005: 349–53), Kamtekar (1998, 2001, 2004: 150–5), Klosko (2006: 79–83), Kraut (2010), Vasilou (2008 and 2012), Vlastos (1973: 136–9), and Wilberding (2009).

[4] Commentators who argue or accept that musical education is to a large extent aimed at spirit include Destrée (2011: 268–73), Gill (1985 and 1996: 268–70), Gosling (1973: 44–5), Hobbs (2000: 11–14), Irwin (1977: 194–5), Kamtekar (1998), Klosko (2006: 124–6), Lear (2006 and 2004: 140–4), Moss (2005: 163 and n. 53), Nehamas (2007a: 130–2), Pracuscello (2014: 35, n. 43), Reeve (2013b: 99), Renaut (2014: 246–61), Vasilou (2012: 28–9), Weinstein (2018: 17), and Wersinger (2001: 173). Most of these commentators explicitly or implicitly advocate some version of the idea that music's axiological effects are registered on *thumos*.

adult. Because *thumos* acquires the right values through musical training, it supports reason once the latter is capable of generating or endorsing correct ethical judgments on its own. Recent commentators, however, have challenged this traditional view on two main grounds.[5] First, they point out that traditional interpretations often fail to account for music's effects on the reasoning element of the soul, which is explicitly "nurtured" and "aroused" by music, weakened by neglect of it, and trained by "admirable speeches and learning."[6] Second, traditional interpretations often grant a high degree of cognitive independence and sophistication to spirit by characterizing its moral orientation in terms of value judgments, a self-conception, or a set of personal ideals that rival, or are the same in kind as, the beliefs and views of reason.[7] Many traditionalists suggest that music inculcates in spirit correct *judgments* about moral domains relevant to its desires and emotions, and that the aim of musical education is to make sure that spirit's beliefs about what is, say, honorable or *kalon* align with reason's own eventual true beliefs about what is morally good. Thus Douglas Cairns, for example, writes, "Reason supplies judgements about the better and the worse, spirit about the honourable and dishonourable, and a judgement that *x* is dishonourable may or may not be

---

[5] Most notably, Singpurwalla (2013) and Wilberding (2009) both defend a line of interpretation according to which music has *two* main parts: stories and poetry on the one hand, and rhythm and harmony on the other. The former is the axiological component that fosters correct values, and it is directed at reason. The latter—call it the "melodic" part—is directed at spirit but does *not* shape its values; rather, it makes *thumos* inclined or able to listen to and obey reason. At this point their views diverge. On Wilberding's account, spirit is naturally inclined to concern itself with the views of other people in general and to pursue honor and avoid disgrace accordingly. The aim of the melodic part of musical training is to bring it about that the views to which spirit is most sensitive are those of *reason*, which acts as a sort of "person" within the soul itself, rather than to the "fortuitous opinions of one's fellow citizens" (p. 367). Singpurwalla's account differs in that she takes spirit to care *by nature* about reason: it *naturally* seeks what is *kalon*, and what is truly *kalon* is acting in accordance with one's rational views. The axiological side of music, then, ensures reason has the *correct* views about how to live, while the melodic side tempers those aspects of *thumos*—particularly its impetuousness—that might interfere with its inborn inclination to listen to reason. Although I admire aspects of both views, they do run into problems. On Wilberding's account, it is mysterious what exactly hearing the right rhythms and melodies has to do with turning spirit's attention *away* from external sources and *toward* an internal one. It also ignores Plato's emphasis on the social dimensions of moral education (see the final paragraphs of Section 3 in the main text below). Meanwhile, Singpurwalla's idea that spirit naturally seeks obedience to reason makes it hard to explain Plato's emphasis on the similarity between human spirit and that of dogs and horses. Her view evidently entails either that human *thumos* differs fundamentally from non-human *thumos*, or that bestial spirited desires aim at obedience to reason too. The former alternative severs the close connection between human and animal spirit, and the latter seems implausible as an analysis of bestial desire. See also Kamtekar's suggestion that Singpurwalla's view does not adequately account for spirit's social nature (2017: 182, n. 3).

[6] See Wilberding (2009: 363–4 and n. 53) and Singpurwalla (2013: 49–50).

[7] See, for example, Annas (1981: 127–8), Cooper (1984: 16), Destrée (2011: 270), Hobbs (2000: 57–9), Kahn (1987: 85), and Russell (2005: 235). For commentators who attribute sophisticated forms of cognition to spirit, see Ch. 8, n. 4.

congruent with the judgement of reason as to what is best."[8] This picture, however, is potentially at odds with Socrates' characterizations of spirit's psychic behavior in terms of its responsiveness directly to reason and *its* value judgments and practical commands,[9] and thus makes it more difficult to explain spirit's "natural" support for reason.[10]

My own account is a version of the traditional interpretation, although it will be distinguished by its details, which draw on the resources of previous chapters, and it avoids the two objections just stated. Regarding the first, my account acknowledges and even emphasizes the effects of music on reason, but denies that they occur *instead of*, rather than *alongside*, important axiological effects on the spirited part of the soul. Regarding the second, the account of early education I develop makes only minimalist assumptions about spirit's cognitive resources. According to my interpretation, spirit's moral or axiological orientation consists not in a self-conception or set of principles, ideals, or robust beliefs, but rather in dispositions or habits of response to people, actions, or things with certain kinds of morally relevant features. In other words, what *thumos* acquires through musical education is not the correct *judgment* that some actions are, for example, disgraceful, but rather the tendency to react with appropriate shame or contempt when faced with disgraceful behavior. Its "values" consist not in sophisticated judgments, but rather habitual inclinations to find certain kinds of things attractive or repulsive. On my reading, *reason* is responsible for making judgments in the soul, and those judgments in turn influence, or can influence, the motivational or emotional responses of spirit. In Chapters 7 and 8 I will defend and fill in the details of this account, while also addressing the inflationary view of spirited cognition more directly. For now, it suffices to note that my interpretation of musical education and the psychological relationships it fosters will not, unlike many of its competitors, rest on any ambitious assumptions about spirit's cognitive capacities or activities.

I turn now to the positive case for thinking that musical education (*including* its axiological components) aims largely to shape spirit and its motivations. My first argument is a relatively familiar one: Socrates emphasizes that musical training is supposed to begin when children are very young, which suggests that it affects a component of human psychology that is present and fully

---

[8] 1993: 386. Cf. Kamtekar (1998: 334), who argues that early education aims to impart true beliefs about what is fearful and *kalon* to the spirited part.

[9] Wilberding (2009: 362–5). This objection is less explicit in Singpurwalla, although she does deny any need to attribute reasoning of its own to spirit, since that is "reason's job" (2013: 56, n. 13; cf. 63).

[10] Wilberding (2009: 364–5) and Singpurwalla (2013: 48).

active during early development. This points to *thumos* rather than reason, for on Plato's view, children do not yet possess the complete rational capacities of an adult. Whereas infants are "full of spirit" from the time they are born, according to Glaucon, reasoning is something that takes time to mature and develop (441b–c). This idea receives further support from 401e–402a, where Socrates explains that music affects the guardians while they are still young and hence "unable to grasp reason." The implication is that music's influence on the soul is in some sense a pre- or non-rational one.[11] Now, this line of argument has its limits because, as I acknowledged above and will discuss below, music *also* affects the developing reasoning part of the soul. Children are not, on Plato's view, entirely irrational throughout childhood.[12] However, the contrast between the fullness of *thumos* at birth and the comparative deficiency or immaturity of reason, combined with Socrates' insistence that the *beginning* stages of education are the most important, suggests that many of music's effects, especially its earliest ones, are registered largely on the spirited part of the soul. A later passage from Book 7 reinforces this idea. When Socrates introduces the need for philosophical studies that direct the soul away from the world of "becoming" and toward that of "being," he first considers whether the guardians' training in music might constitute such a study. He quickly rules out that possibility, however:

> But [music], if you remember … educated the guardians through habits (*ethesi*). Its harmonies gave them a certain harmoniousness, not knowledge; its rhythms gave them a certain rhythmical quality; and its stories, whether fictional or nearer to the truth, cultivated other habits (*ethē*) akin to these. But as for the subject you're looking for now, there's nothing like that in music. (522a3–b1)

The mere fact that music does not "turn" the soul toward being does not by itself entail that it has no effects on reason at all, of course. However, the fact that Socrates characterizes the main effects of music, even of poetic *speeches*, as mere "habits," *ethē*, is not the characterization one would expect if those effects

---

[11] Cf. Lear (2006: 117) and Kamtekar (1998: 334 and n. 38).

[12] Traditional interpretations sometimes overemphasize the irrationality of children and downplay or ignore reason's role in early moral development. While we need not (and should not) think reason is *fully* developed in young children, however, neither need we conclude that it is entirely absent or inactive. Indeed, Plato provides evidence that children do in fact engage in activities that involve reason and are made possible by the reasoning part of their souls. Most notably, they learn reading, writing, and mathematics, all of which are rational activities for Plato. See Jenkins (2015) on mathematical education during childhood in the *Republic*.

were primarily matters of rational value judgment. The word instead suggests acquired non-rational habits or tendencies, which points toward the emotional and motivational habits of the spirited part of the soul.

Next, the metaphors Socrates invokes in describing the psychological effects of musical education are especially apt for characterizing the spirited part. In particular, he adopts the language of hardness and softness and chooses metaphors informed by that opposition. This is significant because, as we have seen in Chapter 2, both in Plato and early Greek literature generally, *thumos* is standardly described with terms that denote softness on the one hand or hardness on the other: a "soft" *thumos* is (among other things) warm, affectionate, yielding, or merciful, and a "hard" one is cold, aggressive, inflexible, or cruel. In his discussion of early education Socrates applies exactly this language, with those connotations, to the spirited aspect of the soul. Excessive gymnastic training makes *thumos* savage and "hard," while excessive musical training makes it cowardly and "soft." Likewise, Socrates indicates that *some* amount of music makes spirit soft and useful, like "iron that is tempered." The comparison of *thumos* to a metal once again reflects well-established Greek literary tradition, but the ferric metaphor has additional significance as well.[13] What makes tempered iron useful, of course, is its malleability: because it is soft, it can be shaped into valuable tools and instruments. Likewise, Socrates suggests, what makes a softened *thumos* useful is *its* malleability: spirit can also be "shaped," so to speak, and presumably this "shaping" is what takes place through early education. Talk of shaping or molding pervades Socrates' discussion and confirms this idea. Notably, immediately after asserting that musical education must begin from an early age, he asks, "You know, don't you, that the beginning of any process is most important, especially for anything young and tender (*hapalō*)? For that is the time when it is molded (*plattetai*) the most and takes on any stamp (*tupos*) one wishes to impress (*ensēmēnasthai*) on it" (377a12–b3). That is why nurses and mothers must tell young children only "admirable" stories, "since they will shape their souls (*plattein tas psuchas autōn*) with stories much more than they shape their bodies by handling them" (377c3–5). Here Socrates invokes the metaphor of a wax seal: like the soft wax impressed by a stamp, the "soft" souls of the young are impressed or molded by the stories they hear as they grow up. This idea, then, anticipates the language of malleability that Socrates explicitly applies to

---

[13]   Kamtekar (2006: 188–90) discusses Plato's use of the metaphor of "molding" *thumos* and treats it as an *explanandum*, but she does not consider the immense historical precedent for it in her explanation.

thumos leading up to and in passage T1, and by doing so it suggests that stories and poetry directly shape the emotional habits of the spirited part.[14] In other words, the earlier passage identifies "molding" with the presentation of appropriate poetic content, and subsequent passages indicate that *thumos* is the thing in the soul there to be molded.[15]

Perhaps the most substantial argument is that Socrates' discussion of music overwhelmingly focuses on cultivating motivations and virtuous qualities that Plato associates with, or explicitly attributes to, the spirited part of the soul. Most obviously, many of his restrictions on poetic content are designed to make the guardians courageous and promote endurance. The youths must be told stories that make them "least afraid of death," because mortal fear is incompatible with courage. Contrary to what Achilles' soul tells Odysseus from the afterlife, therefore, they should fear slavery and defeat in battle rather than death at the hands of their enemies (386a–387b). They must imitate courageous individuals, but not cowards (395a–396a), and they must be kept away from the "soft" flute music that would turn them into "soft warriors." Instead they should hear musical modes that imitate "a courageous (*andreiou*) person who is active in battle (*polemikēi*) or some other violent deed (*biaiōi*), or who is failing and faces wounds, death, or some other misfortune, and who, in all these circumstances, is defending against his fate from his assigned post on the battlefield with endurance (*karterountōs*)" (398e–399c). Poetry must also promote mastery over one's appetites, which is itself understood as a kind of strong-willed fortitude. The young guardians cannot hear stories of heroes celebrating the pleasures of food and wine or gods being overcome by sexual passion. Instead, they should see and hear "words or deeds of famous men who are exhibiting endurance (*karteriai*) in the face of everything" (390a–d). That Plato has *thumos* firmly in view at this point in the text is made especially conspicuous by the fact that the Homeric lines he quotes approvingly as an example of heroic endurance are precisely the ones he uses later to establish spirit's and reason's distinctness from one another: Odysseus' rebuke to his angry heart (390d).

Music and poetry also aim to foster spirited motivations associated with friendship and civic unity. To begin with, the young guardians must avoid hearing stories about the gods warring, fighting, or plotting against one another. Socrates explains:

---

[14] Cf. 381d–e, as well as 387b–c, where Socrates worries that if children hear horrifying stories, their fear will make them θερμότεροι καὶ μαλακώτεροι than they should be. Adam (1902, i: 133) comments, "Plato is thinking of the softening effect of heat upon iron."
[15] Cf. Annas (1981: 128).

> The battles of gods and giants, and all the various stories of the hostilities (*echthras*) among gods and their relatives (*sungeneis*) or friends (*oikeious*), should neither be told nor even woven into embroideries. If we're to persuade our people that no citizen has ever hated another and that it's impious to do so, then *that's* what should be told to children from the beginning.
>
> (378b8–d1)

Stories of strife among the gods and heroes suggest the permissibility of strife among human beings and thereby undermine the political unity for which Socrates' city strives. Such stories must be replaced with morally edifying ones for youths "if they are to honor (*timēsousin*) the gods and their parents and not take their friendship (*philian*) with one another lightly" (386a1–4). Along similar lines, poetry and music should instill moderation in young people, understood as obedience to rulers. Stories of soldiers marching in silent obedience to their commanders, for example, or of inferior men obeying their superiors, encourage moderate behavior among young people. The guardians must not hear stories of insubordination, however, "or any other insolent words spoken by private citizens against their rulers" (389b–390a). They should imitate people who are moderate in these ways, but not women who insult their husbands or quarrel with the gods, or inferior men who "slander and ridicule each other using shameful language while drunk or sober, or wrong themselves and others" (395d–396a). Finally, as a complement to the "courageous" musical modes, they should hear "moderate" ones that depict interactions between people at peace (*eirēnikēi*), who use persuasion and exhortation rather than violence, and who treat one another moderately (*sōphronōs*) and with measure (*metriōs*) (390b–c).[16] If the guardians are properly educated in this way, they will be "gentle" (*hēmeroi*) to one another and to their fellow citizens (416b–c).

Here it is worth pausing to note how neatly the motivations surveyed so far, which constitute much of Socrates' focus, correspond to the two faces of *thumos* as Socrates introduces them in Book 2. This constitutes an ancillary argument to our main one. Socrates introduces spiritedness into the text in order to establish the dual attributes guardians must possess *by nature*:

---

[16] Schofield (2010: 233), who discusses the role of music proper in early education, contrasts the "courageous" and "moderate" musical modes, suggesting the former imitates behavior expressive of *thumos*, and the latter behavior expressive of reason. On my view, both modes express (and can benefit) both aspects of psychology simultaneously: peaceful discussion has an affective component that requires gentle spirited feelings, and truly courageous behavior, for Plato, has an intellectual component that involves reason.

aggression, which is necessary for courageous fighting, and gentleness, which is necessary for friendship and political fellowship. The fact that the discussion of their upbringing and education that follows prominently focuses on cultivating precisely those two kinds of attributes, therefore, shows that Socrates' musical program aims to train and refine natural qualities that he locates squarely in *thumos*.

Socrates' account of poetry and music also emphasizes the proper cultivation of spirited motivations that involve an emotional response to the *kalon* or the *aischron*—in particular, feelings of admiration, shame, and disgust. In his discussion of poetic content and appropriate imitative behavior, Socrates shows fastidious concern for what kinds of people, behavior, and things the young guardians admire and honor, and what kinds disgust them and make them feel shame. For example, regarding displays of grief in poetry, Socrates says that only inferior women and cowardly men should be depicted as weeping or lamenting. That way, he explains, the young guardians will be "disgusted" (*duscherainōsin*) to display grief themselves. Stories of "renowned" (*onomastōn*) men, heroes, or gods indulging in sorrow, by contrast, must be expunged from early education (387e–388d):

> If our young people listen to these stories without ridiculing (*katagelōien*) them as unworthy (*anaxiōs*) of hearing, it's hardly likely that they'll consider the things described in them to be unworthy (*anaxion*) of mere human beings like them or that they'll rebuke themselves for doing or saying similar things when misfortune strikes. Instead, they'll feel neither shame (*aischunomenos*) nor endurance (*karterōn*) and lament at even insignificant misfortunes.   (388d2–7)

Here Socrates seeks to make sure that the young guardians would be *ashamed* to engage in behavior that is, in fact, shameful. To that end, he is attentive both to which characters are presented in ways that are likely to elicit responses of admiration and disgust from young people in the first place, as well as to the effects that their admiration and disgust for those characters will have on their own feelings of pride and shame in their personal lives and actions.[17] If famous men, heroes, and gods—that is, characters who are praised and hence inspire the admiration and awe of young people—act in morally reprehensible ways, the youths will come to view such behavior itself as admirable (or at least, *not*

---

[17] For other examples of appropriate and inappropriate "praise" (*epainein*), "disparagement" (*loidorein*), or "blame" (*memphesthai*), see 377d–e, 386b, and 390e–391a.

shameful). Conversely, if only characters who are treated with contempt act viciously, the young will consider such behavior disgraceful. The underlying idea is that if guardians feel ashamed of certain kinds of actions and admiration for others, they will be motivated to avoid the former and perform the latter. In another passage, Socrates explains that an educated and measured man would not be ashamed (*aischuneisthai*) to imitate the words or actions of a good man. He would, however, be ashamed (*aischuneisthai*) to imitate someone unworthy (*anaxion*) of himself, because he finds doing so disgusting (*duscherainōn*) and holds it in dishonor (*atimazōn*) (396c5–e1). Once again, when a virtuous man feels contempt for someone else, he will consider their actions shameful and dishonorable, and his sense of shame will prevent him from performing, or even *imitating*, such actions himself.

Socrates' concern for this class of moral emotions culminates in another important passage to which I will return in the next chapter. He insists not only that music and poetry reflect standards of what is admirable and beautiful, but also that the city's artifacts—its buildings, embroideries, paintings, furniture, and other products of crafts—reflect those same standards as well (401a–c). He explains:

T3

Then our young people will dwell in a healthy place and be benefited on all
    sides, and so something of those admirable works (*tōn kalōn ergōn*) will
    strike their eyes and ears like a breeze that brings health from a good place,
    leading them unwittingly, from childhood on, toward similarity and
    friendship and harmony with admirable reason (*homoiotēta te kai philian
    kai sumphōnian tōi kalōi logōi*)? . . . Aren't these the reasons, Glaucon, that
    education in music is most important? First, because rhythm and harmony
    permeate the inner part of the soul more than anything else, affecting it
    most strongly and bringing it grace, so that if someone is properly educated
    in music, it makes him graceful, but if not, then the opposite. Second,
    because anyone who has been properly educated in music will perceive it
    acutely when something has been omitted from a thing and when it hasn't
    been admirably (*mē kalōs*) crafted or admirably made by nature. And since
    he has the right feelings of disgust (*duscherainōn*), he will praise (*epainoi*)
    admirable things (*kala*), and, being pleased by them and receiving them
    into his soul, he will be nourished by them and become admirable and
    good (*kalos te k'agathos*) himself. He'll rightly blame (*psegoi*) what is
    shameful (*aischra*), hating (*misoi*) it while he's still young and unable to
    grasp reason (*logon*); but, having been reared in this way, he will warmly

welcome reason (*tou logou aspazoit'*) when it comes, recognizing (*gnōrizōn*) it easily because of its familiarity (*oikeiotēta*). (401c6–402a4)

Here Socrates identifies two main ways in which in which admirable musical and cultural influences benefit young people. The first operates independently of voluntary or conscious experience: beautiful sights and sounds in the young person's environment "permeate" their souls and directly foster psychological harmony, grace, and rhythm without their noticing it. This process is likened to the effects of air on the body, an analogy which invokes the medical climatology of the Hippocratic school.[18] Just as breathing salubrious or noxious air over time produces health or disease in the body, so exposure to virtuous or vicious culture during youth produces a "healthy" or "diseased" condition of the soul.

The second way is that a homogeneously virtuous culture promotes the correct emotional responses to what is truly admirable or shameful. The terms Socrates uses here to characterize those responses, moreover, are strongly associated with *thumos*: the youths will hate, blame, and be disgusted by the *aischron*, and they will love and praise the *kalon*.[19] The spirited nature of their emotional reactions is also confirmed by the language with which Socrates characterizes their response to admirable *logos* or reason in particular. The young guardians will feel "friendship" for it and "warmly welcome" it because they "recognize" it on account of its "familiarity." Likewise, he goes on to say, those trained in this way will love and "warmly welcome" (*aspazesthai*) someone who possesses admirable character (402d–403a). The language he uses here exactly parallels his description of a spirited dog's response to the familiar in Book 2.[20] Thus Plato signals to the reader in an especially striking way that the psychological habits music aims to instill prominently involve spirit's natural affection for the *oikeion*. In Chapters 7 and 8, I will provide an account of the *internal* case—what it means for spirit to "recognize" reason itself as *oikeios*, and how that recognition results from musical training. In the

---

[18] See *Airs Waters Places* 3–6 on the effects of various kinds of airs or winds on human health. For general discussion of the medical influence on Plato's understanding of psychic harmony/health and disharmony/disease, see Brill (2016), Kenny (1973), and Renaut (2019).

[19] Additional examples of Socrates' effort to shape the guardians' reactions to the admirable and shameful: the stories they hear must be καλόν (377c1; cf. 377d9, 377e7); they must consider it αἴσχιστον to be easily provoked into hating each other (378c1–3); poets must not depict ἀξίους people being overcome by laughter (388e9–389a1); Odysseus cannot be heard saying that indulgence in food and wine is κάλλιστον (390a8–b2); they should hear of acts of endurance by ἐλλογίμων ἀνδρῶν (390d1–3); they must imitate only virtuous people, if anyone, but never τῶν αἰσχρῶν (395b8–c7); and they should adopt the narrative style of the true καλὸς κἀγαθός (396b10–c1).

[20] Cf. Weinstein (2018: 176–7).

case of the person's response to their *external* environment, however, it is not difficult to fill in the details. If the young guardians are surrounded with people and things that are admirable, then what is *kalon* will be familiar to them, and that familiarity will in turn activate the spontaneous spirited feelings of affection and admiration that people have for the *oikeion*. If young people are surrounded by what is *kalon*, therefore, then they will come to love and admire what is *kalon*.[21] Conversely, vicious and shameful influences must be removed from, or at least minimized in, their cultural environment, so that what is *aischron* is unfamiliar or alien to them. When they do encounter shameful people or things, consequently, they will feel hate and disgust toward them. That is to say, they will experience spirited feelings of aversion and hostility toward someone or something that is *allotrion* to them. In T3, then, Socrates alludes to spirit's natural sensitivity to the familiar and the foreign, and he identifies that sensitivity as a basis for cultivating appropriate moral attitudes, feelings, and emotions in the young.

This discussion also points to a fourth and final argument: much of musical education has a distinctively social and interpersonal character, which suggests that it affects the distinctively social part of the soul, spirit, with its character-istic concern for other people and the individual's relation to them. As we saw in Chapters 3 and 5, some of Plato's most pressing objections to traditional democratic education concern the distribution of praise and blame, honor and dishonor. The poets cast praise and blame on characters and things that do not deserve them in their stories, and other people in the city—the young person's family, friends, and fellow citizens—also voice admiration and disdain incor-rectly both in private households and in public venues like the assembly, theater, or army camp.[22] Because *thumos* is the part of the soul sensitive to social influences, it is the part most immediately harmed by the morally corrupt social world of places like Athens. Socrates' musical proposals for the Kallipolis constitute Plato's antidote to traditional Athenian culture and education. Importantly, however, he does not aim to *eliminate* social influ-ences or modes of influence from education, but rather to curate and control them. Socrates seeks to surround children with *kaloi* and *kala*—admirable

---

[21] Note that the processes of loving what is admirable and becoming more virtuous are mutually reinforcing: the young person is surrounded by admirable people and things, which therefore become familiar to them; the youth consequently absorbs their influence, both unconsciously and as a result of conscious emotional responses; the young person becomes increasingly admirable themselves as a result of this influence; and the more admirable they become, the more similar they are to—and hence the deeper the kinship they have with—other admirable people and things, which will in turn intensify their feelings of admiration and love for them.

[22] Lear (2004: 141–2) also emphasizes that Socrates' educational program is designed as a response to Glaucon's and Adeimantus' characterizations of contemporary education.

people and things—so that they become familiar, and hence dear, to them, and he seeks to provide them with a morally homogeneous culture in which their families, fellow citizens, poets, and storytellers agree in their assessments of what is *kalon* or *aischron* and are univocal in their expressions of honor and dishonor. As a result of these extraordinary social and cultural conditions, the young guardians will grow to have the appropriate reactions of admiration or disgust toward other people and actions that they encounter in poetry or real life, and they will imitate virtuous individuals, act in morally admirable ways, and become increasingly virtuous and good themselves.[23]

Another succinct way of putting this line of argument is that musical education in the Kallipolis is largely designed to exploit two interrelated facts about human psychology that Plato attributes to our social and spirited nature. First, we tend to feel friendship for, love, and admire what is *oikeion* to us; and second, we tend to absorb the influence of the people we feel friendship for, love, and admire—through obedience, absorption of their views about what is admirable and shameful, and imitation of their behavior. Conversely, we tend to hate and feel disgust for the unfamiliar, and we tend to repel the influence of those we hate or abhor.[24] These psychological facts motivate much of Socrates' careful attention to the social and political conditions in which young people are raised. Musical education, for Plato, is necessarily a public and interpersonal process that exploits the desires, emotions, and sensitivities of *thumos*.

3. Musical Education and Reason

Musical education does not *only* affect the spirited part of the soul, however. It also has concomitant effects on the developing reasoning part—I will drop the

---

[23] Cf. *Rep.* 500b–d: it is "impossible" "for someone to spend time with things he admires without imitating them." Antiphon the Sophist expresses a similar idea: "Whoever one spends most of the day with, one necessarily becomes similar to in character" (DK B62). The importance of imitation in Socrates' account of education is discussed in Lear (2011), Schofield (2010: 236–8), Vasilou (2008: 215–19), and Weinstein (2018: 255–6). Kamtekar (1998: 336 and n. 42) notes the mutually reinforcing nature of imitation and admiration.

[24] The word "tend" in these claims matters, since Plato recognizes exceptions. Most obviously, Socrates lived his whole life in Athens and among its citizens, yet did not become attached to the culture and character of his surroundings. (What he found truly *oikeion* instead, we might say, was his own soul, or reason, or virtue and wisdom.) Importantly, however, Plato seems to think such cases are incredibly rare: "You should realize," Socrates himself says, "that if anyone is saved [from the influence of the many] and becomes what he ought to be under our present constitutions, he has been saved— you would rightly say—by divine dispensation" (*Rep.* 492e–493e). Exceptions evidently require anomalous divine intervention or extraordinary, idiosyncratic personal circumstances (496a–e). The educational program of the Kallipolis, therefore, is required in order to produce any kind of consistent or reliable results, given the *nearly* universal tendencies of human social nature. I'm grateful to Rachel Singpurwalla for encouraging me to address this point.

qualifier "developing" in the rest of this section, but let it be assumed, as discussed above, that during most of early education reason is nascently present to some degree but still in the process of maturing—and those effects are crucial to understanding the close psychic relationship between reason and *thumos*.

Music influences the rational part of the soul in two discernible ways. First, it provides something analogous to *exercise* for reason: it stimulates and strengthens it. In the background here is a Platonic view about the effects of stimulation and inactivity on the parts of the soul:

> **Stimulation Principle.** A part of the soul becomes stronger when it is exposed to, and indulged in, the objects that it characteristically and by nature desires; and it becomes weaker when it is kept away from, and deprived of, those objects.

This principle is evident, for example, in the *Timaeus*, where Socrates explains that there are three distinct "types of soul" within us, each with its own peculiar motions (*kinēseis*), and that "any type which is idle (*en argiai*), and keeps its motions inactive cannot but become very weak (*asthenestaton*), while one that keeps exercising (*en gumnasiois*) becomes very strong (*errōmenestaton*)" (89e–90a). He emphasizes the importance of "caring" for the divine or reasoning part of our souls and explains, "Now there is only one way to care for anything and that is to provide for it the nourishment (*trophas*) and the motions (*kinēseis*) that are proper to it" (90c). The idea here is that indulging a soul part in its proper or distinctive objects and activities has quasi-gymnastic effects on it: just as feeding and exercising the body—i.e. providing the food and activities proper to it—makes *it* stronger, so "feeding" and "exercising" a part of the soul makes it "stronger" as well. "Strength" in this context (to anticipate the next chapter) is measured by a soul part's influence on the person's psychological economy, behavior, and way of life—that is, by the extent to which it can and does influence, control, or "rule" the other two parts of the soul, and how efficacious the motivations it generates are in producing actions and determining how the person lives their life.

Plato also presents and draws on the Stimulation Principle throughout the *Republic*, including in his characterization of music's effects on reason. This is most evident in T1, where Socrates describes what happens to a person's soul when they are alternately deprived of or exposed to learning, inquiry, and participation in *logos*. Neglect of these activities, Socrates says, causes the person's "love of learning" to become weak, deaf, and blind, such that they become "ignorant," "stupid," and incapable of using persuasive speech. Conversely, practicing or engaging in them "nurtures" and "arouses" a person's "love of learning," which Socrates then equates with "stretching" or "straining" the philosophic aspect of the soul. He echoes this idea in T2, where he reiterates that musical education "stretches" and "nurtures" the reasoning part of the soul with admirable speeches and learning. The idea is that exposure to poetic speeches and the lessons they impart constitutes an important antecedent to the characteristic activities of the mature reasoning part of the soul. Reason by nature seeks knowledge, and it is the part of the soul responsible for a person's capacity to learn, use speech, and articulate rational accounts. Plato plausibly thinks that psychological engagement with speeches (*logoi*) during childhood, therefore, is a way of primitively exercising and nurturing what will eventually become reason (*logos*) in the soul, and hence of preparing it for its role in learning and the pursuit of wisdom. On the other hand, in young people who fail to exercise their nascent capacity to learn and reason, that psychic part will, like an unused muscle, atrophy from inactivity.

Musical education also benefits the rational part of the soul in another way: it influences reason's *beliefs or judgments* about what is valuable. Here I take it for granted that on Plato's view, the reasoning part naturally makes such judgments. Reason inherently seeks knowledge and wisdom, and for Plato that means above all knowledge of things like justice, moderation, admirableness, courage, piety, and especially *goodness*. Because human beings have this rational desire, they naturally try to figure out what is good and consequently form beliefs about what is good or otherwise valuable in the world around them. This is true not merely of philosophers, moreover, but of *everyone*. Most people in most cities do not form reliably true or stable beliefs about value, on Plato's view, but they form such beliefs all the same, and their doing so involves a defining activity of the reasoning part of their souls: the pursuit (however misguided it may be) of what is good. I also take it for granted that it is beneficial for a person to hold *true* rational beliefs about what is valuable. Such beliefs play a determining role in how a person acts and lives their life—and hence whether they live well and happily—and they are a necessary condition of, and facilitate, the person's attainment of actual *knowledge* or *wisdom* about goodness, justice, and so on. By that I have in mind simply the uncontroversial point that on Plato's view, no one who believes, for example, that the best things in human life are pleonectic goods like wealth and power can possibly achieve genuine wisdom with those views intact. Conversely, those who place value on the right things and evaluate people and actions correctly, will be well-positioned to make progress toward the fulfillment of reason's ultimate desire, given a suitable natural endowment and further education.

With this picture in mind, we can see how musical education not only stimulates and exercises reason, but exercises it in ways that conduce to making *correct* value judgments and choices. It does so, first of all, by establishing *environmental* conditions that foster true beliefs. It provides young people with an intellectual and cultural setting in which examples of people, behavior, and things that are truly admirable and good are ubiquitous, and in which they are encouraged to judge them to be such by their educators. The poetry and stories they hear accurately depict what just and virtuous people are like and how they behave, as well as what is worthy of pursuit or avoidance. Likewise, the music they hear and cultural products they encounter reflect standards of beauty and harmony that are consonant with truly good ethical character. In a city like Athens, young people are presented with false and misleading examples of putative virtue and value, and they encounter a diverse and confusing collection of competing candidates for goodness—some of them truly good, perhaps, but many or most of them actually bad. In the Kallipolis, by contrast, the uniform world around them is filled with models and illustrations of what is genuinely valuable, which means that when young people begin the rational activity of trying to look for what is good, they will readily find it.[25]

Music also provides *psychological* conditions that promote correct rational judgment. One of the key features of Plato's theory of tripartition is that the three parts of the soul can and do influence and affect one another's activities and motivations in various ways. That is to say, the tripartite soul is the integrated soul of an embodied *person*, not a collection of three discrete souls that each has its own several condition and moral fate in isolation from the others. These interrelations among the three parts are also reflected in the ability of spirited and appetitive motivations to affect a person's rational beliefs about what is good. In many cases, especially those involving appetite (as I discuss in Section 1 of the next chapter) the influence is ethically harmful. However, our *spirited* motivations can, and virtually inevitably *do*, influence our reasoning as well (as I discuss in Sections 2 and 3 of the next chapter), and

---

[25] The fact that spirited admiration for truly beautiful people and things can help direct reason's attention toward truly good ones is grounded at the metaphysical level in Plato's view that the forms of the *kalon* and the *agathon* are closely connected, such that truly admirable and truly good things in the perceptible world are coextensive with each other. On the relation between beauty and goodness, see Barney (2010), Ferrari (1987: 144–7), Harris (1930), Hobbs (2000: Ch. 8), Kahn (1996: 271 and 2004: 12–13), Lear (2006 and 2007: 101–11), Reeve (2013b: Ch. 6), Santas (1980), and Singpurwalla (2013: 52–6).

under the right circumstances, that influence can be beneficial. Socrates' musical program, therefore, is designed to create precisely such circumstances through education of *thumos* and spirited emotions. The idea is that if we antecedently love, admire, or feel drawn to something out of spirited attachment, then we will naturally tend to pay attention to it and judge it to be admirable and good when we begin making rational judgments about such things.[26] Conversely, if we antecedently hate or disdain something, then we will naturally tend to avoid it and judge it to be shameful and bad. In general, the way we *feel* about things can affect the way we *think* about them. If we are trained to feel anger or outrage in response to a given type of behavior, we will tend to rationally judge that such behavior is unjust and deserving of anger; if we feel afraid of something, we will be inclined to judge it to be fearful; if we admire someone, we will tend to judge them to be noble; and so on. Musical education, then, not only supplies abundant exemplars of virtue and goodness for reason's consideration, but also makes sure that we rationally notice them and evaluate them appropriately. It cultivates spirited emotions and attachments that direct our attention to the right people and things and exert internal psychological pressure on us to judge them the way we are supposed to.[27]

4. Gymnastic Education

Gymnastic education has two main psychological benefits, both of which involve the Stimulation Principle, but only one of which is explicitly emphasized by Socrates. According to him, the primary effect of gymnastic training is that it "stimulates" or "stretches" the spirited part of the soul. Gymnastics

---

[26] See also Lear (2006), who emphasizes spirited love of the *kalon* as a basis for rational deliberation. Cf. Gallaher (2004: 10–14). Jimenez (2020) focuses on the role of spirited *anger* in particular in moral and intellectual development.

[27] Does musical education benefit appetite at all? Much of what I go on to say in this chapter and the next might seem to suggest that it does not and cannot. Note, however, that when Plato talks about appetites in the *Republic*, he focuses on desires connected with the pleasures of bodily *taste* and *touch*: food, drink, sex, and ultimately the money that facilitates increasingly luxurious versions of them. By contrast, he has little to say about appetitive pleasures connected with the senses of sight and sound. Maybe that is because he thinks none exist. I find it plausible, however, that on Plato's view it can feel good *in an appetitive way* to listen to certain music or see certain sights (beyond those that are sexually or gastronomically stimulating), and that unlike the pleasures of taste and touch, such pleasures do not necessarily stand in the same inexorable tension with virtue. If Plato does think something like that, then there is room for musical education to benefit appetite after all by cultivating habits of feeling appetitive pleasure in the sounds and sights of the virtuous. In any event, though, Plato is far more concerned with what he considers morally hazardous forms of appetite in the *Republic*, and my account of his educational program answers to that focus. Cf. Ch. 10, n. 35, in connection with the *Laws*.

energizes *thumos* through military labor, athletic training and contests, and various other feats of endurance that require activity of the spirited part and that appeal to, and indulge, its competitive desire for honor. In other words, gymnastics affects the *thumoeides* in a way that parallels the effect of music on reason: it exercises it in some of its characteristic activities and thereby makes it stronger. This is confirmed by Socrates' description of the effects of gymnastic training, as well as deficiency or excess of it, in T1. Gymnastics makes a person "proud," "full of *thumos*," and "courageous," but in excess it makes a person "violent" and "savage." Those who *neglect* gymnastics, on the other hand, become "cowardly" and have a "weak" *thumos* or become altogether "unspirited." Gymnastic education, then, is necessary for exercising *thumos* and making it "strong" enough to fulfill its psychic role in courage. Too little of it makes it too weak to fulfill that role; too much of it makes spirit's influence in the soul excessive relative to that of reason, such that the person becomes not courageous, but simply truculent and barbaric.

Gymnastic education also has important psychological effects on the *appetitive* part of the soul that again involve the Stimulation Principle. In this case, however, Plato's aim is not to strengthen appetite, but rather to *weaken* it. Through deprivation and moderation, gymnastics stymies appetite's growth and thereby minimizes its influence in the soul.[28] Recent work by James Wilberding provides a useful starting point for understanding how gymnastics accomplishes this.[29] His interpretation is based on important connections between Socrates' discussion of early education and his detailed remarks on appetite in Books 8 and 9. In Socrates' analysis of the psychology of the oligarchic individual, he distinguishes necessary appetites from unnecessary ones. The former are those "from which we cannot desist," because we are "compelled by nature to satisfy them" and die if we do not; their satisfaction is "beneficial" and promotes bodily "health (*hugieias*) and well-being (*euexias*)"; and they include "the appetite for food and prepared dishes" and "the desire to eat to the point of health and well-being." *Unnecessary* appetites, by contrast, are ones that "someone could get rid of if he practiced from youth on" or that "most people can get rid of" if their desires are "restrained and educated while they're young"; they lead to "nothing good," but rather are "harmful to the body and to the prudence and moderation of the soul"; and they include appetites for "other foods" that exceed the limits of health and well-being

---

[28] Commentators who take the "training" of appetite to involve deprivation or forcible suppression include Gill (1985: 11), Nussbaum (1986: 155), Reeve (2013b: 98–9), and Russell (2005: 216).

[29] 2012.

(558d–559c). Later, in his image of the three-part soul, Socrates likens appetite to a beast with a mix of "gentle" and "savage" heads, and he insists that the just and happy person must "take care of the many-headed beast as a farmer does his animals, feeding and domesticating the gentle heads and preventing the savage ones from growing" (588b–589b).

According to the general picture that emerges from these passages, some of our appetites are both ineliminable *and* good for our health and well-being, while others are both bad for us and eradicable through education and restraint during youth. Wilberding argues that *gymnastics* is the component of early education that achieves this training of the appetites. Gymnastic education aims to eliminate or occlude unnecessary appetites from our psychology through moderate practices, while satisfying only the necessary ones that benefit us. As Wilberding points out, many of Socrates' gymnastic guidelines concern the characteristic objects of appetitive desire: food, drink, and sex. Thus the city's warriors are assigned a simple diet and lifestyle and are forbidden from eating extravagant foods, getting drunk, or hiring prostitutes. In other words, they are prescribed exactly the sorts of moderate practices that Books 8 and 9 recommend for nurturing beneficial appetites and eliminating harmful ones. They are not permitted to "feed" their unnecessary appetites for indulgent foods, wine, and illicit sex, but rather only their necessary appetites in accordance with prudence (403d–404e). Indeed, Socrates' dietary and lifestyle guidelines explicitly aim at promoting bodily "health" and "well-being," precisely the terms he uses to characterize the effects of satisfying necessary appetites in Book 8.[30] These guidelines, therefore, aim at promoting healthy appetites and excluding all unhealthy, excessive ones from the soul.[31]

I accept the account just sketched: Socrates' dietary and lifestyle guidelines directly affect the appetitive part of the soul in these ways. According to Wilberding, however, they affect *only* appetite, and on this point I disagree. He comments, "It is easy enough to see how *exercise* could arouse the spirited part of the soul and promote courage, but how does a simple lifestyle of moderation do this? The answer is: it *doesn't.*"[32] On Wilberding's view, gymnastic education is subdivided into two components: one part is athletic and military exercise, and the other is diet and lifestyle. The former *exclusively* affects the spirited element of the soul, while the latter *exclusively* affects the appetitive. My own interpretation dissents on both counts: athletics also

---

[30] As Wilberding notes, Socrates uses forms of ὑγιεία or εὐεξία five times in total at 404a–e to characterize the goals of his policies.

[31] For a different perspective on the benefits of gymnastic education, see Reid (2007).

[32] 2012: 246.

affects appetite, and diet and lifestyle also affect *thumos*. More to the point, there is no sharp distinction between the two components of gymnastics posited by Wilberding. Rather, gymnastic education is a unified discipline that has psychological effects on *both* the spirited and appetitive parts of the soul. To see this point, note Socrates' characterization of spirit's psychic role in T2 above: it is supposed to "govern" and "watch over" the appetitive part of the soul in cooperation with reason, and its unique function in the individual virtue of courage consists in its preservation of reason's declarations "through pleasures and pains." According to Socrates, then, the proper activity of *thumos* in the soul involves the management and suppression of appetite and of appetitive impulses related to pleasure and pain. With this background in mind, consider again the gymnastic regulations on diet and lifestyle. The simple and austere regimen that Socrates prescribes requires that the guardians resist any desires they may have for quantities or kinds of pleasurable food, drink, or sex that exceed what is required and beneficial. The gymnastic diet and lifestyle, in other words, require psychological feats of endurance and resistance in the face of malignant bodily pleasures. Such activities, moreover, are precisely the ones Socrates assigns to the *thumoeides* for its role in courage, which means that maintaining proper diet and lifestyle requires and involves one of the defining activities of the spirited part of the soul. This point allows us to see how diet and lifestyle contribute to making *thumos* "courageous," which Socrates explicitly identifies as the goal of gymnastics: in guarding and fighting against excessive appetites, spirit is actively practicing for its psychic function. The dietary and lifestyle aspect of gymnastics, therefore, not only checks and weakens appetite, but also stimulates and strengthens *thumos*.

A converse point can also be made about military and athletic exercises. These activities stimulate and satisfy spirit's competitive desires in obvious ways, by providing opportunities for individuals to distinguish themselves and earn honor through contests, martial skill, and acts of nobility. Importantly, though, these activities also involve spirit's opposition to appetite. As Socrates explains, military training for the guardians must make them capable of tolerating various kinds of physically painful or unpleasant circumstances: frequent changes to their food and water, extreme heat and cold, and lack of sleep (404a–b). Indeed, for the Greeks, military and athletic training *in general* involved the risk and endurance of painful or disagreeable bodily conditions: injury, physical exertion, discomfort, strenuous labor, exhaustion, and so on. Hence in the *Protagoras*, for instance, Socrates classifies gymnastic and military training as "painful" activities that involve "intense pain and suffering" (354a–b). Because the appetitive part of the soul is innately averse to bodily pain and discomfort, therefore, this means that success in athletic and military training requires resistance to appetite. The individual must overcome and resist natural appetitive desires to avoid or desist from activities that are physically unpleasant. In other words, the stimulation of *thumos* through competitions, athletics, and martial training is simultaneous with, and inextricable from, a corresponding deprivation of the appetitive part. Spirit's pursuit and fulfillment of its competitive desires *requires* that appetite's aversion to bodily pain be suppressed and ignored. The athletic and military component of gymnastics, therefore, provides training for the appetitive part of the soul just as diet and lifestyle do: by depriving appetite of what it wants (when it wants something incompatible with education and virtue), and thereby making sure it remains weak. If any difference is to be detected between the two "parts" of gymnastic training, it is perhaps that athletics and martial training involve spirit's opposition to the appetitive aversion to pain, whereas diet and lifestyle involve its opposition to the appetitive desire for pleasure. Gymnastic education as a whole, however, essentially involves *both* the stimulation and strengthening of spirit and the concurrent deprivation and weakening of appetite.

Having now determined the effects of music and gymnastics on *thumos* and the other two parts of the soul, I next examine how the soul's parts are supposed to function and interact with one another in a virtuous soul, as well as how the effects of early education are related to and designed to promote those proper relationships.

7

Oikeion and *Allotrion* in the City and Soul

The Psychology of Virtue and Civic Unity

In this chapter I examine the psychology of virtue and civic unity. As we saw in the last chapter, musical and gymnastic education aim at producing a properly ordered soul in which reason rules, spirit supports reason, and the two of them together supervise appetite and keep it in check. In this chapter I first offer a closer analysis of the nature of these relationships and how they are connected to the goals of early moral education. I will begin in Section 1 by discussing the distinctive danger posed by the appetitive part to reason and its authority in the soul. I then analyze spirit's support for reason in combating this danger, focusing especially on Socrates' characterization of courage, in Sections 2 and 3. Finally, in Section 4 I turn to the civic harmony and fellowship that Socrates aims to produce through his social and economic policies. Speaking generally, my main thesis in this chapter is that at the intrapsychic and interpersonal levels alike, Plato's proposals are designed to exploit the two primitive faces of spirited motivation: its aggression toward the *allotrion*, and its fondness, protectiveness, and friendship toward the *oikeion*. His educational proposals produce psychic harmony in large part by making correct reason familiar to spirit and vicious appetites foreign to it, and his policies on family and private property promote political harmony by instilling emotional bonds of familiarity and friendship among citizens.

1. The War against Appetite

Because spirit's role in the psychology of virtue is characterized in terms of its support for reason in opposing vicious appetites, understanding that role requires closer attention to the specific kind of danger posed by appetite. Once we understand *how* the appetitive part threatens to subvert reason's influence in the soul, we will be able to fill in further details about spirit's role in guarding against that threat. My goal in this section is to show that the psychic strength of appetite and reason—their capacity to influence a person's

The Political Soul: Plato on Thumos, *Spirited Motivation, and the City*. Josh Wilburn, Oxford University Press.
© Josh Wilburn 2021. DOI: 10.1093/oso/9780198861867.003.0007

behavior and lives—are inversely related to one another, and that when appetite is too "strong," it has the potential to "enslave" the rational part in the long-term or make it "abandon" its true beliefs in the short term. Both of these forms of domination, moreover, involve destabilizing or corrupting rational judgment. Spirit's psychic function, consequently, will largely involve keeping reason's true judgments safe and intact in the face of problematic appetites.

The caution with which Plato treats appetite in the *Republic* reflects his view that the appetitive and reasoning parts of the soul stand in a special tension to one another. One of the especially worrisome features of appetite, as Plato understands it, is that the stronger the appetitive part becomes, the *worse* it becomes. As we have seen, the only appetites it is beneficial for a person to satisfy are necessary ones, which promote bodily health and are an ineliminable part of our nature. If we consider this point in light of the Stimulation Principle, it follows that there is some *minimal* degree of psychic strength that the appetitive part of the soul should, and presumably *must*, possess. In virtue of being embodied human beings, we cannot help but experience certain appetitive urges such as hunger and thirst. What is more, it would be *bad* for us to avoid experiencing them entirely even if we could. We need to satisfy our necessary appetites for food and drink in order to survive, and in doing so we stimulate, at least to some extent, the appetitive part of the soul. Plato's theory does not merely grudgingly grant that some appetites are necessary, therefore; it recognizes that they positively contribute to a person's well-being. It is *good* for the appetitive part of the soul to be strong enough to motivate us to satisfy bodily needs.[1]

It is only good for appetite to be *just* strong enough to do so, however, and no stronger. When its strength exceeds its necessary lower limit, appetite motivates us to pursue unnecessary quantities and types of pleasure, along with the wealth and material resources that facilitate their attainment. If *those* desires are satisfied, appetite becomes stronger yet again and motivates us to pursue even more wealth or even more harmful pleasures. Socrates' account of moral degeneration in Books 8 and 9 reflects the danger of this process. The increasingly vicious oligarchic, democratic, and tyrannical personality types are each defined in large part by the increasingly prominent role appetites play in their psychologies and lives. As they become stronger and exert more

---

[1] Because necessary appetites are ineliminable, Plato evidently does not think there is any pressing danger that appetite might become too weak to accomplish this basic biological task. Likewise, Aristotle notes that necessary appetites are natural and that "few people go wrong in the natural desires, and only in one direction: excess" (*NE* 1118b15–16).

influence on the individual's behavior, appetites become progressively more diverse and morally destructive—a process that ultimately leads to the frenzied mass of criminal appetites that distinguishes the soul of the tyrant. Presumably, this tendency of appetite to become worse the more it is stimulated is connected to its *insatiability*, which for Plato is another of the defining characteristics of appetitive desire. In T2, for instance, Socrates describes appetite as "by nature absolutely insatiable (*aplēstotaton*) for money," and he later refers to the same "insatiability" (*aplēstias*) of the appetitive beast within (590b8).[2] The ethical problem, then, is that in principle there is no upper limit to the amount of wealth or perceived bodily pleasure that a person can appetitively desire and pursue: the more of it they get, the more they want.[3] By definition, though, it is morally harmful for a person to satisfy any appetites that exceed what is necessary—and the more they exceed it, the more harmful it is to them. As appetite becomes "bigger and stronger," the more corrupt it, and the individual *themselves*, becomes.

These facts about appetite provide resources for explaining the unique threat it poses to reason. The aims of a life determined by a person's rationality are virtue, wisdom, and goodness, but the more appetite grows, the more the person will be motivated to pursue and value unnecessary or vicious objects that compete with those goals. Socrates alludes to precisely this issue when he discusses the oligarchic city, which has its origin in the rising value its citizens place on wealth. He explains, "They proceed further into money-making, and the more they honor it, the less they honor virtue. Or aren't virtue and wealth so opposed that if they were set on a scale, they would always incline in opposite directions?" (550e4–7). Here Socrates insists on the incompatibility of two competing goals of action. The aim of maximizing wealth and profit is distinctive of the appetitive part, while that of living virtuously is proper to the rational part (and, presumably, a well-trained spirited part)[4] in its pursuit of

---

[2] Those who spend their lives occupied with "feasts and the like" are similarly "insatiable"—literally, "unfillable"—because "the part they're trying to fill is like a vessel full of holes" (586a–b). Cf. *Gorg.* 492d–494a and comments in Moss (2007: 238).

[3] Aristophanes' *Wealth* anticipates Plato's characterization: "No one ever gets their fill (μεστός) of you [Wealth]. There can be enough (πλησμονή) of anything else: of love (ἔρωτος) . . . music (μουσικῆς) . . . honor (τιμῆς) . . . manliness (ἀνδραγαθίας) . . . ambition (φιλοτιμίας) . . . generalship (στρατηγίας) . . . But no one ever gets his fill (μεστός) of you" (188–97). Cf. (ps.-)Plato, *Hipparch.* 226d–e, as well as Aristotle's distinction between a "natural" or "limited" form of wealth acquisition that is part of household management, and the more common, unnatural form of it that aims at physical gratification and is "limitless" (ἄπειρον) (*Pol.* 1256b40–1258a19).

[4] Note that Plato portrays morally beneficial expressions of *thumos*, especially friendship and shame, as standing in the same inverse relation to money-making and unnecessary appetites as do reason and virtue. Hence the deterioration of cities and souls culminates in the completely friendless and shameless tyrant of Book 9. Cf. *Critias* 120e–121a, where "friendship and its companion, virtue" thrived as long as citizens did not value money, but declined and vanished once they did. Likewise, in Academic texts,

wisdom and the good. The metaphor of a scale is particularly emphatic: there is a zero sum between the value a person places on virtue and the value they place on money.

This point reflects a more general principle that governs the dynamic between reason and appetite, on Plato's view, which is that the psychological power of each is inversely related to that of the other. Simply put: the stronger one part becomes, the *weaker* the other tends to become. Socrates provides a foundation for this line of thought in his description of philosophical nature in Book 6:

> Now, we surely know that, when someone's desires incline strongly (*spho-dra*) for one thing, they are thereby weakened (*asthenesterai*) for others, just like a stream that has been partly diverted into another channel . . . So, when someone's desires flow toward learning and everything of that sort, he'd be concerned, I suppose, with the pleasures of the soul itself by itself, and he'd abandon those pleasures that come through the body—if indeed he is a true philosopher and not merely a counterfeit one . . . Surely, then, such a person is moderate and not at all a money-lover. He is less likely than anyone else at all to take seriously the things for which money and large expenditures are needed.   (485d6–e5)

Socrates' hydraulic metaphor suggests that each person has something like a fixed treasury of motivational energy, at least when it comes to dividing up their devotions between appetitive and rational ends. The stronger a person's rational desires are—the more efficacious they are in making the person pursue learning and wisdom—the weaker their appetitive desires to pursue physical pleasures and money will be.[5] Socrates clearly means to imply the converse as well: the stronger a person's appetites are, the weaker their rational desires.[6]

"shamelessness" (ἀναισχυντία) is defined as "the state of soul which endures dishonor (ἀδοξίας) for the sake of profit (κέρδους)" (*Def.* 416a14–15), and it "makes [people] dare to be greedy (τολμᾶν φιλοκερδεῖν)" (*Hipparch.* 225a8–b3).

[5] Cf. Democritus, DK B72: "Intense desires (σφοδραὶ ὀρέξεις) for one thing blind (τυφλοῦσιν) the soul to everything else."

[6] Other passages reflect and confirm this idea, e.g. 328c–d and 605a–c, and cf. *Tim.* 88a–b. For discussion of 485d–e, see Gill (1985: 19–21), Klosko (2006: 98–100), and Weinstein (2018: 262). Some commentators take the passage to suggest a general principle that governs the relationships among all three soul parts' desires. Kahn (1996: 276–81), by contrast, offers a "cognitive" reading that takes only *rational* desire, not desire generally, to be limited and dirigible. I take no stand dogmatic on the issue; what matters most for my purposes is simply the passage's illustration of the competition between appetitive and rational ends and pursuits.

The language of "strength" and "weakness" might suggest that the primary danger appetite poses to reason is that it will overpower it with something like brute psychic *force*. On this way of understanding their relationship, situations in which appetite prevails over reason in the soul would look like cases of *akrasia*, or lack of self-control: a person tries to resist satisfying one of their appetites on the basis of reasoning, but their appetitive desire is *stronger* than their rational one, and they end up acting on their appetite *while continuing to believe rationally that they should not*. The akratic model as defined in this way also appears to receive support from the fact that Socrates uses the language of "enslavement" (553d2), "force" (440b1), and "compulsion" (519a4, 587a4) to describe appetite's treatment of reason, and he characterizes conflict between appetite on the one hand and reason and its helper spirit on the other in martial terms: reason and spirit engage in "civil war" against appetite, and spirit is reason's "ally" or "fellow fighter" against it (440b2–4, 440c8). Likewise, as we saw in Chapter 1, Plato often characterizes desires themselves in the language of "pushing," "pulling," or "dragging," which suggests that conflicts between desires are like games of tug-of-war in which the stronger party wins.

The akratic model is misleading, however. On Plato's view, appetite ordinarily overcomes reason not by "dragging" it along toward indulgence, but instead by corrupting or destabilizing its practical judgments, values, and desires so that it stops resisting or never resists in the first place.[7] The appetitive agent is not typically an akratic, therefore, but rather someone in whom the rational part has been perverted. Or, to put the point in terms of a classic Greek distinction: when reason cedes psychological control of a person's behavior to appetite, it is not normally because it is brutely "forced" to do so, but because it has become (perhaps only temporarily) "persuaded" that it should, or at least is no longer persuaded that it should resist.

To see why, it will be useful to consider the two main types of cases in which appetite prevails over reason. The first involves the long-term patterns of behavior that constitute a way of life: the person lives the life of a hedonist or money-lover, rather than a life of virtue or philosophy, because the appetitive part of their soul and its desires are "stronger" than the reasoning part

---

[7] Others who recognize that Plato is less concerned about *akrasia* (as just defined) than he is about other ways non-rational motivations subvert reason include Kahn (1996: 254), Penner (2003: 205, n. 5), Price (1995: 98–100), Scott (1999: 35–6), Shields (2007: 82–6), Stalley (2007: 80–1), Weinstein (2018: 210–11), and Whiting (2012: 175). By contrast, many commentators take *akrasia* to be a central preoccupation of Platonic philosophy, and many developmentalists, e.g. Reeve (1988: 134), even attribute the shift they perceive in Plato's psychology from early dialogues to the *Republic* largely to his desire to allow for the possibility of akratic action. I argue against such interpretations in Wilburn (2014a), on which some of the arguments of this section are based.

and its desires. Let us call this a *global* failure of reason. In Books 8 and 9 Socrates discusses just such cases: he explains the etiology and psychology of various character types who are "ruled" or dominated by elements of their souls other than reason and who live inferior lives as a result. Significantly, in his analyses of all three character types who are in one way or another dominated by the appetitive part of the soul and its desires—the oligarch, democrat, and tyrant—Socrates emphasizes ways in which the individual's rational judgments and values are compromised and corrupted in accordance with the aims of appetite. The most striking example is Socrates' theatrical description of the origin of the oligarchic individual:

> Don't you think that this person would establish his appetitive and money-making part on the throne, setting it up as the Great King within himself?...He makes the reasoning and spirited parts sit on the ground beneath appetite, one on either side, reducing them to slaves (*katadoulōsamenos*). He won't allow the first to reason about (*logizesthai*) or investigate (*skopein*) anything except how a little money can be made into great wealth. And he won't allow the second to admire (*thaumazein*) or honor (*timan*) anything but wealth and wealthy people or to have any ambition (*philotimeisthai*) other than the acquisition of wealth or whatever might contribute to getting it.   (553c4–d7)

The oligarch lives the life of a money-lover, according to Socrates, because the money-loving appetitive part of his soul "rules" over reason and spirit. Importantly, though, the fact that reason is "enslaved" does not mean that it *resists* appetite's domination. It is not that the oligarch's reasoning part judges that he should live the philosophical life of a Socrates, but simply motivates him too weakly to overcome the greater force of his appetitive desire to live life as a profiteer. Rather, the rational part itself, under the influence of appetite, comes to judge that the money-making life is best and devotes its powers of reasoning and calculation to fulfilling the avaricious goals of such a life.[8] The oligarchic individual does not pursue profit or live a life of greed akratically, but rather with reason's full endorsement.[9]

---

[8] Carone (2001: 135) similarly draws on the description of the oligarch to support the view that non-rational domination of reason involves affecting its judgment. My understanding of appetite's "rule" in the oligarchic soul is consistent with the accounts of Brown (2012: 68–9), Lorenz (2006b: 157–8), and especially Johnstone (2011 and 2013), who responds to an alternative view in Irwin (1995a: 284–7).

[9] Cf. Book 9: when the spirited or appetitive part of the soul rules the soul, it "compels" (ἀναγκάζειν) the other parts to "chase after" (διώκειν) untrue pleasures (587a3–5).

Other passages suggest a similar story. In Book 7 Socrates describes rational education as a process of "turning the soul around" so that its power is directed toward the true objects of knowledge. The problem is that "feasting, gluttony, and other such pleasures" drag its vision downward and "chain" it to the flawed and fleeting material world (518b–519b). He asks:

> Have you never noticed this about people who are said to be vicious but clever: how keen the vision of their little souls is, and how sharply it distinguishes the things toward which it is turned? This shows that its sight isn't inferior but rather is forced to serve evil ends, so that the sharper it sees, the more evil it accomplishes,   (519a1–6)

Crafty evildoers use their intellectual endowments to pursue unjust objectives associated with physical pleasure. However, that clearly does not imply that reason, so to speak, actively "resists" or "fights" against directing its thoughts toward such aims. Rather, bodily pleasures have the effect of corrupting reason's values so that instead of focusing on and trying to obtain wisdom, it turns its attention and desires toward appetitive objects. This reading is confirmed by the passage's context. It is a commentary on Socrates' image of the cave and refers to its pitiable residents, who are chained down in such a way that they "see" and care only about the shadows on the cave wall. This matters because the prisoners are explicitly "uneducated" or "ignorant": they do not know or have correct beliefs about what is truly valuable. Indeed, they are not even aware that anything of value *exists* beyond the chimerical world of shadows with which they concern themselves (514a–515e, 517d–e).[10] Similarly, in Book 9 Socrates indicates that when the reasoning part is "weak" (*asthenes*) in someone, it "serves" the other two parts of the soul and "learns" (*manthanein*) only about the things that flatter them (590c2–6). Reason evidently continues to pursue its desire for learning even when subjugated by appetite or spirit, but due to its "weakness," the only subjects it judges worth "learning" are those that promote the attainment of pleonectic goods. Its innate desire to seek goodness and knowledge presumably continues to influence the person's actions and decisions in life, but that desire is oriented toward meretricious values and forms of knowledge. These passages all show that global failures of reason, for Plato, characteristically involve the long-term perversion of reason and its values. When people live inferior lives

---

[10] Cf. Wilberding (2004: 135).

under the influence of appetite, reason is typically a consenting accomplice in that life.[11]

The second main type of case in which appetite prevails over reason involves specific or isolated instances of behavior: on a given occasion the person rationally judges that they should not φ—drink a glass of wine, for instance—but they appetitively desire to φ and end up φ-ing anyway under the influence of that desire. Let us call this a *local* failure of reason. Here my argument is more controversial, because many commentators have argued or assumed that local failures of reason are paradigm cases of akratic behavior as defined above. However, the text itself provides strong reasons for thinking that, even if agents in the *Republic* do sometimes act akratically, Plato is arguably much *more* concerned about local failures of reason that the akratic model fails to capture.[12] The key evidence in this regard is an important passage from Book 3 that immediately follows Socrates' account of musical and gymnastic training. Having determined how the young guardians are to be educated, he and his interlocutors must next determine who among them are well-suited for becoming rulers—the "true guardians" of the city. Socrates claims that rulers are distinguished by their exceptional commitment to certain kinds of civic *beliefs*, especially the belief that they must always do what is best for the city as a whole (412d–e). Evaluating which citizens should rule, therefore, requires observing them throughout their lives to make sure they do not "abandon" (*ekballousin*, 412e7) their correct judgments. Socrates elaborates: all "abandonment" of true belief is *involuntary*, he says, and it occurs due to one of three causes: theft (*klapentes*), force (*biasthentes*), or magical spell (*goēteuthentes*):

> By "the victims of theft" I mean those who are persuaded to change their minds or those who forget, because time, in the latter case, and argument, in

---

[11] Cf. Shaw (2015: Ch. 6), who examines Plato's view of how pleasure distorts judgment and leads people to accept hedonistic or appetitive world views.

[12] If Plato acknowledges *akrasia* anywhere in the *Republic*, it is most likely in the story of Leontius. That, at any rate, is how most commentators interpret his case. I have argued in previous work (2014a: 61–2, 82–4, and n. 40; and 2015a: 12–14 and nn. 39–40) that the text does not necessitate the akratic reading of Leontius, but nothing in my arguments here turns on that issue. My interpretation requires only the moderate claim that—*whatever* Plato may think about the possibility of *akrasia* in the *Republic*—he also recognizes the prevalence of, and demonstrates more concern about, other *non-akratic* ways in which appetites subvert reason's authority and judgments. For interpreters who assume or argue that Leontius is akratic, see Bobonich (2017: 2–6), Brickhouse and Smith (2007: 16), Dorion (2012: 37–8 and n. 20), Gardner (2002: 200–1), Gerson (2003a: 105), Gosling (1990: 21), Irwin (1977: 192–3), Kahn (1996: 254–5), Lesses (1987: 148), Reeve (1988: 134), and Rowe (2003: 27). For critics who reject or doubt the akratic reading, see Bloom (1968: 375–7), Crombie (1962: 346–7), and especially Carone (2001: 136–41) and Bieda (2012), who concludes of Leontius, "Su apetito no vence a la razón, sino a la impulsividad que lucha por escapar del escarnio público y personal" (p. 147).

the former, takes away their opinions without their realizing it.... By "the forced" (*biasthentas*) I mean those whom pain or suffering causes to change their mind (*metadoxasai*)... The "victims of magic," I think you'd agree, are those who change their mind because they are under the spell of pleasure or fear (*metadoxasōsin ē huph' hēdonēs kēlēthentes ē hupo phobou ti deisantes*).

(413a4–c3)

In order to determine which citizens will be "good guardians" of their beliefs, Socrates proposes that contests and competitions be devised to "test" them throughout their lives. These should include not only subjection to labors and pains, but also, and most importantly, exposure to pleasures and fears. The citizens must be tested "more thoroughly than gold in fire," and those who prove immune to the spell of pleasure and fear throughout their lives will be selected as candidates to become rulers (413c–414b).

This passage offers an informative picture of the relationship between non-rational motivation and reason. The cases of "force" and "magic" explicitly concern what happens when a person's true rational belief about how to act comes into conflict with motivations like pleasure, pain, or fear. Note that Socrates' focus is on specific circumstances and actions: he is dealing with local cases in which some occurrent non-rational feeling or desire conflicts with a person's practical judgment. This is confirmed by the fact that he seeks to simulate such conflicts with tests that are repeated on different occasions throughout their lives. Although he does not provide examples of the kinds of challenges he has in mind, he offers one useful analogy: testing young people against fear or pleasure is like "leading colts into noise and tumult to see if they're afraid" (413d9–10). Just as colts "fail" this test if they become agitated or attempt to run away, so the guardians fail their own tests if they behave in accordance with their non-rational motivations—say, by fleeing what is fearful, avoiding what is painful, or pursuing what is physically pleasant. That is to say, the criterion of someone's success or failure in the tests Socrates has planned is how they *act*. This means that, in this passage at least, Socrates is identifying correct action with the perseverance of true belief, and incorrect action with the abandonment of it. Those who act well hold on to their correct rational judgments about how to behave, while those who act badly give up those judgments. In other words, non-rational motivation prevails not by making an individual act against a rational belief (and corresponding rational desire) that they continue to hold *even while they are acting*, but instead by causing the person, at least temporarily, to relinquish their opposed belief all together. Those who make the right judgments about

how to act prior to acting but nonetheless behave wrongly under the influence
of pain, pleasure, or fear do not do so *akratically*, but because their feelings and
desires cause them to "change their minds" (*metadoxasai*, literally "change
their beliefs") about what to do.[13] In the local failures of reason that are of
primary ethical concern to Socrates, therefore, non-rational motivations prevail against rational judgment by destabilizing or corrupting it.[14]

The akratic model, therefore, fails to account for much of the *Republic*'s
treatment of the relationship between reason and appetite. If that is the case,
however, then why does Plato use the language of strength, force, violence, and
physical or martial struggle to describe their relationship at all? The answer is
that such language is useful and illuminating in ways that do not depend on, or
necessarily imply, the akratic model. To begin with, as I argued in Chapter 1,
Plato thinks of the soul's parts as sources of motion, and of motivations as the
type of psychic motion that causes human behavior. It makes sense, therefore,
for Plato to characterize parts of the soul and their desires as "strong" or
"weak" (since motion can vary in its force or intensity), or in terms of "pulling," "pushing," and "dragging" (since such language refers to obvious forms
of bodily motion). Such language also captures something about the *experience*
of motivation: to desire something is to feel "drawn" to it. What is at issue in
my arguments above, therefore, is not whether soul parts can "pull" us
strongly or weakly toward certain behavior or ways of life—my view assumes
that they do—but rather how it typically affects reason when appetite is the
part that pulls the hardest. What I have tried to show is simply that in the
Republic, the competing "strengths" of appetite and reason are correlated with
the extent to which appetite is able or unable to affect rational beliefs and
values. The stronger appetites are, the more capable they are of influencing
reason's judgments, and the weaker reason is, the more vulnerable it is to
appetite's influence. Conversely, the stronger reason is, the more impervious it
is to appetitive influence, and the weaker appetites are, the less capable they are
of affecting rational judgments. The strength of rational desire and belief, then,
is often closely connected with its *content*. To put the point in Plato's language:
when reason is incapable of "pulling" forcefully, it also tends to be bad at

---

[13] Passages in early Greek literature suggest similarly beguiling effects of greed and pleasure, but
often those effects are characterized in terms of emotions or language associated with *thumos*. For
example: the goddess *Aidōs* urges *thumos* on in battle, but "the sense of shame that brings fame is
secretly stolen by the greed for profit" (Pindar, *Nem.* 9.33–6). Cf. Hesiod, *WD* 323–4 and Archilochus,
fr. 191.
[14] Cf. Scott (1999: 29–31).

figuring out, or maintaining a correct view about, which direction is the right one in which to pull.[15]

The usefulness of the language of force, strength, and struggle is also especially clear in occurrent cases of psychic *conflict*, by which I mean an instance of active opposition between one motivation and another that is part of the agent's conscious experience. This is the sort of conflict to which Socrates appeals in Book 4 in his argument for tripartition, and it is also at issue in the Book 3 passage on how true beliefs are lost. In such contexts, the language of physical and martial struggle—of "tug-of-war" and war itself—captures the fact that when we experience psychic conflict, we often feel "pulled" in two directions, and often as if we are fighting or struggling against the appetite of which we disapprove. Hence even though appetite's ultimate "victory" over reason in cases of conflict does not typically involve *akrasia*, the initial conflict *itself* can still aptly be described using the language of war and struggle.

Note also that for Plato, there appears to be an interesting asymmetry in the relationship between reason and appetite. Whereas appetite's control of reason is more akin to persuasion than brute force, reason's control of appetite often looks like just the opposite. In non-metaphorical terms, when we succeed in resisting our appetites, our appetites often persist *while* we do the resisting. Whereas local failures of reason are not typically instances of *akrasia*, local *successes* of reason often do take the form of *enkrateia* or self-control.[16] In the

---

[15] Plato also seems to think appetite's domination of reason has something in common with violent force: when reason adopts corrupt values, its doing so is in a sense *involuntary* for the person. In the *Gorgias* Socrates distinguishes between doing what one *believes is best* and doing what one *wants*. Although everyone ultimately *wants* happiness and what is truly good for them—namely, *virtue*, on Plato's view—many people act in unjust ways that are bad for them, and hence *involuntarily*, under the false impression that doing so is in their best interest (466d–468e). When people live and behave badly out of ignorance, therefore, they always in some sense do so against their own will. This idea continues to operate in the *Republic*. Hence in the Book 3 passage discussed above, Socrates says that all loss of true judgment is "involuntary," and in Book 9 he claims that the soul of a tyrannical person, dominated by appetitive *erōs*, "least of all does what it wants" (577e1–2). Despite the fact that appetite typically corrupts reason through something analogous to persuasion, then, Plato thinks some persuasion can be "force-like" in one important sense. Cf. *Laws* 863b, where he oxymoronically describes pleasure as a force that overcomes us πειθοῖ μετὰ ἀπάτης βιαίου.

[16] Plato's portrayal of this asymmetry is especially clear in the *Phaedrus* in the struggle between the bad appetitive horse, which seeks "the gratification of sexual pleasure," and the charioteer and good horse which resist it (253e–254e). Although Plato characterizes the behavior of both parties using language of struggle that befits the equine image of the chariot—they "draw," "drag," "force," and "pull against" one another—he also draws some contrast in the methods by which they attempt to control one another. The bad horse uses insidious rhetoric to try to persuade the charioteer and good horse: it "reproaches," "argues," and secures an "agreement" from them. The charioteer, meanwhile, employs violence, intimidation, and pain to keep the bad horse in check (254e2–8). Rachana Kamtekar comments, "One point this makes is that our being rational allows our appetitive desires to appear to us as reasons, and our being appetitive allows our reasons to appear to us as violent forces."

self-restrained thirsty person of Book 4, for instance, reason "masters" (*kratoun*, 439c7) appetite and "drags it away" (*anthelkei*, 439b3) from drinking: appetite is evidently defiant to the end. Likewise, Plato often likens reason and spirit's control of unruly appetites to forms of violence or threats.[17] The notion of physical struggle or force, then, accurately captures one possible outcome in conflicts between the rational and appetitive parts.[18]

Finally, Plato's use of the language of physical conflict and war is informed in part by the role of *thumos* in the psychology of virtue. In short, he appropriates the martial language associated with spirit's role in fighting external enemies on the battlefield and applies it to its psychic function of protecting reason and fighting "enemy" appetites within the person's own soul. I turn now to the details of that account.

2. The Ally of Reason

By contrast to the antagonism that characterizes reason's relationship to appetite, its relationship with spirit is markedly cooperative. As we have seen, Socrates describes *thumos* as the "ally" or "auxiliary" of the reasoning part and attributes to it a unique responsibility for the virtue of courage that involves its support for reason. A person is courageous, T2 tells us, when spirit "preserves through pains and pleasures the declarations of reason about what is fearful and what is not (*diasōizēi dia te lupōn kai hēdonōn to hupo tou logou parangelthen deinon kai mē*)." In this section I examine spirit's relationship with reason and its role in the psychology of courage in closer detail. According to my interpretation, what it means for spirit to act as reason's "ally" and "preserve" its declarations is for it to provide motivations that are sensitive to and reinforce correct rational judgments about how to live and act in the face of recalcitrant appetites.[19] When spirit is successful in this role, the person maintains their rational judgments in the face of conflicting appetitive

---

(2006: 196). I think this is exactly right. The passage reflects what Plato takes to be the complicated and messy phenomenology that results from our being both rational and appetitive creatures. Cf. discussion in Ferrari (1987: 185–90).

[17] E.g. at *Rep.* 554c–d, a passage I analyze in Wilburn (2014b); and *Tim.* 70a.

[18] Interestingly, an inverted version of this asymmetry seems to apply between reason and spirit: reason "overcomes" spirit by calming it down, whereas spirit averts reason's control through impetuous violence (e.g. in cases of impulsive anger).

[19] I defend this view at greater length in Wilburn (2015b). Weinstein (2018) defends a similar interpretation that takes courage to consist in spirit's opposition to appetites that threaten to destabilize reason's judgments, but he develops the details differently in light of his distinctive understanding of tripartition. On his view, the three soul parts are defined by their different relationships to *time*:

motivations and acts accordingly. This interpretation involves four main claims. (1) The "declarations of reason" that spirit preserves are rational beliefs about how to act. (2) The "pleasures and pains" through which it preserves them are appetitive motivations associated with pleasurable and painful bodily feelings. (3) Spirit's successful "preservation" of the reasoning part's declarations consists, first and foremost, in ensuring that reason does not alter its beliefs under pressure from those appetites.[20] And (4) spirit accomplishes this task by—and its work as the "ally" or "auxiliary" of the rational part consists in—supplying motivations that are supportive of, and responsive to, reason's beliefs.

One of the main argument for claims (1), (2), and (3) of this interpretation takes as its starting-point the conclusion of the previous section: that the main ethical threat appetite poses is that it will corrupt or destabilize a person's reasoning about what is valuable and how to act and live. Since *that* is the main danger appetite poses, and since spirit's role as reason's ally is to help guard against the danger of appetite, it follows that spirit's psychic function is (at least in large part) to protect against the corruption or destabilization of rational judgment. In other words, T2 specifies that spirit's job is to make sure appetite and its desires do not disrupt reason's rule in the soul or interfere with reason's declarations, and the passages surveyed above in Section 1 indicate exactly what appetite's enslavement of reason looks like and how desires associated with pleasure and pain affect rational beliefs. The appetitive part of the soul and its motivations imperil a person's reasoning about what is valuable and how to act, and spirit's job is to help keep that from happening.

We can say more in support of this reading, however, by considering the relationship between Socrates' account of individual courage in T2 and his description of the courage of the *polis* earlier in Book 4. There he claims that the city's fighting class is responsible for the city's possession of courage and, more specifically, that the city is courageous when its auxiliary class "has the

---

appetite is concerned with the short-term or finite, *thumos* with the stability of the long-term or indefinite, and reason with the permanent or infinite. Cf. Reeve (2013b: 99). On this view, spirit "preserves" reason's judgments because it fundamentally seeks stability in a changing world and wants to make sure that outcomes in the future correspond to our (rational) plans and expectations about them. I find this analysis illuminating, although I am not persuaded that time is the central factor in Plato's *own* thinking about or presentation of the three parts of the soul.

[20] In Ch. 8 I argue against the view that spirit (or appetite) holds "beliefs" of its own in any robust sense. However, the present argument does not depend on that claim. What matters here is simply that, regardless of whether spirit *can* hold beliefs, the beliefs it is supposed to "preserve" in the case of courage belong to reason. Other commentators who attribute the courageous beliefs in question to reason include Kamtekar (2017: 169–70), Renaut (2014: 192–5), Singpurwalla (2013: 57), and Weinstein (2018: 204–16). For commentators who attribute the beliefs to spirit itself, see Bobonich (2002: 288), Hobbs (2000: 22–3), and Jansen (2015: 4).

power to preserve (*sōsei*) through everything the belief (*doxan*) about what is fearful." This means, in particular, the belief that fearful things are as the lawgiver "announced" (*parēngellen*) them to be in the course of education. Courage, then, is "a certain sort of preservation (*sōtērian*)" (429a–c). When Glaucon asks what sort of preservation he has in mind, Socrates responds:

> The preservation through everything of the belief that has been produced by law through education about what things and what sorts of things are to be feared. And by preservation (*sōtērian*) of this belief "through everything" I mean preserving (*diasōizesthai*) it and not abandoning (*ekballein*) it because of pains, pleasures, appetites, or fears. (429c7–d2)

Socrates provides an analogy: those who dye wool aim to do so in such a way that the color is completely absorbed and cannot be washed out. In educating the young guardians, he says, they were partly aiming to do something similar—namely, ensure that the youths would "absorb" lawful beliefs "about the fearful and everything else" so thoroughly that "even such extremely effective detergents as pleasure, pain, fear and appetite wouldn't wash it out." Courage, on Socrates' view, is "this power" of "preservation through everything of the correct and lawful belief about what is fearful and what isn't (*sōtērian dia pantos doxēs orthēs te kai nomimou deinōn te peri kai mē*)" (429d–430b).[21]

The passage is important because it directly informs Socrates' account of courage in T2. Of course, that is precisely what it is supposed to do given Socrates' stated methodology in Books 2 through 4. He begins by examining and outlining the virtues of a city in the hopes that doing so will illuminate the virtues of a person. It is here in his discussion of "political" courage, then, that Socrates introduces the idea of courage as a kind of "preservation." In this earlier context, moreover, he is explicit about what that "preservation" consists in: it means holding on to a rational belief, *doxa*, in the face of pleasures, pains,

---

[21] Socrates quickly clarifies that he refers here only to "political courage" (430c), a qualification that is ambiguous: it could indicate either (a) the type of courage possessed by the *polis* itself (rather than the kind possessed by individual souls), or (b) a *political* form of courage possessed by the auxiliaries themselves (by contrast to unqualified or true courage). Cf. discussion in Adam (1902: 231–2), Annas (1981: 114), Bobonich (2002: 44–5), Irwin (1977: 329–30, n. 26), and Kamtekar (1998: 318). While I concur with Adam and Kamtekar that Socrates may invoke both senses, Glaucon seems to have sense (b) most in mind, given that he contrasts the courage Socrates has just described with "the correct belief about these same things which you find in animals and slaves, and which is not the result of education." This contrast makes the most sense if he assumes Socrates is attributing political courage to properly educated *people*. What matters for my purposes, however, is simply that the Book 4 characterization of individual courage is clearly informed by the account of "political" courage, and that the latter is understood in terms of stable belief.

fears, and appetites. Significantly, Socrates identifies *failing* to preserve one's beliefs in this way with "abandoning" them, an unmistakable reference to his earlier discussion of the ways in which true beliefs are abandoned. As we saw above, in that Book 3 passage Socrates explained how non-rational impulses can cause a person to change their mind and "abandon" their judgments about what is valuable and how to act. He now identifies a form of courage with the ability to *prevent* such impulses from affecting beliefs in that way. Talk of "preservation" and "abandonment" in Books 3 and 4, in other words, concerns the relationship between rational judgments and the non-rational motivations that put them in jeopardy.

The implications for Socrates' account of individual courage support my proposed interpretation. The "declarations of reason" about what is fearful are clearly parallel to the "beliefs" about what is fearful from earlier in Book 4. Both are practical value judgments. The main difference, I take it, has to do with their source. In the political case, the *laws* supply the content of the beliefs; in the individual case, the person's own *rational part* supplies the content of the beliefs on the basis of its reasoning. On this view, a "declaration" in the individual case is something like the conclusion of a rational argument or outcome of a person's deliberation. The rational part considers what is good, beneficial, fearful, and so on for the whole soul and arrives at a belief about how to act on the basis of that reasoning. The "pleasures and pains" that need resisting in individual courage, likewise, are parallel to the various appetitive motivations—which earlier explicitly include fears and appetites— that have the potential to destabilize reasoning and make a person "abandon" their judgments. For the spirited part of the soul to "preserve" reason's declarations through pleasures and pains, therefore, is for it to prevent appetitive impulses from interfering with a person's true rational beliefs. The person is courageous when *thumos* ensures that reason does not change or lose its correct judgments under the influence of appetite.[22]

But by what means, exactly, does the spirited part of the soul accomplish this feat? The answer I suggest is claim (4) above: *thumos* supports reason by providing motivations that are responsive to, and reinforce, rational judgments about how to act in the face of problematic appetites. In other words, its support for reason operates on the same model as appetite's defiance of reason. When appetite motivates a person to act in a way that is contrary to their

---

[22] Balot (2014: 41–3) notes aspects of this Platonic reimagination of the traditional Greek concept of courage that are anticipated in Thucydides. Cf. discussion of Thucydides on courage in Rorty (1986) and Renaut (2014: 29–36), who draws on Huart (1968) and de Romilly (1980).

rational judgment, spirit motivates them to act *in accordance with* it. And just as recalcitrant appetites exert psychological pressure that can destabilize rational belief, supportive spirited desires and emotions exert psychological pressure that can *stabilize* and *fortify* reason's beliefs and make sure the person acts on them.

The language Plato uses in Book 4 to characterize the roles of reason and *thumos* supports this interpretation by emphasizing the cognitive nature of the former and the motivational nature of the latter. The rational part "decides what must not be done" (440b5), "reasons about better and worse" (441c1–2), is "wise" and "exercises foresight" (441e4–5), takes care of "planning" and issues "deliberative judgments" (442b7–9), makes "declarations" (442c2), and has "knowledge" (442c6). The spirited part, meanwhile, "boils," "gets angry," "conquers," "endures," persists in "noble actions," "calms down," acts as a "fellow fighter" (440c7–d2), and "wages war" and "executes" the decisions of reason with its "courage" (442b7–9). This language supports the view that the reasoning part thinks and arrives at beliefs about how to act, and the spirited part forms desires and emotions that motivate the person to act in that way. This is not to say that reason does not *also* motivate—it "fights" too, after all— but only that its relation to spirit is distinguished by the latter's motivational responsiveness to its practical judgments.

To give a more concrete example of how this all works, recall Socrates' description of the noble man's response to justice and injustice. "When someone believes he is the victim of injustice," he explains, his spirit will become angry and fight "for what is believed to be just" even in the face of "hunger, cold, and the like." Although spirit is the only part of the soul mentioned by name here, Socrates clearly thinks all three parts are involved, because he takes such cases as evidence that "in the civil war in the soul [the spirited part] aligns itself far more with the rational part [than with the appetitive]" (440b–e). With that in mind, we can see that the reasoning part is responsible for the beliefs about injustice in question. Socrates attributes those beliefs only to "the person" ("someone," *tis*), but in order for his remarks to count as evidence for spirit's alliance with reason, spirit must be responding to *rational* beliefs.[23] That is to say, when the *person* judges he has suffered injustice in this case, he is doing that judging with his reasoning part. Likewise, the references to "hunger, cold, and the like" clearly allude to the appetitive part, especially since Socrates has just identified hunger and the desire for warmth as basic appetitive urges. The idea, then, is that when we are hungry

---

[23] *Pace* Kahn (1987: 85), who attributes the beliefs in question directly to the spirited part.

and cold, we appetitively seek food and warmth. Sometimes, however, acting in accordance with rational judgment requires endurance of hunger and cold. In such instances, appetite will be opposed to reasoning, and as we have seen, its opposition has the potential to cause a person to change their mind about how to act. The spirited part, however, is sensitive to and reinforces reason's assessments by providing additional motivation—in this case, through the emotion of anger—to endure hunger and cold and thereby resist appetite's aversion to them. This, then, is how spirit acts as reason's "ally," and how it executes the task of "preserving" the rational part's "declarations" in a courageous soul.

3. *Oikeios Logos*

In this section, I address the questions of *why* spirit is distinctively responsive to reason and *how* its responsiveness is related to the effects of early education. To set the stage for that discussion, it will be useful to note some unique features of spirit's status as a target of early education. First, note that the centrality of the *thumoeides* in early moral training is related to the fact that reason's power or influence in the soul is limited during youth, when the rational part is still immature and incompletely developed. Although reason (rather than appetite) is the dominant part of psychology in virtuous *adults*, no amount of education or quality of upbringing can make it the strongest or ruling part within an individual's soul during childhood. The best educators can do is provide training and environmental conditions that promote reason's healthy development and prepare it for its proper role later in life. This is where *thumos* comes in, however. In the absence of a mature reasoning part, the psychology of children and adolescents is necessarily dominated by their non-rational elements. This means that during that time, the non-rational spirited part and its motivations provide the only alternative to appetite's control over a young person's soul and behavior. This is precisely why Plato considers it imperative that early education devote much of its attention to *thumos*.

The education of spirit is complicated in an important respect that does not apply to either appetite or reason, however. In their cases, moral education proceeds more or less on the basis of a simple mandate: *make appetite as weak as possible, and make reason as strong as possible*. As we saw in the last chapter, gymnastic training partly aims to eliminate or occlude unnecessary appetites from the soul through deprivative practices, and music partly aims to nourish and invigorate the rational part with speeches and learning. This approach is justified by the inverse relation or competition between the strength of rational and appetitive desires. However, whereas a person becomes more vicious the stronger their appetitive part becomes, and more virtuous the stronger their reasoning part becomes, no such straightforward principle applies in the case of *thumos*. On the one hand, it is true that having a *weak* spirited part constitutes a moral deficiency, on Plato's view. However, a strong spirited part is not necessarily a moral asset. First of all, it is a good thing only if it has the right moral orientation. If a young person experienced emotions such as shame, anger, and admiration in ethically inappropriate ways, then it would be morally *harmful* for those emotions to be powerful and motivationally efficacious. Moreover, although *thumos* needs to be strong in order for a person to obtain virtue, it must not become so strong that it inhibits the development or empowerment of the reasoning part. Its strength must be appropriately calibrated relative to that of reason. This means that training spirit involves a complex process of negotiation between excess and deficiency—the precarious threading of a needle—in a way that education of appetite and reason does not.

Plato's concern for this issue, and his awareness that it is a problem peculiar to the spirited part, is evident in T1. Excessive devotion to physical training, according to Socrates, has negative effects on both spirit and reason: hypertrophy for the former and atrophy for the latter. Note, however, that in the case of excessive musical training, Socrates mentions only negative effects on *spirit*: it becomes enervated and weak. He mentions no corollary harm to the rational part of nature.[24] The reason for his omission, I propose, is that there is no *direct* harm to reason at all. On Plato's view, reason should be as strong and psychologically dominant as possible, and there is no principled upper limit (though there may be practical ones related to embodiment) on how strong it should become. That is, there is no such thing as *hypertrophy* in the case of the rational part. To be sure, excessive musical training has negative effects on reason, but the harms are indirect. Because the person does not stimulate spirit and practice resistance to appetite through gymnastic training, the former becomes an impotent and ineffective ally against the latter during a crucial stage of life. The spirited part of the soul, then, poses a special set of problems that inform the task of the moral educator. The *thumoeides* must be trained to be strong, but it must also be trained in such a way that it is prepared to serve as reason's subordinate and obedient auxiliary.

---

[24] Cf. discussion in Renaut (2014: 255–61).

Exactly how does Plato's program of early education, as described in Chapter 6, foster spirit's proper relationship with the reasoning part of the soul? In what follows I argue that it does so by shaping and exploiting expressions of spirit's two-sided nature that are directed *inwardly* toward elements of the person's own psychology. Through successful musical and gymnastic training, reason and its judgments become *oikeion* to spirit, while unnecessary appetites become *allotrion* to it; and as a result, spirit responds with natural affection for the former and hostility toward the latter. These feelings of affection and hostility make spirit inclined to obey, support, and defend rational judgments, while resisting and opposing vicious appetitive desires. The clearest evidence is passage T3, where Socrates explicitly states that musical education culminates in the young person's "similarity and friendship and harmony with admirable reason," and guarantees that they will "recognize" and "warmly welcome" reason because of its "familiarity." As I noted in the last chapter, Socrates' language unmistakably alludes to his earlier discussions of spirited psychology, and we should, therefore, take the person's friendship for and warm welcoming of reason as emotional responses for which *thumos* is responsible. In order to understand how and why reason becomes reliably familiar to spirit in this way, however, some further details are necessary.

My explanation will rely on two background assumptions. The first has already been established in the previous chapter: musical education and culture in the Kallipolis make admirable people, behavior, and cultural products familiar to spirit, and vicious ones unfamiliar or alien to it. The city is filled with carefully curated and uniformly virtuous influences, and the result of the young person's rearing in such an environment is that they respond to what is *kalon* around them with the friendship, love, admiration, and praise that characterize spirited reactions to the *oikeion*. Conversely, they respond to what is *aischron*—or at least, become *inclined* to respond to it (since they will not, ideally, encounter much that is vicious in their city)—with the hate, disgust, and blame that characterize spirited reactions to the *allotrion*.

The second is that admirable things in the world—poetry, music, speech, laws, artifacts, people, and so on—are all "akin" to one another in an important sense. Precisely what this kinship consists in raises complicated metaphysical questions, but it clearly involves some kind of discernible likeness, similarity, or family resemblance among seemingly diverse sorts of things.[25] Plato, for his part, describes this kinship or resemblance using a variety of

---

[25] Cf. Thaler (2016: 421–8).

terminology in Book 3. In the discussion that immediately precedes T3, Socrates explains that harmony, gracefulness, and rhythm are found not only in music and poetry, but also in admirable painting, weaving, embroidery, architecture, products of craft, and physical bodies. All of these various types of admirable things and their qualities, moreover, "accompany" (*akolouthei*, 400e1; cf. 398d8, 400c8, 401d5), "follow" (*hepetai*, 401d2; cf. 400a1, 401d6), "liken themselves" to (*homoioumenon*, 401d2), are "akin" to (*adelpha*, 401a8; cf. 401a7), are "imitations" of (*mimēmata*, 401a8; cf. 399a7), or are stamped with the "images" of (*eikona*, 401b2, b9), admirable speech and admirable character, which are akin or similar to one another as well. By contrast, shameful things and their qualities are "akin" to or "images" of vicious speech and character in the same way.[26] Admirable cultural products, admirable speech, and the character or souls of admirable people themselves, therefore, all bear some kind of recognizable aesthetic, quasi-aesthetic, or moral resemblance to one another.[27]

For Plato, these two assumptions explain spirit's receptiveness to *logos* when it eventually arrives in full maturity in the person's soul. Reason is familiar and recognizable because of its likeness or similarity to the admirable people and things to which the young person's *thumos* has grown accustomed—and indeed, because of its similarity to or kinship with the admirable person the youth themselves is becoming.[28] As a result, spirit reacts to reason with characteristic expressions of its response to the *oikeion*, such as gentleness, love, loyalty, honor, and obedience. This means that as the young person's rational part develops and begins issuing its own practical judgments—which will, due to its own proper education, be *true* ones—spirit reacts with solicitous deference to those judgments and supportively motivates the person to act in accordance with their reasoning.[29]

The idea that spirit's support for reason is closely connected to its instinctive response to the *oikeion* appears to be at the heart of a later passage at the closing of Book 7 (537e–539a). Socrates notes that a young person "honors" and does not "disobey" (those he believes to be) his father, mother, and relatives, but that if he discovers they are not his real family, he will become

---

[26] In his remarks following T3, Socrates further explains that virtuous qualities like moderation, courage, and magnificence are themselves "akin" (ἀδελφά, 402c3) to one another; that "images" (εἰκόνας, 402c6) or "forms" (εἴδη, 402c2) of these qualities appear everywhere; and that admirable character in the soul and admirable body "agree" (ὁμολογοῦντα, 402d2) or are "consonant" (συμφωνοῦντα, 402d3) with each other because they bear the same "stamp" (τύπος, 402d3).

[27] Cf. Burnyeat (1999: 282–5) and Janaway (1995: 103–4).   [28] Cf. Hobbs (2000: 227–30).

[29] Cf. Euripides, *Supp.* 913–17: "Even a baby learns to speak and hear things it cannot comprehend; and whatever someone has learned, this he loves (φιλεῖ) and preserves (σώζεσθαι) up till he is old."

disobedient and inclined to keep company with flatterers instead. Likewise, Socrates says:

> We hold certain beliefs from childhood about just and admirable things; we're raised with them as with our parents, and we honor (*timōntes*) them and obey them like rulers (*peitharchountes*) ... There are other ways of living, however, opposite (*enantia*) to these and full of pleasures, that flatter the soul and drag (*helkei*) it to themselves, but which don't persuade sensible people, who continue to honor (*timōsi*) and obey their fatherly convictions like rulers.   (538c6–d4)

If a young person of this sort is subjected to questioning and argument that undermine his beliefs, however, he will come to consider them illegitimate and consequently no longer honor and obey them, adopting a lawless life of pleasure instead. Now, the immediate aim of this passage is to warn against the dangers of exposing young people to the practice of dialectic, and Plato does not explicitly identify parts of the soul. The theory of tripartition is clearly in the background, however. The opposition between our "beliefs" and "pleasures" alludes to the familiar opposition between evaluative rational judgments and appetitive desires for pleasure (note that pleasures "drag" us in an "opposite" way, just like appetite in Book 4). It is significant, then, that Socrates likens our beliefs to parents or *oikeioi* that we are inclined to "honor" and "obey as rulers" precisely *because* they are family- or parent-like to us. The language he uses unmistakably refers to spirited psychology—all the more so because, just a few Stephanus pages later, Socrates will identify concern for honor and obedience to rulers as distinctive features of the timocratic man ruled by *thumos*. In other words, our impulse to honor and obey our own rational beliefs against the conflicting pull of pleasures is rooted in the spirited part of the soul and its instinctive response to the *oikeion*. This relatively unremarked passage, therefore, reinforces my reading of T3.

The same line of interpretation also accounts for spirit's complementary opposition to unnecessary appetites, which are similar or akin to the shameful people and things that have been expunged from the person's environment as much as possible. If any such appetites arise in the young person's soul, therefore, their spirited part will find them alien and react with characteristic hostility. Although Socrates does not use the term *allotrion* in T3 itself, it appears in a relevant context later in Book 3, where Socrates contrasts good doctors with good judges (408d–409c). Whereas the former need to have encountered bodily diseases of every kind, both in others and in themselves, from the time they are young, good judges must be kept away from "diseases" or vices of the soul until late in life. They cannot "be nurtured among vicious souls from childhood," associate with unjust people, or perform acts of injustice themselves:

> Rather, if [a soul] is to be admirable and good...it must itself be unmixed with bad character and have no experience of it while it's young... Therefore, a good judge must not be a young person but an old one, who has learned late in life what injustice is like and who has perceived it not as something familiar (*oikeian*) in his own soul, but as something alien in alien others (*allotrian en allotriais*)—someone who, after a long time, has recognized that injustice is bad by nature, not from his own (*oikeiai*) experience, but from knowledge.   (409a5–c1)

This passage appeals to the same view of environmental influence that Socrates describes in T3. Because people absorb the influence of the familiar, young people who are exposed to vicious characters will become vicious themselves, which in turn means that vice or injustice will become welcome in their own psychology. For that reason, Socrates insists they be kept away from such influences so that injustice is *allotrion* to their souls.[30] Given the role of appetite in motivating acts of injustice, this unfamiliarity of vice presumably means that any unnecessary or morally bad appetitive desires that might arise in the soul (if any do at all) would be alien and unknown there, and consequently would activate spirit's natural opposition to the *allotrion*.[31]

According to this view, then, Plato's program of early education carefully and deliberately exploits the two faces of spiritedness in order to cultivate important aspects of the psychic relationships that constitute virtue. It aims to make correct reason familiar to *thumos* and unnecessary appetite unfamiliar to it, thereby ensuring that *inward* expressions of spirit's primitive impulses are directed in the right ways toward other elements of the person's own soul. Socrates' account of courage of the individual provides further evidence for this reading, as it reflects Plato's attention to ways in which spirited motivation is manifested, and can be shaped, at the intrapsychic level. Recall that in

---

[30] Thaler (2015) anticipates my account in emphasizing the passage just quoted and suggesting that early musical education exploits our natural attachment to the familiar and aversion to the foreign. Curiously, though, he takes this as evidence *against* the view that spirit is the target of the education; he thinks it is directed at reason instead. Although we clearly disagree on that point, his account of how music benefits reason actually fits well with my discussion in Ch. 6 of how a morally good cultural environment benefits reason.

[31] Cf. Euripides, *Hec.* 599–602.

popular Greek ethics, courage is paradigmatically exemplified by, and often even *identified* with, "rescuing" or "preserving" one's *oikeioi* in the face of danger. In Book 4, Plato appropriates this traditional idea and reshapes it for his own philosophical purposes.[32] He continues to define courage as a form of "preserving" the *oikeion*, but for him this means above all what is familiar within our own souls, reason, rather than the family and friends outside of ourselves. Likewise, the "enemy" or *allotrion* against whom we must protect the familiar are not the external adversaries of war or political enmity, but our own dangerous appetites. And of course, this idea is reinforced by the martial metaphors Plato employs to describe spirit's "alliance" with reason: the rational part is a companion and fellow fighter on the intrapsychic battlefield, while appetite is the assailing enemy. Moral education in the *Republic*, then, seeks to make sure that spirit comes to love and protect reason the way a spirited person loves and protects their family.

This account explains how proper early education makes spirit the reliable auxiliary of reason in the soul. But there is an issue I have not yet addressed that concerns an important exchange between Socrates and Glaucon at 440a–b, following their discussion of Leontius. After observing that spirit "in many other cases" fights with reason against resistant appetites, Socrates asks, "But I don't believe you can say that you've *ever* seen spirit, either in yourself or anyone else, ally itself with an appetite to do what reason has decided must not be done?" to which Glaucon responds, "No, by god, I haven't." These remarks draw attention to spirit's typical cooperativeness with reason and complementary opposition to appetite. It is the *typicalness* of those relationships that requires comment, however. The group of people on whom Socrates and Glaucon are basing their observations are not citizens of the Kallipolis, but simply ordinary Athenians and the rest of their contacts in the actual world. In other words, spirit's cooperative relationship with reason is not merely a normative ideal found only in the virtuous, but evidently something that, as a matter of empirical fact, tends to arise in morally average or inferior people as well.[33] This raises a potential worry about my account of musical and gymnastic training. In what sense can Socrates' program of early education be said to foster spirit's proper relationship with reason, if spirit naturally tends to align itself with reason even in the *absence* of that education?[34]

---

[32] Hobbs (2000: 163) suggests that Plato's reinterpretation of courage is designed to make it a virtue that *philosophers* preeminently display.

[33] Cf. Moss (2005: 153).

[34] For discussion of this issue and spirit's characteristic responsiveness to reason, see Gosling (1973: 50–1), Kamtekar (2017: 166–72), and Reeve (2013b: 14–49).

The short answer is that there is more to spirit's proper relationship with reason than simply its tendency to act as reason's psychic ally. I want to concede, then—indeed, *emphasize*—that even in the non-virtuous and badly educated, spirit tends to be responsive to rational judgment and to take sides with reason in conflicts against the appetites. My account of early education, moreover, provides useful resources for explaining why this should be the case. For the same community that shapes our spirited motivations during youth is always *also* the one in which the reasoning part of the soul matures and develops. This means that the ostensible examples of virtue and vice a given culture or social group provides—what it praises as good and denigrates as bad—will both mold spirit's emotional orientation and at the same time provide the environmental resources from which reason's burgeoning values and beliefs must draw. Because a person's emotional and intellectual development take place in the same social and cultural setting, therefore, it is natural that spirited motivation and rational judgment will tend to be closely aligned. Moreover, we have seen that there are also *intrapsychic* mechanisms that promote and intensify this tendency. Spirited emotions like shame, disgust, and admiration arise in the soul prior to rational judgment, and as our rational capacities develop, those emotions influence our reasoning about what is good by drawing our attention to people, actions, and things in motivationally charged ways. In other words, the spirited part of the soul exerts direct *internal* pressure on reason that reflects and reinforces the *external* influences to which both parts are subject. When reason starts issuing practical judgments, therefore, those judgments will generally tend to be agreeable to *thumos*, because the values on which they are based are informed by the same society that shaped spirit's motivational dispositions, as well as by spirited emotions themselves. All of this is true, finally—and this is the crucial point—not only in the Kallipolis, but in corrupt cities as well. Hence, as we saw in Chapter 3, spirited motivation is often subordinated to appetite and its desires in corrupt cities like Athens, and reason tends to be subordinated right along with it, which is why the "majority" of people judge things like bodily pleasure and material resources to be the ultimate good for human beings. Likewise, in the case of the oligarchic individual discussed above, appetite enslaves not only reason, but also *thumos*, which "admires" and "honors" nothing but money and wealthy people.[35] Regardless of whether an individual receives a proper

---

[35] Note that according to Socrates, the oligarchic man has allowed *unnecessary* appetites to arise in his soul but does not typically *act* on them: usually he "forcibly" restrains them with ἐπιεικεῖ τινὶ ἑαυτοῦ (554b–e). It is not difficult to see that this restraint will likely consist in the joint resistance of both reason and spirit. When the oligarchic individual has an appetite for something unnecessary and

upbringing or not, it will be true of them that their spirited and intellectual development occurred alongside one another in the same community, and that their spirited emotions influenced the development of their reasoning about what is good and bad.[36]

Virtue requires more than just this *typical* alignment between reason and spirit, however. The two parts must also have the appropriate degrees of strength relative to one another, which for Plato means that reason is the ruling or dominant part of the soul and spirit its subordinate. We have seen in T1 and T2 that Socrates pays special attention to this point, characterizing early education as a delicate process of "stretching" and "relaxing" the two parts so that they are in harmony with one another. Socrates also alludes to this idea in his discussion of spirit in Book 4. After Glaucon notes the similarity between the auxiliaries of the Kallipolis and the *thumos* of a noble man, Socrates refers to the spirited part as "a third thing in the soul that is by nature the auxiliary of the rational part, *provided that it hasn't been corrupted by a bad upbringing*" (441a2–3). Unlike 440a–b, Socrates here acknowledges the role of education in spirit's relationship with reason and concedes the possibility of a breakdown in it. As Rachana Kamtekar points out in recent work, however, there is a subtle shift in terminology on Plato's part between 440a–b and 441a. The latter claims not that spirit is reason's natural "ally" (the term used in 440a–b) unless it is corrupted by bad upbringing, but rather that spirit is the natural *auxiliary* of reason if it is not corrupted. Whereas the term "ally" (*summachos*) designates only that one person or thing is a "fellow fighter" of another, implying nothing about the power relation between the two parties, the term "auxiliary" or "helper" (*epikouros*) indicates that the adjuvant party is subordinate to the person or thing it is helping.[37] In other words, whereas being an ally is a reciprocal relation—if *x* is the fellow fighter of *y*, then *y* is also the fellow fighter of *x*—being an auxiliary is not symmetrical in this way: spirit is by nature reason's obedient helper in the soul, but the reverse does not apply. As Kamtekar argues, what it means for spirit to be the subordinate of reason in the relevant sense is for the rational

---

extravagant, his reasoning part will calculate the monetary loss involved and resist the desire accordingly, and spirit's admiration for wealth will make it inclined to serve as reason's ally in motivating frugality. Hence even in a non-virtuous soul, spirit will tend to be responsive to rational judgment.

[36] Significantly, in Socrates' account of the tyrannical individual, the last step in his transformation is that he purges from his soul "any beliefs or desires that are thought to be good or still admit of shame" (573a–b). Even in someone as vicious as the (soon-to-be) tyrant, it seems, rational beliefs about the good and spirited feelings of shame stand united as the last line of defense against his descent into wickedness.

[37] 2017: 165–8. Cf. Arruzza (2018: 51).

part to be ruling (or in a young person, we might say, at least *ascendant*) in the soul, and for spirit to support the practical judgments reason issues from that position of psychic authority. If this is right, then 441a is affirming not that proper education is required to produce patterns of cooperation between reason and spirit *in general*, but rather to produce the naturally appropriate relation of power or control between them. In other words, spirit may act as an ally of reason even in many vicious souls, but it is reason's *auxiliary*, strictly speaking, only in virtuously organized ones.

This point has corollaries or consequences that concern the value of early education. To begin with, it is important to note that Socrates' musical program aims not simply to make reason *simpliciter* familiar to spirit, but rather to make *admirable* reason familiar to it. Although spirit often or typically supports reason even without a proper upbringing, only with the right education will it welcome, obey, and defend *logos* that consistently issues true and virtuous judgments. This is related to the previous point, because part of what it means for the rational part to be *strong* is for it to be capable of reasoning effectively and reaching correct practical conclusions. An early education that makes reason the strongest part of the soul (or at least prepares the way for it to become the strongest), therefore, is also one that both guides it toward *true* moral reasoning and that makes such reasoning *oikeion* to the spirited part.

Furthermore, the fact that spirit tends to act as reason's ally regardless of upbringing leaves open the possibility that in non-virtuous souls, that tendency is less reliable. Although commentators have sometimes taken 440a–b to suggest that spirit is *always* reason's ally,[38] that is not actually what Socrates and Glaucon say. Instead, they affirm only that it is often ("in *many* other cases") reason's ally, and that it is *never* the ally of *appetite against reason*.[39] This difference matters, because there are ways spirit could fail to behave as reason's ally that do not involve its instead aligning with appetite.[40] First, most obviously, it could simply side with neither, indifferent both to rational

---

[38] See, for example, Gerson (2003a: 243).

[39] I take Socrates and Glaucon at their word when they make this claim. In context they have just described Leontius' reaction to indulging his base appetite. Their exchange makes the point that whereas we often feel ashamed or angry with ourselves for acting on appetitive impulses, we *never* feel ashamed or angry with ourselves for doing what we believe (and continue to believe) is right. This is an interesting and plausible empirical claim. I am preceded in my reading by Galen (*PHP* 5.7.57–8), as well as by Craig (1994: 98) and Cross and Woozley (1964: 120–1) among recent commentators. Some interpreters, however, think the claim in question is implausible, that Plato himself rejects it, and that it is quickly contradicted or qualified by other passages like 441a. See, for example, Allen (2006: 139, n. 14), Guthrie (1975: 474), Hobbs (2000: 17–18), and Irwin (1995a: 212).

[40] Hence Robinson (1970: 44–5) is wrong to equate spirit's occasional failure to act as reason's ally with its siding *with appetite* against reason. Scott (1999: 31–2, n. 31) gets this point right.

judgment *and* to appetitive desire. That is to say, spirit may sometimes fail to be moved by reason's declarations, or it may be moved by them only weakly, rendering it either no ally at all or an ineffective one. And secondly, *thumos* could also fail to be reason's ally by motivating the person to act brutishly and impetuously in ways that do not serve the desires of appetite. Consider, for example, a variation of the Odysseus case in which he kills the maidservants and suitors impulsively out of rage without ever pausing to reconsider, or in which he does attempt to subdue his spirit "with word," but fails and kills them all anyway.[41] In such cases Plato surely would not want to characterize *thumos* as reason's "ally," yet neither is its defiance of the rational part rooted in support for appetite instead.

We can identify two interrelated reasons why these types of disharmony between spirit and reason might arise. The first is a simple matter of *misalignment*: reason judges that some action is good or bad, but for whatever reason spirit has an apathetic or contrary reaction to it. Although such cases may be atypical, presumably they become more common in places like Athens that foster a heterogeneous, incoherent, and unstable set of values. The musical education of the Kallipolis, by contrast, prevents misalignment of this sort by promoting a uniform and consistent set of values that fosters reason's development. The second explanation involves an improper balance of power between spirit and reason. If spirit is too weak, then even if it *is* aligned with reason, its motivational support will be slight and inadequate. If it is too strong, then the person becomes rash and violent, acting on the basis of *thumos* without ever stopping to think about whether it is good to act that way. This latter case is not, strictly speaking, a case of misalignment, but rather a case in which reason never has a chance to issue an action-guiding judgment at all. Socrates' careful balance of music and gymnastics, however, makes sure that spirit is strong enough to support reason effectively, but not so strong, nor reason so weak, that it does not still answer to rational judgment. Or, to put all of this in the language of spirited psychology: musical education makes sure that spirit consistently admires and honors the same people, actions, and things that reason judges good, and that spirit is both tame enough to

---

[41] The *Laws* shows that Plato recognizes precisely such cases. In the Athenian's discussion of the causes of criminal behavior, he considers the case of homicide motivated by impetuous anger or *thumos*, which causes the killer to act ἐξαίφνης, παραχρῆμα τῆς ὁρμῆς, and ἀπροβουλεύτως. He contrasts such murders with those that are performed μετὰ ἐπιβουλῆς or ἐκ προνοίας, making it clear that their defining feature is that the enraged agent acts impulsively without reasoning about their action (866d–867b, 869e, 871a). I discuss the *Laws*' theory of criminal psychology in relation to tripartition in Wilburn (2013a). See also Aristotle's discussion of impetuous anger (*MM* 1202b12–21; cf. *NE* 1149a25–b1).

recognize and respond to reason as *oikeion*, but also tough enough to fight off an *allotrion* appetite that challenges reason's authority.[42]

4. Civic Unity in the Kallipolis

As we saw in Chapters 3 and 5, the problem of civic strife is closely related to, and exacerbated by, improper moral education. In corrupt cities, people are educated to value finite pleonectic goods, and that ethical orientation leads them to treat one another as competitors for those goods and to feel the spirited rivalry and aggression that accompanies such competitiveness. The same interconnectedness applies to Plato's solutions to these two problems: his positive educational proposals for the Kallipolis *also* contribute to the goal of civic unity. Musical education itself, we have seen, partly aims at fostering friendship and gentleness toward one's fellow citizens. More importantly, early education aims to replace pleonectic values with genuinely morally good ones, thereby putting spirit in the service of rational ends instead of appetitive ones that promote conflict. When citizens are not motivated by *pleonexia* in the first place, then they are much less likely to experience the jealousies, resentments, and hostilities that inevitably accompany an appetitive value system.

Plato's efforts to promote civic unity extend beyond education, however, to the social, economic, and political policies of the Kallipolis. My central thesis here is that through his policies on property and family, Socrates aims to make citizens *oikeioi* to one another so that they are bound together by the spirited feelings of friendship that arise in response to the familiar. His proposals are

---

[42] Russell (2005: 207–18)—and cf. Gill (1985: 22–3)—argues that Plato presents two competing and irreconcilable models of reason's relationship to spirit in the *Republic*. The first, "agreement" model involves a cooperative relationship that is captured by talk of spirit as the dog-like loyal "ally" to the "shepherd" reason in Book 4. The second, "control" model involves reason's forcible suppression of spirit's innate brutality and is captured by the image of spirit as a lion in Book 9. Russell comments, "A shepherd chooses a certain breed of dog because of its natural cleverness and cooperation...but one can direct a lion only by *overpowering* its natural tendencies" (pp. 209–10). I am skeptical that Plato intends the lion analogy in the way Russell takes it, however. Whatever may be true about the differences between dogs and lions, the language Plato uses to characterize the lion's ideal relationship with its "tamer" echoes Book 4 and suggests the same cooperativeness: the virtuous person "nurtures" the lion so that it becomes his "friend" ($\varphi i \lambda a$) and "ally" ($\sigma \dot{\upsilon} \mu \mu a \chi o \nu$) (589a–b). Plato is hardly at pains, then, to emphasize a model of forcible and coercive control here. My suspicion is that the shift to the metaphor of a lion is due to the fact that Book 9's image of the soul is supposed to illustrate cases of *both* virtue *and* vice. To that end, the choice of a lion is useful because although a lion can be tamed, it can also be dangerous and savage. By contrast, a dog would be a less suitable animal to illustrate the dual possibilities of virtue and vice, as shown by the fact that when Socrates wants to draw a contrast to the positive case in which spirit and spirited people are analogous to noble dogs, he likens them not to "bad" dogs, but to a different animal entirely: the wolf (e.g. at 416a).

best understood a direct challenge to the traditional Greek household or *oikos*, which is distinguished by two important features: private ownership of the physical estate itself, along with the dwellings, property, wealth, and possessions associated it; and private families who live there, consisting of the landowner, his wife and children, and other members of the household such as relatives, servants, nurses, and slaves. Because the household is the most basic social or political unit out of which larger communities are composed, it is also the basic social unit of pleonectic competition. As Lin Foxhall argues, the *oikos* serves for the Greeks as the practical "limit of trust," or the boundary within which members of the household can rely on one another's affection and loyalty, but beyond which trust becomes less reliable and secure.[43] Consequently, as we have seen, the *oikos* as the site of private life often has an uneasy or even antagonistic relationship with the *polis*. In the popular ethical and political mind, the *idia* or private is contrasted with and opposed to the *koinon* or public: to devote oneself to the city means neglecting one's personal affairs, and to pursue advantages for one's household means disregarding the wellbeing of the city and one's fellow citizens. The private *oikos*, therefore, is the elementary social institution that threatens civic unity and the public good.[44]

Socrates undermines the tension between *idia* and *koinon* by rejecting both key aspects of the conventional household through policies of *de*-privatization for his guardians. First, when he turns to address the guardians' living conditions, Socrates explains that they are not permitted to possess any private property beyond what is absolutely necessary. They have no private homes or treasuries of their own; they are not allowed to possess money or even *touch* gold or silver; and they have no resources for luxuries like buying expensive furniture or jewelry, entertaining guests, making extravagant sacrifices to the gods, giving gifts to mistresses, or making private trips away from the city. Instead, they will live together austerely in a military camp and share meals that will be provided for them through a tax on the craftspeople and farmers they protect (416d–417b, 419a–420b). Second, Socrates also eliminates private families from his guardian class. In place of traditional households and family structures which sharply distinguish husbands' and wives' roles, he argues at length that men and women should "share" the same upbringing, education,

---

[43] 1998: 53–5 and 2007: 51–2. For additional discussion of the *oikos* and its relation to the *polis* in Greek and Athenian life, see Foxhall (1989) and Roy (1999).

[44] Arruzza (2011) offers a penetrating discussion of Plato's abolition of private households, families, and property with which my own is aligned on several points, although she does not draw connections between these policies and *thumos*.

and civic work, including fighting as warriors and serving as guardians (451c–457c; cf. 423e–424b).[45] Moreover, he explains, "All these women are to belong in common to all the men, none are to live privately with any man, and the children, too, are to be possessed in common, so that no parent will know his own offspring or any child his parent" (457c10–d3). Reproductive sex is no longer the private right or responsibility of individual household owners and their wives, but rather must be sanctioned by the city itself. When approved children of good parents are born, they are taken to a special "rearing pen" to be raised by nurses who will make sure that parents cannot identify their biological children, nor children their parents. The system of conjugal unions and child-rearing is maintained through a clandestine system of secrecy and deceit, and in place of private families, it is supposed to create something like a large "public" family that extends throughout the whole guardian class (457c–461d). Socrates explains:

A man will call all the children born in the tenth or seventh month after he became a bridegroom his sons, if they're male, and his daughters, if they're female, and they'll call him father. He'll call their children his grandchildren, and they'll call the group to which he belongs grandfathers and grandmothers. And those who were born at the same time as their mother and fathers were having children they'll call their brothers and sisters.   (461d2–e1)

This "civic" model of the family is anticipated earlier, moreover, by the "noble lie" (414d–415c), which teaches citizens that they are all born autochthonously, the progeny of the earth itself: they are all brothers and sisters, and the earth their mother. Together, then, the noble lie and the social organization of the

---

[45] Natali (2005) discusses the close connection between elimination of separate social roles for women and the abolition of the private household: "Platon pense que la division la travail entre hommes et femmes est liée d'une manière essentielle à l'existence de *l'oikos*...[S]i l'on confie à la femme les mêmes occupations qu'à l'homme, *l'oikos* est destiné à disaparaître" (p. 212). For further discussion of Plato's policies on women in the *Republic*, their significance in historical and political context, and controversy regarding Plato's supposed "Feminism," see Annas (1976), Brisson (2012a), Buchan (1999), Copland (1996), Deretic (2013), Forde (1997), Haarman (2016: Ch. 3), Hobbs (2000: 245–9), Kochin (2002), Lesser (1979), McKeen (2006), Murray (2011), Okin (1977), Salkever (1990: Ch. 4), Saxonhouse (1976), Serban (2014), Smith (1980), Spelman (1994), and Vlastos (1994b). Most of these commentators focus their discussion of Book 5 on ways in which Plato attributes to women courageous or aggressive psychological qualities in virtue of which they are included in martial and political activities ordinarily reserved for men in Greek culture. The converse point is underappreciated (though Kochin and Salkever are important exceptions): Plato also insists that the guardian *men* must share in warm, moderate, and gentle feelings and virtues that Greeks associate with women and the household. I pursue this line of thought in more detail in work with Kirsty Ironside.

guardian class are designed to foster a sense of family among all the citizens, especially among the warriors and rulers themselves.[46]

As noted in Chapter 2, the connection between the household and *thumos* is an immediate one for Plato that reflects the linguistic relationship between *oikos* and *oikeion*: one of the most primitive manifestations of spirited desire, on his view, calls to mind precisely the sorts of feelings a person has about their *oikos* and its members and contents. It is no surprise, then, that the reasoning Socrates offers in favor of his property and family policies is, as Tad Brennan remarks, "shot through with the terminology of the *oikeion* and a few other phrases equivalent to it."[47] Socrates explains that the greatest good for a city is the sharing—literally, *community* (*koinōnia*, 462b4)—of pleasures and pains. When citizens feel pleasure and pain together in response to the same events, their shared experiences "bind" the city together and make it one, which is the greatest good for a city. Conversely, when they react differently to the same things, some rejoicing and others grieving, this "privatization" (*idiōsis*) of pleasure and pain destroys the city. What produces the unifying condition of sharing or community, moreover, is when citizens use the phrases "my own" (*to emon*) and "familiar" (*oikeion*), along with "not mine" (*to mē emon*) and "other" (*allotrion*) unanimously, applying them to the same things and—very importantly—the same *people* in the same situations (462a–e, 464c–d).

Socrates defends the benefits of both his social and economic policies in terms of this unanimity about the familiar, as well as spirited desires and emotions associated with familiarity. He and Glaucon note that in other cities like democracies, the citizens who share in ruling consider some of their co-rulers *oikeioi* and "their own," but others of them *allotrioi* and "not their own." In the case of the guardians of the Kallipolis, however, *no one* will consider anyone else "other" in this way (463b–c). "There's no way he could," Glaucon assures, "for when he encounters any of them, he'll believe that he's meeting a

---

[46] Plato's policies have a few noteworthy historical and literary precedents. (1) Many of them represent more radical or extreme versions of Spartan social and political practices. For parallels, see, e.g., Xenophon, *Lac.*, esp. 1.4–10, 5.1–4, 6.1–2, and 7.1–6; and Plutarch, *Lyc.*, esp. 8.1–10.3, 14.1–4, 15.6–10, 24.1–4, and 25.3–4. For discussion of Spartan customs see Kennel (1995), Powell (2015), and Rahe (2016: Ch. 1). On the influence of Spartanism on Plato, see Futter (2017), Jaeger (1944a: 246–58), and Menn (2005). (2) Several of them echo, allude to, or parallel ideas and reforms proposed by Praxagora in Aristophanes' *Assemblywomen* (which itself appears to parody Spartan policies)—e.g. at 590–602, 613–14, 635–43, 673–6. For further discussion, see Nightingale (1995: 177–80) and n. 51 below. (3) Herodotus' description of the Agathyrsi people anticipates both Socrates' family policy and the reasoning behind it: "They have wives in common, so that they may all be brothers, and, since they are all familiar (οἰκήιοι), will neither envy (φθόνῳ) nor hate (ἔχθεϊ) one another" (*Hist.* 4.104). Perhaps of some significance, Herodotus likens the Agathyrsi to the Thracians, whom Socrates associates with *thumos* at *Rep.* 435e. Cf. Thomas (1997: 345, n. 2).

[47] 2012: 118. For general discussion of the social policies of Book 5, see Klosko (2006: Ch. 9), and on the importance of *philia* in the Kallipolis, see Prauscello (2014: Ch. 1).

brother or sister, a father or mother, a son or daughter, or some ancestor or descendant of theirs" (463c5–7). And citizens will not only "mouth the names of family (*oikeia onomata*)" but also *act* in ways that reflect their perceived kinship with one another. They will treat all of their parents with a sense of shame, care, obedience, and justice (463c–d), and they will show "honor" to their elder relatives and act as shame requires toward them, fostering political "peace" instead of "faction" among them (465a–b). In addition, whenever one of their fellow citizens is faring well or badly, they will say that "mine" is doing well or badly (463e). Importantly, Socrates has earlier identified this perceived sharing of another's success or failure with *friendship*. In the passage that precedes the noble lie, he explains, "One cares (*kēdoito*) most for what one loves (*philōn*)... and someone loves (*philoi*) something most of all when he believes that the same things are advantageous to it as himself and supposes that if it does well, he'll do well, and that if it does badly, then he'll do badly too" (412d2–7). By producing unanimity about the *oikeion*, therefore, Socrates aims to bind the guardians together with spirited feelings of friendship and familial love.

The complementary benefit, Socrates explains, is that they will martial the aggressive resources of *thumos* in defense of one another and the city when they are threatened either by outsiders or by anomalous enemies within the city itself. If an older citizen were to be attacked by a younger one, for example, the rest of the citizens would "come to the rescue of the victim" like family (465a–b). In the case of war, "The guardians would be excellent fighters against an enemy because they'd be least likely to desert each other, since they know each other as brothers, fathers, and sons, and call each other by those names" (471c8–d3). The fact that children will accompany their warrior parents on military expeditions will intensify this effect, for "every animal fights better in the presence of its young" (467a10–b1).

Because of the noble lie, moreover, the guardians' political "family" also extends beyond their own class to the craftspeople and farmers. Unlike rulers and their subjects in unjust cities, who often think of one another antagonistically as "despotic rulers" or "slaves," respectively, the guardians and producers of the Kallipolis share mutual feelings of appreciation and fellowship. The craftspeople and farmers think of the guardians as "auxiliaries" and "preservers"—literally, "those who keep them safe"—while the guardians think of the producers as their "providers" and "friends" (*philous*) (463a–b, 547c1–2).[48] Because the guardians think of *all* their fellow citizens as earthborn kin,

---

[48] Cf. discussion in Kamtekar (2004: 156–60).

moreover, they will "care (*kēdesthai*) more for the city and each other" (415d). Again, this will be reflected in the spiritedness with which they fight to protect everyone in the city. "If anyone attacks the land on which they live," Socrates explains, "they must make a plan on its behalf and defend it as their mother and nurse, and think of all the other citizens as their earthborn brothers" (414d–e).[49]

Socrates' explanation of his economic policies for the guardians follows a similar logic. If they are permitted to possess their own private land, houses, and money, they will become "savage despots" (*despotais agriois*) or "enemies" of the other citizens instead of their "friendly allies" (*summachōn eunmenōn*): "They'll spend their whole lives hating (*misountes*) and being hated (*misoumenoi*) . . . more afraid of internal than of external enemies (*polemious*)" (417a6–b6, 416b5). Later he elaborates:

> If different people apply the term "mine" (*to emon*) to different things, one would drag into his own house whatever possessions he could separate from the others, and another would drag things into a different house to a different wife and children, and this would make for private (*idias*) pleasures and pains at private things (*idiōn*). But our people, on the other hand, will think of the same things as familiar (*oikeiou*), aim at the same goal, and, as far as possible, share feelings (*homopatheis*) of pleasure and pain . . . And what about lawsuits and mutual accusations? Won't they pretty well disappear from among them, because they have everything in common (*koina*) except their own bodies? Hence they'll be spared of all the faction that arises between people because of the possession of money, children, and families.
>
> (464c8–e2)

Private ownership of material possessions produces spirited anger, hatred, and faction among the citizens, while having things in "common" fosters the sharing of pleasures and pains that conduces to mutual care and friendship.[50] Socrates' goal, therefore, is to reduce privatization to the minimum level possible for human beings, such that only their physical bodies are uniquely "their own." Socrates concedes, moreover that even this relatively slight

---

[49] Socrates even makes a panhellenic appeal to the idea that all Greeks are in a sense *oikeioi* to one another, and hence that fighting among them is a matter of civil *stasis*, rather than *polemos* proper, which is strictly limited to conflict against *allotrioi* (470a–e). For similar panhellenic themes, see Gorgias' *Olympic Speech* (DK B7, B8, B8a) and Isocrates' *Paneg*. (e.g. 3, 173–4), as well as discussion in De Romilly (1992: Ch. 8).

[50] Strauss (1964: 103) astutely comments, "In the city of the armed camp there does not exist that approximation to the ring of Gyges which is the private home."

element of privacy in their lives can generate hostility if citizens cause bodily injury or offense to one another. Notably, his response to this possibility reiterates the centrality of spiritedness in his thinking. In order to prevent lawsuits, citizens should be encouraged to stay fit enough to defend themselves against personal assaults of this kind by their peers. He explains, "If someone became angry (*thumoito*) and sated his spirit (*thumon*) in this way, it would be less likely to lead him into more serious conflicts (*staseis*)" (465a1–3). This reasoning reflects the idea that spirited feelings of aggression and competitiveness always have the potential to arise whenever things are private rather than shared. When perceived "ownership" is limited to the physical body, however, any hostility that arises among people is minimal enough to be managed through isolated expressions of anger.[51]

---

[51] The "Straussian" reading of Book 5 poses a challenge to my interpretation. According to arguments developed in Strauss (1964) and Bloom (1968), Plato does not earnestly endorse Socrates' proposals; rather, they are designed to demonstrate to his interlocutors the unnaturalness, impossibility, or undesirability of the philosophical city. Their arguments are based largely on Socrates' allusions to Aristophanes' *Assemblywomen*, in which Athenian women, led by Praxagora, take over the assembly and enact a program of communal living that, on the Straussian reading, "extends the principle of Athenian democracy to the extreme and shows that it is absurd" (Bloom [1977: 325]; cf. [1968: 380] and Craig [1994: 204]). Four responses. (1) *Assemblywomen* is not obviously meant to parody distinctively *democratic* ideas. Although Aristophanes' work is complex and surely includes critique of Athenian politics (see Tordoff [2007, 2017]), Praxagora's policies have much more conspicuously in common with, and are better suited to satirize, the *Spartan* system. Several dramatic details in the play support this reading; see David (1984: 25–9), Dettehoffer (1999), Foley (1982: 15–16), Perentidis (2012), and Sheppard (2016). Likewise, by advocating extreme communal living, abolition of private property, "sharing" of wives, and so on, Socrates is hyperbolizing distinctively Spartan ways of life. Book 8 confirms this point: the imperfect regime most similar to the best city is the timocratic one, "which corresponds to the Laconian form of constitution" (545a–b), and which "imitates" several of Kallipolis' social policies (547c–d). The fact that Book 5 presents a Spartanized way of life makes it less clear, then, that neither Plato himself nor his elite readers could have taken it seriously. (2) In response to Bloom, Klosko (1986) rightly grants there is *some* relationship between *Republic* and *Assemblywomen*, but notes that this fact underdetermines how we interpret that relationship. Klosko also draws an important contrast: Plato, but not Aristophanes, recognizes the potential to shape people through systematic moral education. He comments, "Perhaps Bloom is correct that the desires for property and family are ineradicable...But the point at issue is whether Plato believed in their ineradicability, and this Bloom has not demonstrated" (p. 288). To this I want to add that, as a matter of Platonic interpretation, the fact that the *Republic* defends views that are derided in comedy strikes me as, if anything, a *prima facie* reason to suspect Plato's *seriousness* about those views, not his dismissal of them. It seems far more characteristic of Plato to take an idea that is laughed at by the crowd and show we should take it seriously, than for him to pile on to an object of popular ridicule. Cf. Nightingale (1995: 178). (3) Bluestone (1994; cf. 1987: Ch. 1) exposes the ways that modern forms of sexism—including the "blatant sexism" (p. 116) inherent in the Straussian view, with its claim that Socrates' proposals regarding women defy "nature"—have impaired much scholarly assessment of Book 5. Indeed, we seem to learn much more about Strauss' and Bloom's views of women than we do about Plato's from their interpretations. (4) Finally, the arguments of this book show that Book 5's policies are not frivolous comic suggestions, but rather motivated and supported by careful reflection on human psychology. For additional criticism of the Straussian view, see Hall (1977), as well as Burnyeat's (1985) intemperate review of Strauss, to which Cropsey et al. (1985) and Levine (1991) respond. Ferrari (1997) offers a fair-minded assessment of Strauss's work; see also Lane (1999). Others who doubt the seriousness of Book 5's proposals, though not from a Straussian perspective, include Annas (1999: Ch. 4) and Waterfield (1993: xiv–xx).

Socrates also reinforces his social and economic policies, as well as the power structure of the Kallipolis itself, through the city's system for distributing honor. Broadly speaking, his proposals make sure that honors and prizes go to those who are *virtuous* in the Kallipolis. The virtuous guardians as a class are considered happier than Olympic victors, for their "victory is more admirable" (465d–e), and among the warriors the honor system is used especially to encourage courageous behavior. Those who excel in war receive "the privilege of more abundant intercourse with women" (460a–b), and soldiers who earn "high reputation" receive crowns of victory and are permitted to "kiss, and be kissed" by any and all of the young people on the campaign, men and women alike, and they are "honored" in rites and hymns (468b–d). Those who die nobly in battle will be considered members of the "golden" race (468e), who themselves receive the city's greatest distinctions. The golden race are awarded "honors" for passing the trials in pleasure, pain, and fears by which they are selected for rule (414a); they are the "most honored" people in the city throughout their lives (415a); and for their outstanding virtue they are glorified with distinguished burials, tombs, and memorials and are worshipped as divine guardian spirits after their deaths (468e–469b).

This system of honor has several valuable political effects that complement and fortify Socrates' policies on family and property. To begin with, by rewarding the bravest soldiers with sanctioned sexual intercourse, Socrates notes, they are thereby ensuring that the best individuals have a greater share in producing the city's children, which means that the children themselves will tend to be endowed with the best possible natures (460a–b, 468c). In general, the erotic and osculatory rewards exploit the feelings of attachment that soldiers have to one another: a person who feel especially strong love or sexual attraction for someone else will be more spiritedly eager (*prothumoteros*, 468c3) to excel in virtue. Furthermore, by reserving the greatest honors for the most virtuous and wisest, the philosopher kings and queens, Socrates' policies also reinforce the obedience, respect, and reverent awe that the citizens are supposed to feel and show toward their rulers, and that promote the unanimity about who should rule that constitutes the city's moderation. Indeed, assigning the highest honors to philosophers is designed not so much to gratify the rulers themselves, who presumably value such acclaim least of anyone in the city, but rather to steer the veneration of the productive and warrior classes in a direction that both benefits them ethically and fosters civic harmony and friendship with the rulers. The system of honor also bolsters Socrates' policies on private property. As we have seen, Socrates establishes that the pursuit of money-making stands in singular opposition to the pursuit of virtue. If his elimination of private property is designed to make sure that the warriors and guardians do not value and compete for personal wealth, therefore, then his system of honor has the complementary effect of instilling a desire to excel morally. In other words, the honor system directs the ambition and competitiveness of exceptional young people and warriors—the very people most likely to be *corrupted* in unjust societies, we have seen—away from finite material goods and toward the non-finite good of virtue itself, the value of which is shared by the possessors and their fellow citizens alike. To the extent they compete with one another, consequently, it will be for a "prize" that is ethically and politically beneficial to the whole city.

Thumos, then, with its twin capacities either to bind people together through mutual care and friendship or tear them apart through anger and competition, lies at the heart of Socrates' social and economic policies. In the Kallipolis there is no longer competition between private and public, household and city, because the city itself in an important sense *becomes* (especially among the guardians) an expanded civic version of the *oikos*. Socrates aims to make the citizens *oikeioi* to one another and hence to extend the feelings of solicitude and affection that are usually reserved for friends, family, and members of one's household throughout the whole city.[52] Note, by way of conclusion, how in doing so Socrates perfectly undermines the Thrasymachean and popular conception of justice as "the good of another." When every citizen is a friend and familiar, *no one* in the city is an *allotrios* whose successes or failures could come into conflict with one's own. Hence Socrates' social and economic policies inoculate the city against the potentially destructive effects of the ethics of helping friends and harming enemies to which spirited psychology gives rise, while using its advantageous effects in the service of civic unity.

---

[52] Cf. Grube (1980: 270–1).

8

The Spirited Part of the Soul in the *Timaeus*

In Chapters 6 and 7, I examined the *Republic*'s account of moral education and the psychology that underlies and informs it. According to that picture, music and gymnastics aim to foster proper relationships among the three parts of the soul: they prepare reason (at least in preliminary ways) for its job of ruling the soul, train spirit to act as reason's obedient ally in the face of external and internal enemies, and minimize appetite's influence in the soul through practices of abstinence and restraint. In the ideal case, all three parts of the soul will accept reason's psychic sovereignty, but appetite is always at least a *potential* threat to the rule of reason, and the reasoning and spirited parts must, therefore, treat it with vigilance and caution. Musical and gymnastic training, then, aim both to make sure that refractory appetites never or only rarely arise in the first place, and also to make sure that reason and spirit watch out for them and are fit to resist them successfully if they do.

Crucial to this account is the idea that some form of, or something analogous to, intrapsychic interaction and communication takes place among the soul parts. Of special importance for my purposes, the spirited part is supposed to be responsive to, and defensive of, rational judgments issued by the reasoning part: it is trained to treat reason and its desires as *oikeion* and vicious appetitive desires as *allotrion*. This raises a number of questions, however. What exactly is going on internally when the reasoning part makes "declarations" and spirit "listens" to them? How does a rational part of the soul communicate to a non-rational part, and how does the latter comprehend the former? What kind of cognitive processes are involved? Are spirit and reason doing something like "talking" to one another, as the language of declaring, ordering, listening, and obeying suggest, or is a different kind of psychological mechanism at work? Moreover, precisely what does it mean for *thumos* to "recognize" reason as "familiar" or find unnecessary appetites "alien" in the ways I have suggested, and how does early education produce the relevant sort of intrapsychic recognition or non-recognition by the spirited part? What cognitive resources are available to spirit that make its psychic behavior possible, and how, if at all, do those resources differ from the ones Plato is prepared to attribute to reason on the one hand or appetite on the other?

The Political Soul: Plato on Thumos, *Spirited Motivation, and the City.* Josh Wilburn, Oxford University Press.
© Josh Wilburn 2021. DOI: 10.1093/oso/9780198861867.003.0008

I do not think the *Republic* itself provides resources for answering these questions in much detail, in part because it never directly concerns itself with the internal mechanics of communication and cognition among the soul parts, nor with how those mechanics are related to the biological processes involved in cognitive activities like sense-perception. Plato does address these issues in the *Timaeus*, however, and by drawing on what he says there, it is possible to construct an account of the cognitive resources available to the soul parts and how those resources are involved in their communication (or communication-like activity) with one another. My focus in this chapter will be on *spirited* cognition and spirit's interactions with the other two soul parts, although I will also discuss the cognitive resources of appetite and reason. This chapter cuts to the heart of one of the central controversies about Plato's theory of tripartition, which I addressed briefly in Chapter 1: the extent to which the three parts of the soul are or are not "agent-like"—that is, whether, how, and to what extent they should be understood as cognitively independent of one another, with their own discrete faculties, beliefs, conscious experiences, and psychological lives, in the sorts of ways that different animals or human beings are. In that earlier discussion I suggested that the views I defend in this book require only minimalist assumptions about psychic parthood. The three parts of the soul are all discrete, independent sources or subjects of motivation, but they do not have (or at least nothing I say requires them to have) distinct, independent psychological lives. The conclusions I defend in this chapter are consistent with these minimalist commitments.

In what follows I will be advocating an *imagistic* account of spirited cognition, according to which the various activities of the spirited part of the soul—the motivations and emotions it generates, its training through musical and gymnastic education, its responsiveness to rational judgment, and its resistance to offensive appetites—can all be explained at the cognitive level by appealing only to the resources of sense-perception, memory, and imagination.[1] That is to say, we need not attribute to spirit any cognitive resources

---

[1] Lorenz (2006a: Ch. 7 and 2012) and Moss (2012a) develop imagistic accounts of the *Timaeus* in detail but focus on the appetitive part. Gerson (2003a: 239–50), Kahn (2004: 353–9), Kamtekar (2017: 175–6), Renaut (2020), and Russell (2005: 233–4) also consider or sketch imagistic interpretations. Bobonich (2010) criticizes the accounts offered by Lorenz and Kahn, claiming that an imagistic account of *spirited* cognition and motivation in particular is "very implausible" (p. 158). Fletcher (2016), too, criticizes the accounts of Lorenz and Moss and questions whether appetite is aware of (visual) images, but her view seems to rely in part (e.g. pp. 418-9, 426-7) on the idea that appetite in human beings must have the same limitations Timaeus attributes to (exclusively appetitive) plants. I would suggest as an alternative, however, that appetite shares in awareness of *whatever* perceptual experiences a given organism has, but that since plants, unlike people and animals, lack the physiological equipment for sight and hearing, botanical appetite does not share in the corresponding experiences. Cf. Thein (2019: 22).

beyond imagistic perceptual ones in order to account for everything Plato needs spirit to do in his psychological theory. I will begin in Section 1 with an overview of the relevant sections of the *Timaeus*, before turning to an explanation and defense of the imagistic account in Section 2. I will argue that because it is non-rational, spirit neither makes judgments of its own, nor has the capacity to understand the linguistic or propositional content of rational judgments themselves. Rather, reason communicates its judgments to spirit through the medium of imagination, and it is to that imagistic content that spirit directly responds. This view also has a physiological component: perceptual and imagistic content, according to the *Timaeus*, is conveyed by means of the blood. Plato, we will see, continues in the Homeric and poetic tradition of associating *thumos* with the heart and circulatory system (as well as with the lungs and respiratory system), and he makes use of that association as a biological foundation for his theory of spirited cognition and intrapsychic communication. Finally, in Section 3, I will project the imagistic account of the *Timaeus* onto the *Republic*'s account of early education and virtue. Although I will neither assume nor argue that Plato already had the cognitive theory of the *Timaeus* in mind when he wrote the *Republic*, I *will* argue that the *Republic* is consistent with and helpfully illuminated by that imagistic theory.

1. The Mortal Soul

In his cosmological account of the origins of human psychology, Timaeus explains that the creator Demiurge crafted the "divine" part of the human soul himself, but subsequently turned over what remained of human creation to the Lesser Gods. The fact of embodiment, he informs them, means that the human soul will necessarily be subject to "irrational sense-perception" and the feelings, desires, and emotions associated with it, especially pleasure, pain, boldness, fear, anger, hope, and lust. These "disturbances," which are caused by, or arise in connection with, the chaotic motions of the material world, threaten to disrupt the "circular" motions of the immortal soul that constitute rational thought and on which a virtuous and happy life depend. The Lesser Gods address this problem in their creation of embodied human beings by designing them in a way that enables and promotes the divine element's proper circular movement. They encase the rational soul in the spherical human head, create the rest of the body as its vehicle, and in the lower sections of the body build "another kind of soul as well, the mortal kind, which contains within it those dreadful but necessary disturbances" (69a–e).[2] Timaeus continues:

Inside the chest, then, and in what is called the trunk, they proceeded to enclose the mortal type of soul. And since one part of the mortal soul was naturally better than the other, they built the hollow of the trunk in sections, dividing them the way that women's quarters are divided from men's. They situated the midriff between the sections to serve as a partition. Now the part of the mortal soul that shares in courage and spirit (*thumou*), the victory-loving part, they settled nearer to the head, between the midriff and the neck, so that it might listen to reason (*tou logou katēkoon*) and together with it restrain by force the part consisting of appetites, should the latter at any time refuse to voluntarily obey (*mēdamēi peithesthai hekon etheloi*) the command (*epitagmati*) of reason coming down from the acropolis. The heart, then, which ties the veins together, the spring from which blood courses with vigorous pulse throughout all the bodily members, they set in the guard-house. That way, if the might of spirit (*thumou*) should boil over at a declaration from reason (*tou logou parangeilantos*) that some injustice (*adikos*) concerning its members is taking place—something being done to them from outside or even something originating from the appetites within—everything in the body that is perceptive (*aisthētikon*) may sharply perceive (*aisthanomenon*), through all the narrow vessels, the encouragements or threats (*tōn te parakeleuseōn kai apeilōn*), and so listen (*epēkoon*) and follow completely. In this way the best part among them all can be left in charge ... The part of the soul that has appetites for food and drink and whatever else it feels a need for, given the nature of the body, they settled in the area between the midriff and the boundary toward the navel. In the whole of this region they constructed something like a trough for the body's nourishment. Here they tied this part of the soul down like a wild beast that they could not avoid feeding if a mortal race were ever to exist. They assigned it its position there, to keep it ever feeding at its trough, living as far away as possible from the part that takes counsel, and making as little clamor and noise as possible, thereby letting the superior part deliberate in peace about what is beneficial for one and all.   (69e3–71a3)

---

[2] I follow commentators such as Robinson (1970: 105–6) and Sedley (1997: 329–30) who take Timaeus' teleology seriously, including its assignment of the soul's parts to bodily locations associated with physiological phenomena. For commentators who doubt the literalness of Timaeus' account, however, see Steel (2001) and Grube (1980: 143–4).

The general picture that emerges from this passage is familiar. As in the *Republic*, spirit has a supportive relationship with reason, while appetite is a potential enemy or unruly animal that the two of them must sometimes forcibly restrain.[3] Like Socrates in the *Republic*, moreover, Timaeus uses the personifying language of communication to describe reason's interactions with the lower soul parts. Reason issues "commands," which appetite is evidently prone to "refuse to voluntarily obey," but which spirit is disposed to "listen to" and enforce. Reason also makes "declarations" (echoing the *Republic*'s account of courage) about acts of injustice, which provoke a motivational response from spirit in the form of anger. And finally, Timaeus indicates that reason issues "threats and encouragements" that spirit plays some role in administering, and to which "everything in the body that is perceptive" is supposed to "listen."

The main issue here is how to understand the talk of communication, and what it implies about the cognitive resources of the non-rational soul parts, in particular *thumos*. One possible way of understanding it is on the model of literal verbal communication between human beings. On this reading the parts of the soul engage in something like a "conversation" (though perhaps a one-sided one) in which reason communicates judgments that have linguistic, propositional structure and content—call this sort of content "logistic"—and the lower parts comprehend that content *as such* just as one human being understands the speech of another. Often versions of this interpretation also include the idea that spirit and appetite make judgments or hold logistic beliefs of their own, and that intrapsychic communication involves, or can involve, a form of *persuasion* in which reason secures the obedience and support of the lower soul parts (when it does) by changing their beliefs.[4] Many literalist commentators adopt some such reading of intrapsychic communication in the *Republic*, and some also explicitly defend the same analysis of the *Timaeus*.

---

[3] Taylor (1928: 496–9) makes an especially strong case for continuity between the tripartite theory of the *Republic* and the version of it we find in the *Timaeus*. Cf. Guthrie (1971a: 233), Johansen (2004: 152–8), Renaut (2014: 221), and Robinson (1970: 104).

[4] Commentators who attribute seemingly logistic forms of belief or persuadability to the lower soul parts in the *Republic* include: Barney (2016: 59), Bobonich (2002: 219–20, 243–7; 2017: 8, 18), Brickhouse and Smith (2010: 199–213), Cairns (1993: 385–8 and n. 131), Carone (2001 and 2005b), Cooper (1984: 16), Irwin (1977: 193–5; 1995a: 211–13), Kamtekar (1998: 324–30; 2006: 189), Lesses (1987: 149–54), Moline (1978), Morris (2006: 218–25), Moss (2005: 156; 2008: 64–6; 2014b: 14–16), and Reeve (1988: 139, 164). Commentators who reject or are skeptical of such attributions include Anagnostopolous (2006: 176–8), Gerson (2003a: 107–8), Renaut (2014: 135–7), Stalley (2007), and Storey (2014).

Hence Gabriela Roxana Carone argues that according to Timaeus' account, non-rational parts of the soul or their motivations "share in doxastic structure," hold "beliefs," are "capable of participating in judgmental attitudes," have "propositional structure" or even "some sort of rational structure," and "can listen to reason and be persuaded" by it.[5]

Strong evidence tells against this line of interpretation. But first, a caveat. In the passage quoted above, Timaeus notes that appetite will sometimes fail to "voluntarily obey" the commands of reason. The implication is that other times, appetite *will* voluntarily obey those commands. Now, the word that I am translating as "obey" here is *peithesthai*, which is the passive form of *peithō*, a verb sometimes appropriately translated as "persuade." This is the translation favored by Carone, who appeals to this passage as straightforward evidence that the lower parts can, in fact, be persuaded. My response to this argument is to accept that appetite can *peithesthai*, but to deny that we should translate the term as "be persuaded" in this instance, if by that we have in mind (as Carone does) a change in belief brought about through convincing speech. The problem is that the Greek *peithō* has a significantly wider usage than the English term "persuade." As Glen Morrow comments, "It means getting a person to do something that you want him to do, by the use of almost any means short of physical compulsion."[6] Such means certainly *include* actual persuasion through speech, but they encompass much more as well. Hence, for example, bribery counts as a form of *peithō*, as in the *Republic*, where Socrates objects to the poets' suggestion that "gifts persuade (*peithei*) gods and venerable kings" (390e3). Likewise, in Xenophon's treatise on equestrianism, he freely speaks of horses as *peithesthai* with respect to the pulls of their reins.[7] In many cases, like this last, the passive form of the verb indicates simply compliance without resistance and is most accurately translated with a word like "obey."[8] The passage from the *Timaeus*, then, certainly implies that the

---

[5] 2007. Bobonich, however, who attributes an extravagant range of agent-like capacities to all three soul parts in the *Republic*, takes Plato to *reject* agent-like psychology in the *Timaeus*, supposedly as a step toward rejecting tripartition entirely in favor of an undivided soul in the *Laws* (2002: Ch. 4). I reject both Bobonich's agent-like interpretation of the *Republic*'s psychology (see Sect. 3 below) as well as his interpretation of the *Laws* (see Ch. 10.1). Lorenz (2004b: 565) succinctly states the problem with Bobonich's developmentalist view: "The *Timaeus* explicitly denies the capacity for reasoning to the soul's lowest part...On Bobonich's view, this is a devastating blow to tripartition...If, however, the nonrational soul-parts of the *Republic* are already conceived of as incapable of reasoning, the *Timaeus* simply makes fully explicit what has been assumed all along." Cf. Taylor (2003).

[6] 1953: 236. Cf. Gerson (2003a: 108, n. 20).

[7] E.g. *Eq.* 3.6.2, 3.12.3; cf. 6.10.1 and Xenophon, *Symp.* 2.10.6, as well as Socrates' description of the good horse as εὐπειθής in Plato's *Phaedrus* (254a1).

[8] Indeed, the fact that *peithesthai* is paired with "command" suggests that "obey" captures the sense Timaeus has in mind: one *obeys* commands; one is not "persuaded" by them.

appetitive part (and *a fortiori* the spirited) can *peithesthai* in this sense: it sometimes conforms to reason's judgments without (so to speak) putting up a fight. But we cannot infer that its obedience consists in anything like persuasion by speech, any more than does the behavior of a yielding horse.[9]

Timaeus, moreover, gives us good reasons for doubting that the mortal parts of the soul are capable of comprehending logistic content, and for thinking they respond only to imagistic content instead. He is especially clear in the case of appetite:

> [The gods] knew that this part of the soul was not going to understand (*sunēsein*) reason (*logou*), and that even if it were in one way or another to have some perception (*aisthēseōs*) of rational judgments (*logōn*), it would not be in its nature to care about any of them, but it would be much more enticed by images and phantoms (*eidōlōn kai phantasmatōn*) night and day. Hence the god conspired with this very tendency by constructing a liver, a structure which he situated in the dwelling place of this part of the soul. He made it something dense, smooth, bright, and sweet, though also having a bitter quality, so that the power of the thoughts sent down from the mind might be stamped upon it as upon a mirror that receives impressions and returns visible images (*eidōla*). So the power of the mind's thoughts could frighten this part of the soul whenever it could avail itself of a congenial portion of the liver's bitterness and threaten (*apeilēi*) it with severe command ... And again, whenever thought's gentle inspiration should paint pictures (*phantasmata apozōgraphoi*) of the opposite sort, its power would bring respite from the bitterness.   (71a3–c5)

Timaeus goes on to reiterate that the appetitive part "has no share in reason (*logou*) and understanding (*phronēseōs*)," but indicates that it can see "images" (*phantasmata*) and perceive the "sights and sounds" (*ta phanenta kai*

---

[9] Likewise, Plato undeniably attributes *doxa* to the lower parts of the soul in the *Republic*. The question, however, is whether the term there refers to beliefs with logistic content, as it does in the *Timaeus*. As I propose in Sect. 3 below, the *Republic* seems to indicate that the "beliefs" of the lower parts can be cashed out entirely in terms of their access and responsiveness to perceptual or imagistic content. On my view, then, the two dialogues are perfectly compatible, and even complementary. Lorenz (2006a: Chs. 5–7) similarly finds that the term *doxa* in the *Republic* is more elastic than it is in later dialogues like *Theaetetus* and *Timaeus*. In its looser sense it includes "beliefs" of the lower parts that consist in some form of "acceptance" of, or disposition to act on the basis of, content provided through sensory appearances. Cf. like-minded suggestions in Kamtekar (2004: 154, n. 139), Gerson (2003a: 107, n. 18), and Storey (2014).

phōnēthenta) that occur in dreams (71d–72a).[10] Later, moreover, he seems to attribute the cognitive deficiencies of plants largely to the fact they possess only appetitive soul: "This type [of soul] is totally devoid of belief (*doxēs*), reasoning (*logismou*), or understanding (*nou*), though it does share in perception, pleasant and painful, and appetites" (77b3–7).[11] In all of these passages Timaeus denies that appetite understands *logos* or shares in rational capacities associated with it, and he contrasts these cognitive limitations with appetite's share in sense-perception and its responsiveness to various sorts of imagistic or quasi-perceptual content: images, visions, pictures, sights, and sounds. The contrast is emphatic, and it tells strongly against the literalist model of communication. If appetite cannot hold beliefs or understand speech, then reason can neither communicate its commands logistically to appetite nor use anything like persuasion on it. Evidently, moreover, the alternative is that reason must communicate with appetite quasi-perceptually.

Still, one might think that even if this assessment of appetitive cognition is correct, Plato means to allow more sophisticated capacities to spirit. Some commentators have drawn exactly this conclusion.[12] After all, spirit is much more responsive to reason than appetite; perhaps its responsiveness is due to superior cognitive abilities. Even if reason must interact with appetite through images, then, perhaps it can communicate to or persuade *thumos* directly by means of *logos*.

There are significant obstacles to this view, however. Although Timaeus devotes less attention to spirit's cognitive resources than to appetite's, he provides reasons for thinking that the limitations he places on appetitive cognition apply generally to both parts of the mortal soul.[13] To begin with, early in his cosmology, Timaeus characterizes rational thought processes in

---

[10] Carone (2007: 112) claims that Timaeus does not deny comprehension of *logos* generally to appetite, but only *logos* in the limited sense of "what looks after the interest of (or what is better for)... all parts in common." As Bobonich (2002: 557, n. 45) notes, however, because the contrast case is imagistic, the distinction is clearly between "anything linguistic and something non-linguistic."

[11] Cf. Russell (2005: 233–4) and Grönroos (2013: 17). Carone (2007: 114–16) is correct to caution that the appetitive part of plants may function differently from that of human beings (cf. n. 1 above). Nonetheless, the specific limitations of botanical appetite Timaeus identifies simply echo and confirm the ones he has already attributed to human appetite.

[12] Steel (2001: 117) comments, "Unlike the *thymos*, which can have direct communication with the *logistikon* and even collaborate with it, the appetitive part is a purely irrational force and can neither hear nor obey a rational commandment." See similar ideas in Archer-Hind (1888: 262–3), Brennan (2012: 123), Fermeglia (319–20), Gill (1997: 268–70), and Karfík (2005: 210–12). Moss (2012a: 275; cf. 2007: 522–3 and n. 38) also entertains this line of thought. Finally, the accounts of Irwin (1995a: 211–13) and Reeve (1988: 136–7), which distinguish spirited desires from appetites on the grounds that the former, but not the latter, depend partly on the agent's conception of the good, suggest this sort of interpretation as well.

[13] Renaut (2020: 112–18) defends the same conclusion.

terms of the immortal soul's circular orbits. The soul produces a *logos*—it "speaks" or "declares" to itself "without utterance or sound"—when it comes into cognitive contact with a perceptible or intelligible object and determines in which respects that thing is the same as or different from other things. Timaeus describes belief or *doxa*, moreover, as *logos* of this sort that results from or is identified with the revolving motion of the soul's Circle of the Different, and *nous* or knowledge as *logos* that results from or is identified with the revolving motion of the Circle of the Same (37a–c).[14] Importantly, these psychic motions evidently require rather fussy and specific physiological conditions in order to occur in embodied creatures. They are possible in human beings only because of the spherical shape of the human head, which (thanks to the wise design of the gods) is suited to their circular motion and provides protection against the chaotic rectilinear motions of the sensible world (42e–44c, 69c–e). Conversely, Timaeus connects the irrationality of non-human animals to the anatomical fact that their heads have taken on "all sorts of irregular shapes" (91e6–92a2), and he explains that human infants at first lack reason and understanding because the disturbances of the perceptible world overwhelm the immortal soul's revolutions (43a–b, 44a–b). All of this matters because the physiological circumstances of spirit and appetite are decidedly *not* the special ones favorable to rational thought, *doxa*, and *logos*: they are located in parts of the body other than the spherical head, and they are subject to the same rectilinear motions that initially disorient the immortal soul upon its embodiment. Indeed, the mortal parts of the soul are specifically created by the Lesser Gods for the purpose of "containing" those disturbances. This makes it unclear how spirit or appetite could possibly share in anything approximating the logistic activities of reason, given that those activities require some degree of isolation from the very motions it is the mortal soul's job to experience and contain. And if even the elongated or imperfectly spherical heads of non-human animals are unfit to house the motions that constitute *logos*, *doxa*, and understanding, then *a fortiori* the human chest and abdomen are. When Timaeus explicitly denies these very capacities to appetite, therefore, we have every reason to believe that the same applies to *thumos*, which shares its kinetic constraints. To this we might add that Timaeus accounts for the cognitive powers of the immortal soul in part by appealing to its cosmic composition out of Sameness, Difference, and Being. By contrast,

---

[14] This is in line with Plato's characterization of *doxa* in his late dialogues as the soul's "silent speech" to itself, speech which has propositional structure and requires cognitive contact with the Forms (especially those of Being, Sameness, and Difference), since it involves attributing "being" to things (*Tht.* 186a–187a; *Soph.* 262a–264b; *Phdr.* 249b–c).

he is conspicuously silent on the composition of the *mortal* soul, which leaves open the possibility that its cognitive limitations are determined not just by its contingent location in the body, but also by its very constitution.

Furthermore, Timaeus' description of the creation of the mortal soul makes no discrimination between spirit and appetite when it comes to cognitive resources. He says only that the mortal soul contains sense-perception, but he does not equip it or any part of it with further capacities that could account for comprehension or use of *logos*. In fact, he explicitly says that the sense-perception the gods grant them is "irrational," *alogos* (69d4, 28a3; cf. 43e3, 47d4), and he calls the affective states, emotions, and desires to which spirit and appetite are subject "a turbulent, irrational mass" (42d1). This language is important. The positive term *logos* has a famously broad range of meanings that prominently includes both "reason" as well as "word" or "speech." This reflects the fact that for the Greeks, rationality and language are tightly bound together, as are irrationality and lack of linguistic capacity. Hence one of the primary denotations of the privative term *alogos* is simply "speechless" or "without speech." Therefore, if appetite and spirit—as well as sense-perception itself, the only cognitive capacity they are expressly granted—are non-rational, then we have strong grounds for doubting that they use or understand logistic content, and thus for doubting that reason communicates to them through internal "speech."

2. An Imagistic Account of Spirited Cognition

The alternative I would like to defend assumes only that spirit and appetite have cognitive access to the resources of perception with which Timaeus explicitly endows them. That is, my account assumes only that the mortal soul parts are responsive to the sort of imagistic content that can be acquired through sense-perception and reenacted or simulated through the connected faculties of memory and imagination. If a paradigm example of logistic content is a written sentence, then a paradigm example of imagistic content is a painted picture. Note, however, that despite the visual connotations of the term, imagistic content is not restricted to the visual. We perceive through all five senses, and we are capable of remembering or imagining the complete range of those perceptual experiences. We also often *feel* certain ways when we perceive things—pleased or pained, happy or sad, proud or ashamed—and we are fully capable of remembering or imagining those feelings as well. The main claim of my account, then, is that reason communicates with spirit and appetite by means of imagistic content of this sort. The commands, declarations, threats, and encouragements issued by the reasoning part take the form of, or are accompanied by, mental images or "imaginings" that represent their content, and that is the content to which the mortal soul parts respond. Spirit and appetite become aware of reason's messages, in other words, because they "perceive" them.

One argument in favor of the imagistic interpretation concerns the spirited part's relation to the heart, which Timaeus identifies as the central organ of circulation.[15] The heart "ties the veins together," he says, and its "pulsing" sends blood "throughout all the bodily members." This blood, moreover, is the vehicle by which reason's messages are distributed throughout the body, and Timaeus explains spirit's bodily location near the heart in terms of the goal of facilitating intrapsychic communication by means of the blood: the force of spirited anger helps make sure that reason's "encouragements and threats" are distributed throughout the body "through all the narrow vessels." He goes on to explain that the heart's "pounding" occurs "when one expects what one fears or when one's *thumos* is aroused" (70a–c). Spirit's emotional excitement, then, is correlated with the heart's beating faster, which in turn accelerates the distribution of reason's messages throughout the body in threatening situations that call for fast and decisive action.

The fact that reason's threats and encouragements are delivered by means of the blood is significant. In his account of sense-perception, Timaeus characterizes blood as the primary carrier of perceptual experiences and information, and blood vessels as the conduits for the transmission of that information.[16] He describes taste, for example, as the process in which "earth-like particles penetrate the area around the tiny vessels that act as testers for the tongue and reach down to the heart" (65c–d), and sound is "the stroke of air inflicted by way of the ears, brain, and blood to the soul" (67b). Sight occurs when the "internal fire" within us, coming into contact with external objects and the "kindred fire" outside, "transmits the motions of whatever it comes into contact with to and through the whole body until they reach the soul." Dreams, he says, are caused when this internal fire is shut up inside us and produces "visions" (*phantasmata*) similar to the ones produced from outside

---

[15] For discussion of Hippocratic or Pythagorean influences on Timaeus' cardiological account of *thumos*, see Frère (1997), Kamtekar (2017: 183, n. 9), and Renaut (2014: 215–16).

[16] Brisson (1999: 157–9) helpfully discusses this feature of Timaeus' account. Cf. Ganson (2005: 2), Lautner (2005: 236–7), and Solmsen (1961: 159–67). On this reading, Timaeus' account has obvious connections to Empedocles' theory of thought and perception, which makes blood the primary agent of these processes (e.g. DK B105, B107)

(45d–46a). Later he tells us that this internal fire is localized around, and associated with, the blood and veins, the blood itself consisting primarily of fire (78a–79d). Finally, speaking more generally about the construction of the blood vessels, Timaeus explains:

> [The Lesser Gods] next split these veins in the region of the head and wove them through one another, crossing them in opposite directions. They diverted the veins from the right toward the left side of the body, and those from the left toward the right... They did this especially to make sure that the stimulations received by the senses (tōn aisthēseōn), coming from either side of the body, might register clearly to the whole body.
>
> (77d6–e6)

These passages show that Timaeus takes the blood to have a prominent role in transmitting sensory experiences and information.[17] This provides additional support for the imagistic interpretation. Spirit helps transmit the "threats and encouragements" of reason by means of circulation, which suggests that their content is the same in kind as the perceptual or imagistic information the blood conveys during sensory experiences. This idea is confirmed by the language Timaeus uses in characterizing the process. Reason's messages are delivered to "everything in the body that is perceptive" (pan hoson aisthētikon en tōi sōmati), which is in turn described as "perceiving" (aisthanomenon) them (70b6–7).[18]

From all of this we may conclude that the commands, declarations, threats, and encouragements of reason are communicated in the form of mental images with perceptual content. The idea is this: the reasoning part deliberates about which actions are beneficial and best and which should be avoided, and the judgments at which it arrives through deliberation have the form of logoi. These logoi, in turn, are accompanied by mental images that illustrate at least some of their content, and it is those images that the mortal parts perceive and

[17] As discussed in Solmsen (1961), the blood serves functions that are eventually attributed to the nervous system in early Greek thought. Cf. Masi (2001: 85, n. 57).

[18] The phrase πᾶν ὅσον αἰσθητικόν ἐν τῷ σώματι refers to, or is meant to include, the soul that is present in the marrow distributed through the body. As Timaeus explains, the gods "implanted" τὰ τῶν ψυχῶν γένη throughout the marrow and "bound" them to it (73c–d). Johansen (2004: 150–2) persuasively argues that the "types" of soul Timaeus refers to here are the three soul-types of tripartite psychology: appetitive, spirited, and rational. Cf. Carone (2007: 110), Miller (1997: 180–1), and Steel (2001: 122 and n. 41). Johansen also responds to Cornford (1937: 294–5), who argues instead that τὰ τῶν ψυχῶν γένη refers to the various souls of future living species (described at 91d–92c). Pace Bobonich (2002: 556, n. 43), Fletcher (2016: 425), and Renaut (2014: 218–19), there is no reason to take πᾶν ὅσον αἰσθητικόν ἐν τῷ σώματι to refer (or at least, refer exclusively) to the physical matter or organs of the body itself.

to which they are capable of responding. But what exactly does it mean for mental images to depict the logistic content of reason's beliefs? What do such images look like? Although Timaeus does not make this part of his account explicit, the *Philebus* illuminates how we might fill in some of the details.[19] In his discussion of "false pleasures," Socrates explains that (at least some of) our perceptual experiences and affective states involve both a "scribe" and a "painter" in our souls (38c–40e). For example, if a man sees something standing in the distance, he might question what it is and silently conclude to himself, "It is a man." This conclusion, Socrates says, is "written" in our souls by the scribe, and that inscription constitutes a belief (*doxa*) and a *logos*. But there is also a "painter" in our souls, who follows the scribe and illustrates the scribe's *logoi*. This process, moreover, occurs not just in the case of present perceptual experiences, but also in cases of remembering the past or imagining the future. Thus, for instance, Socrates says that "hopes" often involve *logoi* that assert our expectations about the future. "But there are also those painted images (*phantasmata ezōgraphēmena*)," he explains, "and someone often envisions himself in the possession of an enormous amount of gold and a lot of pleasures as a consequence. And in addition, he also sees, in this inner picture (*enezōgraphēmenon*), that he is beside himself with delight" (40a9–12). Socrates goes on to explain that the same sort of analysis applies "in the case of fear, *thumos*, and everything of that sort" (40e2–5).

This account has several striking points of contact with the *Timaeus*. Both draw a distinction between *logoi* on the one hand and mental images on the other; both describe those images as "visions" (*phantasmata*) or "painted pictures"; both characterize belief or *doxa* as a form of *logos*; and the *Philebus* explicitly applies its dualistic painter-scribe account to same class of states that Timaeus attributes to the mortal soul: pleasures, pains, hopes, fears, and anger.[20] The account of the *Philebus*, therefore, provides useful resources for reconstructing a like-minded interpretation of intrapsychic communication in the *Timaeus*. According to the model that Socrates' characterization of hope suggests, a person's mental images can depict the agent themselves, along

---

[19] My reading of the *Philebus* largely follows the more detailed accounts offered by Lorenz (2012; cf. 2006a: 99–110), Moss (2012a), and Russell (2005: 176–83). For discussions of, and controversy related to, the content of the scribe's and painter's products, see Butler (2007: 111–15 and nn. 40–2), Dybikowski (1970), Evans (2008), Frede (1985), Gosling (1959), Gosling and Taylor (1982: 431–44), Harte (2004), Kenny (1960), Penner (1970), and Thein (2012). Thein's account, which downplays the role of mental images and even takes the content of the "painter's" illustrations to be propositional or (in my terms) logistic, represents the sharpest contrast to my interpretation.

[20] In fact, the only states Timaeus lists that the *Philebus* does not are boldness and *erōs*, but presumably they are counted under Socrates' "everything of that sort."

with their behavior and affective responses in relation to objects that are motivationally salient (that is, provocative of desire or aversion). Bringing this model to bear on the *Timaeus*, it is reasonable to conclude that rational "commands" involve mental images that depict the agent engaging in the behavior mandated by reason. When we rationally judge that we should or should not do something, in other words, we also *imagine* acting or not acting in those ways, pursuing or not pursuing the objects deemed valuable or disvaluable by reason. Spirit and appetite cannot comprehend the logistic content of reason's beliefs, but they *are* capable of responding to the perceptual content of the visions entertained in the faculty of imagination. Reason communicates its commands to the lower parts of the soul, then, by using mental images to *show* them how the person is supposed to act.

Consider next reason's "threats and encouragements," which seem to be directed especially at the appetitive part when it is disinclined to obey rational commands. Its disobedience, I take it, consists in its resistance to the recommended course of action depicted in imagination. Reason determines that the person should submit to a painful medical procedure, for instance, but appetite motivates the person to forego the treatment out of its aversion to pain; or reason demands abstinence from drinking wine on a given occasion, but appetite motivates the person to indulge anyway because of its desire for pleasure. In cases like these, reason can use the faculty of imagination to draw appetite's attention *either* to features or effects of the action it commands that are likely to be attractive to appetite, *or* to aspects of the proscribed alternative that are likely to be repulsive to it. Mental images of this sort, I am suggesting, constitute reason's "encouragements" or "threats." Hence, for example, reason might draw attention to desirable feelings that the medical procedure will bring about—like the alleviation of whatever present discomfort the treatment is designed to address—or it might highlight the painful headaches or nausea that follow a bout of drinking. Just as hopeful images in the *Philebus* depict the agent's enjoyment of a future pleasure, therefore, reason's "encouragements" involve picturing experiences of appetitive satisfaction that are associated with the beneficial action in question. Conversely, reason's "threats" involve imagining experiences of appetitive *dis*satisfaction associated with a forbidden course of action, and thereby "frightening" appetite into submission.[21] Reason's "commands," therefore, can be reinforced by rational thoughts about features of available courses of action that are

---

[21] The nature of these mental images is also reflected in actual physical feelings that reason is able to produce by means of the liver.

motivationally salient to appetite, which can then be illustrated through imagination in ways that attract or repel appetite and thereby mitigate its resistance to what reason judges best.

The spirited part, meanwhile, is naturally inclined to obey reason's initial commands in the first place, and in addition responds with anger to reason's "declarations" about acts of injustice. The latter, we can speculate, involve remembering some offensive action that the agent has suffered or perpetrated in the past, or imagining an offensive action the agent anticipates suffering or considers perpetrating in the future. Reason issues the judgment that the person has done or suffered (or that they might do or suffer) wrong, and when it does the person also remembers or imagines the injustice in question. Such memories or anticipatory visions may also involve, as in the case of appetite, imagining features of the experience or action that make it especially motivationally salient to spirit, along with associated feelings of spirited satisfaction or dissatisfaction. If an individual has been insulted by another agent, for instance, they might hold the insulting behavior before their memory, while also remembering, say, the presence of their peers at the time and their feelings of embarrassment. If they seeks retribution for the injustice, they might imagine both their intended act of vengeance as well as the spirited enjoyment and pride they would feel in executing it. Similarly, if reason determines that the appetites themselves are motivating the person to act unjustly—for instance, indulging in an illicit sexual act—the individual might imagine not only the act itself but also the looks of disgust they would receive from others if they were caught, or the feelings of shame they would experience having acted that way. The effect of those mental images is that the individual's spirited part will be roused to support reason in retaliating against the offending agent or in resisting their own appetitive urges.[22]

Here I would like to consider a potential objection to the imagistic interpretation. If reason communicates by means of mental images, and spirit and appetite are incapable of comprehending logistic content, then why does Plato regularly characterize intrapsychic communication using the language of interpersonal speech? Why does reason "command," "declare," or "threaten," and why is spirit described as "listening" or "obeying"? There are three points

---

[22] As I discuss in Wilburn (2014c: 641–5), Plato's imagistic account as I present it has important points of continuity with related views found both in Aristotle and in later thinkers like Posidonius and Galen, who interpret and borrow from Platonic psychology. See, for example, *PHP* 5.6.23–8, where Galen approvingly cites Posidonius' suggestion that it is impossible to "move the irrational with reason" (λόγῳ κινήσειε τὸ ἄλογον) unless one places before it "some kind of painted picture that resembles a perception" (τινα ἀναζωγράφησιν αἰσθητῇ παραπλησιαν).

to note here. The first is that Timaeus makes heavy use of martial metaphors throughout his cosmological account. For example, he explains that the "bile and serum and phlegm of every sort" that contaminate our veins in times of disease "are hostile to one another...and they wage a destructive and devastating war against the constituents of the body that have stayed intact and kept to their post" (82e–83a). This language is especially prevalent in Timaeus' characterization of the spirited part of the soul, whose function is clearly supposed to parallel that of the "guardians" of the city whom Socrates describes at the beginning of the dialogue.[23] Just as their job is to protect the *city* against injustice "whether it be from someone outside or even from someone within" (17d2–4), so spirit is stationed in the "guardhouse," where it protects the *individual* against injustice, "whether it be from someone outside or even from one of the appetites within" (70b5). The martial metaphor justifies the language of "listening to" or "obeying" reason's "commands," but it need not suggest that spirit responds directly to a verbal order in the same way a soldier does.

The second point is that early Greek literature often characterizes *thumos* as a participant in internal dialogue. In Homer especially, *thumos* often serves an interlocutory function, particularly in times of crisis or indecision: it can be the recipient of speech—as implied when Odysseus "rebukes his heart with word"—and sometimes it is even itself described as "having spoken" to the person (although no quoted speech is ever attributed to it).[24] This Homeric use of *thumos* makes it natural for Plato to describe spirit's relationship with reason using the language of interpersonal conversation, but we need not conclude he thereby commits himself to thinking *thumos* can do all the same things it can do in epic literature. On the contrary, Plato's theory of tripartition, unlike Homer's fluid and poetic use of psychological terminology, represents a self-conscious effort to provide a worked out *account* of the human soul. Its philosophical ambitions mean that it is informed by many of Plato's theoretical commitments (including his conception of the rational/-non-rational distinction), and those commitments naturally place limitations on the extent to which he accepts earlier uses of *thumos* exactly and literally as he finds them. According to my interpretation, then, the Homeric depiction of

---

[23] Taylor (1928: 500–4) describes these parallels in detail.

[24] For examples from Homer, see Intro., n. 23. Outside of Homer, too, spirit can both be affected by someone else's speech as well as motivate a person to deliver (typically angry) speech to another person. For example: "These [prophecies] are the arrows which, like an archer, since you have provoked me, I have shot in anger (θυμῷ) at your heart (καρδίας)" (Sophocles, *Ant.* 1084–6). See also Theognis, *El.* 2.1321–2; Sophocles, *Ajax* 1124 and *Oed. Tyr.* 334–44; Aeschylus, *Supp.* 446–8; Euripides, *Electra* 577–8; Praxilla, fr. 748; and Stesichorus, fr. S11.5–6.

thumos' participation in internal discourse does indeed find its way into Plato's account, but Plato fills in the cognitive details in a way that fits with the rest of his theory.

The third, and most important, reason for Timaeus' use of language that implies verbal or logistic content is that such content *does*, in fact, have a central role in reason's communications with spirit and appetite. According to the imagistic account, rational judgments *themselves* take the form of speech, and it is those judgments that are in turn depicted by imagination. Just as the writings of the scribe determine the painter's illustrations in the *Philebus*, so the logistic content of reason's judgments informs the mental images that accompany them. Therefore, while Timaeus' account may preclude the possibility that spirit understands logistic content as such, there is no need to explain away the presence or significance of such content. On the imagistic account, speech plays an integral part in intrapsychic communication.

I would now like to highlight an aspect of the imagistic account that I take to be one of its strengths, which concerns what I have been referring to as its "minimalism." Simply put, my account permits that each of the person's cognitive capacities—belief, sense-perception, and so on—is a single, integrated, undivided capacity. In that respect my interpretation can be contrasted with pluralistic accounts that assign to each separate soul part (at least some) discrete cognitive faculties of its *own* that can operate independently of duplicate faculties of the other parts. On my interpretation, each part of the soul is a distinct source or subject of *motivations*, but not of a separate cognitive life. The soul's motivational faculty is complex, but each one of its cognitive faculties is simple.

Consider the following sketch of this minimalist picture. As I argued above, some of our cognitive faculties are rational in the sense that they require and are constituted by the motions and activities of the reasoning part of the soul. This prominently includes the capacities to form propositional beliefs and make use of speech, as well as related faculties like knowledge, understanding, deliberation, and thought. Because these are rational faculties, and because the person has only one reasoning part of the soul, the person possesses only one of each of them. Spirit and appetite, therefore, neither possess their own separate faculties of belief or speech or the rest, nor do they comprehend the logistic content that comprises or is generated by reason's use of those faculties. When the person believes or knows or deliberates, only the reasoning part of their psychology is directly involved in and responsible for that believing or knowing or deliberating.

The non-rational faculties of sense-perception, memory, and imagination are also unified, but unlike the rational powers, they and their content are cognitively available to all three parts of the soul. This means that when one of these faculties is in use, all three parts of the soul experience or have access to its content. When we sense or remember or imagine something, in other words, we do not experience three separate perceptions or memories or mental images of the object, one for each part of the soul; rather, we have *one* perception, memory, or mental image that is common to all three parts. Indeed, Timaeus' characterization of sensory processes throughout his discussion emphasizes the unity of perception: a single perceptual experience registers simply on the *soul*.[25]

On the minimalist account, therefore, the soul's motivational complexity does not require a corresponding cognitive complexity. Rather, the motivational threeness of the soul is due to the fact that each of its parts—through a combination of nature, habit, and education—is "wired up" to desire and be averse to different sorts of things. When the person as a whole perceives, remembers, or imagines something, certain features of the perceptual experience or mental image will be motivationally salient to one part, but might not be salient, or be salient in an oppositely charged way, to one or more of the other parts. Leontius, for instance, has just a single, integrated perception that constitutes his experience of seeing the corpse lying by the executioner, but his appetite and spirit react differently to that perceptual content: what he sees activates an appetitive desire but spirited disgust. In any given case, then, there is just *one* perception or memory or mental image, but potentially three distinct motivational responses to it.

Note, however, that there is an important difference between sense-perception on the one hand and memory and imagination on the other: the latter but not the former are (at least partly) within our voluntary control. As Aristotle points out, we cannot see or hear or taste things at will, because perception depends on the presence of external objects, but by contrast, "imagining lies within our own power whenever we want."[26] According to the imagistic account, one way of exercising this power or control over the imaginative faculty occurs when reason issues judgments about how to act and

---

[25] Cf. Lorenz (2012: 242–3), and for textual examples, see the citations above in the main text, as well as 64a–c, where Timaeus contrasts unperceived and perceived forms of bodily disturbances and takes the latter to be "passed on in a chain reaction" that extends throughout the body to the entire soul, resulting in perception. For further discussion of Plato's theory of perception in the *Timaeus*, see Silverman (1990 and 1991) and Fletcher (2016).

[26] *DA* 417a1–9, 427b17–18.

thereby causes memory or imagination to illustrate the content of its thoughts. Because there is just one integrated faculty of imagination, the mortal parts of the soul immediately become aware of, and can therefore react to, that content.

In short, the minimalist imagistic account is an economical one that permits the unity of human cognition and consciousness. By contrast, pluralistic accounts are theoretically expensive in their doubling or tripling of each of our cognitive powers, tend to raise more questions than they answer, and are difficult to square with human experience.[27] If each of the three parts of the soul possessed its own discrete cognitive powers, especially ones like belief and speech, our psychology would be fragmented in ways that defy the phenomenology of consciousness.[28] For while we are certainly familiar with multiplicity and conflict among our desires, most of us do not experience similar disunity in cognition. For example, we do not experience three separate, simultaneous "seeings" when we look at something; we have just *one* visual experience. The same goes when we remember something or make use of our imagination. Likewise, we do not typically find ourselves with three simultaneous internal dialogues that can be at odds with one another, or three

[27] Cairns (2014) presents a compelling skeptical challenge to commentators on both sides of the literal and deflationary debate. He claims that Plato's approach is *always* metaphorical: we only hear what the soul is *like*, never the full and true account of what it by nature *is*, and Plato always flags his discussions as contextually useful approximations to the truth (para. 80). Cairns is pessimistic about the project of trying to "get behind" these metaphors, however: "To attempt to sort out what is and is not literal about these metaphorical agents is a confusion" (para. 77), and "The only answer to the question of what these metaphorical agents *really* do is 'nothing'. The only real agent in all of this is the person as such" (para. 73). I have a few responses. (1) First, I am not entirely persuaded that Plato's accounts of psychology are always and exclusively metaphorical. Cairns sometimes seems to conflate Plato's uses of metaphor with his concessions of fallibility. For Timaeus to say that his account is only "likely," for example, is not the same as indicating that everything he has said about the soul is mere metaphor. (2) Second, it is worth noting that Plato's own students and successors show no hesitation about interpreting his metaphors. Aristotle's psychology is clearly influenced by his understanding of how to cash out the details of Plato's theory, for instance, and Platonist commentators readily interpret Plato's myths and metaphors in precisely the sorts of ways Cairns criticizes. (See, e.g., Galen, *PHP* 6.2.4.) (3) Finally, however, I am actually sympathetic to Cairns' main point. As I understand my project in this chapter (and other relevant sections of this book), my goal is not to figure out what kinds of "agents" appetite and spirit are. Like Cairns, I am not committed to, and am skeptical of, their being agents of *any* kind. My primary interest, rather, is in determining what Plato thinks about the cognitive conditions that give rise to motivations generated by the different parts of our souls. My claims can all be reframed (quite happily, as far as I am concerned) in terms of what *we the agent* experience and do. My main thesis in this chapter, then, would be that our appetitive and spirited *motivations* are stimulated by images and sense-perception, rather than by speech and reasoning as such.

[28] Cf. Price (2009: 10), who takes the unity of consciousness, or "co-consciousness" of the soul's three parts, to be a decisive obstacle to identifying them as agent-like. Weinstein (2018: 260–1) concurs, taking the three parts to share a "common awareness" of the world. Note that in what follows I make general claims about conscious phenomenology, but I do not mean to disallow the possibility of exceptions or different ways of experiencing mental life. The important point is simply that the unity of consciousness is at least a *common* and *widespread* experience, and hence that it would be a glaring strike against Plato's theory (and one we have no reason to believe would escape him) if it could not account for such unity.

competing sets of potentially conflicting (conscious, occurrent, propositional) beliefs. We can certainly experience uncertainty, vacillate in our commitments, engage in a scattered or erratic train of thought, and change our minds, but such variability in our thinking is diachronic, not synchronic. Importantly, moreover, I see no grounds for thinking that Plato would have rejected these general claims or that he viewed psychological life differently. The minimalist line of interpretation, then, makes sense of human cognition and intrapsychic communication at a low theoretical cost, while also preserving the unity of conscious experience.[29]

3. Cognition and Communication in the *Republic*

Finally, I would like to consider how this understanding of intrapsychic communication relates to the *Republic*'s account of early education as sketched

---

[29] Note that my view does *not* require a "good-dependent" or agathistic understanding of non-rational motivation, according to which appetite and spirit do some combination of the following: pursue or aim at the good, represent or conceive of their objects as good, or believe or judge their objects to be good. Indeed, my interpretation is straightforwardly *incompatible* with some such views: if appetite and spirit cannot form concepts or beliefs with logistic content, it follows trivially that they cannot form them about the good. However, my account *is* compatible with at least two weaker kinds of good-dependence. First, Kamtekar (2017: Ch. 4) defends an agathistic reading and suggests ways that desires or actions can count as aiming at the good without requiring the soul parts or agents involved to conceive of their objects in terms of goodness. One such proposal appeals to the teleology of the *Timaeus*: because having non-rational parts is beneficial to us (given necessary facts of embodiment), their motivations are in an important sense good-directed, regardless of how appetite and spirit themselves perceive their objects. My interpretation is compatible with (and I myself accept) this weak sense of good-dependence. A second, more complicated case concerns a line of interpretation developed by Jessica Moss (2006: 524–30; 2008; 2012a; forthcoming). She accepts, as I do, that appetite and spirit are limited to resources of images and perception, but argues that they *perceive* their objects as good. She explains, "'Good' here is relatively undemanding: it certainly need not mean 'morally good,' nor 'beneficial,' nor 'best all things considered,' but it does mean more than simply 'desired'" (2008: 62). I have two main worries about this view. (1) First, once one subtracts morality *and* benefit *and* optimalness from the good, I start to wonder how much the notion that remains resembles anything that *Plato* would recognize as goodness. (2) Moreover, whatever *is* left of goodness becomes explanatorily idle. On my interpretation, we can explain why appetite motivates us to pursue a pleasant object simply in terms of the dual facts that appetite desires physical pleasure, and physical pleasure and its sources are perceptible. No additional work is done by insisting that we perceive the object not only as pleasurable, but also as *good*. Cf. Renaut (2020: 104, n. 2). All of that said, nothing in my account *requires* me to deny the perceptibility of (at least some forms of) goodness, and if goodness turns out to be perceptible in some way, then my imagistic minimalism can accommodate this further sense of good-dependence. For various agathistic interpretations, see Bobonich (2002: 252–3 and 2017: 10–16), Brickhouse and Smith (2010: 211–12), Carone (2001), Hoffman (2003), Lesses (1987: 149), Morris (2006: 220), and Weiss (2006: Ch. 6). For anti-agathistic or good-*independence* views, see Ganson (2009), Gosling (1990: 20–2), Kahn (1987), and Penner (1971: 103–11 and 1990: 49–61). Irwin (1977: 191–5 and 1995a: 209–17) and Reeve (1988: 135–40) both advocate "mixed" views according to which appetites are good-independent, but spirited desires *partially* aim at the good. Finally, Weinstein (2018: 71–8 and n. 37; cf. 226–7) makes a convincing case that the dispute between the two camps is largely verbal.

in Chapters 6 and 7, focusing on the relationship that music is designed to foster between spirit and reason. Note that we have good reason for thinking Plato continues to have something like the *Republic*'s early educational program in mind when he writes the *Timaeus*. The dialogue begins with a recapitulation by Socrates and Timaeus of a conversation they had the day before about "the kind of political structure cities should have and the kind of men who should make it up so as to be the best possible" (17c–19a). The political system they describe bears striking resemblance to that of the Kallipolis on several points. It consists of a guardian class that is separated from the rest of the citizens; the guardian class includes women among its warriors; the guardians are forbidden from owning private property; and spouses and children are to be shared in "common" so that the guardians all consider one another family. Of special importance for present purposes, the education of the guardians consists of a combination of musical and gymnastic training that aims at producing the same psychological profile we find in the Kallipolis: the guardians must be both "spirited" and "philosophical" so that they are "gentle" (*praioi*) to "friends" (*philoi*) and "harsh" (*chalepoi*) to their "enemies" (*echthroi*).[30] Just like the noble dogs and warriors of *Republic* 2, then, the guardians of the *Timaeus* must possess a combination of spirited gentleness and harshness. Socrates and Timaeus provide only a brief sketch, and we need not think the city they are describing is supposed to be identical with the Kallipolis, or that the previous conversation to which they are referring is the very one Socrates recounts in the *Republic* itself.[31] Nonetheless, it is reasonable to conclude that Plato means to put the reader in mind of the Kallipolis and some of its outstanding political features, including its account of early education.[32] If that is right, then we are justified in considering how the *Timaeus*' account of cognition and intrapsychic

[30] For discussion of education in the *Timaeus* and its relation to the program of the *Republic*, see Scolnicov (1997) and Sedley (1997). Gill (2000: 68) and Johansen (2004: 155–6) both note that at *Tim.* 88b–89a Timaeus characterizes gymnastic training as training for the *body*, rather than explicitly for the spirited part of the soul as in the *Republic*. This merely represents a difference in emphasis, however (as Johansen agrees, p. 158). Even in the earlier dialogue, Socrates never denies that gymnastics benefits the body. He thinks its more important effects are on the soul, but grants that it also trains the body "as a byproduct" (πάρεργον, 411e7). It makes sense, therefore, that Timaeus, whose focus is on the relation between psychology and *physiology*, would highlight that aspect of gymnastic education.

[31] Johansen (2004: 9–11) claims the city's political structure differs from that of the Kallipolis, in that the *Timaeus*' guardians are described as a single class, with no mention of a distinction between philosophers and auxiliaries. I am not entirely convinced by this point, however. Even in the *Republic*, including in Book 5, Socrates sometimes uses the term "guardians" to refer to auxiliaries and philosophers collectively. Cf. Popper (1962: 46–7).

[32] Cf. Sedley (2007: 95–6).

communication might be informed by, or usefully applied to, the musical and gymnastic program of the *Republic*.

Of course, this argument establishes at most that when Plato wrote the *Timaeus*, he took its cognitive theory to be consistent with and relevant to the sort of educational system he outlined in the (presumptively) earlier dialogue. It does not show that when he wrote the *Republic*, Plato already had that cognitive theory in mind. And I do not intend to argue that he did. However, I do think the account of the *Republic* fits remarkably well with the cognitive account of the *Timaeus*, that nothing in the former contradicts the latter, and that the two theories are mutually illuminating. Note, moreover, that the *Republic* seems to be committed to two central assumptions on which the imagistic account of the *Timaeus* rests. The first is that (at least some of) the content of rational *logoi* can be represented in the form of images or other perceptual content. In the *Republic* this idea seems to be anticipated by Socrates' view (discussed in Chapter 7.3) that paintings and other cultural products are "similar to," "akin to," or "imitations of" corresponding types of speech, and that speech in turn is akin to or modeled on corresponding types of behavior and character. Indeed, poetry itself is a form of speech that "imitates human beings acting voluntarily or under compulsion ... and experiencing either pleasure or pain in all this" (603c4–8). However the details of this theory of imitation or kinship are to be filled in, Socrates clearly appeals to some version of the idea that similar content can be represented in both perceptible and logistic forms.

The second assumption is that the non-rational parts of the soul have cognitive access to, and are especially responsive to, the content of sense-perception and imagination. To begin with, Socrates is explicit in the *Republic* that the *entire* soul shares the perceptual experiences that constitute pleasure and pain. In Book 5 he explains that when someone hurts their finger, "the entire community that binds body and soul together into a single system under the ruling part within it perceives this, and the whole feels the pain along with the part that suffers." The same is true anytime someone experiences bodily pleasure or pain, Socrates says, and this is precisely why such pleasure or pain is attributed to the *person* as a whole (462c10–d5). On this account, all three parts of the soul are evidently aware of and affected by the person's sensory perceptions. Socrates hints at a similar understanding of the faculty of imagination. In Book 9 he distinguishes "lawless appetites" from lawful ones, and when Adeimantus asks what he means by the former, Socrates responds:

Those that are awakened in sleep, when the rest of the soul—the rational, gentle, and ruling part—slumbers. Then the beastly and savage part, full of food and drink, casts off sleep and seeks to find a way to gratify itself. You know that there is nothing it won't dare to do at such a time, free of all control by shame (*aischunēs*) or thought (*phronēseōs*). It doesn't shrink from trying to have sex with a mother, as it supposes, or with anyone else at all, whether man, god, or beast. It will commit any foul murder, and there is no food it refuses to eat. In a word, it omits no act of folly (*anoias*) or shamelessness (*anaischuntias*).   (571c3–d4)[33]

Here Socrates, like Timaeus, establishes a special connection between appetite and the mental images that constitute dreams: the appetitive part is stimulated by, and somehow responsible for, oneiric content.[34] Appetite's ability to produce and indulge in perverse dreams, moreover, is due to the inactivity or dormancy of the other two parts during sleep. The implication is that when the person is awake, all *three* parts of the soul have access to, and play some part in controlling, imagination. The reason the person does not fantasize about unspeakable behavior and experiences while awake is that spirited shame and reason do not permit it. If this is right, then Socrates' brief comments here suggest that the faculty of imagination is a unified one to which all three soul parts have cognitive access, just as in the *Timaeus*.

The *Republic* also provides reason for thinking the non-rational parts of the soul are especially sensitive to and impressed by imagistic or perceptual content.[35] In the case of appetite, of course, many of its desires are direct responses to, or aim at, bodily feelings associated with pleasure and pain. Note also that Leontius' appetite is a desire to "look" (*idein*) at a "spectacle" (*theama*), having "perceived" (*aisthomenos*) the corpses, which is why his anger is directed at his *eyes* (439e8–440a3). *Thumos*, for its part, is similarly oriented toward the perceptible world. The primitive spirited gentleness and aggression of noble dogs is a reaction to the "sight" (*opsis*, 376b7) of a perceived friend or enemy, and more generally, the spirited part is concerned with the world of appearances—with reputation, how things seem, conspicuous signs of

---

[33] When a moderate man sleeps, by contrast, "the visions that appear in his dreams are least lawless" (571d6–572b1).

[34] Thein (2019) offers an interpretation of dreaming in *Republic* and *Timaeus* that is informed by a different understanding of tripartite theory than my own, but his view does not contradict the modest point that appetite can be responsive to, or involved in the production of, dream content.

[35] Cf. Renaut (2020: 115).

honor and victory (or dishonor and failure), public signs and expressions of approval, and the safety of their *oikeioi* and triumph over threatening *allotrioi*. Hence it is the part that is shaped by the resounding "shouts and claps" (*ekboōntes kai krotountes*, 492b9) of the many's praise and blame. In Book 10, moreover, Socrates seems to confirm a cognitive picture in which the non-rational parts of the soul are especially responsive to perceptual or imagistic content.[36] He begins by describing cases in which the way things appear—in particular, how they *look* or *sound*—differ from the way they actually are. For example, objects "appear through the faculty of sight (*tēs opseōs*)" to be different sizes when they are close than they do when they are far; the same thing appears crooked in the water but straight outside of it "to those who are looking" at it; and paintings produce illusory appearances "because our eyes our misled by its colors" (602c7–d4). Poetry, meanwhile, "paints colored pictures (*epichrōmatizein*) with words and phrases" using "the colors of music" (601a4–b4), just as painters do with "shapes and colors"; it both imitates and produces "images" (*eidōla*) (600e5); and it is an "imitation we hear" that has deceptive effects analogous to those of painting (603b6–7). In this context Socrates distinguishes between the "foolish," "inferior," or "irrational" part of the soul on the one hand and the "best" or "rational" part on the other. The latter is able to use measurement, weighing, and calculation as correctives against perceptual illusion, and thereby to and judge things as they truly are. The irrational part, however, "cannot distinguish large from small," is unaffected by measurement and reasoning, accepts "images that are far removed from truth," and as a result "believes" that things are the way they look or sound (602c–605c).[37] Importantly, Socrates later explicitly identifies this "foolish" part as the psychic source of sexual desire, appetites, and anger (*thumos*), which suggests that it is meant to encompass both non-rational parts of the soul (606d1–4). If that is right, then Socrates depicts the spirited and appetitive parts as subject to the illusory effects of images, appearances, sights, and sounds.[38] Although this passage is the subject of a great deal of controversy,

---

[36] Cf. Gerson (2003a: 244–5 and n. 9).

[37] Cf. Storey (2014), who argues that perception in the *Republic* has an assertoric character that supplies the content of the lower parts' "beliefs." He draws special attention to 523a–524e, where perception "gives reports," "declares," "says," "gives interpretations," and makes "announcements" to the soul (pp. 110–13).

[38] Bobonich (2017: 17) raises a challenge for the view that the lower parts are *always* taken in by perceptual illusions: "Could Plato have really supposed that Greek soldiers on seeing hordes of Persian troops at a great distance suddenly found that their fear vanished and their spirited parts gloated in the belief that the Persians were literally the size of ants?" I agree with him that the answer here clearly must be "no." The reason for that, however, can still be explained in terms of imagistic content. They have access both to memories of nearby soldiers based on past experience, as well as to the content involved in anticipating and imagining the soldiers up close in the imminent future, and on that basis (rather

this much, at least, should not be especially contentious: that in Book 10 Socrates depicts the irrational element of the soul as being especially reliant on, and responsive to, perceptual content, while being comparatively unmoved by rational thought as such. This modest conclusion, in conjunction with the fact that appetitive and spirited desires are oriented toward the perceptible world of human affairs, hints at similar commitments to those that animate the cognitive account of the *Timaeus*.

Let us, then, consider how the theories of the two dialogues bear on one another. As we have seen, in its training of the spirited part, Socrates' musical program focuses on what the young guardians "see" and "hear," curates their environment with "images" of virtue rather than vice, and aims to ensure that "admirable works will strike their eyes and ears." Those images of virtue are, in turn, akin to virtuous *logoi*. When the person begins reasoning, their rational part starts issuing its own *logoi* about how to act, which spirit "recognizes" and "warmly welcomes" as *oikeioi*, and which it is disposed to support and obey (400e–402d). In the *Republic* itself, Plato never addresses the intrapsychic mechanics of spirit's "recognition" and comprehension of reason, but the imagistic account of the *Timaeus* allows us to supply the missing details. When the person reasons, their *logoi* are accompanied by mental images that depict their content. Importantly, moreover, those mental images have the same kind of perceptible content as the "images of virtue" that have become *oikeia* to the person through their socialization and musical education. Spirit "recognizes" reason, then, because the visions that illustrate rational content in the person's imagination *look like* the external images that constitute the person's familiar social and cultural environment. When reason recommends an act of courage in a given instance, for example, the person imagines that action, and the content of that mental image resembles not only the acts of courage that have been praised and held up as examples of admirable behavior in the Kallipolis, but also the "imitations" of courage that are found in the city's artifacts and music. Presumably, we can add, the mental image might also prominently involve picturing any of the person's own actual *oikeioi*—their family, friends, or fellow citizens—who are associated with the action in question, either because the courageous act involves protecting or saving them, or because the act is likely to result in their approval and praise. It might also, conversely, include imagining the *allotrion* enemy

than, say, mathematical calculations of size), appetite and spirit are capable of responding in the expected ways. Even many non-rational animals, it should be noted, have perceptual (including size) constancy.

that needs to be resisted. Because the behavior commanded by reason is "familiar" to spirit in these ways (and may involve aggression against the unfamiliar), *thumos* will be inclined to obey and execute it. This point, furthermore, fills in something that is missing from the *Timaeus*' account, which is an explanation of *why* spirit tends to obey reason's orders and to "boil over" at its declarations about injustice. The answer is that the mental images associated with rational communication depict actions that are "familiar" to spirit and involve protecting what has come to be *oikeion* to it. Where the *Timaeus* provides the resources for explaining how spirit understands reason in the first place, therefore, the *Republic* provides the resources for explaining why, having understood it, spirit is disposed to support and obey it. In these ways the theories of the two dialogues are complementary.

PART IV

9

Spirited Psychology and Civic Temperament in the *Statesman*

In preceding chapters I have argued that Plato conceives of *thumos* as the social and political part of the soul. Within the framework of his tripartite theory, it is the part responsible for the motivations that make political communities possible, and addressing central problems related to social and civic life requires attention to the spirited desires, emotions, and tendencies of human beings. In the remaining two chapters, I aim to show that Plato continues to conceive of spirited motivations in these ways in two of his late political works, the *Statesman* and the *Laws*. In both dialogues, I argue, the psychological phenomena Plato attributes to *thumos* under tripartite theory play a crucial, and often underappreciated, role in his characterization and treatment of social and political issues. Like the dialogues I discussed in Chapters 4 and 5—ones traditionally assumed to *predate* the *Republic*—these later works do not explicitly mention or endorse tripartition of the soul. There is an important asymmetry between the earlier works and the later, however, which makes the case for concluding that Plato accepted tripartite theory when he wrote the *Statesman* and *Laws* stronger than it was in the case of dialogues like *Protagoras* and *Gorgias*. In the case of the later works we know that Plato had *already* conceived of the three-part soul, thought about it at great length, and worked out many of its details. Because we cannot know that about him in the case of his early works, it is plausible that his treatment of spirited motivations in those dialogues represented beginning stages in his thinking about *thumos* that would eventually culminate in, but did not yet reflect, his worked-out conception of a tripartite soul. It is comparatively *less* likely that Plato did not still have tripartition in mind when he wrote the later works, however, given how strikingly they appear to take for granted, and to draw on the resources of, precisely that theory and its understanding of spirit. Indeed, I aim to show that aspects of both dialogues make more sense if we consider Plato's thinking about *thumos* and spirited motivation.

The Political Soul: Plato on Thumos, *Spirited Motivation, and the City*. Josh Wilburn, Oxford University Press.
© Josh Wilburn 2021. DOI: 10.1093/oso/9780198861867.003.0009

In this chapter I focus on the *Statesman*. My main thesis is that the dialogue characterizes the task of the statesman or *politikos* as one that prominently requires attention to distinctively spirited aspects of the human soul. My arguments will be based on two key passages from the text—the Myth of Cronus and the final discussion of civic temperament. In Section 1, I examine the myth and argue that it deliberately depicts a human-like race that is devoid of any spirited motivations (or any need for them) and likewise any social or political relationships. The Myth of Cronus is designed to expose the inadequacy of the notion of politics as mere "herding," which is explored early in the dialogue but which does not give due attention to the *social* desires and emotions of human beings. Such motivations, however, are precisely the ones with which politics must deal first and foremost. This prepares the way for the second key passage, the Eleatic Visitor's treatment of civic unity at the dialogue's conclusion, which I examine in Sections 2 and 3. On the Visitor's view, the primary problem of politics is that of producing harmony between, or "weaving" together, two main types of citizens: the "courageous" and the "moderate." Tension between the two groups is the source of political conflict, and civic unity and stability, therefore, require reconciliation between them. On my interpretation, the Visitor's treatment of civic unity is largely a discussion of spirited political psychology: the "courageous" citizens incline toward behavior associated with the aggressive side of *thumos*, while the "moderate" tend toward behavior associated with its gentle side. On this view, the central problem of politics turns out to demand attention to the role spirit plays in human behavior and civic relationships.[1]

1. The Myth of Cronus

The Athenian Visitor and his interlocutor, Young Socrates, conduct their investigation into the nature of the statesman by means of a taxonomical

[1] Several commentators draw on the language of tripartition in their interpretations of the *Statesman*—for example, Arends (1993: 174), Dorter (1994: 227), Márquez (2012: 86), Miller (1980: 86, 105), and Rosen (1995: 154)—but most stop short of explicitly affirming Plato's continued commitment to the theory. Miller (1980: 135, n. 44) is an exception. Skemp (1952: 229, n. 1) and White (2007: 125) deny that tripartition plays a role in the *Statesman*, while Annas (1995: x), Bobonich (1995: 328–9), and Lane (1995: 277) all perceive at least a shift in Plato's psychology. For general discussion of the place of the *Statesman* in Plato's *political* thought in relation to *Republic* and *Laws*, see Annas (1995), Kahn (1995 and 2008: 160–1), Klosko (2006: Ch. 11), Lane (1998: 3–6), Márquez (2012: 11–22), McCabe (1997: 97–8, 112–17), Rowe (1995: 27–8, n. 98 and 2000: 238–9), and Skemp (1952: 40–7). I concur with Kahn's (1995: 54) assessment that "at the high level of theory . . . Plato's political ideal shows no change or development between the *Republic* and the *Statesman* or between the *Statesman* and the *Laws*"; cf. Gill (1995: 301).

method of collection and division. At the beginning of the dialogue, they pursue a line of inquiry that culminates in a characterization of statesmanship as a form of "herd-maintenance" (*agelaiotrophikē*, 261e8) or shepherding (*nomeutikē*, 267b7) that renders the *politikos* analogous to "stock-farmers of horses or cattle" (261d–e).[2] In particular, statesmanship is the branch of knowledge concerned with the herding of hornless, non-interbreeding, two-footed animals (267a–c). The Visitor, however, is dissatisfied with this definition, noting a crucial disanalogy between ordinary shepherds and statesmen. The former have uncontested, exclusive responsibility for maintaining their herds, whereas the statesman faces a wide variety of rivals—doctors, gymnastic trainers, farmers, and merchants, for instance—who *also* claim responsibility for human maintenance (267c–268c). Their conclusion therefore, was premature: their discussion has failed to differentiate statesmanship sufficiently from other human occupations.

In response the Visitor proposes they make a fresh start, beginning with a bit of "play" in the form of a myth in which he distinguishes two alternating cosmological epochs (268d–274e).[3] During the first, the universe is under the direct supervision of the god Cronus, who is personally responsible for its revolving motion and who guides and manages the world and its inhabitants. The god cannot supervise the universe interminably, however, and when the "right moment" (*kairos*) arrives he withdraws his direct control and lets go of the *cosmos*, which then begins revolving backwards in the opposite direction. During this second cosmic epoch, the *cosmos* becomes increasingly chaotic and filled with wickedness and "whatever is harsh (*chalepa*) and unjust (*adika*)" in it, until at last the god intervenes and resumes his control, and the cycle repeats itself.

The crucial details of the myth for present purposes concern the Visitor's contrasting descriptions of life in the Age of Cronus versus in the second era, commonly referred to as the Age of Zeus. To begin with, biological processes

---

[2] The Athenian uses numerous forms of, and terms related to, ἀγειλαιοτροφική and νομευτική throughout this early discussion (e.g. ἀγειλαιοτροφία, 263c4; τοῖς περὶ τὰ ἀνθρώπινα νομεύσιν, 267e9). Cf. also ἀνθρωπονομική, 267c2, 266e8; and κοινοτροφική, 261e2, 264b6, 264d6, 267d11.

[3] Here I follow the majority of scholars in identifying *two* stages in the myth's cosmic cycle. A few commentators, however—notably Brisson (1995), Carone (2005a: Ch. 6), and Rowe (2001)—argue that there are *three* cosmic stages. The two-stage reading is by far the more natural, however, whereas arguments for the three-stage reading seem strained and face compelling objections, many of which are presented in Horn (2012), Kahn (2008: 150–2), Márquez (2012: 128–9), McCabe (1997: 102–8), and Verlinsky (2008 and 2009). Márquez and Kahn, for example, draw attention to features of the myth that are clearly modeled on specific *two*-stage processes: the characterization of the cosmic "long year" in terms of *tropai* encourages comparison to the summer and winter solstices (Márquez), and the myth draws on the two-phase cycle of reversals in Empedoclean cosmology (Kahn). Cf. Skemp (1952: 147, n. 1) and Grube (1980: 278).

themselves were different under Cronus' reign: creatures aged in reverse, growing younger instead of older, all the way through infancy until their bodies simply disappeared. In place of reproduction, moreover, full-grown "grey-haired" adults were born (and reborn) directly from the earth. The god's oversight of living things also meant striking differences in their living conditions:

> A different divine spirit was assigned to every species and every flock, to act as its herdsman, so to speak. Each spirit had sole responsibility (*autarchēs*) for supplying all the needs of the creatures in his charge. As a result, there was no such thing as creatures feeding on one another or savageness (*agrion*) in general, and war (*polemos*) and faction (*stasis*) were completely unknown... God himself was directly responsible for managing the human herd, just as nowadays humans herd inferior species because they are closer to godhood. With the god as their herdsman, there were no governments (*politeiai*), and no possession of wives and children (*ktēseis gunaikōn kai paidōn*), since everyone just came back to life out of the earth, with no memory of their past lives. But even if these kinds of things played no part in their lives, trees and other plants produced huge crops and grew in abundance, without needing to be farmed: the soil yielded them automatically. People spent most of their time roaming around in the open air without clothes or bedding, since the climate was temperate and painless (*alupon*), and the earth produced more than enough grass to provide soft beds.   (271d6–272b1)[4]

Finally, during this time human beings were able to use speech to communicate not only to one another, but with other animals as well.

At the beginning of the Age of Zeus, which the Visitor identifies with the current epoch, human and animal life shifted in the opposite direction toward the familiar conditions of the present time. Creatures began aging from younger to older again, and the ordinary processes of reproduction, birth, and child-rearing replaced autochthonous generation. Because Cronus and his divine assistants stopped supervising living things and providing for all their needs, moreover, humans and animals were left to their own devices, and their experiences and behavior changed dramatically:

> Most animals became wild (*apagriōthentōn*), because they were harsh (*chalepa*) by nature, and started to prey on the weak—and now unguarded

---

[4] Translations of the *Statesman* are from Annas and Waterfield (1995), with modifications.

(*aphulaktoi*)—human race. In these early days, human beings had not yet developed their tools and technical skills; they had been used to being maintained without having to do anything themselves, but now they were deprived of that; they didn't yet know how to provide resources for themselves, since no need had ever forced them to learn in the past. As a result of all this, they were in a very bad way indeed. That is why the gods gave us the gifts we hear about in the ancient tales, along with the necessary teaching (*didachēs*) and education (*paideuseōs*)—fire from Prometheus, the crafts from Hephaestus and the goddess who shares his skill, seeds and plants from others.   (274b6–d2)

This, the Visitor concludes, is the origin of human life as we know it, in which people have to watch over *themselves* in the absence of direct divine control.

The Visitor immediately draws two main lessons from the Myth of Cronus (274e–275c). First, the true "shepherd" or "herdsman" of the human flock is divine and belongs to the Age of Cronus, whereas their goal was to define the *human* statesman on the basis of "how things are today." Because the statesman is human, moreover, it is much more difficult to distinguish him from his subjects either in terms of nature (since they are also human) or in terms of nurture (since he generally receives the same sort of upbringing and education as they do). This, of course, relates to the initial worry that prompted the myth in the first place, which was that the statesman is challenged by various competitors who also claim responsibility for managing human beings. Second, the Visitor concludes, they failed to explain *how* the statesman rules over his fellow human beings, which means their account so far has been incomplete.

My main interpretive claim is that the myth illustrates these shortcomings in large part by depicting humanoid beings who, in the Age of Cronus, live under conditions that do not require spirited motivations and who, accordingly, show no sign of having any.[5] The idea is that the conception of statesmanship as human herding, as it is developed early in the dialogue, fails to account for the spirited nature of the statesman's subjects (and of the

---

[5] Both the myth itself and the Visitor's use of it are complex. My aim is to highlight one important and neglected feature of its role in the dialogue, but my interpretation is compatible with others. For general discussion of the myth, see Ambuel (2013), Blondell (2005), Campbell (1867: xxvii–li), Clark (1995), Cole (1991: 196–201), Dillon (1995), Dorter (1994: 191–5), Ferrari (1995), Hemmenway (1994), Kahn (2008), Klosko (2006: 203–4), Lane (1998: 99–136), Márquez (2012: Chs. 2–3), McCabe (1997), Nightingale (1996), Schäfer (2002), Scodel (1987: Ch. 2), Vidal-Naquet (1978), Weiss (1995), and White (2007: Ch. 2). I have benefited especially from the work of Hemmenway, Kahn, and Márquez.

statesman himself, for that matter), as well as for the conditions of human life that call for social and political motivations associated with *thumos*. The need for (and possibility of) statesmanship only arises in the first place, however, *given* those facts about the role of spirit in human life and psychology. What distinguishes humans in the actual world from the quasi-human wards of the divine shepherd, in other words, is precisely their spiritedness. The job of the *politikos*, therefore, necessarily involves attention to spirited psychology, and to the extent that their earlier definition failed to account for that point, it failed to specify who the statesman is and how he rules.[6]

The case is best articulated in terms of the two faces of *thumos*: the gentle side rooted in affection for the familiar and the aggressive side rooted in hostility toward the foreign. Simply put, under Cronus' rule human beings have nothing *oikeion* to love and care for, nor anything *allotrion* that requires defending against or attacking. Consequently, they possess none of the psychological traits associated with either side of spirit, nor do they engage in any behavior that displays those traits. Consider first the aggressive side, the most primitive expressions of which in the animal world are based on bodily needs: animals prey on one another because they need food and seek sexual partners, and those attacks in turn prompt the need for defense in the service of self-preservation. Divine management of living things, however, means that all creatures' physical needs are met automatically, rendering violence unnecessary and out of place. Indeed, the Visitor explicitly states there is no "savageness" in the Age of Cronus—using one of Plato's favorite terms for primitive spirited aggression—by contrast to the Age of Zeus, in which animals become "savage" and "harsh." Likewise, there is none of the behavior, human or otherwise, that results from feelings of hostility: there are no wars or factions of any kind.

Consider now the gentle side of spirit, which is characteristically expressed in the forms of political fellowship, friendship, love of one's family, emotional attachment to one's private property, and, at the most basic level, protective care for one's own physical body. None of these expressions of spirited affection appears in the Age of Cronus, and the living conditions of that era actually make them all unnecessary or even impossible. First, there are no constitutions, and hence no *cities*, under Cronus' supervision, nor would they

---

[6] Márquez (2012: Ch. 2) similarly suggests that the myth shows that focusing on rationality or appetitive needs omits what is most central to human politics: human sociality and *thumos*. Márquez does not, however, develop this idea as I do. Cf. Rosen (1995: 55), who thinks the Cronus nurslings "lack at a minimum two-thirds of the soul as it is described in the *Republic*" (making them, on his view, appetitive only).

serve any purpose. Here it is useful to call to mind some of Plato's earlier depictions of incipient human communities. In both the myth of the *Protagoras* and *Republic* 2, Plato characterizes the first cities as arising out of human *needs*.[7] People need one another, first of all, for the purpose of protecting themselves against predatory animals or other aggressors. In a world without fighting, however, no such need arises. People also need one another in order to satisfy the exigencies of human life, which diverse individuals with different kinds of technical knowledge collectively provide. In the *Republic*, Socrates identifies the three most basic needs of this sort as food, shelter, and clothing, which are provided through the skills of farming, building, weaving, cobbling, and the like. Yet these are all redundant in the Age of Cronus due to provisions arranged by divine oversight: the earth yields crops automatically, and the temperate climate means that people remain naked and sleep outside. Because human beings lack nothing and have no enemies under the god's supervision, they have no needs which would prompt them to form communities. Likewise, because there are no organized political arrangements, there is also no culture or education, *paideia*. In the absence of cities, people lack the need and opportunity to shape the values of one another through social means. Given the prominent role of spirited motivation in Plato's understanding of education, this once again points to living conditions in which *thumos* appears inconsequential. Second, the Visitor indicates there are no families—no "possession of wives and children"—in the Age of Cronus. The absence of children, of course, follows directly from the biological facts of the time: without sexual reproduction there can be no offspring.[8] Third, the myth strongly implies that people possess no property of their own. Of special note, there are no private homes during this epoch, since people roam from place to place and use only the beds of grass supplied by nature, having none of their own. Finally, perhaps the only candidate for something that counts as *oikeion* for Cronus' humans is their own bodies. Even here, however, spirit's usual roles in relation to physical security and personal well-being appear to have no place. People have no need to protect themselves from other animals

---

[7] Barney (2002: 222–3) discusses the Myth of Cronus in relation to the "healthy" city of pigs of *Republic* 2. I concur with her suggestion that the myth depicts what a community dominated by appetitive life would have to look like in order for it to be self-regulating in the way assumed in the healthy city. On her view, the myth confirms the impossibility of the city of pigs by showing that self-regulation is impossible without radical changes both to the conditions of human existence and to human nature itself. Cf. Márquez (2012: 102–3) and Dorter (1994: 185–6, n. 4), who note other possible allusions to the "city of pigs."

[8] Blondell (2005: 33) even suggests that, given the Greek view that women's primary function is reproduction, women may not exist at all in the Age of Cronus.

or each other, and no need to assert themselves against or compete with others for the sake of resources. There is also no *injustice* in the universe during this time, which means no place for spirited anger. Even spirit's function as a source of endurance has no obvious use, since there appears to be no pain or discomfort in human life. It is especially relevant that the Visitor describes the mildness of the climate as making life "painless" for them, since Plato associates exposure to extreme weather with the development of spirited fortitude.

An additional line of argument emerges out of the relationship between the Cronus myth and the *Theaetetus*, which is the first dialogue, followed by the *Sophist*, in the philosophical trilogy of which the *Statesman* is the conclusion.[9] In the digression of the *Theaetetus*, Socrates sketches a characterization of the philosopher that the mathematician Theodorus enthusiastically endorses, *despite* its being a caricature, and which anticipates the Myth of Cronus in several respects.[10] Socrates indicates that the philosopher does not know his way "to the marketplace, the lawcourts, the assembly, or any other community meeting place in the city"; he knows nothing of "laws (*nomous*) or popular votes"; and he "pays no honor" (*atimasasa*) to "political offices" (*archas*) or "good reputation" (*eudokimein*), nor bothers with "get-togethers, dinners, or revelry." He is incapable of joining his fellow citizens in casting "blame" or "praise" (*en tais loidoriais ... en tois epainois*) and does not especially care about unjust acts among his fellow citizens—the game of "I did you injustice (*adikō*) or you me". He is ignorant of "matters of birth" and finds talk of mothers, fathers, and other ancestors "trivial" and "silly," just as he disdains concerns about personal property and possessions. He is socially inept in both private (*idiai*) and public (*dēmosiai*) life, does not even notice his own next-door neighbor, and ultimately "barely knows whether he is a man or some other kind of creature." Indeed, the "mind" (*dianoia*) of the philosopher is detached from the political world that seems so insignificant to him, and "in reality it is only his body (*sōma*) that lives and sleeps in the city." Not surprisingly, the philosopher holds political activity in no esteem: "When he

---

[9] The opening section of the *Statesman* (257a–258a) establishes a dramatic connection to Plato's *Theaetetus* and *Sophist*, and the *Statesman's* philosophical agenda is established by the opening of the *Sophist*: when the Eleatic Visitor claims that the philosopher, sophist, and statesman are three distinct kinds, Socrates requests to hear each of them distinguished (216a–217b). The *Sophist* and *Statesman*, consequently, each take up the task of analyzing its professional namesake. The three dialogues also share key characters in common—Theaetetus, Young Socrates, Socrates, and Theodorus—and the *Statesman* contains two internal references to the conversation of the *Sophist* (284b7 and 286b9). For discussion of Plato's "trilogy," see Kahn (2007) and Miller (1980: Ch. 1).

[10] My reading of the digression and its relation to the myth mainly echoes, and is heavily indebted to, the excellent work of Hemmenway (1994). Blondell (2005: 26) and Benardete (1984, III: 94) also note or imply connections between the digression and the Cronus myth.

hears the praises of a despot or a king being sung, it sounds to his ears as if some shepherd were being congratulated—some keeper of pigs, or sheep, or cows," and he thinks rulers are destined to become as "provincial and uneducated (*apaideuton*)" as any actual herdsman (173c–176d). On this Theodoran view of philosophy, human reason is exercised in theoretical activities like mathematics, and politics, by contrast, is merely the uninteresting business, akin to animal herding, of meeting the human bodily needs.[11] This conception of the rational but apolitical philosopher strikingly foreshadows the misunderstanding of Young Socrates, who not coincidentally is Theodorus' ambitious young student and is a bystander during the conversation of the *Theaetetus*. For Theodorus and Young Socrates alike, human life consists of a duality between the divine rationality that concerns philosophers and the bestial biological needs that concern politicians. Their conception entirely ignores the social and political, or spirited, dimension of human life and psychology. The Myth of Cronus, therefore, dramatizes that omission and in doing so exposes the shortcomings of their conception of politics. The emphasis on lack of social or political desires and behavior in the digression of the *Theaetetus*, then, combined with obvious echoes of that digression in the Cronus myth, provides further evidence that one of Plato's main concerns in the *Statesman* is to highlight the centrality of spirit in understanding politics.

If the Protagorean myth discussed in Chapter 4 presented pre-political human beings who *needed* to form communities and protect themselves, but lacked the spirited motivations required for social and military life, then the myth of the *Statesman* presents pre-political human beings who had no reason to form social groups or defend themselves, and who therefore had neither need nor opportunity to feel or behave in any characteristically spirited ways.[12] For contrast, note that the Visitor goes out of his way to make it clear that the humans of this time possessed distinctively appetitive and rational desires and capacities. They eat and drink, after all, and the Visitor leaves open the possibility that they might spend all of their time "stuffing themselves with

---

[11] Cf. Hemmenway (1994: 254–5).

[12] Other commentators who draw attention to the lack of family, social life, and politics in the Age of Cronus include Ambuel (2013: 222–3), Barney (2002: 222–3), Ferrari (2005: 393–4), Hemmenway (1994: 261–2), Márquez (2012: 152–4), McCabe (1997: 109–10), Nightingale (1996: 84), Rowe (2000: 242–4), and Vidal-Naquet (1978: 137). For commentators who discuss the relation of the Cronus myth to the Great Speech, see Blondell (2005: 35, 45–6), Friedländer (1958: 369, n. 9), Hemmenway (1994: 267, n. 24), McCabe (1997: 101, n. 33; 108, n. 62; and 110, n. 68), Miller (1980: 45–51), Narcy (1995), and Scodel (1987: 84, n. 84). One key difference between the two myths is that in the *Statesman* the gods do not grant "shame and justice" to human beings. Presumably, this is partly due to the fact that Protagoras appeals to Zeus' allotment in the service of his argument that *everyone* possesses a share of political expertise, an idea the *Statesman* emphatically denies. Cf. Márquez (2012: 167, n. 166) and Rowe (2000: 243–4; cf. 2015), who calls the Cronus myth "a kind of counter to the democratic myth."

food and wine." They also have the capacity for speech or *logos*, and the Visitor leaves open the possibility that they might spend their time in conversation or even the philosophical pursuit of wisdom (272b–d).[13] In the case of spirit, the myth leaves only two possibilities: that humans in the Age of Cronus lacked *thumos* and spirited motivation entirely, or that spirit was simply latent and idle in them during a time in which it had no use. We need not decide between these options, because the outcome is the same: they fail to exhibit any of the interpersonal spirited desires and emotions that define humans as social and political creatures. The myth shows what human life, psychology, and behavior would have to be like in order for the conception of statesman-ship as human herding to be appropriate, and what it depicts is a world without *thumos*.[14] The Myth of Cronus suggests, then, that the positive conception of the *politikos* that still needs to be developed must account for human spiritedness. And that is precisely what the dialogue does.

2. Courage and Moderation

In the discussion following the myth the Visitor attempts to refine their understanding of the statesman and distinguish him more sharply from his rivals, who include not only the imposter politicians of inferior and unlawful regimes—whom the Visitor describes as mere "factionists" and "imitators" of true statesmanship (303b–d; cf. 291a–b)—but also those who *genuinely* con-tribute to the city in various ways, but whose branches of knowledge are nonetheless distinct from and subordinate to statesmanship. These genuine contributors include, first of all, those who produce or provide the city's resources, possessions, and services: builders, carpenters, potters, painters, farmers, retailers, heralds, priests, and so on (287b–291a). It also, however, includes three political professions that the Visitor actually identifies as "akin" (*sungenē*) to statesmanship and hence more difficult to separate clearly from it: rhetoricians, generals, and judges (303d–304a). Key to distinguishing the statesman from all these various craftspeople and experts is his knowledge of

---

[13] I concur with the majority of scholars, however, who judge it unlikely—some commentators claim *impossible*, which seems too strong—that the Cronus nurslings actually engage in philosophy. See Barney (2002: 222–3 and n. 17), Blondell (2005: 36–7, 47–8), Cole (1991: 197–8), McCabe (1997: 105–9), Nightingale (1996: 83–4), Rosen (1995: 55–6), and Scodel (1987: 81). Márquez (2012: 150–1 and n. 149) expresses agnosticism on the issue, while Carone (2005a: 247, nn. 60–1) and Van Harten (2003: 131) dissent from the majority view.

[14] By contrast, Blondell (2005: 44–5) takes *rationality* to be what humans gain in the Age of Zeus that turns them into political creatures.

"due measure" or the *metrion*. The Visitor draws a distinction between judgments of things based on their relation to one another (for instance, a smaller object in comparison to a larger) and judgments of them in relation to "due measure." All branches of knowledge and their practitioners, he claims, are concerned with the latter and its various expressions, which also include the "fitting" (*prepon*), the "needed" (*deon*), and the "opportune moment" (*kairos*).[15] Knowledgeable experts necessarily recognize the existence of the *metrion*, aim at it in their work, and use it as the criterion for judging excess and deficiency (283c–284e). And it is this knowledge that distinguishes the statesman from all other experts in the city: whereas they each know the subjects of their crafts alone, he also knows *whether* and *when* those subjects should be taught, learned, and used. The rhetorician, military commander, and judge know how to persuade crowds of people, conduct a battle, and identify lawful or unlawful behavior, respectively, but they do not know when and how it is appropriate to use persuasion or wage war, or which specific laws are fitting and best for the city (304a–305d). Socrates explains, "Genuine kings do not actually *do* things themselves; they *rule* people whose domain is doing, and they know the opportune moments (*enkairias*) and inopportune ones (*akairias*) for embarking on and initiating courses of action" (305d1–4). Statesmanship, he concludes, "is the branch of knowledge that rules over all of them, as well as over the laws and every other aspect of the city as well, and which creates the best possible fabric out of all these materials" (305e2–5).

This last idea represents the culmination of an analogy the Visitor develops in the second half of the dialogue between the statesman's expertise and weaving, which he says "involves the same activity as statesmanship" (279a–b), and which he examines dialectically in detail in order to illustrate methodological and other points relevant to investigating the nature of the *politikos*. This analogy, moreover, sets up the dialogue's concluding discussion: having distinguished the statesman from his rivals, the Visitor remarks that what is left for them to do is "describe what kind of weaving together kings do, how they do it, and what the resulting woven fabric is like" (306a1–3). It is here that we find the second key passage of the dialogue in which spirited psychology plays a central role.

The Visitor begins with the "daring" assertion that courage and moderation, despite both being "parts" of virtue, are actually "in some sense" (*kata tina tropon*) in tension with one another: there can be "hostility" (*echthran*),

---

[15] For further discussion of the *metrion*, the *kairos*, and related terms in the *Statesman*, see Lane (1995: 278–80 and 1998: 125–46) and Márquez (2012: 218–31 and 315–18).

"faction" (*stasin*), and "disagreement" (*diaphoran*) between them (306a–c).[16] This tension is grounded, he suggests, in the fact that the two virtues are each associated with different sets of opposed qualities—courage with speed, intensity, hardness, sharpness, and loudness, and moderation with slowness, tameness, steadiness, softness, and quietness. All of these qualities, moreover, can be met with praise or blame depending on their perceived relation to due measure in a given context. When the former qualities are appropriate and praiseworthy, they are courageous, but when they appear at inopportune times, they are violent and mad. When the latter are praiseworthy, they are moderate and orderly, but when they are excessive, they are cowardly and lazy. These two classes of qualities in both their admirable and defective forms, therefore, are "in a way separated by mutual war and faction, so that we never find the two of them mixed together in any relevant activity."[17] Not only that,

---

[16] Some commentators take this claim to contradict Plato's treatment of the virtues in earlier dialogues, or even to constitute a rejection of the earlier Platonic or Socratic doctrine of the unity or reciprocity of the virtues. See esp. remarks in Penner (1992: 128), Scodel (1987: 161), and Skemp, (1952: 223, n. 1), who calls the passage "a frontal attack" on the *Republic*'s account of the virtues. Cf. remarks in Benitez (2014: 126), Klosko (2006: 210), Mishima (1995: 309–11), Irwin (1995a: 339–41), and Pradeau (2002: 92). However, the Visitor's claim about courage and moderation need not refer to *true* virtues rather than to "natural" versions of them, understood as untutored instincts or qualities that somehow resemble, or provide psychic resources for developing, true virtues, but which creatures possess by nature rather than as a result of education. Since the earlier doctrines with which the *Statesman* is supposed to conflict concern *true* virtues (or demotic or civic approximations of them), therefore, the apparent tension dissolves. The Visitor provides strong evidence for the "natural" interpretation. The moderation and courage at issue are transmitted from parents to children by birth, which shows he is focused on inborn nature, and moderate individuals who receive a good education become "*truly* (ὄντως) moderate" only ὥς γε ἐν πολιτείᾳ (309e5–8), making it clear that their "raw" moderation falls short of true or even civic virtue. My account adds further support to this reading: it shows that the "courage" and "moderation" in question are natural *spirited* dispositions. For examples of Plato's distinction between true vs. natural virtues, see the *Laws*, where the Athenian acknowledges a "popular" moderation, "the sort that blooms naturally, from the beginning, in children and beasts," but contrasts it with a "solemn" moderation that involves prudence (710a3–b2; cf. 696d4–e6 and *Epin.* 977b9–d1); he also recognizes a form of courage that exists without reason in beasts and young children (963e3–8). Even in the *Republic*, Socrates and Glaucon recognize animal forms of courage (375a, 430b), and Socrates claims that philosophers must be born with a nature that includes both moderation and courage (487a; cf. 491b), by which of course he cannot mean virtues that require the rigorous early and/or higher education he describes in the text. Outside of Plato, Aristotle is especially clear in distinguishing between natural and real virtue, and he explicitly attributes the former to children and beasts (*NE* 1144b1–9). Other commentators who defend a "natural" reading of the *Statesman*'s courage and moderation include Dorter (1994: 225–7), Márquez (2012: 320–1, n. 298), Miller (1980: 107), North (1966: 184), and Weiss (2005: 221, n. 31).

[17] Plato's interest in the association of certain descriptive qualities with courage and moderation, and in potential conflict between the two sets, is evident throughout his career; cf. North (1966: 184, n. 69). This interest is hinted at in early dialogues like the *Laches*, where Socrates compares courage and quickness (ταχυτής) (192a–c), or *Charmides*, where the first proposed definition of moderation is that it consists in doing things in an orderly (κοσμίως), quiet (ἡσυχῇ), or slow (βραδέως) way, rather than quickly (ταχέως) or sharply (ὀξέως) (159b–160b). These ideas also underlie the musical theories of both the *Republic* and *Laws*, which associate courageous musical tones with sharp, fast sounds, and moderate tones with soft, slow ones. In the *Republic*, Socrates also notes the difficulty of finding all

but human beings who possess these qualities are themselves at odds with one another as well (306c–307c). The Visitor explains:

> We don't need to look any further than the cases we mentioned a moment ago (although I'm sure there are plenty of others too), because it's their own kinship (*sungenneian*) to one or the other set of qualities which makes people praise (*epainountes*) things that are familiar (*oikeia*) to them and their own (*sphetera*), and blame (*psegontes*) those that are foreign (*allotria*) to them. This is what causes so much enmity (*echthran*) between people over all sorts of issues... Now, when the disagreement between the two groups occurs in the human sphere like that, it remains trivial; but when it occurs in serious contexts, there's no more hateful disease (*nosos*) for cities... You see, people who are particularly orderly (*kosmioi*) always like to live a quiet (*hēsuchon*) life, keeping to themselves and doing their own thing (*ta sphetera autōn prattontes*); that's how they deal with everyone at home, and by the same token they like to find a way to be on peaceful terms with other cities abroad. And because this desire of theirs is often inopportune (*akairoteron*) and excessive, when they get their own way in politics, they unconsciously become unwarlike (*apolemōs*) and make the younger generation that way too. Then they are at the mercy of aggressors, and before too many years have passed, they themselves and their children and the whole city have gone from being free (*eleutherōn*) to being slaves (*douloi*), without even realizing it... But what about people who incline toward courage (*andreian*)? Aren't they constantly working their city up for war (*polemon*), because of their excessive enthusiasm for the military life? This leads them to enmity (*echthran*) with many powerful opponents, and consequently they cause their fatherland to be either completely destroyed or, again, to be plunged into a state of slavery and submission to their enemies.   (307c9–308a9)

The natural opposition of courage and moderation and their associated qualities in human beings, the Visitor concludes, is the source of perpetual conflict and hostility among citizens. The primary task of the statesman, therefore—his role as political "weaver"—is specified in terms of the two

---

the elements required for philosophy, including moderation and courage, in the same person's nature, because its parts "mostly grow in separation." Those who are quick (ὀξεῖς) and thus quick learners tend not to live in an orderly way with quiet and stability (κοσμίως μετὰ ἡσυχίας καὶ βεβαιότητος), while those who are stable and calm tend to be slow learners, due to their sleepiness and sluggishness (503b–d; cf. *Epin.* 989b4–d4). The distinction between moderate and courageous citizens also reappears in the *Laws* (as I discuss in Ch. 10.2).

opposed types of character. The courageous citizens are the "firm" or "stiff" (*stereon*) warp of the city and the moderate ones its "soft" (*malakōi*) weft, and the *politikos* must "find a way to link and weave them together" (308d–309b), with the ultimate aim of producing civic unity and friendship in place of discord (311b–c).[18]

3. Statesmanship and *Thumos*

The central thesis of my interpretation is that the passage draws heavily on Plato's reflections on the two faces of *thumos*: the courageous citizens are defined by tendencies and motivations that Plato associates with the aggressive side of spirit, while the moderate are defined in terms of its gentle side.[19] On this reading, the dialogue's final analysis of the *politikos* answers to the need to address spirited psychology that is dramatized by the Myth of Cronus. Note that the weaving metaphor itself is already suggestive. The contrast between the tough or strained warp and the soft or slack weft fits naturally with familiar metaphors associated with the two aspects of *thumos* in early Greek thought. The most obvious evidence for my interpretation, however, is Plato's conspicuous use of terminology that echoes his accounts of *thumos*. Courage itself is an unmistakable example, and the Visitor associates it with additional spirited qualities like boldness, hardness, violence, and a propensity for war. Likewise, we have seen, moderation often prominently involves spirited motivation in Plato as well, and here it is associated with qualities of *thumos* like softness, tameness, cowardice, and unfitness for war. Perhaps most notably, the Visitor invokes the two most fundamental expressions of spirit's dual nature, affection for the familiar and hostility toward the unknown. People praise what is

---

[18] For general discussion of the dialogue's concluding section on "weaving" citizens together, see Arends (1993), Balot (2014: 333–6), Blondell (2005), Bobonich (1995), Cole (1991), Cooper (1997), Klosko (2006: 208–9), Lane (1998: 163–82), Marqez (2012: Ch. 6), Miller (1980: 107–10), Mishima (1995), North (1966: 183–5 and nn. 69–70), Pradeau (2002: 90–9), Rosen (1995: 154), Scodel (1987: Ch. 4), Skemp (1952: 232, nn. 1–2), Taylor (1961: 242–5), and White (2007: Ch. 5).

[19] Márquez (2012: 322–4) also recognizes the importance of *thumos* in the discussion, but seems to think only courageous citizens are characterized in terms of spirited qualities, as does Hobbs (2000: 264). Rosen (1995: 154) similarly takes the Visitor's talk of "hard" and "soft" natures to refer to "something like the degree of spiritedness" in the citizens. These interpretations all reflect the traditional view of spirit as defined only by its aggressive side. Understood in that limited sense, Rosen's idea that "hard" characters display a high degree of (the aggressive side of) *thumos* while "soft" ones display a low degree of it is correct. However, it misses the converse point that "soft" natures display a high degree *of the gentle side* of spirit, while "hard" natures display a low degree of it. The fact that moderate types experience strong versions of *gentle* spirited emotions is evident, among other ways, in the fact that (as noted below in the main text) one of their flaws is that their shame can become *excessive* (they become "too full" of it, 310d–e).

similar or *oikeion* to them, he says, and blame what is different or *allotrion*. The defining qualities and propensities of the two types of citizens, therefore, are couched in terms of spirited motivation.[20]

The language and logic of spirited psychology also appear in the Visitor's discussion of precisely *how* the statesman "weaves" together the moderate and courageous citizens. The process begins in childhood with playful tests and education designed to identify and expel individuals who are incapable of sharing in civic virtue, and to train those who *are* capable of it and "prepare" them for the statesman's weaving (308d–309b). The weaving itself is a twofold method. First, the statesman binds together the "eternal part" of citizens' souls by instilling stable true beliefs about what is admirable or shameful, just or unjust, and good or bad (309c–310a).[21] These true beliefs serve to check or mitigate the instincts of each character type and produce agreement (*homodoxiais*, 310e9–10) and like-mindedness (*homonoiai*, 311b9) among the citizens.[22] Although the "eternal part" surely refers to the reasoning element of psychology, we have seen in earlier chapters that spirited motivation is closely connected with rational judgment: emotions shaped during early education, like shame and admiration, influence a person's maturing reasoning about what is valuable and disvaluable, and rational judgments, in turn, can guide and influence *thumos*. We have reason for thinking this close connection persists in the *Statesman*. First, note that the citizens' shared beliefs are supposed to correct their *natural* inclinations to "praise" and "blame" what is *oikeion* or *allotrion* to them, respectively. This suggests that the importance of correct belief is not merely about purely rational assessments, but also their spontaneous spirited feelings of admiration and disgust. This idea receives further support from the fact that in his recapitulation of the statesman's weaving methods, the Visitor includes the use of "honors (*timais*) and dishonors (*atimiais*)" alongside "shared beliefs" (310e9–11). Furthermore, it is significant that the process of instilling true beliefs can take place only *after* the preparation and training provided by early education, which occurs when reason is undeveloped. The Visitor says nothing about what this early training

---

[20] Lane (1998: 174–7) discusses the role of natural reactions to the familiar and foreign in citizens' evaluative judgments, but she does not make an explicit connection to *thumos*.

[21] Annas (1995: xxi) curiously claims that Plato here "softens" his earlier view that only knowledge is stable, and belief inherently *un*stable. Already in the *Republic*, however, the guardians' early education aims to instill "lawful beliefs" as securely as "dye in wool."

[22] *Pace* Arends (1993: 163–4), who claims that by contrast to the shared values and fellowship of the Kallipolis, in the *Statesman* there are two conflicting "communities of value," and "the emotional unity of the citizens is missing." On the contrary, the Visitor emphasizes the citizens' unanimity and friendship, and they come to share "a single opinion about what is admirable and good."

consists in, but it is reasonable to suppose it involves music and gymnastic education—just as in the *Republic*, *Timaeus*, and (as we will see in the next chapter) the *Laws*.[23] The Visitor actually provides some corroboration for this idea in his comparison of the psychology of those who are educated and those who are not. Naturally courageous citizens who acquire true belief become "tame" (*hēmeroutai*) while those who never acquire it become "bestial"— language which echoes exactly Socrates' characterization of the effects of music and its lack on *thumos* in *Republic* 3. Educated "orderly" citizens, meanwhile, become sufficiently moderate and intellectually fit to share in civic life, whereas the uneducated become stupid (309d–e). Again, this recalls the *Republic*'s idea that a proper balance of music and gymnastics makes people "moderate," while neglect of music makes them feeble-minded and ignorant. This parallel suggests that citizens' true rational beliefs are possible in part because of the effects of early education on *thumos*, and that spirited motivation continues to be closely connected with those beliefs throughout their lives.

Second, the statesman uses "human bonds" by making sure moderate and courageous types are joined together in marriage with one another. This practice contributes to civic unity in two ways, both of which reflect a concern for *thumos*. The first is that intermarriage results in children with a better "mixture" of the two character types. When courageous individuals reproduce only with one another in generation after generation, their undiluted vigor eventually turns into madness (310d). Notably, this biological point antici- pates Aristotle's claim that "honor-loving" families eventually degenerate into madness, citing the descendants of the notoriously spirited and ambitious Alcibiades as an example (*Rhet.* 1390b16–29). By contrast, when moderate types reproduce only among themselves, the result is excessive shame (*aidōus*), deficiency of daring (*tolmēs*) and courage (*andreias*), and general sluggishness and ineptitude (310d–e). This description highlights one of the most distinc- tive expressions of spirit's gentle side, a sense of shame, while also drawing attention to the privation of two of its *positive* aggressive qualities.

The other benefit of intermarriage is that it produces the "bonds" (*desmous*) and "partnerships" (*koinōnēseōn*) that result from marriage, having children in common, and making marriage arrangements with other families for one's children (310b). In other words, marriage produces the ties of affection that characterize communities by creating families, extended families, and

[23] Márquez (2012: 326–35) discusses education in the *Statesman* and similarly concludes that the early stage likely involves a mix of musical and gymnastic training. He suggests (plausibly, I think) that naturally "moderate" youths might be stimulated with a greater share of martial or physical activities, and the naturally "courageous" youths calmed with more music and poetry.

friends.[24] By uniting moderate individuals and families with courageous ones, therefore, intermarriage gives rise to feelings of love and friendship between two groups who might otherwise be naturally disposed to disagree with and dislike one another. This brings us to the Visitor's account of why the statesman *needs* to intervene in marital and reproductive relationships in the first place. Left to their own devices, he explains, people tend to marry (or arrange for their children to marry) people who are *similar* to themselves: people "warmly welcome" (*aspazesthai*) those who are "similar" (*prosomoious*) to them, and "reject" (*mēstergein*) and feel "disgust" (*duschereiai*) for those who are different (310c–d). Once again, the Visitor uses language that invokes two fundamental expressions of spirit's dual nature in order to explain social behavior. On his view, affection for the familiar usually causes courageous people to marry and reproduce with other courageous people, and moderate people to seek out other moderate types. The statesman's use of intermarriage is necessary to counteract this instinct.

The Visitor's account of courageous and moderate character types, then, reflects Plato's understanding of *thumos* in two main ways. First, it defines each of the two types of people in terms of motivations and qualities, and using language, that Plato strongly associates with spirit. Second, the two methods of "weaving" people together are also described in terms that invoke spirited psychology, and, most importantly, both methods are explicitly designed to regulate impulses that, by the lights of tripartition, constitute classic expressions of the two faces of *thumos*. The bond of true belief is a remedy for citizens' natural spirited inclination to praise and admire what is *oikeion* to them and blame what is *allotrion*, and the bonds of intermarriage similarly account for their spirited affection for what is similar to themselves and disgust for what is dissimilar. All of this results, moreover, in civic "bonds" and friendship, *philia*—social ties that have their affective source in and are made possible by human spirit in works like the *Republic*. And here, finally, it is important to reiterate that this weaving together of the two types is *the* definitive task of the statesman in the dialogue's final analysis. In the Visitor's closing remarks, he concludes:

> The work of a weaver-statesman is complete when he has woven these two types of human character—the courageous and the restrained—into a well-knit fabric. It is complete when a king with his knowledge makes sure that

---

[24] Cf. the use of δεσμοὶ φιλίας in Protagoras' Great Speech (322c3).

agreement (*homonoiai*) and friendship (*philiai*) are the materials out of which he constructs their community, and so creates the most magnificent and excellent fabric there can be.   (311b7–c3)

What this means is that the knowledge that defines statesmanship is in large part a knowledge of *thumos*. The statesman understands the spirited tendencies and motivations that define human social and political life, and he knows how to guide and exploit those tendencies in the interest of civic unity. The Myth of Cronus illustrates that spirit is a dominant psychological force in politics which must be accounted for, and the Visitor's analysis of the *politikos* does the accounting.

4. Political Psychology in Contemporary Greek Thought

Contemporary Greek sources provide additional evidence for this interpretation. In short, the Visitor's treatment of courageous and moderate citizens is in keeping with a deep tradition of understanding dichotomies of character types in terms of *thumos* and associated traits. This tradition is evident in discussions of the contrast between masculine and feminine, or between young and old (see Chapter 10.3), and in political contexts it also features prominently in analyses of opposed types of citizens and civic temperaments.[25] Most obviously, as discussed in the Introduction, Plato's term *thumoeides* has its origin or precedent in the Hippocratic text *Airs Waters Places*. There the author draws a contrast between Asiatic and European dispositions, and between the dispositions of groups that inhabit different regions within Europe, in terms that anticipate both the Visitor's distinction between courageous and moderate citizens, as well as the two faces of Platonic spirit more generally. Asiatics and other mild types are described as unwarlike (*apolemoteroi*), gentle (*hēmerōteroi*), and lacking nerve (*atalaipōroi*); they are inactive (*atremizein*), are unwilling to take risks (*kindunein*), lack courage (*to andreion*) and

---

[25] The masculine/feminine dichotomy is especially relevant to the *Statesman*'s metaphor because men and women are typically associated with the "toughness" and "softness," respectively, that characterize the two sides of spirit. As Blondell (2005: 67–8) notes, the *Statesman* replaces male and female with the two temperaments as the "warp" and "weft" of the political fabric. This makes Plato's choice to echo Aristophanes' *Lysistrata* (536–8, 567–86) in selecting weaving, a paradigmatically feminine activity for the Greeks, as a metaphor for statesmanship all the more striking. For further discussion, see Balot (2014: 257–67 and 334), Blondell (2005), Cole (1991: 195–6 and 207, n. 12), Lane 1998: (164–71), Miller (1980: 118), and Skemp (1952: 44, n. 1). For examples of the masculine/feminine dichotomy in Greek literature that use the language of *thumos* and spirited motivation, see Euripides, fr. 362.33–4; Xenophon, *Oec.* 7.23; and Aristotle, *HA* 608a22–b19.

industry (*to emponon*), have slavish souls (*hai psuchai dedoulōntai*), and are subject to the rule of despots; and they exhibit cowardice (*anandreia, deilia*), laziness (*argia*), lethargy (*to hupnēron*), and quietness (*hēsuchia*). Europeans and other aggressive types, meanwhile, are anti-social (*to amikton*), militant (*machimōteroi*), tough (*sklēroi*), and quick or sharp (*oxuteroi*); they excel in matters of war (*ta polemia*), eagerly pursue victory (*nikē*), readily rush into danger (*deinon*) and face risks (*kindunoi*), and lack gentleness (*to hēmeron*); and they exhibit courage (*andreia, eupsuchia*), savageness (*to agrion*), endurance (*to talaipōron*), energy (*to ergatikon*), and stubborn tempers (*orgai authadeai*).[26] Both the *Statesman* and the Hippocratic author, then, draw political contrasts that assume connections between aggressive spirited qualities and quickness or activity on the one hand, and gentle ones and quietness or torpidity on the other. The Hippocratic author, moreover, is explicit that these opposed kinds of qualities involve conditions of *thumos*: Asiatics are defined by spiritlessness (*athumia*, 16.3), *lack* of spiritedness (*to thumoeides*, 12.41, 16.11), or *soft*-spiritedness (*rhaithumia*, 23.26, 23.28–9, 24.50), whereas Europeans are characterized by their spiritedness (*to thumoeides*, 23.20) and are eager-spirited (*prothumeuntai*, 23.38). In his *Politics*, Aristotle confirms this assessment: Europeans are naturally "full of spirit" (*thumou plērē*) but "apolitical" and incapable of ruling others, whereas Asiatics are unspirited (*athuma*) and subject to being ruled and enslaved by others (1327b19–28).[27] To be clear, the point here is not that Plato's moderate and courageous citizens are exactly like Asiatics and Europeans as the Hippocratic author and Aristotle conceive them, but simply that the parallels are sufficient to show that Plato's analysis is part of the same tradition of political analysis as theirs—namely, one that makes *thumos*, along with motivations and behavioral qualities associated with it, central to distinguishing psychological types of citizens and their relation to political arrangements.

Thucydides provides further examples. His *History* is full of dichotomous characterizations that anticipate the Visitor's account in the *Statesman*, and he even makes some use of *thumos* and its cognates (though he generally favors other related terms instead). Two examples stand out. First, Thucydides uses a series of speeches by various individuals to draw a contrast between Spartan and Athenian temperament. The Spartans are distinguished by their slowness

---

[26] These descriptors all appear in sections 12, 16, and 23–4 of the text, several of them repeatedly and in various cognate forms. Skemp (1952: 225–6, n. 1) notes the Hippocratic influence on the *Statesman*'s characterization of civic temperaments.

[27] Notably, these remarks immediately precede the passage discussed in Chapter 2 in which Aristotle comments on Plato's view that guardians must be both "friendly" and "savage."

(*bradutēs*), quietness (*hēsuchia*), order (*kosmon*) or orderliness (*to eukosmon*), a tendency toward hesitation (*mellēsis*) rather than action or haste, and a sense of moderation (*sōphrosunē*) closely bound up with their sense of shame (*aidōs, aischunē*). The Athenians, by contrast, are characterized by their speed (*to tacheion*), courage (*andreia*), daring or boldness (*tolma*), and spirited enthusiasm (*prothumia*); they are arrogant (*hubrizomenoi,*), quick (*oxeis*), and prone to war and violence; they are motivated by the pursuit of reputation (*doxa*), honor (*timē*), and vengeance (*timōria*); they are unhesitating (*aoknoi*), feel sanguine in the face of danger (*en tois deinois euelpides*), take senseless risks (*para gnomēn kinduneutai*), and in general face peril and endure hardships (*ponoi*) readily; they favor active struggle over inactive peace; they press their victories (*nikōmenoi*) to the limit in conquering (*kratountes*) enemies; and, finally, their belief in their right to rule (*archein*) makes them exceptionally inclined to act out of anger (*orgē*) or spirit (*thumos*) without thinking.[28] Thucydides, speaking in his own voice toward the end of his work, endorses this general dichotomy between the two cities. He writes, "The Spartans proved themselves to be the best possible opponents for the Athenians to be at war with. They were completely different from the Athenians in temperament—the latter quick (*oxeis*), the former slow (*bradeis*), the latter adventurous (*epicheiretai*), and the former cautious (*atolmoi*)" (8.96.5.1–6).[29] The second example is the contrast between two Athenian leaders, Nicias and Alcibiades, in the debate over whether Athens should pursue a military expedition in Sicily. The elder statesman Nicias presents the case for caution, criticizing Alcibiades' jingoism, encouraging moderation (*sōphronoumen*), and warning against acting too quickly (*oxeōs*), on the basis of "swift deliberation" (*bracheia boulē*), or hastily at the wrong moment (*oute en kairō speudete*). Alcibiades, meanwhile, is especially enthusiastic (*prothumotata*) about the expedition, success in which will allow Athens to "rule" (*arxomen*) over all of Greece, and he criticizes Nicas for counseling quietness (*to hēsuchon*) and inactivity (*apragmosunē*).[30] In Thucydides too, then, aggressive spirited traits and courage are associated with qualities like speed, haste, and

---

[28] The various Greek terms referred to in parentheses in this summary are all found in sections 1.68.1–76.2, 1.84.1–85.1, 1.143.5, 2.11.7–9, and 2.39.2–44.4. Most of them are used multiple times and in various cognate forms to characterize the relevant parties.

[29] Speakers also describe the dangers of erring in the direction of either of the two extremes represented by the Spartans and Athenians—cautious hesitation or aggressive risk-taking—in terms that parallel the Visitor's warning in the *Statesman*: the former results in passive enslavement, the latter in unnecessary defeat. See esp. 1.120.3–4 and 2.65.2–3.

[30] See esp. *Hist.* 6.9.1–3, 6.11.7, 6.15.2, and 6.18.3–6 for use of these terms and phrases.

activity, while gentle ones and moderation are associated with slowness, quietness, and inactivity.[31]

These historical examples illustrate the centrality of *thumos*, along with motivations and behavior associated with it, in Greek presentations of character dichotomies that closely parallel the Visitor's own. This historical point supplements the strong evidence within the *Statesman* itself for thinking Plato has spirited psychology in mind in his treatment of moderate and courageous citizens, by showing how natural such thinking would be for a Greek political philosopher. Like Plato, moreover, other early authors not only present similar dichotomies between opposed political types, but as the selections from Thucydides make especially clear, they also problematize conflicts between the two types. Indeed, concern for this tense dichotomy is so central to Greek ethical and political thought both before and after Plato that Helen North, in the preface to her groundbreaking work on *sōphrosunē*, writes:

> Among certain persistent themes that are discussed, the most important is the polarity between sophrosyne and the opposing principle—variously called *andreia* ("manliness"), *to eugenes* ("nobility"), *to drastērion* ("the active principle"), or *megalopsychia* ("greatness of soul")—and the attempts made at various stages of Greek and Roman thought to reconcile the two. This antithesis lies at the very core of Hellenism.[32]

Note, by way of conclusion, that Plato alludes to and engages with this very problem in the opening passage of the *Theaetetus*, where Theodorus commends the young Theaetetus to Socrates by commenting on his remarkably balanced nature. He is particularly struck by the fact that he is both "gentle" (*praion*) and "courageous" (*andreion*). Courageous people tend to be sharp-minded and fast learners, but unstable and impetuous, whereas gentle types tend to be steady and reliable, but dull-minded and forgetful. Until he met Theaetetus, Theodorus did not believe the combination of gentleness and courage could coexist in a single individual (144a1–b6). Plato's "trilogy," in other words, is framed by an opening passage that draws attention to the difficulty of reconciling the opposed traits associated with courage and

---

[31] North (1966: 184) comments that Plato's analysis of the "moderate" civic disposition "reads like a commentary on the remarks about the danger of *apragmosynē* and *hēsychia* attributed by Thucydides to Pericles and Alcibiades." Cole (1991: 203) and Lane (1995: 280–1) also note this connection. On the dichotomy of character types in Thucydides, see Balot (2014: 119–28), Jaeger (1939: 394–7), and North (1966: 100–15).

[32] 1966: ix.

moderation, and by a closing passage that offers a political solution to that problem.[33] His answer, and hence his contribution to this persistent theme in Greek thought, draws on the resources of his worked out views about *thumos*, its double nature, and its role in social life—views which reveal statesmanship to be an art of dealing with human beings as they are defined and distinguished by *spirited* desires and dispositions.[34]

---

[33] The distinction between temperaments is also reflected in Plato's contrasting characterizations of Theaetetus and Young Socrates throughout the trilogy. Despite Theodorus' suggestion that Theaetetus embodies a mix of gentleness and courage, the youth lacks confidence and needs frequent encouragement to keep participating in discussion. By contrast, Young Socrates' "courage," confidence, haste, and eagerness often need to be checked. For commentators who discuss these characterizations in connection with the final argument of the *Statesman*, see Benardete (1984: III.142–9), Hemmenway (1994: 256), Lane (1998: 34 and n. 48), Márquez (2012: 86), Miller (1980: 24–9, 111–12), and Scodel (1987: 61 and n. 63).

[34] Some commentators, e.g. Bobonich (1995: 317–19) and Annas (1995: xxi–xxii), criticize the distinction between courageous and moderate citizens as implausible or underdeveloped. Bobonich notes that the *Statesman* does not work out the details of the distinction and suggests that "any attempt to do so faces serious difficulties." In particular, the supposed relationships between courage and quick/sharp qualities, and moderation and quiet/slow ones, are "too crude to be plausible." My survey of Greek literature in this chapter, however, shows that such ideas were already widespread in early Greek thought and not at all implausible to Plato or his contemporaries. Moreover, although the Visitor does not fill in the psychological details of his account, Plato himself *does* work out many of those details. Once we recognize that the two civic temperaments are defined in terms of spirited motivation, we can see that Plato is drawing on the account of *thumos* he has already thoughtfully developed and explored in previous work.

10

Politics, Education, and Spirit in the *Laws*

The *Laws* is an important test case for some of the main ideas of this book. It is Plato's longest work and one of his last, and its central concern is politics. If the account of spirit I have defined and defended in previous chapters continues to play a prominent role in the arguments of the *Laws*, therefore, then we will have especially strong confirmation that that account is a fixed and enduring feature of Platonic psychological, social, and political theory. My aim in the present chapter is to defend the antecedent of this conditional. I will argue that the dialogue treats spirited motivation as crucial for political unity and friendship, as well as for the development of civic virtue through moral education. Not only does the text echo the *Republic* in these respects, moreover, but actually expands the political role of spirit by subordinating it to the reason embodied in law itself.

There are obstacles to this line of interpretation, however. Some commentators have argued that Plato treats spirit primarily as a *negative* psychological force in the dialogue and relegates it to a demoted status alongside problematic appetitive urges. According to this view, Plato abandons tripartite theory in the *Laws* in favor of a *bi*partite soul, or at least no longer grants to spirit the capacity to make valuable contributions to moral and political life in the ways it did in earlier texts. In Section 1, I clear the way for my interpretation by responding to this developmentalist line of criticism. I will argue that the text gives no reason for thinking Plato has abandoned either tripartite theory or his views about spirit. Part of my response will involve an examination of the relationship between tripartition and bipartition in Plato's thought. The rest of the chapter lays out my positive case, beginning in Section 2 with the issue of civic unity. I argue that Plato's thinking about spirit is evident in the *Laws* through the Athenian Visitor's response to what he perceives as undue Cretan and Spartan emphasis on cultivating courage, competitiveness, and martial virtue at the expense of moderation, cooperation, and friendship. Much of the text is designed to stress the importance of the latter set of civic qualities and offer proposals for developing them, and the details of this endeavor reflect the influence of Plato's two-sided theory of spiritedness. Sections 3 and 4 turn to the topic of moral education and show that Plato continues to view spirited

The Political Soul: Plato on Thumos, *Spirited Motivation, and the City*. Josh Wilburn, Oxford University Press.
© Josh Wilburn 2021. DOI: 10.1093/oso/9780198861867.003.0010

motivation as the primary target of both musical and gymnastic education. In fact, I suggest, the Athenian's account of early education supports an especially strong conclusion here: Plato continues to accept the existence not only of distinctively spirited motivations, but of a distinct, spirited *part of the soul* like the one found in the *Republic* and *Timaeus*. Finally, in Section 5, I will examine the educational role given to the laws themselves in Magnesia and argue that many of their prominent effects are directed at spirited motivations as well. If all of this is right, then the *thumoeides* remains at the heart of Plato's reflections on human social and political nature—and on the necessary conditions for just, unified, and flourishing cities and citizens—all the way to the end of his career.

1. *Thumos* and the Bipartite Soul

Commentators who perceive a change in spirit's status in the *Laws* appeal to two main lines of argument. The first is based on the image of the puppet, which the Athenian offers in Book 1 for the purpose of explaining the notion of being "stronger" or "weaker" than oneself. We are all like divine puppets, he says, pulled in opposite directions by "cords" within us. Our "iron" cords— associated with non-rational motivations like pleasure and pain, fear and boldness, feelings of anger (*thumoi*), and sexual desires—pull us toward vice, while our "golden" cord associated with reasoning and law pulls us toward virtue (644c–645d). When the former prevail, we are "weaker" than ourselves and act badly; when the latter prevails, we are "stronger" than ourselves and act in accordance with virtue. Many commentators have emphasized that in this passage Plato draws no qualitative distinctions among the various non-rational impulses. There are simply iron cords and a golden cord, and as Christopher Bobonich puts it, "Plato makes no room here for silver cords."[1] Instead, *thumos* is included indiscriminately among the recalcitrant and disruptive irrational forces that pull against reasoning. The bipartite nature of this image has, consequently, been taken to show that Plato has repudiated spirit's intermediate status between appetite and reason, and hence has come to reject the tripartite soul as we know it from earlier works. In its place he

---

[1] Bobonich (2002: 264). Cf. Frede (2010: 118), Gill (1985: 11), and Sassi (2008: 133). I argue against Bobonich's reading of the puppet passage in Wilburn (2012).

offers a dichotomous or two-part model of psychology: there is just reasoning on the one hand and all of our non-rational motivations on the other.[2]

The second argument reinforces this one. Not only in the puppet passage, but throughout the *Laws*, the Athenian frequently characterizes *thumos* as a destructive force in our psychological lives. He identifies it as one of three main causes of criminal behavior (863b); it can lead to violent acts like murder (866d–869e) or to slanderous verbal abuse (934e–935c); it can cause various kinds of ignorance or madness (934a–e); and it typically needs to be restrained or extinguished (731c–d).[3] Spirited motivations like envy (870c–d) and love of victory (938b–c), meanwhile, are also sources of vicious behavior. Those who take the dialogue to reject tripartite theory take this critical portrayal of *thumos* as further evidence for the alternative twofold division of the soul. Even commentators who reject this sort of developmentalism, however, tend to think that the spirited element has at least been demoted in the text. Hence R. F. Stalley, who takes tripartition to be compatible with the dialogue's psychology, comments, "In the *Republic* it is the positive role of spirit that is emphasized; its task is to come to the aid of reason and help it overcome the temptations of appetite. In the *Laws*, on the other hand, it appears in a negative role as the source of irrational passions which oppose the reason."[4] According to many commentators, then, *thumos* is no longer an educable psychological force that can be trained to support reason and contribute to moral development; for the most part, it is simply one more dangerous impulse or psychic influence that needs to be controlled and resisted.

My response to both of these arguments is to grant their major premises but deny the inferences commentators draw from them. The puppet passage does present a bipartite psychology, but that provides no reason for thinking Plato has abandoned tripartition; and the text does typically (but not always, we will see) treat *thumos* as a vicious emotion, while also highlighting the dangers of motivations like envy and competitiveness, but that provides no reason for thinking that Plato has come to reject a positive moral role for spirited

---

[2] Commentators who take the *Laws* to abandon tripartition in favor of bipartition include Fortenbaugh (1975: 23–5), Laks (1990: 221), Rees (1957), Robinson (1970: 145), and Sassi (2008). Bobonich (2002: 260–7) is distinct in taking the *Laws* to replace tripartition with an undivided, *unitary* view of the soul and is followed by Feitosa (2017: 216). Kamtekar (2006: 180–2 and 2010: 141–3) and Gerson (2003b) argue against Bobonich's developmentalist view.

[3] For discussion of *thumos* as a cause of wrongdoing, see Woozley (1972), Saunders (1973), and Wilburn (2013a: 119–23).

[4] 2003: 181, n. 6. Cf. Brisson (2012b: 298–9), who defends the presence of tripartition in the *Laws*, but states that "spirit displays a primarily negative role" in the dialogue. Sassi (2008) argues at length that spirit has a demoted status in the *Laws* and that there is "no trace" of its positive role in resisting appetites (p. 140). Cf. Bobonich (2002: 343).

motivation or a spirited part of the soul.[5] The reason why these conclusions do not follow, moreover, is more or less the same in the two cases: both of the supposedly heterodox features of the *Laws*—bipartite characterizations of the soul and a critical attitude toward *thumos*—also appear prominently in works that endorse tripartition. If those ideas sit comfortably alongside the three-part theory of the soul in Plato's mind, then their appearance in the *Laws* cannot show Plato has come to reject that theory.

Consider first the characterization of *thumos*. Here there are two main issues. First, as discussed in Chapters 1 and 2, Plato himself (by contrast to modern commentators, including me in this book) rarely uses the term *thumos* to refer to the spirited part of the soul itself in his accounts of tripartition. Instead—in line with one of its poetic uses—he most commonly employs *thumos* as a synonym for *orgē* to refer to the emotional state of anger, rage, or belligerent passion. When he wants to refer to the part of the soul responsible for that anger, by contrast, he prefers other expressions or terms like *to thumoeides*. In other words, *thumos* typically refers not to the spirited part of the soul, but only to one specific kind of spirited motivation. This distinction is clearest in the *Timaeus*, where Plato refers to the spirited element of the soul as "the part that shares in courage and *thumos*" (70a2–3). Plato's critical attitude toward *thumos* in the *Laws*, therefore, cannot be taken as a critical attitude toward the spirited part of the soul, but only toward the emotion of anger. Furthermore (and this is the decisive point), even in the works that feature tripartition, Plato always treats spirited motivation, *especially* anger, with caution, recognizing that it can be a dangerous and destructive force. In the *Timaeus*, Plato twice includes *thumos* among the irrational affections of the mortal soul, and he even emphasizes the unruliness of *thumos* by calling it "difficult to soothe" (42a7, 69d3), but the dialogue nonetheless remains committed to spirit's positive psychic role as the ally of reason. Likewise, the very case of opposition Plato uses in *Republic* 4 to distinguish between the spirited and reasoning parts of the soul presupposes the negative potential of *thumos*. Odysseus must restrain his anger precisely because it is "irrational" and pulls him contrary to his better judgment. In *Republic* 9, moreover, Socrates warns that love of honor and victory, when unchecked

---

[5] Other commentators who defend Plato's non-abandonment of, continued commitment to, or use of tripartite theory in the *Laws* include Brisson (2012b; cf. 2015), Kahn (2005: 356–7), Mackenzie (1981: 175), Meyer (2012; cf. 2015: 172–3), Pfefferkorn (2020), Prauscello (2014: 13–15), Price (1995: 90), Renaut (2014: 306–13), and Saunders (1962). Commentators (e.g. Saunders) sometimes cite the three causes of criminal behavior—pleasure, anger, and ignorance (863b–d)—as a direct reference to tripartition. I argue against that reading in Wilburn (2013a), although I also argue the passage is *consistent* with tripartition.

by rational thought, leads to grievous envy (*phthonos*), violence (*bia*), and anger (*thumos*) (586c7–d2). Indeed, Socrates' whole program of early education in the *Republic* is predicated on the idea that the spirited part is morally beneficial only when it is properly trained and subjugated to reason. In the wrong circumstances, we have seen, spirit can just as easily become a source of morally and politically pernicious impulses that serve the aims of human *pleonexia* or impetuous vengefulness. In the works that defend tripartition and affirm the value of an educated spirited part, then, Plato *also* emphasizes the potential for that same soul part, and motivations like anger, to contribute to the worst of human vice and unhappiness. The fact that the *Laws* highlights those dangers as well, therefore, does not imply any change in Plato's thinking about *thumos* or spiritedness. On the contrary, it demonstrates continuity.

Similar considerations apply in the case of the bipartition of the puppet image. Simply put, Plato freely makes use of bipartite characterizations of the soul in the works that feature tripartition, and those characterizations often have important features in common with the version we find in the *Laws*. First, consider again the *Timaeus*, where the only psychological distinction that is relevant for much of the text is between the immortal element of the soul, which is crafted by the demiurge himself and is divine, and the mortal element designed by the lesser gods.[6] When Timaeus describes the latter, he initially says only that the mortal soul contains a variety of "dreadful but necessary affections: pleasure, first of all, evil's most powerful lure; then pains, that make us run away from what is good; besides these, boldness also and fear, foolish counselors both; then also anger (*thumon*) difficult to soothe, and expectation easily led astray" (69c7–d4). Note that the list of "dreadful" motivations bears a striking resemblance to the one in the *Laws*, and that, like the Athenian, Timaeus does not mention soul parts and draws no distinctions among the affections, relegating spirited impulses like "boldness" and *thumos* to the same class as appetitive ones: they all have the potential to interfere with reasoning and lead us toward vice instead of virtue.[7] Nonetheless, Timaeus goes on to draw a clear qualitative distinction between two psychic elements *within* the mortal soul. The spirited part is "by nature superior" to the appetitive part (69e5), and, as we saw Chapter 8, it retains its role as the ally of reason in resisting unjust and harmful appetites.

Two further examples appear in the *Republic* itself, one prior to Socrates' introduction of the tripartite soul and the other subsequent to it. The first,

---

[6] See e.g. 41e–42e, 61c–d, and 69b–e.
[7] Brisson (2012b: 286–7) also draws attention to parallels between the two passages.

from Book 4, offers an analysis of the very same concept the Athenian is attempting to illuminate with his puppet metaphor: the popular notion of being "stronger than oneself." Socrates explains this perplexing turn of phrase:

> The expression is apparently trying to indicate that, in the soul of that very person, there is something better (*to beltion*) and something worse (*to cheiron*) and that, whenever the naturally better part is in control (*enkrates*) of the worse, this is expressed by saying that the person is "stronger than himself" (*kreittō hautou*) ... But when, on the other hand, the smaller and better part is overpowered (*kratēthēi*) by the larger because of bad upbringing or bad company, this is called being "weaker than oneself" and is a form of blame.   (431a3–b2)

As in the puppet passage, here there is no threefold distinction in the soul: there are just better and worse desires, and nothing in between. The second example is from Book 10, where (as discussed briefly in Chapter 8), Socrates drops his explicit talk of tripartition and instead focuses simply on a twofold distinction between what is "foolish" in the soul or taken in by the illusory effects of poetry, on the one hand, and what "follows" reasoning and law in the soul or can resist the effects of poetry, on the other. Socrates associates the former, moreover, with "sexual desires, anger (*thumou*), appetites, pains, and pleasures," all of which are stimulated and nourished by poetic performances (606d). Once again, as in the *Laws* and *Timaeus*, we find *thumos* on an undiscriminating list of troublemaking non-rational impulses that, just as in the *Laws*, oppose the dictates of reason and law. In sum, then, we have no justification for taking the puppet passage as a repudiation of the three-part soul. The fact that bipartite conceptions of the soul appear in the very works in which Plato defends tripartition shows he does not take the former to contradict or compete with the latter. Rather, Plato readily makes use of bipartition alongside tripartition when it suits the context or his dialectical aims.[8]

---

[8] Cf. Saunders (1962: 37–8). By contrast, Vander Waerdt (1985a and 1985b) argues that the later Peripatetic characterization of Platonic psychology in terms of a bipartite rational/non-rational division "fundamentally misrepresented" tripartite theory (1985b: 301). However, his position is based largely on the assumption that the innovation in tripartite theory is *thumos*, which Plato was promoting *above* the non-rational to become reason's ally. Therefore, Vander Waerdt takes the assignment of spirit to the ἄλογον portion of the soul to represent a misunderstanding of Plato's position. Thus I take his background view of tripartition to be mistaken on two counts: (1) As I argued in Ch. 5.3, reason was Plato's innovation, not spirit. (2) According to the account I sketched in Ch. 8, spirit's relationship with reason is perfectly compatible with its being just as non-rational as appetite.

What kinds of aims make bipartition rather than tripartition suitable, then? While I think the argument above is sufficient for rejecting the inference from the puppet image to developmentalism, this question is worth addressing, both for its own inherent interest and in order to provide resources for explaining why Plato might have drawn on a dichotomous soul rather than a three-part one at this particular point in the *Laws*.

We can distinguish, I think, two main (sometimes overlapping) motivations for Plato's use of bipartition in his works. The first is theoretical or metaphysical. Plato seems deeply committed to thinking that the rational part of the soul is immortal and has a special affinity to the divine, whereas (as noted in Chapter 1) he is more skeptical and equivocal over the course of his career about whether appetite and spirit share in immortality, and he clearly thinks they lack reason's unique kinship with divinity. For these reasons, the rational part is qualitatively superior to, and quite possibly also separable at bodily death from, *both* the appetitive and spirited parts of the soul. Some commentators conclude from this that Plato's "real" commitment is to bipartition, but that strikes me as misleading. There may be a sense in which the distinction between reason and the non-rational is more metaphysically fundamental, but Plato also thinks embodied human beings *really do* have three sources of motivation within them—three sources of the psychic motions that explain and produce their actions. It is useful to think of Plato's divisions of the soul as a taxonomy in which the soul is divided into rational and non-rational, and the non-rational is in turn subdivided into its appetitive and spirited parts.[9] In some contexts Plato finds it useful to emphasize the gap between reason on the one hand and the non-rational parts on the other, whereas in other contexts the finer distinctions between appetite and spirit become especially pressing. More specifically, we can say that from the eternal or divine "cosmological" perspective, what is most salient tends to be the distinction between divine reason and the non-rational soul.[10] From the human or "political" perspective, however, the distinction between spirit and appetite is of great importance.[11]

---

[9] Cf. Weinstein (2018: 265). Robinson (1970: 121) makes a similar point but erroneously takes it as evidence *against* Plato's commitment to the tripartite soul. In general, Robinson wrongly takes tripartition and bipartition to compete irreconcilably with one another.

[10] It is no coincidence that in the *Phaedo*, where Socrates is concerned with the soul's immortality and emphasizes its kinship with the divine, desires that are attributed to appetite and spirit under tripartition are ascribed to the "body" instead (e.g. 66b–d, 94c–e).

[11] Robinson (1970: 120–1) notes the importance of *thumos* in political contexts but considers this a "flimsy" foundation for taking it seriously as a part of the soul. It would be flimsy, however, only if Plato took sociality and politics to be unnecessary or insignificant aspects of embodied human life. In a sense, Robinson makes the same mistake as Young Socrates in the *Statesman*, which the Cronus myth is designed to correct (see Ch. 9.1).

This explains why, for instance, much of the *Timaeus* focuses on the distinction between mortal and immortal soul: the former is deeply functionally connected with, or perhaps even ontologically dependent on, the mortal human body, whereas the latter is not.[12] That connection to the body, moreover, is *equally* true of both appetite and spirit, by contrast to reason. From the cosmological perspective, therefore, this metaphysical difference is what is most salient. Only when Timaeus turns to the physiology of the mortal human body and its relationship to moral psychology does he need to attend to the differences between the two mortal parts of the soul.[13]

The second main use of bipartition is practical or moral. Here the dichotomous characterization of the soul is informed by the dichotomous nature of virtue and vice, or of virtuous and vicious action. In some contexts, what matters for Plato's purposes is simply that some of our motivations pull us in the right moral direction and others in the wrong one. Hence in *Republic* 10 the pertinent distinction is between what conforms to reason and law in the soul on the one hand and what opposes them under the deceptive influence of poetry on the other.[14] Because the spirited emotion of anger can motivate ill-advised or illegal behavior just as many of our appetitive impulses do, it belongs in the foolish portion of the soul in this context.[15] Likewise, in Socrates' analysis of psychic strength and weakness, what matters is simply that some of our desires should, and others should *not*, serve as the dominant or ruling force in our psychologies. This practical or moral use of bipartition seems to motivate the two-part nature of the image of the puppet. Given that

---

[12] Lisi (2005: 67–8) defends a strong position to this effect.

[13] A similar shift can be perceived, in the opposite direction, in *Republic* 10. Socrates says that while they have given an adequate account of the *embodied* human soul and its parts, he raises doubt about whether the divine and *immortal* soul is similarly partitioned and πολυειδής (611b–612a). Thus despite the usefulness of tripartition throughout the *Republic*'s discussion of ethics and politics *in the human world*, Plato highlights the fact that, from the divine perspective, reason might be separable from appetite and spirit after all.

[14] Cf. Barney (2016: 58–9, n. 9), Burnyeat (1999: 225), and Nehamas (1982: 67). *Contra* Penner (1971: 96, 113). Book 10 does not try to repudiate or replace Book 4's tripartition.

[15] Many commentators—e.g. Annas (1981: 131), Burnyeat (1999: 223–8), Cairns (1993: 182–3), Kamtekar (2017: 172), Penner (1971: 100), and perhaps Allen (2010: 156)—identify the "foolish" part with appetite alone, taking spirit either to side with reason or simply be left out of the picture. However, this faces the obvious problem that *thumos* is included among the states found in the foolish part, and there are other indications of spirit's presence in Book 10 (see Destrée [2011]). Similarly unsatisfying is Jansen's (2015) argument that the phrase refers primarily to spirit, given that most of the motivations attributed to the foolish part are *appetitive* in nature. More plausible is the view suggested by Nehamas (1982: 66–8), Reeve (2013b: 85), Singpurwalla (2011), Storey (2014: 86, n. 6), and Weinstein (2018: 102, n. 12), and defended at length in Moss (2008), that the irrational part refers jointly to appetite *and* spirit. My own tentative view is a mix of the above: I think spirit falls on the "foolish" side with respect to its susceptibility to perceptual and moral illusion, but that its motivations *can*, given its relationship with reason and the imagistic resources sketched in Ch. 8, nonetheless obey or "follow" reasoning and law in many cases.

Plato finds bipartition useful in illustrating the concepts of being "stronger" or "weaker" than oneself in the *Republic*, of course, it should be no surprise that he continues to find it useful when he returns to them in the *Laws*. In the puppet passage, the Athenian wants to emphasize the moral divide between virtue and vice and between the impulses that draw us toward each of them. In these various contexts, the binaries of lawful/unlawful, virtue/vice, and reason-conforming/reason-opposing make it useful to appeal to a bipartite psychology that splits up our souls and our desires on the basis of which side of these ethical divides they fall on. That does not, however, in the *Laws* any more than in the *Republic*, exclude the possibility of finer or different distinctions among our virtuous or vicious impulses and psychic elements.

This concludes the case against developmentalism. I turn now to my positive arguments concerning spirit's role in the *Laws*.

2. Courage and Civic Unity

Plato's concern with spirited motivation in many ways determines the agenda for the *Laws*. The dialogue begins with the Athenian's interrogation of his Spartan and Cretan interlocutors—Megillus and Kleinias, respectively—regarding the source, substance, and aims of their cities' laws and constitutions. Kleinias' response emphatically identifies martial success as the primary goal of all Cretan legislation: "The lawgiver of the Cretans established all our customs, public and private, with a view to war (*polemon*) ... For according to him nothing is really beneficial, neither possessions nor practices, unless one conquers (*kratēi*) in war" (626a5–b3). Hence Cretan education and practices, as well as like-minded Spartan ones, aim at the cultivation of courage (*andreia*) among citizens through gymnastics, hunting, common meals for soldiers, and various exercises that promote endurance (*karterēsis*) in the face of suffering, pain, and fear (632e–633c). Megillus offers an explanation for the lawgiver's focus, moreover. The prioritization of martial values is due to the ubiquity and unavoidability of conflict. "Endless war exists among all cities," he explains, and even so-called "peace" is mere pretense: "There always exists by nature an undeclared war among all cities." Not only that, but even *within* a city the same thing applies to every village in relation to every other village, every household in relation to every other household, and ultimately to every man in relation to all others, and even in relation to *himself*. He concludes, "All are enemies (*polemioi*) of all in public, and in private each person is an enemy of himself." The world of human affairs, in other words, is distinguished above all by violence, faction, and strife, and the successful city or person, therefore, must cultivate the military fitness and courage required for victory (*to nikan*) (625e–626e).

Much of the rest of the text is concerned with responding to this conception of human life and politics, and Plato's views on the two faces of *thumos* provide a useful resource for understanding both the response itself as well as why it is necessary. Megillus and Kleinias make it clear that their laws and constitutions are devoted entirely to developing the aggressive side of spirited motivation. For Plato this is troubling because it is the gentle side that makes harmonious social groups possible. The Cretan and Spartan perspective takes for granted that communities are full of conflict, but from Plato's point of view, it misunderstands the direction of explanation between militarism and political strife. Megillus and Kleinias justify the exclusive emphasis on developing aggressive and martial traits *because* they take cities and communities to be full of war and faction; Plato, by contrast, takes cities and communities to be full of war and faction in large part *because* citizens have overdeveloped the aggressive side of their spirited nature at the expense of the gentle, friendly, or cooperative side. Indeed, this Platonic diagnosis is in many ways programmatic for the rest of the *Laws*. Broadly speaking, many of the dialogue's discussions and proposals represent the Athenian's attempt to temper his interlocutors' zeal for combative, soldierly qualities with the gentle aspects of spirit that contribute to stable communities and civic unity.[16]

The Athenian's initial reactions to Megillus' characterization of Cretan militarism foreshadow ideas he goes on to develop in more depth. He notes, first of all, that war and violence are not really the most desirable ways to resolve conflict; it is much better for familial or civil strife to be settled peacefully in ways that restore friendship (*philia*). Even reconciliation of this kind, however, is not strictly speaking *good*, but merely a necessary way of dealing with a social and political evil. What is truly good for a city is for there to be no wars or factions in the first place, but instead genuine peace and friendly goodwill (*philophrosunē*). The true legislator, therefore, establishes laws not with a view to war, but with a view to peace (627e–628e). Closely related to this concern, the Athenian strikes at the heart of the Cretan and

---

[16] Cf. remarks in Cleary (2003: 166), North (1966: 171–2), and Grube (1980: 284–5), who suggests that the *Statesman*'s contrast between moderation and courage, or gentleness and spiritedness, reappears in *Laws* 1 as the difference between the Athenian and the Dorian points of view. For a detailed discussion of the Athenian's treatment of *sōphrosunē* in relation to Kleinias' and Megillus' political perspectives, see Taki (2003). For general discussion of the influence of Cretan and Spartan culture and politics on the *Laws*, see Morrow (1960, esp. Chs. 1–2) and David (1978).

Spartan systems by calling into question the supreme value they place on courage: it is actually *last* in importance among the cardinal virtues. Bellicosity by itself is not necessarily a good thing, moreover, but often has morally deleterious side effects. Mercenaries, for instance, are willing to fight, but are almost always rash, unjust, violent, and imprudent (630a–631d). Later, the Athenian issues Kleinias a sharply worded critique of Sparta's neglect of musical education that coincides with its undue preoccupation with war and martial courage:

> Your regime is that of an army encampment rather than of people living together (*katōikēkotōn*) in cities. You keep your young in a flock, like a bunch of colts grazing in a herd. None of you takes his own young aside, all wild (*agriainonta*) and irritated (*aganaktounta*), away from his fellow grazers. None of you gives him a private groom and educates (*paideuei*) him by patting him down and taming (*hēmerōn*) him, giving him all that is appropriate for child rearing (*paidotrophiai*). If you did, he would become not only a good soldier but someone capable of managing a city and towns . . . He would always and everywhere honor the possession of courage as the fourth, not the first, part of virtue, both for private individuals and for the whole city. (666e1–667a5)[17]

Here the Athenian likens children in Sparta to spirited young horses who need to be "tamed." Their military upbringing might turn them into effective and courageous warriors, but inattention to cultivating their gentleness means that they lack the disposition and training required to live together as citizens in a genuine community.[18]

---

[17] Translations of the *Laws* are from Pangle (1980), with modifications.

[18] Note that whereas Plato characterizes Spartans as unduly obsessed with courage, speakers in Thucydides contrast Spartan moderation or caution with *Athenian* courage. My understanding of that discrepancy is based on the fact that Greek treatments of courage—especially in oratorical debates like those in Thucydides—play on its subjective ambiguity: the same actions can be viewed as either courage or rashness, or as either cowardice or prudence, depending on the perspective. The Athenians characteristically rush into conflict eagerly and without hesitation, whereas the Spartans enter into conflict only slowly and carefully. From one perspective, the former can seem courageous and the latter cowardly. On the other hand, Athenian impetuosity also makes them quick to *abandon* a fight, whereas Spartan steadiness makes them much more likely to *remain* in a fight once they have entered it. (Hence Thucydides describes Sparta's surrender at Sphacteria as the Athenians' most unexpected surprise in the war, because they thought the Spartans would "fight any way they could until they died" rather than surrender; 4.40.1–2.) From *this* perspective, the latter clearly seems more courageous than the former. Plato, I take it, is sensitive to the political significance of this ambiguity and the potential for opposed subjective evaluations of actions, as reflected in his discussion of the ways the two civic types of the *Statesman* naturally view one another. Cf. *Laws* 706a–d for a relevant contrast between "steady" soldiers vs. marines who are "quick" to attack but also quick to *retreat*.

The Athenian actually makes the need to balance aggressive traits with gentle ones explicit in a passage from Book 5 that constitutes one of the preambles or "preludes" to the laws. He explains:

> Every man should be spirited (*thumoeidē*), but yet also as gentle (*praion*) as possible. For there is no way to escape from others' injustices (*adikēmata*) that are harsh (*chalepa*) and difficult, or even impossible, to cure, except to secure victory (*nikōnta*) by fighting (*machomenon*) and defending (*amuno-menon*) oneself, not at all slackening (*anienai*) in the punishment; and this no soul can achieve without a noble spirit (*thumou gennaiou*). On the other hand, when people commit injustices that are curable, it is necessary first of all to recognize that no one unjust is voluntarily unjust...The unjust man, like someone burdened by evils, is pitiable in every way, and it is permissible to pity (*eleein*) such a man when his illness is curable, and to restrain one's spirit (*thumon*) and become gentle (*praünein*), instead of continuing on with bitterness and womanly irritation. But in dealing with the purely and inveterately corrupt and wicked man, one must give free rein (*ephieinai*) to one's anger (*orgēn*). This is why we declare that it is fitting for the good man always to be both spirited (*thumoeidē*) and gentle (*praion*).   (731b3–d5)

Notice, to begin with, that the passage supplies an unambiguous counter-example to the idea that *thumos*—even when it refers to the emotion of anger—always belongs indiscriminately among our vicious non-rational impulses in the *Laws*. The Athenian here identifies a morally beneficial use of spirited anger in defense against, and punishment of, the incurably unjust. His unequivocal endorsement of "giving free rein" to *thumos* in such cases (and note the familiar equine metaphor) makes it clear that anger does not always "pull" in the direction of vice. On the contrary, anger is actually "noble" when used appropriately, and citizens must therefore be "spirited." The Athenian emphasizes, however, that people must also possess complementary "gentleness." In context, he has just explained that citizens must strive to "share" their virtues with one another out of "friendship," thereby striving to make one another better (730e–731a). This point, in combination with the curative or rehabilitative principles of the penal code the Athenian advocates throughout the text, suggests that one reason people must be "gentle" is so that they can treat curable wrongdoers with the pity and well-intentioned admon-ishment or punishment due to friends. In this important passage, then, Plato not only uses the same language with which he characterizes the two faces of spiritedness in earlier dialogues—*thumoeidēs* and *praios* describe the desired nature of the warriors in both *Republic* and *Timaeus*—but also associates those two faces with similar psychological and behavioral functions: spirited anger makes people fight well and secure victory, and gentleness makes people treat one another with pity and friendship.

Because Megillus and Kleinias *already* recognize the value of making citizens spirited fighters, however, the Athenian focuses throughout the dialogue on the gentle side of spirit they neglect. The positive political perspective he develops throughout the text, therefore, provides constructive corollaries of his critical assessment of the Cretan and Spartan overemphasis on war and aggression. To begin with, whereas courage is relegated to lowest importance among the virtues, moderation or *sōphrosunē* is elevated to second place behind only prudence or wisdom, with justice following in third (631c–d).[19] He even characterizes moderation as an ethically imperative way of imitating the orderliness of the divine. After stating that everyone should do all they can to become as similar to the god as possible, he specifies, "The moderate man among us is a friend (*philos*) to god, because similar (*homoios*), while the man who is immoderate is dissimilar (*anomoios*) and different and unjust (*adikos*)" (716c1–d4).[20] The Athenian also explains that the quickest and easiest way for a city to change its laws for the better is for "a divine erotic passion for moderate and just practices to arise in some of the great and all-powerful rulers." In general, "When the greatest power coincides in a human being with prudence and moderation, then the best regime is brought forth into being; but otherwise, it will never come into existence" (711c5–712a3). Significantly, these statements parallel and revise the *Republic*'s claim that no city or constitution will ever become perfect until either authentic philosophers become rulers or the present rulers and kings are inspired by a divine "true erotic passion for true philosophy" (499a–c). In other words, in the *Laws* the love of justice and moderation has, at least as a matter of verbal emphasis, taken the place of love of wisdom as the necessary condition of political success. Much could be said about how this shift might relate to other substantive or apparent differences in the political theories of the two dialogues, but the important point here is simply that, given how central philosophy is in the theory of the *Republic*, the close parallel has the effect of

---

[19] Hence courage is ranked below the two "virtues" identified as psychological preconditions of cities in the *Protagoras*.

[20] Note also how the Athenian describes the life of moderation: it is "gentle" (πρᾷον) rather than "sharp" (ὀξύν) and is filled with "mild" or "soft" (μαλακάς) pleasures and appetites rather than "unrestrained" or "violent" (σφοδράς) ones (733d–734e).

amplifying the Athenian's already strong claim about the supreme political value of justice and moderation.[21]

The Athenian also stresses the importance of friendship, which he takes to be inextricably linked with moderation and justice.[22] He claims that a city's laws should be determined in accordance with the goals of prudence, friendship, and moderation, and he adds that these are not really distinct objectives, but rather amount to the same thing (693b–c).[23] In general, the guiding purpose of their laws is to make the citizens "friends with one another to the greatest extent possible" (743c); the laws should promote "friendship between similar people," which is the kind of friendship that is "tame" (*hēmeros*) and "shared" (*koinē*) throughout life for the sake of virtue (837b–d); and they should teach citizens "how to socialize (*homilountes*) with one another and live together in friendly affection (*philophronōs*)" (880d–e). He also stipulates that public sanctuaries in the forms of altars, statues, oracles, and shrines will be located throughout Magnesia to serve as sites for ceremonial events that will bring citizens together and promote social intercourse (738b–d). In terms that echo both Socrates' discussion of spirited dogs in *Republic* 2 and his advocacy for communalism in *Republic* 5, the Athenian explains, "They'll become friendly (*philophronōntai*) at the sacrifices, become familiar (*oikeiōntai*) and get to know (*gnōrizōsin*) one another. There is no greater good for a city that for its inhabitants to be well known (*gnōrimous*) to one another" (738d7–e2).

Related to the goal of civic friendship is the Athenian's emphasis on cultivating not only the political capacity to share in government, but also and especially the willingness to submit oneself to the authority of others. Education, he says, must promote the kind of virtue that motivates a person "to become a complete citizen who knows how to rule and be ruled with justice" (643e3–6), and he is especially keen to emphasize the latter. Again, this makes sense in terms of his dialectical aims in relation to his interlocutors. Whereas the aggressive side of spirit provides the desire for power over

---

[21] Notably, the Athenian earlier insists that the laws must promote moderation and justice coupled with intelligence "rather than wealth or love of honor (μὴ πλούτῳ μηδὲ φιλοτιμίᾳ)" (632c–d), just as philosophy is the alternative to the lives of appetitive greed and spirited love of honor in the *Republic*.

[22] Laks (2007) discusses the interrelations among these objectives, as well as their connection to the value of freedom in the *Laws*.

[23] Stalley (2003: 176–7) argues that moderation plays no significant role in the *Laws*, noting that there are relatively few uses of the term *sōphrosunē* itself. As we have just seen, however, several of the Athenian's references to it are especially emphatic in asserting its value. Stalley's assessment also ignores the fact that the civic virtue of moderation becomes identified or entangled with both friendship and a sense of shame in the *Laws*—concepts that *do* receive verbal emphasis throughout the text. For discussion of *philia* and its importance in the *Laws*, see Sheffield (2020) and Prauscello (2014: Chs. 2–3); cf. Reid (2018) on friendship and sex in the *Laws*.

others,[24] gentleness is what makes people willing to defer to their superiors. Hence the Athenian claims that no one should ever be without a ruler or acquire the habit of independent action. Rather, "at all times, in war and in peace, the soul should live constantly looking to and following the ruler," and "as much as possible everyone should in every respect live always in a group, together and in common (*koinon*)" (942a–d).

Furthermore—to touch briefly on topics I address in the next section—the Athenian identifies a sense of shame (*aidōs* or *aischunē*), which he defines as the fear of bad reputation among one's friends, as the psychological core of moral development and a crucial component of civic unity. The lawgiver "reveres [it] with the greatest honors," while considering shamelessness "the greatest of private or public evils," and he makes pedagogical and legislative use of shame accordingly (646e–647b). Indeed, one of the signature institutions of the Athenian's educational program, the drinking party, is specifically designed to develop and mold a strong sense of shame, while also promoting various qualities related to shame: moderation in the face of appetites (647c–d), obedience to the Dionysian rulers who supervise them (671d–e), and especially *friendship* among the participants.[25] The Athenian explicitly contrasts the function of drinking parties, moreover, with that of the military exercises that instill courage: symposia are concerned not with armies of men "who are fighting enemies in war," but rather "friends sharing in community with friends in peace and friendly affection (*philōn d' en eirēnēi pros philous koinōnēsontōn philophrosunēs*)" (640b6–8; cf. 671e–672a). The striking repetition of the language of *philia* here highlights what the Athenian takes to be the glaring deficiency in the Spartan and Cretan constitutions. His lengthy discussion of drinking parties is largely framed as a response to the skepticism of his interlocutors. Their cities have no such institution—nor any, they confess, that produces similar effects—and as a result they are dubious of its value.[26] In this context, the Athenian's conspicuous emphasis on the crucial contribution symposia make to civic *friendship*, therefore, sends a clear message about what is missing from their constitutions: spirited love of fellow citizens.

---

[24] By contrast, the Athenian attributes the incapacity to be ruled by others to the "pride" (μεγαλαχυίας) of a soul "burning (φλέγεται) with insolence (ὕβρεως)" (716a–b), suggesting an overheated, assertive *thumos*.

[25] Cf. Prauscello (2014: 146–7), who stresses that choral parties promote "social solidarity and cohesion."

[26] See e.g. 633b–c, 636e–637e, and 641a–b, and cf. *Minos* 320a on Cretan and Spartan abstinence from drinking.

Finally, the social institutions of Magnesia are, like those of the *Republic*, designed to promote civic unity and friendship, and evidently they are grounded in the same basic principles that inform the earlier dialogue. The Athenian famously concedes that the city they are constructing will only be a "second-best" city and explains:

> That city and constitution are first, and those laws best, where the old proverb holds as much as possible throughout the whole city: the saying goes that "friends (*philōn*) truly share all things in common (*koina*)." If this situation exists somewhere now, or if it should ever exist someday—if women are common (*koinas*), and children are common (*koinous*), and every sort of property is common (*koina*); if every device has been employed to exclude all of what is called the "private" (*idia*) from all aspects of life; if, insofar as possible, somehow a way has been devised to make common (*koina*) the things that are by nature private (*ta idia koina*), such as the eyes and ears and hands, so that they seem to see and hear and act in common (*koina*); if, again, everyone praises (*epainein*) and blames (*psegein*) in unison, as much as feeling pleasure and pain at the same things, if with all their power they delight in laws that aim at making the city *one* (*mian*) to the extent possible—then no one will ever set down a more correct or better definition than this of what constitutes the extreme of virtue. Whether gods or the children of multiple gods inhabit such a city, they dwell there in good cheer as they live out their lives. Therefore one should not look anywhere else for the model of a constitution, but should hold on to this and seek with all one's power the constitution that comes as close as possible to it. If the regime we've been dealing with now came into being, it would be, in some way, the nearest to immortality and second-place in being *one* (*mia*).
>
> (739b8–e4)

Many commentators have taken this passage as a thinly veiled allusion to the Kallipolis.[27] For the purposes of my argument, however, it is not necessary to make that assumption. What matters is simply that, *whatever* place Plato is referring to here, it shares with the Kallipolis both some of the latter's distinctive social policies—notably, communal possession of wives and children and the elimination of private property—as well as the reasoning that

[27] Kahn (2008: 164–6) provides a compelling defense of this view. For others who view the Kallipolis as the "best" city to which Magnesia is "second-best," or as the ideal or paradigm to which Magnesia is a more practical alternative or approximation, see Adomenas (2001), Fraistat (2014), Kraut (2010), and Laks (1990, 1991, 1998, 2000).

justifies them: sharing things in common promotes friendship and thereby contributes to the political ideal of "oneness" or unity.[28] Although the Athenian thinks the extreme forms of "sharing" found in this best constitution are unattainable for Magnesia, he nonetheless believes they should serve as the "model" for their city's policies and institutions. In other words, in the *Laws* Plato has his main speaker endorse the same kinds of social policies that Socrates advocates in the *Republic*, where they are based on Plato's views about the spirited part of the soul, and he signals to the reader that the Magnesian constitution will strive to approximate those policies to the greatest extent permitted by political reality.[29]

The dialogue makes good on this promise. Although citizens will possess property and have their own families, the Athenian institutes restrictions that are designed to subordinate the private to the public and to limit or mitigate the divisive effects that privatization ordinarily has on a city. In the case of property, citizens receive their own allotments of land and households, but the Athenian repeatedly stresses that "each must consider his share to be at the same time the common property of the whole city" (740a; cf. 877d–e, 923a–b). He is also concerned with preventing acquisitiveness and the wealth disparities that result from it. Money-making is incompatible with justice (736e–737b; cf. 831c–e) and makes a city "friendless" (*aphilon*, 705a–b), he says, and the extremes of affluence and indigence make individuals vicious and fill the city with "civil war and faction" (744d–e).[30] Therefore, he proposes a number of laws aimed at precluding unchecked accumulation or loss of property. Money-making and associated commercial behavior are strictly outlawed, and citizens are forbidden from buying or selling their allotments or possessing more than four times the value of their allotment. And while the citizens are permitted to possess a special Magnesian currency for practical use among themselves, they are forbidden from privately owning any silver or gold, which would have value outside of the city as well (741a–745b).

---

[28] Cf. the description of ancient Athens at *Critias* 110a–d and 112a–c: the military class was separated from the productive class; it included both men and women, who lived, ate, trained, and fought together in "common" and "as if they belonged to a single household"; and the warriors made no use of silver or gold and had no private possessions, but rather thought of their possessions as "the common property of all"

[29] Cf. Macé (2017) and Pradeau (2002: 151).

[30] The Athenian also includes laws throughout the text that aim at regulating property and minimizing property disputes. For example, inheritance laws ensure that the number of allotments remains constant over generations (740b–741a), and citizens are forbidden from loaning money with interest, or to anyone they do not trust (742c). The fixed number of households in Magnesia (737e) also serves the aim of making it possible for everyone in the city to "know" everyone else. I owe this last point to Jeremy Reid.

Family life follows a similar pattern. Citizens have a civic obligation to marry and produce offspring, and they are encouraged to make political expediency a priority in their decision-making about both (772d–774a; cf. 721b–d).[31] In the first instance, this applies to the selection of a suitable partner: what matters most is not what individuals find pleasant, but what benefits the city. Citizens should, therefore, take two main considerations into account for the sake of the common good. First, they should not marry for the sake of money, but should actually privilege the *less* wealthy among their prospective brides in the interest of stabilizing wealth distribution in the city. Second, they should take into account the *character* of their partners. Here the Athenian invokes the same basic account of intermarriage that appears in the *Statesman*. Character falls into two main dichotomous types, which are identified in terms associated with the two faces of spirit, and optimal marriages pair someone from one side of the dichotomy with their opposite.[32] Although people are naturally attracted to what is "most similar" to themselves, the Athenian explains, it is best for "quick (*thatton*) dispositions to join in marriage with those who are slower (*braduteron*), and the slower with the quick." Therefore, "Someone who knows himself to be impatient (*itamōteron*) and quick (*thatton*) in all his affairs should be spiritedly eager (*prothumeisthai*) to make orderly (*kosmioi*) parents his relatives by marriage, and one whose natural disposition is the opposite should ally himself with the opposite sort of in-laws" (773a7–b4).[33] Such unions benefit the city by producing children of a more balanced disposition, and, in general, the couple "should do everything in their power to consider how they can provide the city with noble children" (783d–e). Public officials, moreover, oversee this aspect of their private life. Women who are appointed to supervise marriages are instructed to enter the homes of young couples and "use threats and exhortations to prevent them from doing anything mistaken or foolish" (784b–c). Finally, parents have only limited authority in the upbringing of their own children, and they are not allowed to deny their child a public

---

[31] For discussion of the *oikos* and family in the *Laws* in comparison to the *Republic*, especially with respect to the role of women, see Samaras (2010) and Kochin (2002: Chs. 5–6).

[32] Cf. Campbell (1867: l–li) and Kraut (2010: 61).

[33] At 929e–930b the Athenian considers a case in which husband and wife are both overly spirited types and become incapable of reconciling: "If their souls continue to seethe"—and here the verb κυμαίνω, which means "to swell" or "rise in waves," recalls poetic comparisons of a raging *thumos* to a tumultuous sea—"then they should do what they can to seek partners who will be suitable for each of the parties… They should try to harmonize with those whose character is more sedate and gentle (πρᾳότερα)." Significantly, the Athenian also likens the "mixture" of fast and slow temperaments to the mixture of water and wine (which is said to "boil," ζεῖ) (773c–e), which bears on the connection between wine and spirited emotion discussed in Sect. 3 and n. 49 below. Finally, see also 681a–d on the distinction between "orderly" and "courageous" natures and customs.

education. Rather, every child, both male and female, must necessarily be educated, "on the grounds that they belong more to the city than to those who generated them" (804d–e).

The Athenian, then, allows some privatization of both property and family in Magnesia, but he places limitations on them designed to approximate the social arrangements of the best city. Although there is a sense in which the Magnesian citizens have their own property and families, everything that is theirs privately also, and in a deeper sense, belongs to the public—is "common" after all—and individuals must always subordinate their own proprietary or domestic interests and desires to the good of the city as a whole. As the Athenian later reiterates, "The true political art must care not for the private (*idion*) but for the public (*koinon*)—for the common binds cities together, while the private tears them apart" (875a5–7).

3. Musical Education and the Drinking Party

Spirited motivations also continue to play a prominent role in musical and gymnastic training in the *Laws*, as they did in the *Republic*, and Plato develops spirit's educational role in some new ways as well.[34] The Athenian identifies virtue as complete consonance between correct rational belief and law, on the one hand, and an individual's feelings or emotions of pleasure and pain, "friendship" (*philia*) and "hatred" (*misē*), on the other. Education, he says, is concerned with fostering that consonance on the side of feeling and emotion during a time when they are still incapable of "using reason (*logōi*)". (653b–c). It is "the drawing and pulling of children toward right reason as determined by law" (659d1–3) and it aims at "correct training in pleasures and pains, so that a person hates (*misein*) what he is supposed to hate from the very beginning until the end, and also loves (*stergein*) what he is supposed to love" (653b6–c2).[35] The Athenian goes on to identify education with the

---

[34] Aristotle simplistically claims the Magnesian citizens receive "the same education" as their counterparts in the Kallipolis (*Pol.* 1265a1–10). For discussion of the relation of the early education system of the *Laws* to that of the *Republic*, see Grube (1980: 242–51), Jaeger (1944b: 213–30), Kamtekar (2008: 355–7), Kraut (2010: 64–8), Morrow (1960: 331, n. 117 and 373–5), and North (1966: 186–90). Most commentators take the program of the *Laws* to be broadly similar to that of the *Republic*, although many draw attention to shifts in focus, newly or more deeply developed ideas, or adjustments to its implementation due to the different political structure and circumstances of Magnesia. For general discussion of early education in the *Laws*, see Morrow (1960: Ch. 7) and Stalley (1983: 123–33).

[35] Talk of pleasure and pain might be taken to suggest appetitive rather than spirited motivations. However, throughout the *Laws* the Athenian often uses "pleasures and pains" as a catch-all to refer generally to non-rational motivations, including ones attributed to spirit under tripartite theory. Hence here they include friendship and hatred. Likewise, *aidōs* and *aischunē* are classified as fears (646e–

choral art. Human beings alone among animals perceive and enjoy order in voice and bodily movement ("harmony" is order in voice, "rhythm," order in movement). That is why, from the time they are very young, human beings are incapable of keeping still or remaining silent, but are always moving their bodies around and using their voices. The institution of the chorus attempts to instill proper rhythm and harmony in individuals by directing the delight they take in order and by imposing rhythm and harmony on their own movements and speech (653d–654b). Broadly speaking, music is the vocal part of the choral art concerned with singing and orderly speech, and gymnastics is the bodily part concerned with dancing and orderly movement (664e–665a, 673a). I will first address the role of spirit in musical training before turning to gymnastic education in Section 4.

To begin with, musical education in the *Laws* focuses on the same familiar class of spirited emotions that were the primary target of Socrates' program in the *Republic*—most notably, admiration, disgust, and shame.[36] The choral art as a whole, the Athenian says, and music in particular, aims at a proper appreciation of what is admirable or *kalon*. The correctly educated individual loves (*stergein*) or feels friendship for (*philei*) what is admirable and hates (*misei*) or feels contempt for what is shameful.[37] Someone is well-educated in this sense, the Athenian explains, "who is not fully able to express correctly with voice and body what he understands, yet feels pleasure and pain correctly—warmly welcoming (*aspazomenos*) what is admirable and being disgusted (*duscherainōn*) by what is shameful" (654c9–d3). Song and dance provide means of cultivating the right emotional reactions to the *kalon* and *aischron* because they are "imitations" of moral character: admirable postures

---

647b), and fear, in turn, along with *thumos* itself are both explicitly classified as "pains" (864b). Similarly, lack of self-control with respect to "pleasures and pains" includes unrestrained action due to cowardice, feelings of envy (*phthonoi*), and *thumoi* (934a; cf. 644c–d and 649d). Cf. Prauscello (2014: 80–1). The fact that the Athenian uses the language of pleasure and pain is indeterminate, therefore, and as we will see, his subsequent discussion makes it clear that he has *spirited* emotions like admiration, disgust, and shame prominently in mind. That said, I do not mean to deny that appetitive motivations *also* play a role in early education in the *Laws*. Presumably, they do so at least in the negative sense outlined in Chs. 6 and 7: moral education will aim to moderate appetites. They may also play a more positive role too, however. Plausibly, rhythm and harmony are pleasing to the senses—it "feels good" to perceive, and take part in, song and dance—in such a way that the child takes a distinctively appetitive kind of pleasure in singing, dancing, and playing. Cf. Ch. 6, n. 27. For accounts of early education in the *Laws* that emphasize the role of pleasure, see Annas (1999: Ch. 7), Hatzistavrou (2011), Kamtekar (2010: 128–30 and 146–8), Morrow (1960: 302–18), Stalley (1983: 125–7), and Scolnicov (2003).

[36] Grube (1980: 252) comments: "The 'part' of the soul most directly concerned [in music and gymnastics] is undoubtedly the θυμός, the spirit or feelings." Cairns (1993: 373–8), Cohen (1993), and Renaut (2014: 313–22) also emphasize the Athenian's focus on shaping the sense of shame and honor through early education.

[37] See esp. 654c–d, 655d–e, and 689a–e.

and songs imitate virtue, and disgraceful postures and songs imitate vice (655a–d, 660a). Enjoying the right kinds of songs and dance, therefore, establishes habits of feeling admiration toward *kalon* character and behavior and feeling shame or disgust toward the opposite. The explanation of why attitudes of admiration and disgust are ethically central also echoes the reasoning of the *Republic*: those who admire a certain kind of character or behavior come to acquire that character and behave in those ways themselves. "Surely it is necessary," the Athenian declares, "that one who takes delight in things then becomes similar (*homoiousthai*) to the things he takes delight in ... And what greater good or evil could we say there is for us than such completely necessary assimilation?" (656b4–7). Musical education, then, is designed to make people admire and praise the right kinds of things so that they *become* the right kinds of people.

There are even reasons for thinking not only that musical training aims at spirited motivations, but that it takes for granted the existence of a distinct, independent source of such motivations in our psychology—that is, a spirited "part" of the soul as defined in Chapter 1. This case becomes clearest through the Athenian's discussion of public drinking parties and their relation to the emotion of shame. As noted above, when the Athenian initially suggests that drunkenness can be morally beneficial and praiseworthy under the right circumstances, he meets significant resistance from his more austere interlocutors. In response to their concerns, he provides an extended defense of the practice in Books 1 and 2.[38] He begins by explaining the psychological effects of wine-drinking: wine makes pleasures, pains, feelings of anger (*thumoi*), and sexual desires stronger and more intense, while it causes perceptions, memories, beliefs, and prudent thoughts to "completely abandon" a person (645d–e). The intoxicated individual, the Athenian and Kleinias agree, "arrives at a disposition of the soul that is the same as the one he had when he was a young child" (645e5–6).

Although this constitutes a degenerate condition of the soul, drunkenness can, if practiced under the right conditions and supervision, provide at least two interrelated benefits in a moral educational program. The first is that drunkenness can provide a kind of endurance training for people through which their sense of shame is tested. The Athenian points out that although

---

[38] Belfiore (1986) provides a useful historical analysis of the Athenian's discussion of wine-drinking, but takes his view to assume "a radically different psychological theory" from that of the *Republic*. For further reading on drinking parties in the *Laws*, see Jaeger (1944b: 226–7 and 340, n. 88), Kamtekar (2010: 141–2), Meyer (2015), Morrow (1960: 315–18), Pfefferkorn (2020), Prauscello (2014: Ch. 4), and Stalley (1983: 124–5).

Crete and Sparta have developed many ways of testing their citizens' fortitude in the face of pains—for example, through strenuous physical exercises and exposure to extreme heat and cold—they do not provide any comparable tests for courageous endurance of *pleasures*. This is a troubling omission, the Athenian thinks, especially since it is even *worse* to give in to pleasure than to pain (633b–634c). Alcohol, however, due to its unique properties and psychological effects, provides a means of testing resolve in the face of temptation. Because our pleasures are stronger and more intense when we are drunk, they are also *harder to resist*, and because reasoning "completely abandons" us, we are at an even further disadvantage: we cannot rely on our rational judgments and desires to help us resist them. When we are intoxicated, we are entirely at the mercy of our non-rational impulses; whatever endurance we are able to exercise must have its source among *them*. The solution, for the Athenian, lies in the emotion of shame. Those who have cultivated the proper sense of *aidōs*, he suggests, will continue to find morally objectionable behavior repugnant even while they are drunk and will act accordingly. Those who have not, on the other hand, will indulge their basest pleasures and impulses, having neither shame nor reason to restrain them, thereby revealing their vicious character. Drinking parties, then, provide a way of practicing resistance to pleasures and testing one's sense of shame in the process (647a–650b).

The significance of this discussion is that it clearly assumes a finer division between two types of non-rational impulses: the potentially vicious impulses, particularly those related to pleasure, that need to be resisted, and the better impulses, particularly feelings of shame, that can do the resisting. Thus, although the image of the puppet itself does not explicitly acknowledge a qualitative distinction of this sort, the account of intoxication that immediately follows and is informed by that image *does*. It recognizes that some non-rational motivations—namely, spirited ones—are better than others, and the better motivations serve the same psychological function attributed to the *thumoeides* in tripartite theory: providing courageous resistance to internal threats to virtue.[39] Most importantly, shame is capable of motivating an intoxicated person *independently* both of their reasoning or rational desires, which have "abandoned" them, or of their appetites, which the shame is resisting. In other words, when a drunk person exercises self-restraint, their

---

[39] Meyer (2012: 317–22) presents a similar line of argument, but has a somewhat different focus and draws a weaker conclusion about the role of spirit in the *Laws*. See also Pfefferkorn (2020), whose interpretation overlaps with my own on some key points.

appetitive desires for pleasure pull them in one direction, and spirited emotion pulls them in the opposite. This is, of course, precisely the kind of argument Socrates uses in *Republic* 4 to establish parthood in the soul. Indeed, the Athenian actually defines the emotion of shame in language that echoes Socrates' Principle of Opposites: *aidōs* is "opposed (*enantios*) to sufferings and other fears, but is also opposed (*enantios*) to the most frequent and greatest pleasures" (647a4–6). The discussion of drunkenness, then, points not only to a morally valuable use of spirited motivation, but also to a discrete source of psychic motion and motivation that operates separately from both appetite and reason. It points, in other words, to the existence of a spirited part of the person's soul.

There is a second benefit to drinking parties. If used properly, they do not merely *test* a person's sense of shame, but also *fortify* and *shape* that sense of shame. Although education is supposed to cultivate the proper non-rational feelings and attitudes in individuals, education also "tends to slacken in human beings, and in the course of a lifetime it becomes corrupted to a great extent" (653c7–9). The primary benefit of alcohol, on the Athenian's account, is that it provides a way of correcting this natural tendency through a kind of *re-education* of adults:

> Didn't we assert that... the souls of drinkers, just like some iron (*sidēron*), become fiery (*diapurous*), softened (*malthakōteras*), and youthful, so that they can be easily led—as they were when they were young—by someone who possesses the ability and the knowledge required to educate and mold (*plattein*) souls? Didn't we say that the one who did the molding is the same as he who molded them earlier, the good lawgiver, whose laws must be fellow drinkers at the banquet? They must be able to make whoever becomes hopeful (*euelpin*), bold (*tharraleon*), and more shameless (*anaischuntoteron*) than he should be... willing to act in just the opposite way. When ignoble boldness (*tharros*) appears, these laws will be able to send in as a combatant (*diamachomenon*) the noblest kind of fear accompanied by justice: the divine fear to which we gave the name "awe" (*aidō*) and "shame" (*aischunē*).
>
> (671b8–d3)

According to this passage, wine's usefulness lies in the fact that it makes the souls of drinkers *young* again. Youth is the period of our lives when we are most impressionable and educable, and alcohol evidently simulates that impressionable and educable condition. The primary psychological means by which intoxicated individuals are to be educated, moreover, is *shame*. In a properly run drinking party, individuals will be encouraged to avoid indecorous behavior, and those who succeed in their restraint will be publicly praised and honored and will grow in friendship with one another, while those who fail will be publicly blamed and humiliated. These practices reinforce the correct attitudes of shame, admiration, and so on that were cultivated during early education, but which have since "slackened."

This account provides further reasons for thinking that Plato still takes for granted the centrality of the *thumoeides* in the process of moral education. First, aside from the continued prominence of spirited emotion, note the Athenian's recognizable metaphorical language: he likens the young or drunken soul to soft, fiery "iron" and characterizes education as the process of "molding" that iron. This invokes the metallic metaphor and the dichotomy of hardness or inflexibility and softness or pliability that go all the way back to Homeric descriptions of *thumos*. It is also an exact echo of Socrates' characterization of the effects of early education and music on the spirited part of the soul in the *Republic*, where he says that a young person's *thumos* can be usefully "softened like iron" and then "molded," "stamped," or "imprinted" through musical training. Second, the Athenian's characterization of the relationship between physiology and psychology calls to mind the *Timaeus*. The Athenian explains that every young creature's nature is "fiery" (*diapuros*, 664e4),[40] and young people are full of "fire" (*pur*) in both body *and* soul; wine is also a kind of "fire" that reproduces the same "warm" condition (666a3–b2); and the fire or "heat" in question, we have just seen, is correlated with heightened spirited emotion. Likewise—again, following the tradition of associating of spirit with the heart and circulatory system—Timaeus refers to the blood and veins around the heart as "a kind of fountain of fire" that makes the inner parts of the body its "warmest" (*thermotata*) parts (79d1–2);[41] he explicitly attributes the stirring (*egersis*) or swelling (*oidēsis*) of *thumos* to the "fire" in the blood (70c1–4); and he identifies wine as a fiery (*empura*) agent that has a warming (*thermantikon*) effect on both the body and the soul (59e5–60a5).[42] These parallels suggest that there is a single psychological theory running through all three dialogues, one that takes a spirited element of psychology, as well as biological facts connected with it, to be key to explaining educability during childhood.

---

[40] They are also incapable of "quietness" (ἡσυχίαν).

[41] Cf. 70a7–b3: the heart is the "fountain" of blood that ties the veins together.

[42] Cf. the sudorific effects associated with spirited emotion in the *Phaedrus*: the horse "drenches the whole soul with sweat" out of shame in resisting the bad horse (254c4–5; cf. *Rep.* 350c–d).

The Athenian actually makes several tantalizing references to *thumos* in his discussions of education. For example, he claims that citizens must exercise their sense of shame and practice enduring pleasures in order to avoid "softness of spirit" (*glukuthumia*, 635c8). Likewise, wine makes a person "more eager in spirit" (*prothumoteron*, 666c4)[43] and cures the "toughness" (*austerotetos*) of old age, and when a person drinks, "the soul, by escaping from his dispiritedness (*dusthumia*), has its disposition turned from harder (*skleroteron*) to softer (*malakoteron*), so that it becomes more malleable (*euplastoteron*), like iron when it is plunged into fire" (666b7–c2). Most significantly, when he condemns citizens' use of insulting speech toward one another, he explains that such behavior is due to "the wicked nature (*phusis*) and upbringing (*trophe*) of spirit (*thumou*)" (934d5–6). Here the term *thumos* cannot refer simply to an occurrent feeling of anger, as it does in many other places in the *Laws*. Rather, it clearly refers to something that exists in the soul diachronically, has its own nature, and can be affected by a person's education or rearing. The Athenian continues, "The person who speaks [abusively] is gracious to a graceless thing, spirit (*thumoi*), and gorges his anger (*orgen*) with wicked feasts, making savage (*exagrion*) again that thing in his soul (*tes psuches to toiouton*) that was at one time tamed (*hemerothe*) by education" (935a3–6). Although Plato avoids explicitly acknowledging the existence of soul parts in the *Laws*, this remark comes close with its "that thing in the soul." The Athenian at the very least makes it clear that whatever is responsible for anger in the soul is also a primary target of education. Based on all of the above, we have good reason for thinking that that thing is the spirited part of the soul.

Finally, the Greek poetic and medical traditions provide context for Plato's treatment of wine-drinking that supplements and strengthens the case for this interpretation. To begin with, abundant references to wine-drinking in early poetic literature characterize its effects in terms of familiar spirited motivations and identify *thumos* as the aspect of psychology affected by it. In Theognis, for example:

Whoever exceeds his measure of drink is no longer in command (*karteros*) of his tongue or his mind; he says lawless things which are disgraceful (*aischra*) to the eyes of the sober, and he's not ashamed (*aideitai*) of anything he does when he's drunk. Formerly he was moderate (*sophron*), but now he is

---

[43] Cf. 665e–666a: wine makes those who would otherwise participate in a chorus only "unenthusiastically" (ἀπροθύμως) become 'spiritedly eager" (προθύμους) to do so.

juvenile... That man who will say nothing foolish after drinking many cups is truly unconquerable (*anikētos*). (*Eleg.* 1.479–92)

Here the poet's description of wine anticipates the Athenian's: inebriation impairs a person's sensibility, rendering them childish, and it encourages licentious speech and action, making it more difficult for them to exercise endurance, moderation, and a sense of shame. However, also like the Athenian, Theognis sees in drinking an opportunity to discern a person's character, for those who exercise restraint despite wine's effects prove themselves to be truly self-controlled. If Theognis only hints at *thumos* by referring to endurance and shame, however, Bacchylides is explicit:

When the sweet compulsion of the speeding cups warms (*thalpēsi*) the tender spirit (*thumon*) of the young men, Cyprian hope (*elpis*), mingling with the gifts of Dionysus, makes their hearts flutter. The wine sends him soaring on high: immediately he is destroying the battlements of cities, and he expects to be ruler over all the world... Such are the musings of the drinker's heart (*kear*). (fr. 20b.6–16)

Likewise (to give just a few of many examples from the poets), wine makes a young man "fearless" or "courageous" and nourishes a "sweet *thumos*";[44] it produces a "contented spirit" (*euthumia*);[45] it "gladdens (*euphrane*) the *thumos*";[46] and it is the best remedy (*pharmakon*) for a grieving *thumos*.[47] In all of these passages, drinking has precisely the sorts of effects that it does in Theognis and in the *Laws*: it makes a person bolder and more hopeful and cheerful, and these emotional changes are all expressly registered on the drinker's *thumos*. This strong precedent in poetic folk psychology provides additional reason for thinking that Plato has spirit in mind in his treatment of drunkenness and early education in the *Laws*.[48]

Aristotle corroborates this spirit-centric reading from a different perspective that also provides additional insight into the young/old dichotomy that is at the heart of the Athenian's proposal of drinking parties. In the *Rhetoric*, drawing on ideas from the medical tradition, Aristotle offers some rough-and-

---

[44] Anacreontea, fr. 56.　　[45] Euripides, *Cyclops* 530.　　[46] Stesichorus, fr. S148.8–9.
[47] Alcaeus, fr. 335.
[48] See also Prauscello (2014: 169–73) for illuminating discussion of parallels between the Athenian's account of drinking wine and Euripides' *Heracles*.

ready moral psychological profiles of men at various stages in their lives, including during adolescence and senectitude.[49] He explains:

> Young men... are hot-tempered (*thumikoi*) and quick-tempered (*oxuthumoi*), and apt to give way to their anger (*orgēi*). And they are weaker (*hettous*) than their spirit (*thumou*); for because of love of honor (*philotimian*) they cannot bear being slighted, and are indignant if they think they are being treated unjustly. While they love honor (*philotimoi*), they love victory (*philonikoi*) even more... They trust others readily, because they have not yet often been cheated. They are sanguine (*euelpides*); nature warms their blood as though with excess of wine... They are easily deceived, owing to the sanguine nature just mentioned. Their spiritedness (*thumōdeis*) and hopeful dispositions make them more courageous (*andreioteroi*) than older men are; for the spiritedness prevents fear (*phobeisthai*) and the hopeful disposition makes them feel bold (*tharrein*); we cannot feel fear (*phobeitai*) as long as we are angry (*orgizomenos*), and any expectation of good makes us confident (*tharraelon*). They are full of modesty (*aischuntēloi*)... and love their friends (*philophiloi*) and companions (*philetairoi*) more than at other ages.   (1389a3–b1)

---

[49] Two prominent ideas in contemporary medical theory provide background and theoretical resources on which Aristotle and Plato are drawing. First, early Greek thinkers often understand human physiology in terms of dichotomies like hot/cold and wet/dry and elements associated with those qualities. This way of thinking, which is evident even in early philosophical literature (e.g. Parmenides, Alcmaeon, and Philolaus), receives its most systematic expression in the works of the Hippocratics. On their view, differences in the relative proportions of these four qualities partly explain biological differences among people—between men and women, young and old, healthy and sick. Hence, for example (although the details sometimes vary), women tend to be moister and softer than men (e.g. *Nat. Women* 1, *Reg. in Health* 6.7–11, *Reg.* 1.34.1–10), and children tend to be moister and warmer than adults (e.g. *Reg.* 1.33.1–21). Second, these internal constitutional conditions are not determined exclusively by brute biological facts of nature, but are also affected by external and behavioral factors. This includes environmental influences like air and water quality or seasonal changes in the weather, as well as the individual's own regimen of diet and exercise (see esp. *Reg. in Health* 1–4). Hence winter tends to make people colder and wetter, whereas summer tends to make them hotter and drier, and—of obvious importance here—wine is singularly effective in making people warmer, wetter, and softer, whereas water makes people cooler. Consequently, for instance, as a general rule people should drink nearly undiluted wine in winter to counteract the season's coldness, but only heavily diluted wine, and a lot of it, during the summer. (*Reg.* 35–6 also describes at length a dichotomy between "watery" and "fiery" souls, which can both be affected by water and wine themselves, and which parallels the "slow" and "fast" or "courageous" and "moderate" dichotomies of the *Statesman* and *Laws*. Notably, Aristophanes symbolically associates men with fire and women with water at *Lys.* 319–79.) This view of wine, moreover, is not unique to the Hippocratics, but is widely attested in philosophical and poetic literature. Greek authors frequently note the warming and humidifying effects of drinking—e.g. Aristophanes, *Knights* 89–96, 114; Euripides, *Alc.* 756–9; Diogenes of Apollonia (see Theophrastus, *Sens.* 44); Heraclitus, DK B117; and Xenophon, *Symp.* 2.24. On the Hippocratic and Greek medical view of wine, see Jouanna (2012). For an excellent book-length treatment of Aristotle's conception of the physiology of character and virtue, see Leunissen (2017).

The elderly, by contrast, are "cowardly" (*deiloi*), because "they are chilled (*katepsugmenoi*), whereas the young are hot (*thermoi*), so that old age paves the way for cowardice (*deiliai*), for fear (*phobos*) is a kind of chill (*katapsuxis*)"; they are less likely to have hope (*elpis*); their "feelings of anger (*thumoi*)" are "weak"; "they are not modest (*aischuntēloi*), but rather shameless (*anaischun-toi*)" and do not especially care about what is admirable (*kalon*); they are suspicious and "mistrustful" (*apistoi*); "they neither feel friendship (*philousin*) nor hate (*misousi*) very strongly (*sphodra*)"; and they are less likely to pity others out of friendly feelings of care (1389b13–1390a24).

According to Aristotle, then, physiological conditions at different ages are correlated with psychological ones: youth is characterized by bodily warmth (of the same sort induced by wine) and the concomitant intensity of various spirited motivations like friendship, shame, anger, and boldness—a wide range of both "gentle" and "aggressive" manifestations of *thumos*—whereas old age involves a cooling of the body and a corresponding debilitation of those motivations. The points of contact between the *Rhetoric* and the *Laws* are striking and obvious. Aristotle is clearly outlining the same general account of human physiological and psychological development that animates the Athenian's discussion of education and drinking parties.[50] The fact that Aristotle not only characterizes the psychological differences between young and old in terms of spirited qualities and emotions, therefore, but also repeatedly uses the word *thumos* and terms derived from it (*thumikoi, thumōdes, oxuthu-moi*) in his analysis, adds to the already compelling case for concluding that the Athenian's educational proposals are grounded in Plato's views about spirit.[51]

4. Gymnastic Education in Magnesia

The Athenian returns to the topic of early education in Book 7, where his focus shifts to gymnastic training. As we have seen, he characterizes gymnastics as

---

[50] Aristotle also takes youth to be correlated with increased impressionability (they are "trusting" and "easy to deceive"), whereas the elderly are comparatively inflexible ("untrusting" and "suspicious"). Plato makes use of the same idea in the *Laws* but explicitly connects it to spirited motivation: the young (and the intoxicated whose bodily condition mimics theirs) are more impressionable *because* they have intense spirited emotions that make them susceptible to the influence of others.

[51] Note that this young/old dichotomy differs from both the Greek masculine/feminine dichotomy and the courageous/moderate dichotomy of the *Statesman*. In the case of the latter two, each group is strongly or prominently motivated by one side of spirit or the other, but not both (women and the moderate by the gentle, men and the courageous by the aggressive). By contrast, the young tend to experience *both* gentle *and* aggressive spirited motivations with a great intensity, while the old tend to experience *neither* very strongly. Cf. Ch. 9, n. 19.

the part of early education concerned with order in bodily movement. The Athenian's proposals are founded on the ideas that certain kinds of bodily motions express and imitate corresponding motions and conditions of the virtuous individual's soul, *and* that habituation in the appropriate bodily motions can facilitate acquisition of the corresponding psychic conditions. Hence he reiterates his earlier view that the rhythmic movements of dance are (like the harmonies of song) "imitations of human character" (798d–e). The purpose of gymnastics is to impose the right kind of movements on the body, therefore, so that the corresponding virtuous motions of the soul become inculcated (at least in a preliminary way) in the individual as well.[52]

This process should begin, the Athenian claims, even before the child is born (789a–d).[53] "All bodies benefit from the invigorating stir produced by all sorts of shaking and motions," he says, "whether the bodies be moved by themselves, or in carriers, or on the sea, or by being carried on horses or on any other body" (789d1–5). For that reason, pregnant women must go for regular walks, and once infants are born, their bodies and souls should be kept in motion as continuously as possible, "as if they were always on a ship at sea" (789d–790e). From the ages of three to five or six, children should play games of their own design that are approved and supervised by nurses. At the age of six, boys as well as girls (if they are willing) will begin to learn martial skills such as horseback riding, archery, and javelin-throwing (793e–794d, 804d–805b), and in later years children study the two main branches of gymnastics, dancing and wrestling (795d–e). Dancing must adhere to many of the same guidelines as musical singing—since they are both parts of the single activity of participating in a chorus—and it is divided into two main forms: imitation of admirable bodies in solemn movement, and imitation of shameful bodies in low movement. The youths should be trained only in imitation of the admirable, he says, which in turn has two parts: the Pyrrhic or "warlike" part, which involves imitation of noble bodies engaged in violent martial exertion with courage, and the "peaceful" part, which involves imitation of bodies behaving moderately, lawfully, and in measured ways during times of peace (814e–815b; cf. 660a). As for wrestling, they must avoid practicing techniques that are useless in war, and should instead focus exclusively on those that promote strength, health, and military prowess. Thus, young people—again, including girls and women—should practice wrestling, fighting, and dancing that

---

[52] See discussions of gymnastic education in Morrow (1960: 304–9), Grube (1980: 246–52), and esp. Kamtekar (2010), with whose account I take my own to be largely aligned.

[53] Jaeger (1944b: 246–7) notes that taking measures to improve children during conception and pregnancy was a Spartan practice.

involves heavy armor and weapons, and the movements they learn should be those that are "by far the most akin to fighting in war" (796a–d, 813d–814d).

There are several reasons for thinking gymnastic education is directed at spirited motivation and a spirited part of the soul. First, the Athenian makes it clear that one of the primary aims of gymnastics is to prepare the young citizens for war by making them more *courageous*, where this involves both defense against external foreign enemies as well as the "internal" enemies of pleasure and fear. This, of course, echoes the psychological function of spirit in both *Timaeus* and *Republic*, which the latter explicitly aims to cultivate partly by means of gymnastics. Second, and relatedly, the two types of dance that the Athenian advocates, the "warlike" and the "peaceful," correspond to the two faces of *thumos*. They are designed to imitate and foster courageous and moderate behavior, and they are the terpsichorean counterparts to the two types of musical melodies allowed in the *Republic*'s Kallipolis.[54] Third, the Athenian identifies a cluster of psychic defects that result from inadequate or improper gymnastic education: the young can become ill-humored (*dusko-lon*), irascible (*akrakola*), easily "moved by little things" to anger, violent (*sphodra*), slavish (*aneleutheroi*), savage (*agria*), spoiled by luxury (*truphē*), incapable of "living with others" (*sunoikos*), haters of other people (*misan-thropos*), or subject to cowardice (*deilia*) (791b7–d9). These are recognizably spirited states, and in the *Republic*, several of these exact defects are all explicitly identified as conditions of the *thumoeides*.[55] Fourth, when the Athenian argues that both men and women should share in gymnastic and military exercises, he actually characterizes that as the training of spirit. A common education, he says, makes men and women "united in *thumos*" (*homothumadon*, 805a6).[56]

Finally, we find another important parallel to the psychological theory of the *Timaeus* in the Athenian's explanation of the value of subjecting infants to as much movement as possible. Motion, he says, brings order and quiet to the

---

[54] On the relation of these and other features of Plato's educational program to Damonian musical theory, see Anderson (1955), Lord (1978), and Morrow (1960: 304–5, n. 27).

[55] Excessive music ruins a person's spirit and makes him ill-humored (*duskolia*), irascible (*akrako-loi*), quick-tempered (*orgiloi*), and "quickly inflamed by little things," while excessive gymnastic education makes him savage (*agrion*) (411b6–e2); ill-humor (*duskolia*) produces anger and overstrains the spirited part; luxury (*truphē*) and softness introduce cowardice (*deilia*) into it; and slavishness (*aneleutheria*) turns the *thumoeides* from "lion-like" to "ape-like" (586c6–d2, 590a9–b9).

[56] Two additional pieces of evidence: (1) The use of gymnastic motion on infants is likened to "molding" (πλάττειν) a soft, moist wax (789d–e), the same metaphor applied to *thumoi* earlier in the dialogue (633c–d). (2) Gymnastic games work, the Athenian explains, by making certain habits and practices "familiar" (οἰκείας), "dear" (φίλα), and "known" (γνώριμα) to the souls of the young, just as the body becomes assimilated to the food it consumes (797e–798a).

restlessness of the infant's soul, as evidenced by the fact that mothers use rocking, not stillness, to lull their babies to sleep. He explains:

> The passion being experienced is presumably terror, and the terror is due to some poor habit of the soul. When someone brings a rocking motion from the outside to such passions, the motion brought from without overpowers the fear and the mad motion within, and, having overpowered it, makes a calm stillness (*galēnēn hēsuchian*) appear in the soul that replaces the harsh pounding of the heart (*tēs kardias chalepēs pēdēseōs*) in each case...It thereby replaces our mad dispositions with prudent habits.   (790e8–791b2)

Feelings of fear are associated with certain kinds of motions in the soul, and if those motions become part of the child's settled psychic habits, they become an obstacle to the acquisition of courage.[57] Feeling fear is "practice in cowardice," and for that reason infants should be kept free of terror and suffering as much as possible during the first three years of their lives (791b, 792b). This is accomplished by imposing the right kinds of external motions, which in turn alleviate the *internal* motions that constitute fear and worry. Likewise, as we have seen in earlier chapters, the kinetic psychology of the *Timaeus* characterizes states and disturbances of the soul in terms of psychic motions and conditions that are directly correlated with physiological ones, and it defines education as the process of fostering proper motions in each of the three parts of the soul (89e–90d). The Athenian's explanation of infant care adds to the case for thinking the *Laws* continues to assume the *Timaeus'* account of *thumos* and its connection to the heart. For recall that Timaeus uses the same language to describe the biology of fear as does the Athenian in the passage above: it arises, like anger, in conjunction with the "pounding of the heart" (*tēi pēdēsei tēs kardias*, 70c1), and that pounding is caused by or correlated with the agitation of the spirited part of the soul.[58] The parallel suggests that Plato remains committed to a similar model of the soul's physiological associations in the *Laws*, and that, although the *thumoeides* is not explicitly mentioned, it is still the psychic source of the agitation involved in fear and anger. The Athenian offers a final hint in this direction when he follows up his instructions by asking, "If someone were to apply every device

---

[57] Cf. discussion of this passage in Moutsopoulos (2003: 117), Prauscello (2014: 143–5), and esp. Kamtekar (2010: 143–7).

[58] Kamtekar's (2010) account of gymnastics in the *Laws* is similarly informed by the psychology and physiology of the *Timaeus*. Cf. Naddaf (1997: 35). Saunders (1991: Ch. 5) also draws on the *Timaeus'* physiology in support of his "medical" interpretation of the *Laws'* penology.

in an attempt to make the three-year period for our nursling contain the least possible amount of suffering and fears and every sort of pain, don't we suppose that he would make the soul of the one brought up in this way good-spirited (*euthumon*)?" (792b4–8).

5. The Law

Moral education for the citizens of Magnesia does not end with musical and gymnastic training. Plato also assigns an important pedagogical function to the lawgiver and the laws themselves. Indeed, one of the dialogue's chief innovations is the Athenian's insistence that the laws should employ not only "force," but also "persuasion." He explains that the coercive component of laws, which consists of commands accompanied by threats, should be preceded by "preludes" designed to make listeners more receptive and willingly obedient to the laws (721d–723a). In this final section I argue that the laws of Magnesia, including their preludes, the orders they issue, and the punishments they prescribe, are largely intended to shape and appeal to spirited attitudes, desires, and emotions. To be clear, nothing I say here entails that the laws do not *also* aim at distinctively appetitive or rational aspects of human psychology as well. In fact, I assume they do.[59] My claim, rather, is that much of what the Athenian says about the laws and their contents emphasizes spirited sensitivities and motivations, and that—in combination with the earlier sections of this chapter—this suggests the laws themselves are also partly informed by Plato's thinking about *thumos*.

In several key passages throughout the dialogue, the Athenian characterizes law in terms that call to mind spirited motivation. Early in Book 1 he explains that the lawgiver must watch over the citizens in every aspect of their lives— their relationships and interactions with one another, their emotional experiences, and in any kind of good or bad fortune they might face:

---

[59] Although I take the laws to have effects on all three parts of the soul, including the reasoning, I am skeptical of the rationalist claim advanced by scholars like Bobonich (1991 and 2002: 97–119) and Irwin (2010) that preludes impart genuine *knowledge* or understanding to the citizens, for reasons I explore in Wilburn (2013b: 88–97). My interpretation is not incompatible with such interpretations, however. For other *anti*- or *non*-rationalist interpretations, see Brisson (2005), Dodds (1945: 18 and 1951: 211–12), Görgemanns (1960: 70, 108), Laks (1991), Mayhew (2007), Morrow (1953 and 1960: 557–8), Nightingale (1993 and 1999), Ritter (1896: 13–14), Stally (1983: 43–4 and 1994), and Tarrant (2004).

It is necessary to care for the citizens by apportioning honor (*timōnta*) and dishonor (*atimazonta*) correctly among them...In all their mingling with one another one must keep a guard, blaming (*psegein*) and praising (*epainein*) correctly by means of the laws themselves...What is noble (*kalon*) and what is not must be taught and defined...For those citizens who obey the laws he should ordain honor (*timas*), and for those who disobey he should ordain penalties.   (631d6–632c1)

According to this view, one of the lawgiver's central functions is to assign praise and honor to just or moderate civic behavior and blame and dishonor to the unjust or dissolute, and the laws *themselves* are his medium for delineating the one from the other and his criterion for distributing honor and dishonor.[60] This includes the preludes themselves, which should "reveal which things [the lawgiver] thinks are admirable and which he thinks are not" (823a3–5). The Athenian's focus suggests that the best laws are designed to appeal to citizens' spirited sensitivity to approval and disapproval. The lawgiver seeks to shape their perception of what counts as honorable or dishonorable, which in turn affects the way citizens act and live. In this sense, law is contiguous with and complements early education. It takes for granted that citizens have both the desire for honor and a spirited sense of shame, and it marshals those motivational resources in the service of virtue by establishing what counts as honorable or shameful in the city. The traditional attitude toward incest provides a sort of model for his approach. The reason incest is the one sexual act from which almost everyone refrains "as willingly as possible" is that *everyone* considers it to be "the most shameful of shameful things," and no one ever says otherwise or even so much as "breathes contrary to the law" (838a–e). The lawgiver's goal, then, is to cultivate a proper sense of shame and honor in the citizens by fostering, through the laws themselves, the greatest possible universal agreement about what is praiseworthy and blameworthy.

The content of the laws also reflects and confirms the Athenian's attention to spirited psychology. Many of the punishments prescribed by the laws take the form of dishonor, blame, or public humiliation.[61] To give just a few examples: the penalty for buying or selling an allotted house is that the offender's wrongdoing will be written on tablets to be stored in the temples, "there to be read and remembered for the rest of time" (741c); those reported

---

[60] For further examples, see 711b–c, 757b–d, and 697b–c. Cf. 841c4, where love of honor (*to philotimon*) makes citizens obedient to the laws.

[61] For discussions of punishment and penal theory in the *Laws*, see Mackenzie (1981), Roberts (1987), Saunders (1968 and 1991), and Stalley (1995).

for abandoning their post while serving in the guard will be "held in ill-repute" and have their names "posted in writing in the marketplace," and "anyone they encounter" may strike them with impunity (762b–d); if a citizen attempts to practice a technical skill for the sake of profit, the city regulators will punish him "with blame and dishonors" (847a); and those who are unable to pay fines levied against them are "to be punished with conspicuous, lengthy imprisonments and certain humiliations," which can include "beating" or making the criminal "sit or stand in certain disgraceful ways" (855a–c).[62] These punishments are all designed to prevent or change behavior by exploiting citizens' sense of shame: they all involve degrading expressions of blame or elaborate public rituals of humiliation. Simply enduring a bad reputation, of course, does not cause a person the sort of bodily pain to which appetite is averse, nor does it constitute the kind of rational instruction from which reason might benefit directly. It unmistakably takes aim at the spirited human aversion to dishonor.

Conversely, the laws and preludes place significant positive emphasis on honor, victory, and *good* reputation.[63] Indeed, the argument of the very first prelude the Athenian offers, the preface to his marriage law, appeals to "the desire to become famous and not to lie nameless after one has died" (721b–c). Another prelude refers to "the contest for virtue" and exhorts all citizens to be "lovers of victory" in the "competition" for virtue, which in turn contributes to the "fame" of the whole city (730d–731a).[64] The Athenian's prelude regarding how citizens should think, act, and live with respect to their souls, bodies, and property is especially telling. It begins:

> Of all the things that belong to one, the most divine—after the gods—is the soul, which is the thing that is most of all one's own (*oikeiotaton*). It is the case with everybody that all one's possessions fall into two classes. The superior and better are masterful, while the inferior and worse are slavish. Hence one's masterful possessions should always be honored (*protimēteon*) above one's slavish possessions. So I speak correctly when I urge that one honor (*timan*) one's soul second after the gods, who are masters, and those who follow after the gods. There is no one among us, so to speak, who assigns

---

[62] For further examples of penalties that involve exclusion from honor or fame or subjection to ridicule or bad reputation, see 721d, 761e–762a, 845b–d, 854d–855a, 926d, and 944d–945b.

[63] Avgousti (2018: 97–103) provides a useful discussion of this emphasis. See also Reid's (2020) discussion of the honors granted to exemplary political officials in Magnesia, e.g. the rewards granted to virtuous auditors (pp. 587–8).

[64] Cf. 845d.

honor (*timai*) correctly, though we are of the opinion that we do. For honor (*timē*) is presumably a divine good, and cannot be bestowed by what is bad: he who thinks that he is making his soul greater with words or gifts or certain indulgences, yet fails to change its condition to worse or better, seems to honor (*timan*) it, but in fact is not doing so at all.   (726a2–727a7)

The prelude goes on to explain and elaborate on these claims at great length, consistently—*obsessively* even—speaking in terms of honor and related notions like praise, reputation, blame, and shame (727a–730a). Indeed, forms of the terms "honor" and "dishonor" appear no fewer than twenty-nine times in just over three Stephanus pages. This is especially significant given that this prelude is one of the longest, and for the Athenian clearly one of the most important, in the whole dialogue, because it indicates to citizens what kinds of values and priorities they should hold throughout their lives. The fact that the law communicates those values so emphatically through the language of honor, therefore, suggests that it primarily aims to promote a correct spirited orientation toward the various candidates for "goods" that human beings encounter in their lives. It is noteworthy in this regard that the Athenian begins his prelude by identifying a person's soul as the thing that is "most of all familiar" to them. Citizens who take the prelude to heart, therefore, will ideally feel spirited protectiveness over the virtuous condition of their own souls above all and will be motivated to live accordingly. The prelude also appeals to human ambition and competitiveness, concluding that the best person is "the one who prefers, above any Olympic victories or any victories in contests of war or peace, to be victorious (*nikan*) in having a reputation (*doxai*) for serving his own laws—for being someone who throughout his life served the laws more nobly than any other human being" (729d–e).

This last point draws attention to another notable theme in the dialogue, which is the importance of making citizens view the laws with reverent obedience. The Athenian explains:

Every real man must understand that no human being would ever become a master worthy of praise (*epainou*) unless he has been a slave, and that one should be more attentive to the pride (*kallōpizesthai*) of someone enslaved admirably than to that of the person ruling admirably (*kalōs arxai*). The first enslavement is to the laws (for this is really an enslavement to the gods), and the next is that of the young to their elders at all times, and also to those who have lived their lives honorably (*entimōs*). (762e1–7)

In tripartite psychology, the spirited part of the soul is what makes people both desire to rule and obedient to their superiors, and that obedience is rooted in the spirited sense of shame and respect. Here, then, the Athenian seeks to instill in citizens an especially strong sense of awe for the laws themselves, so that they will willingly comply with them and even take pride in doing so.[65] With this in mind, it is striking to note the Athenian's characterization of the preludes and their intended effects on listeners. The preludes themselves are a form of *paramuthia* or "encouragement" (720a1, 854a6, 880a7, 885b3), and their aim is to make citizens "tamer" (*hēmerōteron*, 718d4, 720d7, 890c8), "more eager in spirit" (*prothumoumenōn*, 718d8) to become good, more "kindly disposed" (*eumenesteron*, 718d3, 718d6, 723a4, 730b6) to the law, and more "obedient" (*eupeithēs*) and "docile" (*euēnios*) (880a7).[66] Meanwhile, citizens who are impervious to the influence of good laws are "savage" (*ōmēs*, 718d3), and in the worst case prove to be completely "impossible to soften (*kerasbolos*)—so hard (*ateramōn*) by nature that they won't melt (*tēkesthai*); just as certain seeds are unmelted by fire, so these men are unmelted (*atēktoi*) by strong laws" (853d1–4). Many of these terms call to mind the familiar qualities Plato associates with *thumos* in the *Republic*, and several are commonly used to describe spirited animals. Hence the term *euēnios*, which literally means "obedient to the rein," is borrowed from equestrian vocabulary; *paramuthia* is what a shepherd uses to calm his herd in the *Statesman* (268b4); and the Athenian himself later identifies "tameness" as the state produced in dogs when they are given food (906d2–4). While the laws and preludes no doubt have effects on appetitive and rational aspects of psychology as well, the Athenian's repetitive description of the preludes in this language throughout the text suggests that they largely aim at promoting the kind of spirited gentleness and shame toward the laws that will incline citizens to obey them readily. In this respect the relation of *thumos* to the laws in Magnesia parallels its relation to reason in the *Republic*, *Timaeus*, and *Phaedrus*. Just as tameness is a precondition of spirit's obedience to the reasoning part of the soul in the latter dialogues, so too in the *Laws* it fosters deference to the authority of law. It is not merely a parallel, however, but rather a manifestation or extension of spirit's subservience to reason. For the Athenian, law itself is supposed to embody divine reason to the greatest extent possible. He identifies reasoning

---

[65] Cf. 700a and 715b–d. For discussion of "enslavement" to the laws, see Annas (2010).

[66] Preludes and/or lawgivers who offer them, moreover, are themselves "tame" (ἡμέρων) and speak "gently" (πράως) with "gentle" words; and they are "without anger" (ἄθυμος), they do not "get angry" (θυμοῦσθαι), and they "extinguish their anger (θυμόν)"; by contrast, the use of commands or threats alone is "savage" (ἀγριώτερον) and done "harshly" (σκληρῶς) (720e3–5, 885c8–e5, 888a1–7).

itself with "the common law of the city" (645a) and conceives of law as "the regulation ordained by intelligence (*nou*)" (714a).[67] In the *Laws*, therefore, spirit is the ally of reason not only within the person's own soul, but also of the reason reflected in the laws of the city itself.

In this late dialogue, then, spirit continues to play a defining, and even expanded, role in musical and gymnastic training, moral education, interpersonal relationships, and politics and civic life. From the beginning to the end of Plato's career, spirit is the social and political component of human psychology on which the moral destinies of cities and individuals largely turn.

---

[67] See also 835e: λόγος "strives to become νόμος." Cf. Adomenas (2001: 37) and Gould (1955: 79).

Works Cited

Adam, Adele Marion and James Adam (1893), *Platonis Protagoras* (Cambridge: Cambridge University Press).

Adam, James (1902), *The Republic of Plato: Edited with Critical Notes, Commentary, and Appendices*, 2 vols. (Cambridge: Cambridge University Press).

Adkins, A. H. W. (1960), *Merit and Responsibility* (Oxford: Clarendon Press).

Adkins, A. H. W. (1970), *From the Many to the One: A Study of Personality and Views of Human Nature in the Context of Ancient Greek Society, Values, and Beliefs* (Ithaca: Cornell University Press).

Adomenas, Mantas (2001), "Self-Reference, Textuality, and the Status of the Political Project in Plato's *Laws*," *Oxford Studies in Ancient Philosophy* 21: 29–59.

Ahbel-Rappe, Sara (2010), "Cross-Examining Happiness: Reason and Community in Plato's Socratic Dialogues," in Andrea Nightingale and David Sedley (eds.), *Ancient Models of Mind: Studies in Divine and Human Rationality* (Cambridge: Cambridge University Press).

Allen, Danielle S. (2002), *The World of Prometheus: The Politics of Punishing in Democratic Athens* (Princeton: Princeton University Press).

Allen, Danielle S. (2004), "Angry Bees, Wasps, and Jurors: The Symbolic Politics of mocratic Athen," in Susanna Morton Braund and Glenn W. Most (eds.), *Ancient Anger: Perspectives from Homer to Galen* (Cambridge University Press), 76–98.

Allen, Danielle S. (2010), *Why Plato Wrote* (Chichester: Wiley-Blackwell).

Allen, Michael J. B. (1981), *Marsilio Ficino and the Phaedran Charioteer: Introduction, Texts, Translations* (Berkeley: University of California Press).

Allen, R. E. (2006), *The* Republic (New Haven: Yale University Press).

Ambler, Wayne H. (1985), "Aristotle's Understanding of the Naturalness of the City," *The Review of Politics* 47/2: 163–85.

Ambuel, David (2013), "Pigs in Plato: Delineating the Human Condition in the *Statesman*," in Ales Havlicek, Jakub Jirsa, and Karel Thein (eds.), *Plato's Statesman: Proceedings of the Eighth Symposium Platonicum Pragense* (Prague: *OIKOYMENH*), 209–26.

Anagnostopolous, Mariana (2006), "The Divided Soul and the Desire for Good in Plato's *Republic*," in G. Santas (ed.), *The Blackwell Guide to Plato's* Republic (Malden, Massachusetts: Blackwell Publishing), 166–88.

Anderson, Warren D. (1955), "The Importance of Damonion Theory in Plato's Thought," *Transactions and Proceedings of the American Philological Association* 86: 88–102.

Andersson, Torsten J. (1971), *Polis and Psyche: A Motif in Plato's* Republic (Stockholm: Almquist and Wiksell).

Annas, Julia (1976), "Plato's *Republic* and Feminism," *Philosophy* 51/197: 307–21.

Annas, Julia (1981), *An Introduction to Plato's* Republic (Oxford: Clarendon Press).

Annas, Julia (1995), "Introduction," in Julia Annas and Robin Waterfield (eds.), *Plato: Statesman* (Cambridge: Cambridge University Press), ix–xxviii.

Annas, Julia (1999), *Platonic Ethics, Old and New* (Ithaca: Cornell University Press).

Annas, Julia (2010), "Virtue and Law in Plato" in C. Bobonich (ed.), *Plato's Laws: A Critical Guide* (Cambridge: Cambridge University Press), 71–91.

Annas, Julia and Robin Waterfield (eds.) (1995), *Plato: Statesman* (Cambridge: Cambridge University Press).

Archer-Hind, R. D. (1888), *The Timaeus of Plato* (London: Macmillan and Co.).

Arends, J. Frederik M. (1993), "Survival, War, and the Unity of the *Polis* in Plato's *Statesman*," *Polis* 12/1–2: 154–87.

Arruzza, Cinzia (2011), "The Private and the Common in Plato's *Republic*," *History of Political Thought* 32/2: 215–33.

Arruzza, Cinzia (2016), "Philosophical Dogs and Tyrannical Wolves in Plato's *Republic*," in Cinzia Arruzza and Dmitri Nikulin (eds.), *Philosophy and Political Power in Antiquity* (Leiden: Brill), 41–66.

Arruzza, Cinzia (2018), "The Lion and the Wolf: The Tyrant's Spirit in Plato's *Republic*," *Ancient Philosophy* 38: 47–67.

Avgousti, Andreas (2015), "Plato's Uneasy Founding: On Reputation in the *Laws*", *Diálogos* 98: 85–110.

Balasopoulos, Antonis (2013), "Pigs in Heaven? Utopia, Animality and Plato's Hūopolis," in Jorge Bastos da Silva (ed.), *The Epistemology of Utopia: Rhetoric, Theory and Imagination* (Newcastle upon Tyne: Cambridge Scholars Publishing), 8–27.

Balot, Ryan K. (2014), *Courage in the Democratic Polis: Ideology and Critique in Classical Athens* (Oxford: Oxford University Press).

Barney, Rachel (2002), "Platonism, Moral Nostalgia, and the 'City of Pigs'," *Proceedings of the Boston Area Colloquium in Ancient Philosophy* 17/1: 207–27.

Barney, Rachel (2006), "The Sophistic Movement," in Mary Louise Gill and Pierre Pellegrin (eds.), *Blackwell Companions to Philosophy: A Companion to Ancient Philosophy* (Malden, Massachusetts: Blackwell Publishing), 77–97.

Barney, Rachel (2010), "Notes on Plato on the *Kalon* and the Good," *Classical Philology* 105/4: 363–77.

Barney, Rachel (2016), "What Kind of Theory Is the Theory of the Tripartite Soul?," *Proceedings of the Boston Area Colloquium in Ancient Philosophy* 31: 53–83.

Beaujeu, Jean (1973), *Apulée: Opuscules Philosophiques (Du dieu de Socrate, Platon et sa doctrine, Du monde) et Fragments* (Paris: Société D'édition "Les Belles Lettres").

Belfiore, Elizabeth (1986), "Wine and Catharsis of the Emotions in Plato's *Laws*," *Classical Quarterly* 36/2: 421–37.

Benardete, Seth (1984), *The Being of the Beautiful: Plato's Theaetetus, Sophist, and Statesman* (Chicago: University of Chicago Press).

Benitez, Eugenio (2014), "Authenticity, Experiment, or Development," in Marguerite Johnson and Harold Tarrant (eds.), *Alcibiades and the Socratic Lover-Educator* (London: Bloomsbury), 119–33.

Bentley, R. K. (2003), "Ruling Oneself: Platonic Hedonism and the Quality of Citizenship," *Polis* 20/1–2: 85–107.

Bett, Richard (1986), "Immortality and the Nature of the Soul in the *Phaedrus*," *Phronesis* 31/1: 1–26.

Bieda, Esteban (2012), "¿Es Leoncio un incontente? Ira y apetito en la *República* de Platón," *Diánoia* 57/69: 127–50.

Blondell, Ruby (2005), "From Fleece to Fabric: Weaving Culture in Plato's *Statesman*," *Oxford Studies in Ancient Philosophy* 28: 23–75.

Bloom, Allan (1968), *The Republic of Plato: Translated with Notes and an Interpretive Essay.* (New York: Basic Books).

Bloom, Allan (1977), "Response to Hall," *Political Theory* 5/3: 315–30.

Blössner, Norbert (2007), "The City-Soul Analogy," in G. R. F. Ferrari (ed.), *The Cambridge Companion to Plato's* Republic (Cambridge: Cambridge University Press), 345–85.

Bluestone, Natalie H. (1987), *Women and the Ideal Society: Plato's* Republic *and Modern Myths of Gender* (Amherst: University of Massachusetts Press).

Bluestone, Natalie H. (1994), "Why Women Cannot Rule: Sexism in Plato Scholarship," in Nancy Tuana (ed.), *Feminist Interpretations of Plato* (University Park, Pennsylvania: The Pennsylvania State University Press), 109–32.

Blundell, Mary Whitlock (1989), *Helping Friends and Harming Enemies: A Study in Sophocles and Greek Ethics* (Cambridge: Cambridge University Press).

Bobonich, Christopher (1991), "Persuasion, Compulsion, and Freedom in Plato's *Laws*," *Classical Quarterly* 4/2: 365–88.

Bobonich, Christopher (1994), "Akrasia and Agency in Plato's *Laws* and *Republic*," *Archiv für Geschichte der Philosophie* 76: 3–36.

Bobonich, Christopher (1995), "The Virtues of Ordinary People in Plato's *Statesman*," in Christopher Rowe (ed.), *Reading the* Statesman: *Proceedings of the III Symposium Platonicum* (Sankt Augustin: Academia Verlag), 313–29.

Bobonich, Christopher (2002), *Plato's Utopia Recast: His Later Ethics and Politics* (Oxford: Clarendon Press).

Bobonich, Christopher (2007), "Plato on *Akrasia* and Knowing Your Own Mind," in Christopher Bobonich and Pierre Destrée (eds.), Akrasia *in Greek Philosophy: From Socrates to Plotinus* (Leiden: Brill), 41–60.

Bobonich, Christopher (2010), "Images of Irrationality," Christopher Bobonich (ed.) *Plato's* Laws: *A Critical Guide* (Cambridge: Cambridge University Press), 149–71.

Bobonich, Christopher (2017), "Agency in Plato's *Republic*," *Oxford Handbooks Online* (DOI: 10.1093/oxfordhb/9780199935314.013.7), 1–31.

Böhme, J. (1929), *Die Seele und das Ich im Homerischen Epos mit einem Anhang: Vergleich mit dem Glauben der Primitiven* (Leipzig: Teubner).

Booth, William J. (1981), "Politics and the Household. A Commentary on Aristotle's *Politics* Book One," *History of Political Thought* 2/2: 203–26.

Brancacci, Aldo (2005), "Musique et philosophique en *République* II–IV," in Monique Dixsaut (ed.), Études sur la *République de Platon*, i: *De la Justice, Éducation, Psychologie et Politique* (Paris: Libraire Philosophique J. Vrin), 89–106.

Brennan, Tad (2012), "The Nature of the Spirited Part of the Soul and its Object," in Rachel Barney, Tad Brennan, and Charles Brittain (eds.), *Plato and the Divided Self* (Cambridge: Cambridge University Press), 102–27.

Brickhouse, Thomas C. and Nicholas D. Smith (2007), "Socrates on *Akrasia*, Knowledge, and the Power of Appearance," in Christopher Bobonich and Pierre Destrée (eds.), Akrasia *in Greek Philosophy: From Socrates to Plotinus* (Leiden: Brill), 1–17.

Brickhouse, Thomas C. and Nicholas D. Smith (2010), *Socratic Moral Psychology* (Cambridge: Cambridge University Press).

Brickhouse, Thomas C. and Nicholas D. Smith (2015), "Socrates on the Emotions," *Plato Journal* 15: 9–28.

Brill, Sara (2016), "Political Pathology in Plato's *Republic*," *Apeiron* 49/2: 127–61.

Brisson, Luc (1995), "Interprétation du Mythe du *Politique*," in Christopher Rowe (ed.), *Reading the* Statesman: *Proceedings of the III Symposium Platonicum* (Sankt Augustin: Academia Verlag), 349–63.

Brisson, Luc (1996), "La notion de *phthonos* chez Platon," in Frédéric Monneyron (ed.), *La jalousie* (Paris: L'Harmattan), 13–26.

Brisson, Luc (1999), "Plato's Theory of Sense Perception in the *Timaeus*: How It Works and What It Means," *Proceedings of the Boston Area Colloquium in Ancient Philosophy* 13 (Leiden: Brill), 147–76.

Brisson, Luc (2005), "Ethics and Politics in Plato's *Laws*," *Oxford Studies in Ancient Philosophy* 28: 93–121.

Brisson, Luc (2012a), "Women in Plato's *Republic*," *Études platoniciennes* 9: 129–36.

Brisson, Luc (2012b), "Soul and State in Plato's *Laws*" in Rachel Barney, Tad Brennan, and Charles Brittain (eds.) *Plato and the Divided Self* (Cambridge: Cambridge University Press), 281–307.

Brisson, Luc (2015), "The Tripartition of the City in Plato's *Laws*," *Diálogos* 98: 111–42.

Brisson, Luc (2020), "The Notion of *Φθόνος* in Plato," in Laura Candiotta and Olivier Renaut (eds.), *Emotions in Plato* (Leiden: Brill), 201–19.

Broadie, Sarah (2012), *Nature and Divinity in Plato's* Timaeus (Cambridge: Cambridge University Press).

Brown, Eric (2004), "Minding the Gap in Plato's *Republic*," *Philosophical Studies* 117/1–2: 275–302.

Brown, Eric (2012), "The Unity of the Soul in Plato's *Republic*," in R. Barney, T. Brennan, and C. Brittain (eds.), *Plato and the Divided Self* (Cambridge: Cambridge University Press), 53–73.

Buchan, Morag (1999), "Plato and Feminism," in Morag Buchan, *Women in Plato's Political Theory* (New York: Routledge), 135–54.

Burnet, John (1902), *Platonis Opera*, iv (Oxford: Oxford University Press).

Burnet, John (1916), "The Socratic Doctrine of the Soul," *Proceedings of the British Academy* 7: 235–59.

Burnyeat, Myles F. (1976), "Plato on the Grammar of Perceiving," *Classical Quarterly* 26/1: 29–51.

Burnyeat, Myles F. (1985), "Sphinx without a Secret," *New York Review of Books* (May 30).

Burnyeat, Myles F. (1999), "Culture and Society in Plato's *Republic*," in G. Peterson (ed.), *The Tanner Lectures on Human Values* (Salt Lake City: University of Utah Press), 20: 215–324.

Burnyeat, Myles F. (2006), "The Truth of Tripartition," *Proceedings of the Aristotelian Society* 106/1: 1–23.

Bury, R. G. (1932), *The Symposium of Plato* (Cambridge: W. Heffer and Sons Ltd.).

Butler, J. Eric (2007), "Pleasure's Pyrrhic Victory: An Intellectualist Reading of the *Philebus*," *Oxford Studies in Ancient Philosophy* 33: 89–123.

Cairns, Douglas (1993), Aidōs: *The Psychology and Ethics of Honour and Shame in Ancient Greek Literature* (Oxford: Clarendon Press).

Cairns, Douglas (2004), "Ethics, Ethology, Terminology: Iliadic Anger and the Cross-Cultural Study of Emotion," in Susanna Morton Braund and Glenn W. Most (eds.), *Ancient Anger: Perspectives from Homer to Galen* (Cambridge: Cambridge University Press), 11–49.

Cairns, Douglas (2014), "*Ψυχη, Θυμος*, and Metaphor in Homer and Plato," *Études platoniciennes*, online, 11 (DOI: https://doi.org/10.4000/etudesplatoniciennes.566).

Calabi, F. (1998), "Andreia/ Thymoeides," in Mario Vegetti (ed.), *Platone: La Republica*, iii, *Libro IV* (Napoli: Bibliopolis), 187–203.

Calogero, Guido (1957), "Gorgias and the Socratic Principle *Nemo Sua Sponte Peccat*," *The Journal of Hellenic Studies* 77/1: 12–17.

Campbell, Lewis (1867), *The Sophistes and Politicus of Plato*, ii: *Politicus* (Oxford: Clarendon Press).

Carone, Gabriela Roxana (2001), "Akrasia in the *Republic*: Does Plato Change His Mind?," *Oxford Studies in Ancient Philosophy* 20: 107–48.

Carone, Gabriela Roxana (2004), "Calculating Machines or Leaky Jars? The Moral Psychology of Plato's *Gorgias*," *Oxford Studies in Ancient Philosophy* 26: 55–96.

Carone, Gabriela Roxana (2005a), *Plato's Cosmology and Its Ethical Dimensions* (Cambridge: Cambridge University Press).

Carone, Gabriela Roxana (2005b), "Plato's Stoic View of Motivation," in Ricardo Salles (ed.), *Metaphysics, Soul, and Ethics in Ancient Thought: Themes from the Work of Richard Sorabji* (Oxford), 365–82.

Carone, Gabriela Roxana (2007), "Akrasia and the Structure of the Passions in Plato's *Timaeus*," in Christopher Bobonich and Pierre Destrée (eds.), *Akrasia in Greek Philosophy: From Socrates to Plotinus* (Leiden: Brill), 101–18.

Caswell, Caroline P. (1990), *A Study of* Thumos *in Early Greek Epic* (Leiden: E. J. Brill).

Cheyns, André (1983), "Le θυμός et la conceptions de l'homme dans l'épopée homérique," *Revue Belge de Philologie et d'Histoire* 61: 20–86.

Clark, Stephen R. L. (1995), "Herds of Free Bipeds," in Christopher Rowe (ed.), *Reading the Statesman: Proceedings of the III Symposium Platonicum*. Sankt Augustin: Academia Verlag, 236–52.

Clarke, Michael (1999), *Flesh and Spirit in the Songs of Homer: A Study of Words and Myths*. (Oxford: Clarendon Press).

Claus, D. B. (1981), *Toward the Soul: An Inquiry into the Meaning of* Ψυχή *before Plato* (New Haven: Yale University Press).

Cleary, John J. (2003), "*Paideia* in Plato's *Laws*," in Luc Brisson and Samuel Scolnicov (eds.), *Plato's Laws: From Theory into Practice: Proceedings of the VI Symposium Platonicum, Selected Papers* (Sankt Augustin: Academia Verlag), 165–73.

Coby, Patrick (1987), *Socrates and the Sophistic Enlightenment: A Commentary on Plato's* Protagoras (Lewisburg, Pennsylvania: Bucknell University Press).

Cohen, David (1993), "Law, Autonomy, and Political Community in Plato's *Laws*," *Classical Philology* 88: 301–17.

Cole, Eve Browning (1991), "Weaving and Practical Politics in Plato's *Statesman*," *Southern Journal of Philosophy* 29/2: 195–208.

Considine, P. (1966), "Some Homeric Terms for Anger," *Acta Classica* 9: 15–25.

Cooper, John M. (1977), "The Psychology of Justice in Plato," *American Philosophical Quarterly* 14/2: 151–7.

Cooper, John M. (1984), "Plato's Theory of Human Motivation," *History of Philosophy Quarterly* 1/1: 3–21.

Cooper, John M. (1996), "An Aristotelian Theory of the Emotions," in Amélie Oksenberg Rorty, *Essays on Aristotle's Rhetoric* (Berkeley: University of California Press), 238–57.

Cooper, John M. (1997), "Plato's *Statesman* and Politics," *Proceedings of the Boston Area Colloquium in Ancient Philosophy* 13: 71–104.

Cooper, John M. (1999), "Socrates and Plato in Plato's *Gorgias*," in John M. Cooper, *Reason and Emotion: Essays on Ancient Moral Psychology and Ethical Theory* (Princeton: Princeton University Press), 29–75.

Cooper, John M. and D. S. Hutchinson (eds.) (1997), *Plato: Complete Works* (Indianapolis: Hackett).

Copland, Amy (1996), "Inchoate Feminism in Plato's *Republic* V," *Episteme* 7/6: 64–78.

Cornford, F. M. (1912), "Psychology and Social Structure in the *Republic* of Plato," *The Classical Quarterly* 6/4: 246–65.

Cornford, F. M. (1929), "The Division of the Soul," *The Hibbert Journal* 28: 206–19.

Cornford, F. M. (1937), *Plato's Cosmology: The* Timaeus *of Plato* (London: Routledge).

Coulter, James A. (1964), "The Relation of the *Apology of Socrates* to Gorgias' *Defense of Palamedes* and Plato's Critique of Gorgianic Rhetoric," *Harvard Studies in Classical Philology* 68: 269–303.

Coventry, Lucinda (1989), "Philosophy and Rhetoric in the *Menexenus*," *The Journal of Hellenic Studies* 109: 1–15.

Craig, L. H. (1994), *The War Lover: A Study of Plato's* Republic (Toronto: University of Toronto Press).

Crombie, I. M. (1962), *An Examination of Plato's Doctrines*, i: *Plato on Man and Society* (London: Routledge & Kegan Paul Ltd.).

Cropsey, Joseph et al. (1985), "The Studies of Leo Strauss: An Exchange," *New York Review of Books* (October 10).

Cross, R. C. and A. D. Woozley (1964), *Plato's* Republic: *A Philosophical Commentary* (London: The Macmillan Press Ltd).

David, E. (1978), "The Spartan *Syssitia* and Plato's *Laws*," *The American Journal of Philology* 99/4: 486–95.

David, E. (1984), *Aristophanes and Athenian Society of the Early Fourth Century B.C.* (Leiden: Brill).

Denyer, Nicholas (2008), *Plato:* Protagoras (Cambridge: Cambridge University Press).

Deretic, Irina (2013), "Plato on the Social Role of Women: Critical Reflection," *Skepsis* 23: 152–68.

Desclos, Marie-Laurence (2007), "Le vocabulaire de l'analyse psychologique chez les sophistes," *Études platoniciennes*, 4: 13–23.

Destrée, Pierre (2011), "Poetry, Thumos, and Pity in the *Republic*," in Pierre Destrée and Fritz-Gregor Herrmann (eds.), *Plato and the Poets* (Leiden: Brill), 1–20.

Destrée, Pierre (2012), "The Speech of Alcibiades (212c4–222b7)," in Christoph Horn (ed.), *Platon: Symposion* (Berlin, Akademie Verlag), 191–205.

Dettehoffer, Maria H. (1999), "Praxagoras Programm: Eine politische Deutung von Aristophanes' *Ekklesiazousai* als Beitrag zur inneren Geschichte Athens im 4. Jahrhundert v. Chr.," *Klio* 81/1: 95–111.

Devereux, Daniel (1995), "Socrates Kantian Conception of Virtue," *Journal of the History of Philosophy* 33/3: 381–408.

Diès, Auguste (2007), *Platon: Œuvres Complètes*, xii, ii: *Les Lois, Livres XI et XII* (Paris: Les Belles Lettres).

Diller, Hans (1966), "Θυμ6erlles LettresI et XIIPhilosophyeh," *Hermes* 94: 267–75.

Dillon, John (1993), *Alcinous:* The Handbook of Platonism (Oxford: Clarendon Press).

Dillon, John (1995), "The Neoplatonic Exegesis of the *Statesman* Myth," in Christopher Rowe (ed.), *Reading the* Statesman: *Proceedings of the III Symposium Platonicum* (Sankt Augustin: Academia Verlag), 364–74.

Dimas, Panos (2008), "Good and Pleasure in the *Protagoras*," *Ancient Philosophy* 28: 253–84.

Dodds, E. R. (1945), "Plato and the Irrational," *The Journal of Hellenic Studies* 65: 16–25.

Dodds, E. R. (1951), *The Greeks and the Irrational* (Berkeley: University of California Press).

Dodds, E. R. (1959), *Plato:* Gorgias (Oxford: Clarendon Press).

Dorion, Louis-André (2007), "Plato and *Enkrateia*," in Christopher Bobonich and Pierre Destrée (eds.), Akrasia *in Greek Philosophy: From Socrates to Plotinus* (Leiden: Brill), 119–38.

Dorion, Louis-André (2012), "*Enkrateia* and the Partition of the Soul in the *Gorgias*," in Rachel Barney, Tad Brennan, and Charles Brittain (eds.), *Plato and the Divided Self* (Cambridge: Cambridge University Press), 33–52.

Dorter, Kenneth (1994), *Form and Good in Plato's Eleatic Dialogues: The* Parmenides, Theaetetus, Sophist, *and* Statesman (Berkeley: University of California Press).

Dorter, Kenneth (2006), *The Transformation of Plato's* Republic (Lanham, Maryland: Lexington Books).

Duncan, Roger (1978), "Courage in Plato's *Protagoras*," *Phronesis* 23/3: 216–28.

Dušanić, Slobodan (1995), "The True Statesman of the *Statesman* and the Young Tyrant of the *Laws*: An Historical Comparison," in Christopher Rowe (ed.), *Reading the* Statesman: *Proceedings of the III Symposium Platonicum* (Sankt Augustin: Academia Verlag), 337–46.

Dybikowski, J. (1970), "False Pleasure and the *Philebus*," *Phronesis* 15/2: 147–65.

Dyson, M. (1976), "Knowledge and Hedonism in Plato's *Protagoras*," *The Journal of Hellenic Studies* 96: 32–45.

Ebert, Theodor (2003), The Role of the Frame Dialogue in Plato's *Protagoras*, in Aleš Havlíček and Filip Karfík (eds.) *Plato's* Protagoras: *Proceedings of the Third Symposium Platonicum Pragense* (Prague: *OIKOYMENH*), 9–20.

Engels, David (2012), "Irony and Plato's *Menexenus*," *L'antiquité classique* 81: 13–30.

England, E. B. (1976), *The* Laws *of Plato*, 2 vols. (New York: Arno Press).

Eucken, Christoph (2010), "Der platonische *Menexenos* und der *Panegyrikos* des Isokrates," *Museum Helveticum* 67/3: 131–45.

Evans, Matthew (2008), "Plato on the Possibility of Hedonic Mistakes," *Oxford Studies in Ancient Philosophy* 35: 89–124.

Feitosa, Zoraida Maria Lopes (2017), "A Questão da Acrasía na Filosofia de Platão," *Prometeus* 10/23: 215–29.

Fermeglia, Francesca (2007), "L'anima 'thymoeides' come 'sýmmachos tōi logoi': ('Tim. ' 69C5–70A7)," in Linda M. Napolitano Valditara (ed.), *La Sapienza di Timeo: riflessioni in margine al Timeo di Platone* (Milan: Vita E Pensiero), 315–30.

Ferrari, G. R. F. (1987), *Listening to the Cicadas: A Study of Plato's* Phaedrus (Cambridge: Cambridge University Press).

Ferrari, G. R. F. (1989), "Plato and Poetry," in George A. Kennedy (ed.), *The Cambridge History of Literary Criticism*, i: *Classical Criticism* (Cambridge: Cambridge University Press), 92–148.

Ferrari, G. R. F. (1990), "*Akrasia* as Neurosis in Plato's *Protagoras*," *Proceedings of the Boston Area Colloquium in Ancient Philosophy* 4: 115–40.

Ferrari, G. R. F. (1995), "Myth and Conservatism in Plato's *Statesman*," in Christopher Rowe (ed.), *Reading the* Statesman: *Proceedings of the III Symposium Platonicum* (Sankt Augustin: Academia Verlag), 236–52.

Ferrari, G. R. F. (1997), "Strauss's Plato," *Arion* 5/2: 36–65.

Ferrari, G. R. F. (2005), *City and Soul in Plato's* Republic (Chicago: University of Chicago Press).

Ferrari, G. R. F. (2007), "The Three-Part Soul," in G. R. F. Ferrari (ed.), *The Cambridge Companion to Plato's* Republic (Cambridge: Cambridge University Press), 165–201.

Festugière, A. J. (1971), "Les trois vies," in A. J. Festugière, *Études de philosophique grecque* (Paris: J. Vrin), 117–56.

Fletcher, Emily (2016), "*Aisthēsis*, Reason and Appetite in the *Timaeus*," *Phronesis* 61: 397–434.

Foley, Helene (1982), "The 'Female Intruder' Reconsidered: Women in Aristophanes' *Lysistrata* and *Ecclesiazousae*," *Classical Philology* 77/1: 1–21.

Foley, Helene (1989), "Medea's Divided Self," *Classical Antiquity* 8/1: 61–85.

Forde, Steven (1997), "Gender and Justice in Plato," *The American Political Science Review* 91/3: 657–70.

Fortenbaugh, W. W. (1975), *Aristotle on Emotion* (London: Duckworth).

Foxhall, Lin (1989), "Household, Gender, and Property in Classical Athens," *The Classical Quarterly* 39/1: 22–44.

Foxhall, Lin (1998), "The Politics of Affection: Emotional Attachments in Athenian Society," in Paul Cartledge, Paul Millett, and Sitta von Reden (eds.), *KOSMOS: Essays in Order, Conflict, and Community in Classical Athens* (Cambridge: Cambridge University Press), 52–67.

Foxhall, Lin (2007), *Olive Cultivation in Ancient Greece: Seeking the Ancient Economy* (Oxford: Oxford University Press).

Fraistat, Shawn (2014), "The Authority of Writing in Plato's *Laws*," 43/5: 657–67.

Frede, Dorothea (1985), "Rumpelstiltskin's Pleasures: True and False Pleasures in Plato's *Philebus*," *Phronesis* 30/2: 151–80.

Frede, Dorothea (2010), "Puppets on Strings: Moral Psychology in *Laws* Books 1 and 2," in Christopher Bobonich (ed.), *Plato's Laws: A Critical Guide* (Cambridge: Cambridge University Press), 108–26.

Frede, Michael (1992), "Introduction," in Stanley Lombardo and Karen Bell (trans.), *Plato: Protagoras* (Indianapolis: Hackett Publishing Company), vii–xxxiv.

Frère, Jean (1997), "Thumós et Kardía (Timée *69c2–70d6*)," *Kleos* 1: 9–16.

Frère, Jean (2004), *Ardeur et Colère: Le Thumos Platonicien* (Paris: Kimé).

Friedländer, Paul (1958), *Plato, i: An Introduction*, trans. Hans Meyerhoff (New York: Bollingen Foundation Inc.).

Fussi, Alessandra (2008), "The Desire for Recognition in Plato's *Symposium*," *Aresthusa* 41: 237–62.

Futter, D. B. (2009), "Shame as a Tool for Persuasion in Plato's *Gorgias*," *Journal of the History of Philosophy* 47/3: 451–61.

Futter, D. B. (2017), "The Dialectic of Community in Plato's *Republic*," *Akroterion* 62: 23–36.

Gagarin, Michael (1987), "Morality in Homer," *Classical Philology* 82/4: 285–306.

Gagarin, Michael (2001), "Did the Sophists Aim to Persuade?," *Rhetorica* 19/3: 275–91.

Gallagher, Robert L. (2004), "Protreptic Aims of Plato's *Republic*," *Ancient Philosophy* 24: 1–27.

Ganson, Todd (2005), "The Platonic Approach to Sense-Perception," *History of Philosophy Quarterly* 22/1: 1–15.

Ganson, Todd (2009), "The Rational/Non-Rational Distinction in Plato's *Republic*," *Oxford Studies in Ancient Philosophy* 36: 179–97.

Gardner, Thomas (2002), "Socrates and Plato on the Possibility of *Akrasia*," *The Southern Journal of Philosophy* 60: 191–210.

Gerson, Lloyd (1987), "A Note on Tripartition and Immortality in Plato," *Apeiron* 20/1: 81–96.

Gerson, Lloyd (2003a), *Knowing Persons: A Study in Plato* (Oxford: Oxford University Press).

Gerson, Lloyd (2003b), "*Akrasia* and the divided soul in Plato's *Laws*," in Luc Brisson and Samuel Scolnicov (ed.), *Plato's Laws: From Theory into Practice: Proceedings of the VI Symposium Platonicum* (Sankt Augustin: Academia Verlag), 149–54.

Gill, Christopher (1983), "Did Chrysippus Understand Medea?," *Phronesis* 28/2: 136–49.

Gill, Christopher (1985), "Plato and the Education of Character," *Archiv für Geschichte der Philosophie* 67: 1–26.

Gill, Christopher (1995), "Rethinking Constitutionalism in *Statesman* 291–303," in Christopher Rowe (ed.), *Reading the* Statesman: *Proceedings of the III Symposium Platonicum* (Sankt Augustin: Academia Verlag, 292–305).

Gill, Christopher (1996), *Personality in Greek Epic, Tragedy, and Philosophy: The Self in Dialogue* (Oxford: Clarendon Press).

Gill, Christopher (1997), "Galen vs. Chrysippus on the Tripartite Soul in Timaeus 69–72," in Luc Brisson and Tomás Calvo (eds.), *Interpreting the Timaeus-Critias: Proceedings of the IV Symposium Platonicum: Selected Papers* (Sankt Augustin: Academia Verlag), 267–73.

Gill, Christopher (2000), "The body's fault? Plato's *Timaeus* on Psychic Illness" in M. R. Wright (ed.), *Reason and Necessity: Essays on Plato's* Timaeus (London: The Classical Press of Wales), 59–84.

Goldberg, Larry (1983), *A Commentary on Plato's* Protagoras (New York: Peter Lang).

Gomperz, Theodor (1896), *Griechische Denker: Eine Geschichte der Antiken Philosophie.* (Leipzig: Verlag von Veit).

Görgemanns, Herwig (1960), *Beiträge zur Interpretation von Platons Nomoi* (Munich: Verlag C. H. Beck).

Gosling, J. C. B. (1959), "False Pleasures: *Philebus* 35c–41b," *Phronesis* 4/1: 44–53.

Gosling, J. C. B. (1973), *Plato* (London: Routledge & Kegan Paul).

Gosling, J. C. B. (1990), *Weakness of the Will* (London: Routledge).

Gosling, J. C. B. and C. C. W. Taylor (1982), *The Greeks on Pleasure* (Oxford: Clarendon Press).

Gould, John (1955), *The Development of Plato's Ethics* (London: Cambridge University Press).

Gribble, David (1999), *Alcibiades and Athens: A Study in Literary Presentation* (Oxford: Clarendon Press).

Griffin, Michael (2016), *Olympiodorus: On Plato: First Alcibiades 10–28* (London: Bloomsbury).

Grönroos, Gösta (2013), "Two Kinds of Belief in Plato," *Journal of the History of Philosophy* 51/1: 1–19.

Grube, G. M. A. (1980), *Plato's Thought* (Indianapolis: Hackett Publishing Company, Inc.).

Gulley, Norman (1965), "The Interpretation of 'No One Does Wrong Willingly' in Plato's Dialogues," *Phronesis* 10/1: 82–96.

Guthrie, W. K. C. (1971a), "Plato's Views on the Nature of the Soul," in Gregory Vlastos (ed.), *Plato II: Ethics, Politics and Philosophy of Art and Religion: A Collection of Critical Essays.* (New York: Doubleday Anchor), 230–43.

Guthrie, W. K. C. (1971b), *A History of Greek Philosophy,* iii: *The Fifth Century Enlightenment Part 1: The Sophists* (Cambridge: Cambridge University Press).

Guthrie, W. K. C. (1975), *A History of Greek Philosophy,* iv: *Plato: The Man and His Dialogues: Earlier Period* (Cambridge: Cambridge University Press).

Haarman, Harald (2016), *Plato on Women: Revolutionary Ideas for Gender Equality in an Ideal Society* (Amherst, New York: Cambria Press).

Hackforth, R. (1952), *Plato's Phaedrus* (Cambridge: Cambridge University Press).

Hainsworth, Bryan (1993), *The Iliad: A Commentary,* iii: *Books 9–12* (Cambridge: Cambridge University Press).

Hall, Dale (1977), "The *Republic* and the 'Limits of Politics'," *Political Theory* 5/3: 219–313.

Hall, Robert W. (1963), "Psyche as Differentiated Unity in the Philosophy of Plato," *Phronesis* 8/1: 63–82.

Halper, Edward C. (2003), "Soul, Soul's Motions, and Virtue," in Luc Brisson and Samuel Scolnicov (eds.), *Plato's Laws: From Theory into Practice* (*Proceedings of the VI Symposium Platonicum, Selected Papers*) (Sankt Augustin: Academia Verlag), 257–67.

Hamblet, Wendy C. (2011), *Punishment and Shame: A Philosophical Study* (Lanham, Maryland: Lexington Books).

Hammond, Scott John (2005), "Spiritedness Incarnate and the Unity of the Soul in Plato's *Republic*," *Polis* 22/1: 60–84.

Hanson, Ann Ellis (2004), "'Your Mother Nursed You with Bile': Anger in Babies and Small Children," in Susanna Morton Braund and Glenn W. Most (eds.), *Ancient Anger: Perspectives from Homer to Galen* (Cambridge University Press), 185–207.

Hardie, W. F. R. (1936), *A Study in Plato* (Oxford: Clarendon Press).

Harris, Marjorie S. (1930), "Beauty and the Good," *The Philosophical Review* 39/5: 479–90.

Harrison, E. L. (1953), "The Origin of Thumoeides," *Classical Review* 3: 138–40.

Harrison, E. L. (1960), "Notes on Homeric Psychology," *Phoenix* 14/2: 63–80.

Harte, Verity (1999), "Conflicting Values in Plato's *Crito*," *Archiv für Geschichte der Philosophie* 81: 117–47.

Harte, Verity (2004), "The *Philebus* on Pleasure: The Good, the Bad, and the False," *Proceedings of the Aristotelian Society* 104/2: 111–28.

Hatzistavrou, Antony (2011), "'Correctness' and Poetic Knowledge: Choric Poetry in the *Laws*," in Pierre Destrée and Fritz-Gregor Herrmann (eds.), *Plato and the Poets* (Leiden: Brill), 361–85.

Hemmenway, Scott R. (1994), "Pedagogy in the Myth of Plato's *Statesman*: Body and Soul in Relation to Philosophy and Politics," *History of Philosophy Quarterly* 11/3: 253–68.

Hobbs, Angela (2000), *Plato and the Hero: Courage, Manliness, and the Impersonal Good* (Cambridge, Cambridge University Press).

Hoffman, Paul (2003), "Plato on Appetitive Desires in the *Republic*," *Apeiron* 36/2: 171–4.

Hooker, J. T. (1987), "Homeric Society: A Shame Culture?," *Greece & Rome* 34/2: 121–5.

Horn, Christoph (2012), "Why Two Epochs of Human History? On the Myth of the Statesman," in Catherine Collobert, Pierre Destrée and Francisco J. Gonzalez (eds.), *Plato and Myth: Studies on the Use and Status of Platonic Myths* (Leiden: Brill), 393–417.

Hourani, George F. (1949), "The Education of the Third Class in Plato's *Republic*," *Classical Quarterly* 43/1–2: 58–60.

Howland, Jacob (2014), "Glaucon's Fate: Plato's *Republic* and the Drama of the Soul," *Proceedings of the Boston Area Colloquium in Ancient Philosophy* 29: 113–36.

Huart, Pierre (1968), *Le Vocabulaire de l'analyse psychologique dans l'œuvre de Thucydide.* (Paris: Librairie C. Klincksieck).

Irwin, Terence (1977), *Plato's Moral Theory: The Early and Middle Dialogues* (Oxford: Clarendon Press).

Irwin, Terence (1983), "Euripides and Socrates," *Classical Philology* 78/3: 183–97.

Irwin, Terence (1995a), *Plato's Ethics* (Oxford: Oxford University Press).

Irwin, Terence (1995b), "Plato's Objections to the Sophists," in Anton Powell (ed.), *The Greek World* (London: Routledge), 568–90.

Irwin, Terence (2010), "Morality as Law and Morality in the *Laws*," in Christopher Bobonich (ed.), *Plato's Laws: A Critical Guide* (Cambridge: Cambridge University Press), 92–107.

Jacquette, Dale (2003), "Plato on the Parts of the Soul," *Epoché: A Journal for the History of Philosophy* 8/1: 43–68.

Jaeger, Werner (1939), *Paideia: The Ideals of Greek Culture*, i: *Archaic Greece, The Mind of Athens* (New York: Oxford University Press).

Jaeger, Werner (1944a), *Paideia: The Ideals of Greek Culture*, ii: *In Search of the Divine Centre* (New York: Oxford University Press).

Jaeger, Werner (1944b), *Paideia: The Ideals of Greek Culture*, iii: *The Conflict of Cultural Ideals in the Age of Plato* (New York: Oxford University Press).

Jaeger, Werner (1946), "A New Greek Word in Plato's *Republic*: The Medical Origin of the Theory of the θυμοειδές," *Eranos* 44: 123–30.

Jaeger, Werner (1948), *Aristotle: Fundamentals of the History of His Development*, 2nd Edn. (Oxford: Oxford University Press).

Janaway, Christopher (1995), *Images of Excellence: Plato's Critique of the Arts* (Oxford: Oxford University Press).

Jansen, Sarah (2015), "Audience Psychology and Censorship in Plato's *Republic*: The Problem of the Irrational Part," *Epochē* 19/2: 1–11.

Jarratt, Susan C. (1991), *Rereading the Sophists: Classical Rhetoric Refigured* (Carbondale, Illinois: Southern Illinois University Press).

Jenkins, Michelle (2015), "Early Education in Plato's Republic," *British Journal for the History of Philosophy*, 23/5: 843–63.

Jeon, Haewon (2014), "The Interaction between the Just City and its Citizens in Plato's *Republic*: From the Producers' Point of View," *Journal of the History of Philosophy* 52/2: 183–203.

Jimenez, Marta (2020), "Plato on the Role of Anger in Our Intellectual and Moral Development," in Laura Candiotta and Olivier Renaut (eds.), *Emotions in Plato* (Leiden: Brill), 285–307.

Johansen, Thomas (2004), *Plato's Natural Philosophy: A Study of the* Timaeus-Critias (Cambridge: Cambridge University Press).

Johnstone, Mark (2011), "Changing Rulers in the Soul: Psychological Transitions in *Republic* 8–9," *Oxford Studies in Ancient Philosophy* 41, 139–67.

Johnstone, Mark (2013), "Anarchic Souls: Plato's Depiction of the 'Democratic Man,'" *Phronesis* 58/2: 139–59.

Jouanna, Jacques (2012), "Wine and Medicine in Ancient Greece," in Jacques Jouanna, *Greek Medicine from Hippocrates to Galen* (Leiden: Brill), 173–93.

Jowett, Benjamin (1892), *Laws* (New York: Macmillan Publishers).

Kahn, Charles H. (1963), "Plato's Funeral Oration: The Motive of the *Menexenus*," *Classical Philology* 58/4: 220–34.

Kahn, Charles H. (1987), "Plato's Theory of Desire," *Review of Metaphysics* 41: 77–103.

Kahn, Charles H. (1995), "The Place of the *Statesman* in Plato's Later Work," in Christopher Rowe (ed.), *Reading the* Statesman: *Proceedings of the III Symposium Platonicum*. Sankt Augustin: Academia Verlag, 49–60.

Kahn, Charles H. (1996), *Plato and the Socratic Dialogue: The Philosophical Use of a Literary Form* (Cambridge: Cambridge University Press).

Kahn, Charles H. (1998), "Pre-Platonic Ethics," in Stephen Everson (ed.), *Companions to Ancient Thought* iv: *Ethics* (Cambridge: Cambridge University Press), 27–48.

Kahn, Charles H. (2004), "Plato on the Good," in Jan Szaif and Matthias Lutz-Bachmann (eds.), *Was ist das für die Menschen Gute?* (Berlin: Walter de Gruyter), 1–17.

Kahn, Charles H. (2005), "From *Republic* to *Laws*," *Oxford Studies in Ancient Philosophy* 26: 337–62.

Kahn, Charles H. (2008), "The Myth of the *Statesman*," in Catalin Partenie (ed.), *Plato's Myths* (Cambridge: Cambridge University Press), 148–66.

Kamtekar, Rachana (1998), "Imperfect Virtue," *Ancient Philosophy* 18: 315–39.

Kamtekar, Rachana (2001), "Social Justice and Happiness in the *Republic*: Plato's Two Principles," *History of Political Thought* 22: 189–220.

Kamtekar, Rachana (2004), "What's the Good of Agreeing?: *Homonoia* in Platonic Politics," *Oxford Studies in Ancient Philosophy* 24: 131–70.

Kamtekar, Rachana (2005), "The Profession of Friendship: Callicles, Democratic Politics, and the Rhetoric Education in Plato's *Gorgias*," *Ancient Philosophy* 25: 319–39.

Kamtekar, Rachana (2006), "Speaking with the Same Voice as Reason: Personification in Plato's Psychology," *Oxford Studies in Ancient Philosophy* 31: 167–202.

Kamtekar, Rachana (2008), "Plato on Education and Art," in Gail Fine (ed.) *The Oxford Handbook to Plato* (Oxford: Oxford University Press), 336–59.

Kamtekar, Rachana (2009), "The Powers of Plato's Tripartite Psychology," *Proceedings of the Boston Area Colloquium in Ancient Philosophy* 24: 127–50.

Kamtekar, Rachana (2010), "Psychology and the Inculcation of Virtue in Plato's *Laws*," in C. Bobonich (ed.), *Plato's* Laws: *A Critical Guide*. Cambridge: Cambridge University Press, 127–48.

Kamtekar, Rachana (2017), *Plato's Moral Psychology: Intellectualism, The Divided Soul, and the Desire for the Good* (Oxford: Oxford University Press).

Karfík, Filip (2005), "What the Mortal Parts of the Soul Really Are," *Rhizai* 2/2: 197–217.

Kennel, Nigel M. (1995), *The Gymnasium of Virtue: Education and Culture in Ancient Sparta* (Chapel Hill: The University of North Carolina Press).

Kenny, Anthony (1960), "False Pleasures in the *Philebus*: A Reply to Mr. Gosling," *Phronesis* 5/1: 45–52.

Kenny, Anthony (1973), "Mental Health in Plato's *Republic*," in Anthony Kenny (ed.), *Anatomy of the Soul: Historical Essays in the Philosophy of Mind* (Oxford: Basil Blackwell), 1–27.

Kidd, I. G. (1972), *Posidonius*, i: *The Fragments* (Cambridge: Cambridge University Press).

Kidd, I. G. (1999), *Posidonius*, iii: *The Translation of the Fragments* (Cambridge: Cambridge University Press).

Klosko, George (1980), "On the Analysis of *Protagoras* 351B–360E," *Phoenix* 34/4: 301–22.

Klosko, George (1986), "The 'Straussian' Interpretation of Plato's *Republic*," *History of Political Thought* 7/2: 275–93.

Klosko, George (2006), *The Development of Plato's Political Theory*, 2nd Edn. (Oxford: Oxford University Press).

Kochin, Michael S. (2002), *Gender and Rhetoric in Plato's Political Thought* (Cambridge: Cambridge University Press).

Konstan, David (2006), *The Emotions of the Ancient Greeks: Studies in Aristotle and Classical Literature*. Toronto: University of Toronto Press.

Kraugerud, Hanne Andrea (2009), "'Essentially Social'? A Discussion of the Spirited Part of the Soul in Plato," *European Journal of Philosophy* 18/4: 481–94.

Kraut, Richard (2010), "Ordinary Virtue from the *Phaedo* to the *Laws*," in Christopher Bobonich (ed.), *Plato's Laws: A Critical Guide* (Cambridge: Cambridge University Press), 51–70.

Kurihara, Yuji (2014), "Socratic Ignorance, or the Place of the *Alcibiades I* in Plato's Early Works," in Marguerite Johnson and Harold Tarrant (eds.), *Alcibiades and the Socratic Lover-Educator* (London: Bloomsbury), 77–89.

Laks, André (1990), "Legislation and Demiurgy: On the Relationship between Plato's *Republic* and *Laws*," *Classical Antiquity* 9: 209–29.

Laks, André (1991), "L'Utopie Législative de Platon," *Revue Philosophique* 4: 416–28.

Laks, André (1998), "In What Sense Is the City of the *Laws* a Second-Best One?," in Francisco Lisi (ed.), *Plato's Laws and Its Historical Significance: Selected Papers of the International Congress on Ancient Thought* (Sankt Augustin: Academia Verlag), 107–14.

Laks, André (2000), "The *Laws*," in C. Rowe and M. Schofield (eds.), *The Cambridge History of Greek and Roman Political Thought*. Cambridge: 258–92.

Laks, André (2007), "Freedom, Liberality, and Liberty in Plato's *Laws*," *Social Philosophy and Policy* 24/2: 130–52.

Lane, Melissa (1995), "A New Angle on Utopia: The Political Theory of the *Statesman*," in Christopher Rowe (ed.), *Reading the* Statesman: *Proceedings of the III Symposium Platonicum* (Sankt Augustin: Academia Verlag), 276–91.

Lane, Melissa (1998), *Method and Politics in Plato's* Statesman (Cambridge: Cambridge University Press).

Lane, Melissa (1999), "Plato, Popper, Strauss, and Utopianism: Open Secrets?," *History of Philosophy Quarterly* 16/2: 119–42.

Lautner, Péter (2005), "The *Timaeus* on Sounds and Hearing with Some Implications for Plato's General Account of Sense-Perception," *Rhizai* 2/2: 235–53.

Lear, Gabriel Richardson (2004), *Happy Lives and the Highest Good: An Essay on Aristotle's Nicomachean Ethics* (Princeton: Princeton University Press).

Lear, Gabriel Richardson (2006), "Plato on Learning to Love Beauty," in G. Santos (ed.), *The Blackwell Guide to Plato's* Republic (Malden, Massachusetts), 104–24.

Lear, Gabriel Richardson (2007), "Permanent Beauty and Becoming Happy in Plato's *Symposium*," in James Lesher, Debra Nails, and Frisbee Sheffield (eds.), *Plato's* Symposium: *Issues in Interpretation and Reception* (Cambridge, Massachusetts: Harvard University Press), 96–123.

Lear, Gabriel Richardson (2011), "Mimesis and Psychological Change in *Republic* III," in Pierre Destrée and Fritz-Gregor Herrmann (eds.), *Plato and the Poets* (Leiden: Brill), 196–216.

Lear, Jonathan (1992), "Inside and Outside the *Republic*," *Phronesis* 37/2: 184–215.

Leroux, Georges (2002), *Platon: La République* (Paris: Flammarion).

Leroux, Georges (2005), "La tripartition de l'âme politique et éthique de l'âme dans le livre iv," in in Monique Dixsaut (ed.), Études sur la *République de Platon*, i: *De la Justice, Éducation, Psychologie et Politique* (Paris: Librarie Philosophique J. Vrin), 123–47.

Lesser, Harry (1979), "Plato's Feminism," *Philosophy* 54/207: 113–17.

Lesses, Glenn (1987), "Weakness, Reason, and the Divided Soul in Plato's *Republic*," *History of Philosophy Quarterly* 4/2: 147–61.

Lesses, Glenn (1990), "Commentary on Ferrari," *Proceedings of the Boston Area Colloquium in Ancient Philosophy* 6: 141–8.

Leunissen, Mariska (2017), *From Natural Character to Moral Virtue in Aristotle* (Oxford: Oxford University Press).

Levine, David Lawrence (1991), "Without Malice but with Forethought: A Response to Burnyeat," *The Review of Politics* 53/1: 200–18.

Liddell, H. G., and Scott, R. (eds.) (1996), *A Greek-English Lexicon*, rev. H. Jones and R. McKenzie, R., 9th ed. (Oxford: Oxford University Press).

Liebert, Rana Saadi (2013), "Pity and Disgust in Plato's *Republic*: The Case of Leontius," *Classical Philology* 108: 179–201.

Lisi, Francisco (2005), "A Alma Do Mundo e a Alma Humana No Timeu: Apontamentos Para uma Reinterpretação da Psicologia Platônica," *Hypnos* 14/1: 57–68.

Lloyd-Jones, Hugh (1980), "Euripides, *Medea* 1056–80," *Würzburger Jahrbücher für die Altertumswissenschaft* 6a: 51–9.

Loraux, Nicole (1974), "Socrate contrepoison de l'oraison funèbre: enjeu et signification du *Ménexène*," *L'antiquité Classique* 43: 172–211.

Lord, Carnes (1978), "On Damon and Music Education," *Hermes* 106/1: 32–43.

Lorenz, Hendrik (2004a), "Desire and Reason in Plato's *Republic*," *Oxford Studies in Ancient Philosophy* 27: 83–116.

Lorenz, Hendrik (2004b), "Review of Christopher Bobonich, *Plato's Utopia Recast*," *Philosophical Review* 113/4: 560–6.

Lorenz, Hendrik (2006a), *The Brute Within: Appetitive Desire in Plato and Aristotle* (Oxford: Oxford University Press).

Lorenz, Hendrik (2006b), "The Analysis of the Soul in Plato's *Republic*," in G. Santas (ed.), *The Blackwell Guide to Plato's* Republic (Malden, Massachusetts: Blackwell Publishing), 146–65.

Lorenz, Hendrik (2012), "The Cognition of Appetite in Plato's *Timaeus*," in Rachel Barney, Tad Brennan, and Charles Brittain (eds.), *Plato and the Divided Self* (Cambridge: Cambridge University Press), 238–58.

Ludwig, Paul W. (2007), "Eros in the *Republic*," in G. R. F. Ferrari (ed.), *The Cambridge Companion to Plato's* Republic (Cambridge: Cambridge University Press), 202–31.

Lynch, John P. and Gary B. Miles (1980), "In Search of *Thumos*: Toward an Understanding of a Greek Psychological Term," *Prudentia* 12/1: 3–10.

Lyons, Dan (2011), "Plato's Attempt to Moralize Shame," *Philosophy* 86/3: 353–74.

Macé, Arnaud (2017), "L'amitié civique: les deux forms du communism chez Platon," *Consecutio Rerum* 2/3: 61–79.

Mackenzie, Mary Margaret (1981), *Plato on Punishment* (Berkeley: University of California Press).

Maguire, Joseph P. (1977), "Protagoras . . . or Plato? II. The *Protagoras*," *Phronesis* 22/2: 103–22.

Mansfield, Harvey C., Jr. (2006), *Manliness* (New Haven: Yale University Press).

Manuwald, Bernd (2000), "Die Schlussaporie in Platons *Laches*," *Rheinische Museum für Philologie* 143: 179–91.

Márquez, Xavier (2012), *A Stranger's Knowledge: Statesmanship, Philosophy, and Law in Plato's* Statesman (Las Vegas: Parmenides Publishing).

Masi, Giuseppe (2001), *Il Timeo: riduzione, traduzione, introduzione e commento* (Bologna: Clueb).

Mayhew, Robert (2007), "Persuasion and Compulsion in Plato's *Laws* 10," *Polis* 24/1: 91–111.

McCabe, Mary Margaret (1997), "Chaos and Control: Reading Plato's *Politicus*," *Phronesis* 42/1: 94–117.

McCoy, Marina (1998), "Protagoras on Human Nature, Wisdom, and the Good: The Great Speech and the Hedonism of Plato's *Protagoras*," *Ancient Philosophy* 18: 21–39.

McCoy, Marina (2008), *Plato on the Rhetoric of Philosophers and Sophists* (Cambridge: Cambridge University Press).

McKeen, Catherine (2006), "Why Women Must Guard and Rule in Plato's *Kallipolis*," *Pacific Philosophical Quarterly* 87: 527–48.

Menn, Stephen (2005), "On Plato's *Politeia*," *Proceedings of the Boston Area Colloquium in Ancient Philosophy* 21: 1–55.

Meyer, Susan Sauvé (2005), "Class Assignment and the Principle of Specialization in Plato's *Republic*," *Proceedings of the Boston Area Colloquium in Ancient Philosophy* 20: 229–43.

Meyer, Susan Sauvé (2012), "Pleasure, Pain, and 'Anticipation' in Plato's *Laws*, Book I," in Richard Patterson, Vassilis Karasmanis, and Arnold Hermann (eds.), *Presocratics and Plato* (Las Vegas: Parmenides Publishing), 311–28.

Meyer, Susan Sauvé (2015), *Plato: Laws 1 & 2* (Oxford: Oxford University Press).

Militello, Chiara (2020), *"A, 0ralloiversity Presson Area ColloquRepublic,"* in Laura Candiotta and Olivier Renaut (eds.), *Emotions in Plato* (Leiden: Brill), 238–51.

Miller, Dana R. (1997), "Commentary on Brisson," *Proceedings of the Boston Area Colloquium on Ancient Philosophy* 13: 177–85.

Miller, Jr., Fred D. (1999), "Plato on the Parts of the Soul," in Johannes M. *Van* Ophuijsen (ed.), *Studies in Philosophy and the History of Philosophy 33: Plato and Platonism* (Washington, DC: The Catholic University of America Press), 84–101.

Miller, Jr., Mitchell H. (1980), *The Philosopher in Plato's* Statesman (The Hague: Martinus Nijhoff Publishers).

Mintz, Avi I. (2016), "The Education of the Third Class in the *Republic*: Plato and the *Locus Classicus* of Formative Justice," *Teachers College Record* 118/10: 1–18.

Mishima, Teruo (1995), "Courage and Moderation in the *Statesman*," in Christopher Rowe (ed.), *Reading the* Statesman: *Proceedings of the III Symposium Platonicum* (Sankt Augustin: Academia Verlag), 306–12.

Mitchell, Lynette G. and P. J. Rhodes (1996), "Friends and Enemies in Athenian Politics," *Greece and Rome* 43/11: 11–30.

Moline, Jon (1978), "Plato on the Complexity of the Psyche," *Archiv für Geschichte der Philosophie* 60: 1–26.

Morr, Josef (1929), "Die Entstehung der Platonischen Apologie," *Schriften der Deutschen Wissenschaftlichen Gesellschaft in Reichenberg* 5: 29–34.

Morris, Michael (2006), *"Akrasia in the* Protagoras *and the* Republic," *Phronesis* 51/3: 195–229.

Morrow, Glenn (1953), "Plato's Conception of Persuasion," *Philosophical Review* 62: 234–50.

Morrow, Glenn (1960), *Plato's Cretan City* (Princeton: Princeton University Press).

Moss, Jessica (2005), "Shame, Pleasure, and the Divided Soul," *Oxford Studies in Ancient Philosophy* 29: 137–70.

Moss, Jessica (2006), "Pleasure and Illusion in Plato," *Philosophy and Phenomenological Research* 72/3: 503–35.

Moss, Jessica (2007), "The Doctor and the Pastry Chef: Pleasure and Persuasion in Plato's *Gorgias*," *Ancient Philosophy* 27: 229–49.

Moss, Jessica (2008), "Appearances and Calculations: Plato's Division of the Soul," *Oxford Studies in Ancient Philosophy* 34: 35–68.

Moss, Jessica (2012a), "Pictures and Passions in the *Timaeus* and *Philebus*," in Rachel Barney, Tad Brennan, and Charles Brittain (eds.), *Plato and the Divided Self* (Cambridge: Cambridge University Press), 259–80.

Moss, Jessica (2014a), "Hedonism and the Divided Soul in Plato's *Protagoras*," *Archiv für Geschichte der Philosophie* 96/3: 285–319.

Moss, Jessica (2014b), "Plato's Appearance/Assent Account of Belief," *Proceedings of the Aristotelian Society* 114/2: 1–27.

Moss, Jessica (forthcoming), "Against Bare Urges and Good-Independent Desires: Appetites in *Republic IV*," *Proceedings of the Keeling Colloquium*, 2011.

Most, Glenn W. (2003), "Anger and Pity in Homer's *Iliad*," in Susanna Morton Braund and Glenn W. Most (eds.), *Ancient Anger: Perspectives from Homer to Galen* (Cambridge: Cambridge University Press), 50–75.

Most, Glenn W. (2011), "What Ancient Quarrel between Philosophy and Poetry?," in Pierre Destrée and Fritz-Gregor Herrmann (eds.), *Plato and the Poets* (Leiden: Brill), 1–20.

Moutsopoulos, Evangelos (2002), "Motions of Sounds, Bodies, and Souls (Plato, *Laws* VII 790e ff.)," *Prolegomena* 1/2: 113–19.

Müller, Carl Werner (1991), "Platon und der 'Panegyrikos' des Isokrates: Überlegungen zum platonischen 'Menexenos'," *Philologus* 135: 140–56.

Murphy, N. R. (1951), *Interpretation of Plato's* Republic (Oxford: Clarendon Press).

Murray, Penelope (1997), *Plato on Poetry:* Ion, Republic *376e–398b*, Republic *595–608b* (Cambridge: Cambridge University Press).

Murray, Penelope (2011), "Tragedy, Women and the Family in Plato's *Republic*," in Pierre Destrée and Fritz-Gregor Herrmann (eds.), *Plato and the Poets* (Leiden: Brill) 175–94.

Naddaf, Gerard (1997), "Plato and the *Peri Phuseos* Tradition," in Luc Brisson and Tomás Calvo (eds.), *Interpreting the Timaeus-Critias: Proceedings of the IV Symposium Platonicum: Selected Papers* (Sankt Augustin: Academia Verlag), 27–37.

Nagle, D. Brendan (2006), *The Household as the Foundation of Aristotle's Polis* (Cambridge: Cambridge University Press).

Narcy, Michel (1995), "La critique de Socrate par l'etrange dans le *Politique*," in Christopher Rowe (ed.), *Reading the* Statesman: *Proceedings of the III Symposium Platonicum* (Sankt Augustin: Academia Verlag), 227–35.

Natali, Carlo (2005), "L'élision de l'*oikos*," in Monique Dixsaut (ed.), Études sur la *République de Platon, i: De la Justice, Éducation, Psychologie et Politique* (Paris: Libraire Philosophique J. Vrin), 199–223.

Nehamas, Alexander (1982), "Plato on Imitation and Poetry in *Republic* X," in Julius Moravcsik and Philip Temko (eds.), *Plato on Beauty, Wisdom, and the Arts* (Totowa, New Jersey: Rowman, and Littlefield), 47–78.

Nehamas, Alexander (1990), "Eristic, Antilogic, Sophistic, Dialectic: Plato's Demarcation of Philosophy from Sophistry," *History of Philosophy Quarterly* 7/1: 3–16.

Nehamas, Alexander (1999), "Socratic Intellectualism," in Alexander Nehamas, *Virtues of Authenticity: Essays on Plato and Socrates* (Princeton: Princeton University Press), 27–58.

Nehamas, Alexander (2007a), "Beauty of Body, Nobility of Soul: The Pursuit of Love in Plato's *Symposium*," in D. Scott (ed.), *Maieusis: Essays in Ancient Philosophy in Honour of Myles Burnyeat*. Oxford, 97–135.

Nehamas, Alexander (2007b), "Only in the Contemplation of Beauty is Human Life Worth Living: Plato, *Symposium* 211d," *European Journal of Philosophy* 15/1: 1–18.

Nettleship, R. L. (1935), *A Theory of Education in Plato's* Republic (Oxford: Clarendon Press).

Nichols, Mary P. (1988), "Spiritedness and Philosophy in Plato's *Republic*," in Catherine H. Zuckert (ed.), *Understanding the Political Spirit: Philosophical Investigations from Socrates to Nietzsche* (New Haven: Yale University Press), 48–66.

Nichols, Mary P. (2006), "Friendship and Community in Plato's *Lysis*," *The Review of Politics* 68: 1–19.

Nicholson, Graeme (1999), *Plato's* Phaedrus: *The Philosophy of Love.* (West Lafayette, Indiana: Purdue University Press).

Nightingale, Andrea Wilson (1993), "Writing/Reading a Sacred Text: A Literary Interpretation of Plato's *Laws*," *Classical Philology* 88/4: 279–300.

Nightingale, Andrea Wilson (1995), *Genres in Dialogue: Plato and the Construct of Philosophy* (Cambridge: Cambridge University Press).

Nightingale, Andrea Wilson (1996), "Plato on the Origins of Evil: The *Statesman* Myth Reconsidered," *Ancient Philosophy* 16: 65–91.

Nightingale, Andrea Wilson (1999), "Plato's Lawcode in Context: Rule by Written Law in Athens and Magnesia," *Classical Quarterly* 49/1: 100–22.

North, Helen (1947), "A Period of Opposition to *Sōphrosynē* in Greek Thought," *Transactions and Proceedings of the American Philological Association* 78: 1–17.

North, Helen (1966), *Sophrosyne: Self-Knowledge and Self-Restraint in Greek Literature* (Cornell University Press).

Nussbaum, Martha (1980), "Aristophanes and Socrates on Learning Practical Wisdom," *Yale Classical Studies* 26: 43–97.

Nussbaum, Martha (1986), *The Fragility of Goodness: Luck and Ethics in Greek Tragedy and Philosophy* (Cambridge: Cambridge University Press).

Nussbaum, Martha (2001), *Upheavals of Thought: The Intelligence of Emotion* (Cambridge: Cambridge University Press).

Nussbaum, Martha (2009), "Commentary on Kamtekar," *Proceedings of the Boston Area Colloquium in Ancient Philosophy* 24: 151–62.

O'Brien, Michael J. (1967), *The Socratic Paradoxes and the Greek Mind* (Chapel Hill: University of North Carolina Press).

Ober, Josiah (1998), *Political Dissent in Democratic Athens: Intellectual Critics of Popular Rule* (Princeton: Princeton University Press).

Okin, Susan Moller (1977), "Philosopher Queens and Private Wives: Plato on Women and the Family," *Philosophy & Public Affairs* 6/4: 345–69.

Onians, R. B. (1951), *The Origins of European Thought: About the Body, the Mind, the Soul, the World, Time, and Fate* (Cambridge: Cambridge University Press).

Pangle, Thomas L. (1980), *The Laws of Plato: Translated, with Notes and an Interpreted Essay* (Chicago: University of Chicago Press).

Parra, José Daniel (2010), "Political Psychology in Plato's *Alcibiades I*," *Praxis Filosófica* 31: 25–44.

Parry, R. D. (2003), "The Cause of Motion in *Laws* X and of Disorderly Motion in *Timaeus*," in S. Scolnicov and L. Brisson (eds.), *Plato's Laws: From Theory into Practice* (Proceedings of the VI Symposium Platonicum) (Sankt Augustin: Academia Verglag), 268–75.

Penner, Terry (1970), "False Anticipatory Pleasure: *Philebus* 36a3–41a6," *Phronesis* 15/2: 166–78.

Penner, Terry (1971), "Thought and Desire in Plato," in Gregory Vlastos (ed.), *Plato: A Collection of Critical Essays* (Garden City, New York: Anchor Books), 96–118.

Penner, Terry (1990), "Plato and Davidson: Parts of the Soul and Weakness of Will," *Canadian Journal of Philosophy*, Supplementary Volume 16: 35–73.

Penner, Terry (1992), "Socrates and the Early dialogues," in Richard Kraut (ed.), *The Cambridge Companion to Plato* (Cambridge: Cambridge University Press), 121–69.

Penner, Terry (2000), "Socrates," in Christopher Rowe and Malcolm Schofield (eds.), *Greek and Roman Political Thought* (Cambridge: Cambridge University Press).

Penner, Terry (2003), "The Historical Socrates and Plato's Early Dialogues: Some Philosophical Questions," in Julia Annas and Christopher J. Rowe (eds.), *New Perspectives on Plato: Modern and Ancient* (Cambridge, Massachusetts: Harvard University Press), 189–212.

Perentidis, Stavros (2012), "La femme spartiate, sujet de conflit entre Aristophane et les Socratiques," in Hélène Ménard, Pierre Sauzeau, and Jean-François Thomas (eds.), *La Pomme d'Éris* (Montpellier, France: Presses universitaires de la Méditerranée), 425–43.

Peterson, Sandra (2011), *Socrates and Philosophy in the Dialogues of Plato* (Cambridge: Cambridge University Press).

Pfefferkorn, Julia (2020), "Shame and Virtue in Plato's Laws: Two Kinds of Fear and the Drunken Puppet," in Laura Candiotta and Olivier Renaut (eds.), *Emotions in Plato* (Leiden: Brill), 252–69.

Popper, Karl (1962), *The Open Society and Its Enemies, i: The Spell of Plato* (London: Routledge & Kegan Paul).

Powell, Anton (2015), "Spartan Education," in W. Martin Bloomer (ed.), *A Companion to Ancient Education* (Chichester, United Kingdom: John Wiley & Sons, Ltd.), 90–111.

Pradeau, Jean-François (2002), *Plato and the City: A New Introduction to Plato's Political Thought* (Exeter: University of Exeter Press).

Prauscello, Lucia (2014), *Performing Citizenship in Plato's* Laws (Cambridge: Cambridge University Press).

Price, A. W. (1995), *Mental Conflict* (London: Routledge).

Price, A. W. (2009), "Are Plato's Soul-Parts Psychological Subjects?," *Ancient Philosophy* 29: 1–15.

Prior, William J. (2002), "Protagoras' Great Speech and Plato's Defense of Athenian Democracy," in Victor Caston and Daniel Graham (eds.), *Presocratic Philosophy: Essays in Honour of Alexander Mourelatos* (Burlington, Vermont: Ashgate), 313–26.

Purviance, Susan (2008), "Thumos and the Daring Soul: Craving Honor and Justice," *Journal of Ancient Philosophy* 2/2: 1–16.

Rahe, Paul A. (2016), *The Spartan Regime: Its Character, Origins, and Grand Strategy* (New Haven: Yale University Press).

Redfield, James (1985), "Le sentiment homérique du Moi," *Le Genre Humain* 12: 93–111.

Redfield, James (1994), *Nature and Culture in the* Iliad: *The Tragedy of Hector* (Durham: Duke University Press).

Rees, D. A. (1957), "Bipartition of the Soul in the Early Academy," *The Journal of Hellenic Studies* 77/1: 112–18.

Reeve, C. D. C. (1988), *Philosopher-Kings* (Indianapolis: Hackett Publishing Company, Inc).

Reeve, C. D. C. (1998), *Aristotle: Politics: Translated, with Introduction and Notes* (Indianapolis: Hackett Publishing Company).

Reeve, C. D. C. (2006), "A Study in Violets: Alcibiades in the *Symposium*," in J. H. Lesher, Debra Nails, and Frisbee C. C. Sheffield (eds.), *Plato's* Symposium: *Issues in Interpretation and Reception* (Cambridge, Massachusetts: Harvard University Press), 124–46.

Reeve, C. D. C. (2013a), "Soul, Soul-Parts, and Persons in Plato," in Anagnostopoulos, Georgios and Fred D. Miller, Jr. (eds.), *Reason and Analysis in Ancient Greek Philosophy: Essays in Honor of David Keyt* (Dordrecht: Springer), 147–70.

Reeve, C. D. C. (2013b), *Blindness and Reorientation: Problems in Plato's* Republic. Oxford: Oxford University Press.

Reeve, C. D. C. (2017), *Aristotle: De Anima* (Indianapolis: Hackett).

Reid, Heather (2007), "Sport and Moral Education in Plato's *Republic*," *Journal of the Philosophy of Sport* 34: 160–75.

Reid, Jeremy (2017), "Unfamiliar Voices: Harmonizing the Non-Socratic Speeches and Plato's Psychology," in Pierre Destrée and Zina Giannopoulou (eds.), *Plato's Symposium: A Critical Guide* (Cambridge: Cambridge University Press), 27–48.

Reid, Jeremy (2018), "Plato on Love and Sex," in Adrienne M. Martin (ed.), *Routledge Handbook of Love in Philosophy* (Routledge: New York), 105–15.

Reid, Jeremy (2020), "The Offices of Magnesia," *Polis* 37/3: 567–89.

Renaut, Olivier (2014), *Platon: La médiation des émotions: L'éducation du thymos dans les dialogues* (Paris: Libraire Philosophique J. Vrin).

Renaut, Olivier (2019), "The Analogy between Vice and Disease from the *Republic* to the *Timaeus*," in Luca Pitteloud and Evan Keeling (eds.), *Psychology and Ontology in Plato* (Cham: Springer International Publishing), 67–83.

Renaut, Olivier (2020), "Emotions and Rationality in the *Timaeus* (*Ti.* 42a–b, 69c–72e)," in Laura Candiotta and Olivier Renaut (eds.), *Emotions in Plato* (Leiden: Brill), 103–22.

Rhodes, P. J. (1998), "Enmity in Fourth-Century Athens," in Paul Cartledge, Paul Millett, and Sitta van Reden (eds.), *KOSMOS: Essays in Order, Conflict, and Community in Classical Athens* (Cambridge: Cambridge University Press), 144–61.

Rickert, GailAnn (1987), "Akrasia and Euripides' *Medea*," *Harvard Studies in Classical Philology* 91: 91–117.

Rist, John (1992), "Plato Says that We Have Tripartite Souls. If He Is Right, What Can We Do about It?," in Jean Pepin (ed.), *ΣΟΦΙΗΣ ΜΑΙΗΤΟΡΕΣ: Chercheurs de sagesse* (Paris: Institute de'Etudes Augustinennes), 103–24.

Ritter, Constantin (1896), *Platos Gesetze: Kommentar zum griechischen Text* (Leipzig: B. G. Teubner).

Roberts, Jean (1987), "Plato on the Causes of Wrongdoing in the *Laws*," *Ancient Philosophy* 7: 23–37.

Robin, Léon (1908), *La théorie platonicienne de l'amour* (Paris, Félix Alcan).

Robinson, Richard (1971), "Plato's Separation of Reason from Desire," *Phronesis* 16/1: 38–48.

Robinson, T. M. (1970), *Plato's Psychology* (Toronto: University of Toronto Press).

Rohde, Erwin (1925), *Psyche: The Cult of Souls and Belief in Immortality among the Greeks*, trans. W. B. Hills (New York: Harcourt, Brace, & Company, Inc.).

Romilly, Jacqueline de (1980), "Réflexions sur le courage chez Thucydide et chez Platon," *Revue des Études Grecques* 93: 307–23.

Romilly, Jacqueline de (1992), *The Great Sophists in Periclean Athens*, trans. Janet Lloyd (Oxford: Clarendon Press).

Rorty, Amélie Oksenberg (1986), "The Two Faces of Courage," *Philosophy* 61: 151–71.

Rosen, Stanley (1995), *Plato's Statesman: The Web of Politics* (New Haven: Yale University Press).

Rowe, Christopher (1986), *Plato: Phaedrus* (Warminster, England: Aris & Phillips Ltd.).

Rowe, Christopher (1995), "Introduction," in Christopher Rowe (ed.), *Reading the Statesman: Proceedings of the III Symposium Platonicum* (Sankt Augustin: Academia Verlag), 11–28.

Rowe, Christopher (2000), "The *Politicus* and Other Dialogues," in Christopher Rowe and Malcolm Schofield (eds.), *The Cambridge History of Greek and Roman Political Thought* (Cambridge: Cambridge University Press), 233–57.

Rowe, Christopher (2001), "Zwei oder Drei Phasen? Der Mythos im *Politikos*," in Markus Janka and Christian Schäfer (eds.), *Platon als Mythologe: Neue Interpretationen zu den Mythen in Platons Dialogen* (Darmstadt: Wissenschaftliche Buchgesellschaft), 160–75.

Rowe, Christopher (2003), "Plato, Socrates, and Developmentalism," in Naomi Reshotko (ed.), *Desire, Identity, and Existence: Essays in Honour of T. M. Penner* (Kelowna, British Columbia: Academic Printing and Publishing), 17–32.

Rowe, Christopher (2007), "A Problem in the *Gorgias*: How Is Punishment Supposed to Help with Intellectual Error?" in Christopher Bobonich and Pierre Destrée (eds.), *Akrasia in Greek Philosophy: From Socrates to Plotinus* (Leiden: Brill), 19–40.

Rowe, Christopher (2015), "Plato Versus Protagoras: The *Statesman*, the *Theaetetus*, and the Sophist," *Diálogos* 98: 143–65.

Roy, J. (1999), "*Polis* and *Oikos* in Classical Athens," *Greece & Rome* 46/1: 1–18.

Russell, Daniel (2005), *Plato on Pleasure and the Good Life* (Oxford: Clarendon Press).

Salkever, Stephen G. (1990), *Finding the Mean: Theory and Practice in Aristotelian Political Philosophy* (Princeton: Princeton University Press).

Samaras, Thanassis (2010), "Family and the Question of Women in the *Laws*," in C. Bobonich (ed.), *Plato's Laws: A Critical Guide* (Cambridge: Cambridge University Press), 172–96.

Santas, Gerasimos (1980), "Plato on Love, Beauty, and the Good," in David J. Depew (ed.), *Greeks and the Good Life* (Fullerton: California State University), 33–68.

Sassi, Maria Michela (2008), "The Self, the Soul, and the Individual in the City of the *Laws*," *Oxford Studies in Ancient Philosophy* 35: 125–48.

Saunders, Trevor (1962), "The Structure of the Soul and the State in Plato's *Laws*," *Eranos*, 60: 37–55.

Saunders, Trevor (1968), "The Socratic Paradoxes in Plato's *Laws*: A Commentary on 859c–864b," *Hermes* 96: 421–34.

Saunders, Trevor (1973), "Plato on Killing in Anger: A Reply to Professor Woozley," *The Philosophical Quarterly* 23/93: 350–6.

Saunders, Trevor (1991), *Plato's Penal Code* (Oxford: Clarendon Press).

Saxonhouse, Arlene W. (1976), "The Philosopher and the Female in the Political Thought of Plato," *Political Theory* 4/2: 195–212.

Schäfer, Christian (2001), "Herrschen und Selbstbeherrschung: Der Mythos des Politikos," in Markus Janka and Christian Schäfer (eds.), *Platon als Mythologe: Neue Interpretationen zu den Mythen in Platons Dialogen* (Darmstadt: Wissenschaftliche Buchgesellschaft), 203–24.

Schiefsky, M. (2012), "Galen and the Tripartite Soul," in Rachel Barney, Tad Brennan, and Charles Brittain (eds.), *Plato and the Divided Self* (Cambridge: Cambridge University Press), 331–49.

Schiller, F. C. S. (1908), "Plato or Protagoras?," *Mind* 17/58: 518–26.

Schofield, Malcolm (2010), "Music All Pow'rful," in Mark McPherran (ed.), *Plato's Republic: A Critical Guide* (Cambridge: Cambridge University Press), 229–48.

Scodel, Harvey Ronald (1987), *Diaeresis and Myth in Plato's* Statesman (Göttingen: Vandenhoeck & Ruprecht).

Scolnicov, Samuel (1997), "Freedom and Education in Plato's *Timaeus*" in Luc Brisson and Tomás Calvo (eds.), *Interpreting the Timaeus-Critias: Proceedings of the IV Symposium Platonicum: Selected Papers* (Sankt Augustin: Academia Verlag), 363–74.

Scolnicov, Samuel (2003), "Pleasure and Responsibility in Plato's *Laws*," in Samuel Scolnicov and Luc Brisson (eds.), *Plato's Laws: From Theory into Practice: Proceedings of the VI Symposium Platonicum: Selected Papers* (Sankt Augustin: Academia Verlag), 122–7.

Scott, Dominic (1999), "Platonic Pessimism and Moral Education," *Oxford Studies in Ancient Philosophy* 17: 15–36.

Sedley, David (1997), " 'Becoming Like God' in the *Timaeus* and Aristotle," in Luc Brisson and Tomás Calvo (eds.), *Interpreting the Timaeus-Critias: Proceedings of the IV Symposium Platonicum: Selected Papers* (Sankt Augustin: Academia Verlag), 327–9.

Sedley, David (2007), *Creationism and Its Critics in Antiquity* (Berkeley: University of California Press).

Segal, Charles P. (1962), "Gorgias and the Psychology of the Logos," *Harvard Studies in Classical Philology* 66: 99–155.

Serban, Silviu (2014), "On Inconsistencies in Plato's Gender Equality," *Journal of Research in Gender Studies* 4/1: 1062–9.

Sesonske, Alexander (1963), "Hedonism in the *Protagoras*," *Journal of the History of Philosophy* 1/1: 73–9.

Sharpe, Matthew (2014), "Revaluing *Megalopsuchia*: Reflections on the *Alcibiades II*" in Johnson and Tarrant (eds.), *Alcibiades and the Socratic Lover-Educator Alcibiades* (London: Bloomsbury), 134–46.

Sharples, R. W. (1983), "'But Why Has My Spirit Spoken with Me Thus?': Homeric Decision-Making," *Greece & Rome* 30/1: 1–7.

Shaw, Clerk (2015), *Plato's Anti-Hedonism and the* Protagoras (Cambridge: Cambridge University Press).

Sheffield, Frisbee (2006), *Plato's* Symposium: *The Ethics of Desire* (Oxford: Oxford University Press).

Sheffield, Frisbee (2012), "*Erōs* Before and After Tripartition," in Rachel Barney, Tad Brennan, and Charles Brittain (eds.), *Plato and the Divided Soul* (Cambridge: Cambridge University Press), 211–38.

Sheffield, Frisbee (2020), "Love in the City: *Eros* and *Philia* in Plato's *Laws*," in Laura Candiotta and Olivier Renaut (eds.), *Emotions in Plato* (Leiden: Brill), 330–71.

Sheppard, Alan (2016), "Aristophanes' *ECCLESIAZVSAE* and the Remaking of the *ΠΑΤΡΙΟΣ ΠΟΛΙΤΕΙΑ*," *The Classical Quarterly* 66/2: 1–21.

Shields, Christopher (2001), "Simple Souls," in Ellen Wagner (ed.), *Essays on Plato's Psychology* (Lanham, Maryland: Lexington Books), 137–56.

Shields, Christopher (2007), "Unified Agency and *Akrasia* in Plato's *Republic*," in Christopher Bobonich and Pierre Destrée (eds.), *Akrasia in Greek Philosophy: From Socrates to Plotinus* (Leiden: Brill), 61–86.

Shorey, Paul (1903), *The Unity of Plato's Thought* (Chicago: Chicago University Press).

Silva, Felipe Gustavo (2018), "O conflito da alma no Livro IV da *República* e sua possível relação com o discurso de Alcibíades no *Simpósio* de Platão," *Ipseitas* 4/2: 92–105.

Silverman, Allan (1990), "Plato on Perception and 'Commons'," *The Classical Quarterly* 40/1: 148–75.

Silverman, Allan (1991), "Plato on *Phantasia*," *Classical Antiquity* 10/1: 123–47.

Singpurwalla, Rachel (2006), "Reasoning with the Irrational: Moral Psychology in the *Protagoras*," *Ancient Philosophy* 26: 243–58.

Singpurwalla, Rachel (2010), "The Tripartite Theory of Motivation in Plato's *Republic*," *Philosophy Compass* 5/11: 880–92.

Singpurwalla, Rachel (2011), "Soul Division and Mimesis in *Republic* X," in Pierre Destrée and Fritz-Gregor Herrmann (eds.), *Plato and the Poets* (Leiden: Brill), 283–98.

Singpurwalla, Rachel (2013), "Why Spirit Is the Natural Ally of Reason?: Spirit, Reason, and the Fine in Plato's *Republic*," *Oxford Studies in Ancient Philosophy* 44: 41–65.

Skemp, J. B. (1952), *Plato's* Statesman (Bristol: Bristol Classical Press).

Smith, Nicholas D. (1980), "The Logic of Plato's Feminism," *Journal of Social Philosophy* 11/3: 5–11.

Smith, Nicholas D. (1999), "Plato's Analogy of Soul and State," *The Journal of Ethics* 3/1: 31–49.

Smith, Nicholas D. (2004), "Did Plato Write the *Alcibiades* I?," *Apeiron* 37: 93–108.

Snell, Burno (1953), *The Discovery of the Mind*, trans. T. G. Rosenmeyer (Cambridge, Massachusetts: Harvard University Press).

Solmsen, F. (1961), "Greek Philosophy and the Discovery of the Nerves," *Museum Helveticum* 18: 150–97.

Sommerstein, Alan H. (2008), *Aeschylus* i: Persians, Seven Against Thebes, Suppliants, Prometheus Bound (Cambridge, Massachusetts: Harvard University Press).

Sorabji, Richard (1993), *Animal Minds and Human Minds: The Origins of the Western Debate* (Ithaca: Cornell University Press).

Spelman, Elizabeth (1994), "Hairy Cobblers and Philosopher-Queens," in Nancy Tuana (ed.), *Feminist Interpretations of Plato* (University Park, Pennsylvania: The Pennsylvania State University Press), 87–107.

Stalley, R. F. (1983), *An Introduction to Plato's* Laws (Indianapolis: Hackett).

Stalley, R. F. (1994), "Persuasion in Plato's *Laws*" *History of Political Thought* 15/2: 157–77.

Stalley, R. F. (1995), "Punishment in Plato's *Protagoras*," *Phronesis* 40/1: 1–19.

Stalley, R. F. (2003), "Justice in Plato's *Laws*," in L. Brisson and S. Scolnicov (eds.), *Plato's Laws: From Theory into Practice* (Proceedings of the VI Symposium Platonicum). Sankt Augustin, 174–85.

Stalley, R. F. (2007), "Persuasion and the Tripartite Soul in Plato's *Republic*," *Oxford Studies in Ancient Philosophy* 32: 63–90.

Steel, Carlos (2001), "The Moral Purpose of the Human Body: A Reading of *Timaeus* 69–72," *Phronesis* 46/2: 105–28.

Stocks, J. L. (1915), "Plato and the Tripartite Soul," *Mind* 24: 207–22.

Storey, Damien (2014), "Appearance, Perception, and Non-Rational Belief: *Republic* 602c–603a," *Oxford Studies in Ancient Philosophy* 47: 81–118.

Strauss, Leo (1964), *The City and Man* (Chicago: The University of Chicago Press).

Sullivan, J. P. (1961), "The Hedonism in Plato's *Protagoras*," *Phronesis* 6/1: 10–28.

Sullivan, Shirley Darcus (1981), "The Function of Θυμός in Hesiod and the Greek Lyric Poets," *Glotta* 59: 147–55.

Sullivan, Shirley Darcus (1988), *Psychological Activity in Homer: A Study of Phrēn* (Ottawa: Carleton University Press).

Sullivan, Shirley Darcus (1993a), "Person and Θυμός in the Poetry of Hesiod," *Emerita* 61/1: 15–40.

Sullivan, Shirley Darcus (1993b), "The Role of Person and Θυμός in Pindar and Bacchylides," *Revue belge de Philologie et d'Histoire* 71/1: 46–68.

Sullivan, Shirley Darcus (1993c), *Aeschylus' Use of Psychological Terminology: Traditional and New* (Montreal: McGill-Queen's University Press).

Sullivan, Shirley Darcus (1994a), "The Relationship of Person and Thumos in the Greek Lyric Poets (excluding Pindar and Bacchylides): Part One," *Studi Italiani di Filologia Classica* 12/1: 12–37.

Sullivan, Shirley Darcus (1994b), "The Relationship of Person and Thumos in the Greek Lyrics Poets (excluding Pindar and Bacchylides): Part Two," *Studi Italiani di Filologia Classica* 12/2: 149–74.

Sullivan, Shirley Darcus (1995), *Psychological and Ethical Ideas: What Early Greeks Say* (Leiden: E. J. Brill).

Sullivan, Shirley Darcus (1999), *Sophocles' Use of Psychological Terminology: Old and New* (Montreal: McGill-Queen's University Press).

Sullivan, Shirley Darcus (2000), *Euripides' Use of Psychological Terminology* (Montreal: McGill-Queen's University Press).

Taki, Akitsugu (2003), "The origin of the lengthy digression in Plato's *Laws*, Books I and II," in Samuel Scolnicov and Luc Brisson (eds.), *Plato's Laws: From Theory into Practice: Proceedings of the VI Symposium Platonicum: Selected Papers* (Sankt Augustin: Academia Verlag), 48–53.

Tarnapolsky, Christina (2007), "The Bipolar Longings of Thumos: A Feminist Rereading of Plato's *Republic*," *Symposium* 11/2: 297–314.

Tarnapolsky, Christina (2010a), "Plato's Politics of Distributing and Disrupting the Sensible," *Theory & Event* 13/4: 1–23.

Tarnopolsky, Christina (2010b), *Prudes, Perverts, and Tyrants: Plato's* Gorgias *and the Politics of Shame*. Princeton University Press.

Tarnopolsky, Christina (2015), "Thumos and Rationality in Plato's *Republic*," *Global Discourse* 5/2: 242–57.

Tarrant, Harold (2004), "Development, Non-Philosophers, and *Laws*," *Polis* 21/1–2: 147–59.

Tarrant, Harold and Terry Roberts (2014), "Report on the Working Vocabulary of the Doubtful Dialogues," in Marguerite Johnson and Harold Tarrant (eds.), *Alcibiades and the Socratic Lover-Educator* (London: Bloomsbury), 223–36.

Taylor, A. E. (1927), *Plato: The Man and His Work*, 2nd edn. (London: Methuen & Co. Ltd.).

Taylor, A. E. (1928), *A Commentary on Plato's* Timaeus (Oxford: Clarendon Press).

Taylor, A. E. (1961), *Plato: The* Sophist *and the* Statesman (London: Thomas Nelson and Sons Ltd.).

Taylor, C. C. W. (1976), *Plato:* Protagoras (Oxford: Clarendon Press).

Taylor, C. C. W. (2003), "Review of *Plato's Utopia Recast*," *British Journal for the History of Philosophy* 11/3: 537–40.

Thaler, Naly (2015), "Plato on the Philosophical Benefits of Musical Education," *Phronesis* 60: 410–35.

Thein, Karel (2012), "Imagination, Self-Awareness, and Modal Thought at *Philebus* 39–40," *Oxford Studies in Ancient Philosophy* 42: 109–49.

Thein, Karel (2019), "Reason and Dreaming in *Republic* IX and the *Timaeus*," *Rhizomata* 7/1: 1–32.

Thomas, Rosalind (ed.) (1997), *Herodotus*: The Histories, trans. George Rawlinson (New York: Alfred A. Knopf).

Tianyue, Wu (2009), "Rethinking Bernard Williams" Criticism of the City-Soul Analogy in Plato's *Republic, The 3rd BESETO Conference of Philosophy* Session 14: 331–46.

Tordoff, Robert (2007), "Aristophanes' *Assembly Women* and Plato, *Republic* Book 5," in Robin Osbourne (ed.), *Debating the Athenian Cultural Revolution: Art, Literature, Philosophy, and Politics 430–380 BC* (Cambridge: Cambridge University Press), 242–63.

Tordoff, Robert (2017), "Memory and the Rhetoric of *ΣΩΤΗΡΙΑ* in Aristophanes' *Assembly Women*," *Histos*, Supplement 6: 153–210.

Trivigno, Franco V. (2009), "The Rhetoric of Parody in Plato's *Menexenus*," *Philosophy and Rhetoric* 42/1: 29–58.

Van Harten, Alice (2003), "Creating Happiness: The Moral of the Myth of Kronos in Plato's Laws (*Laws* 4, 713b–714a)," in Luc Brisson and Samuel Scolnicov (eds.), *Plato's Laws: From Theory into Practice: Proceedings of the VI Symposium Platonicum* (Sankt Augustin: Academia Verlag), 128–38.

Vander Waerdt, P. A. (1985a), "Peripatetic Soul-Division, Posidonius, and Middle Platonic Moral Psychology," *Greek, Roman, and Byzantine Studies* 26: 373–94.

Vander Waerdt, P. A. (1985b), "The Peripatetic Interpretation of Plato's Tripartite Psychology," *Greek, Roman, and Byzantine Studies* 26: 283–302.

Vasilou, Iakovos (2008), *Aiming at Virtue in Plato* (Cambridge: Cambridge University Press).

Vasilou, Iakovos (2012), "From the *Phaedo* to the *Republic*: Plato's Tripartite Soul and the Possibility of Non-Philosophical Virtue," in Rachel Barney, Tad Brennan, and Charles Brittain (eds.), *Plato and the Divided Self* (Cambridge: Cambridge University Press), 9–32.

Vegetti, Mario (1998), *Platone: La Repubblica*, ii: *Libri II e III*. Naples (Napoli: Bibliopolis).

Verdenius, W. J. (1985), *Commentary on Hesiod*, Works and Days, *vv. 1–382* (Leiden: E. J. Brill).

Verlinsky, Alexander (2008), "The Cosmic Cycle in the *Statesman* Myth: Part I," *Hyperboreus* 14/2: 57–86.

Verlinsky, Alexander (2009), "The Cosmic Cycle in the *Statesman* Myth: Part II: The Gods and the Universe," *Hyperboreus* 15/2: 221–50.

Versenyi, Laszlo (1962), "Protagoras' Man-Measure Fragment," *The American Journal of Philology* 83/2: 178–84.

Vidal-Naquet, Pierre (1978), "Plato's Myth of the Statesman, the Ambiguities of the Golden Age and of History," *Journal of Hellenic Studies* 98: 132–41.

Vlastos, Gregory (1969), "Socrates on Acrasia," *Phoenix* 23: 71–88.

Vlastos, Gregory (1973), "Justice and Happiness in Plato's *Republic*," in Gregory Vlastos, *Platonic Studies* (Princeton: Princeton University Press), 111–39.

Vlastos, Gregory (1991), *Socrates: Ironist and Moral Philosopher* (Cambridge: Cambridge University Press).

Vlastos, Gregory (1994a), *Socratic Studies* (Cambridge: Cambridge University Press).

Vlastos, Gregory (1994b), "Was Plato a Feminist?," in Nancy Tuana (ed.), *Feminist Interpretations of Plato* (University Park, Pennsylvania: The Pennsylvania State University Press), 1–24.

Vries, G. J. de (1969), *A Commentary on the Phaedrus of Plato* (Amsterdam: Adolf M. Hakkert).

Waterfield, Robin (1993), *Plato*: Republic (Oxford: Oxford University Press).

Waterfield, Robin (2012), "The Quest for the Historical Socrates" in John Bussanich and Nicholas D. Smith (eds.), *The Bloomsbury Companion to Socrates* (London: Bloomsbury Publishing), 1–19.

Webster, T. B. L. (1957), "Some Psychological Terms in Greek Tragedy," *The Journal of Hellenic Studies* 77/1: 149–54.

Weinstein, Joshua (2018), *Plato's Threefold City and Soul* (Cambridge: Cambridge University Press).

Weiss, Roslyn (1995), "Statesman as *ΕΠΙΣΤΗΜΩΝ*: Caretaker, Physician, and Weaver," in Christopher Rowe (ed.), *Reading the* Statesman: *Proceedings of the III Symposium Platonicum* (Sankt Augustin: Academia Verlag), 213–22.

Weiss, Roslyn (2006), *The Socratic Paradox and its Enemies* (Chicago: University of Chicago Press).

Wersinger, Anne Gabrièle (2001), *Platon et la Dysharmonie* (Paris: J. Vrin).

White, David A. (2007), *Myth, Metaphysics, and Dialectic in Plato's* Statesman (Burlington, Vermont: Ashgate Publishing Company).

White, Nicholas (1979), *A Companion to Plato's* Republic (Indianapolis: Hackett Publishing Company).

Whiting, Jennifer (2012), "Psychic Contingency in the *Republic*," in Rachel Barney, Tad Brennan, and Charles Brittain (eds.), *Plato and the Divided Soul* (Cambridge: Cambridge University Press), 174–208.

Wilamowitz-Moellendorff, U. (1920), *Platon*, i (Berlin: Weidmannsche Buchhandlung).

Wilberding, James (2004), "Prisoner's and Puppeteers in the Cave," *Oxford Studies in Ancient Philosophy* 27: 117–39.

Wilberding, James (2009), "Plato's Two Forms of Second-Best Morality," *Philosophical Review* 118: 351–74.

Wilberding, James (2012), "Curbing One's Appetites in Plato's *Republic*," in Rachel Barney, Tad Brennan, and Charles Brittain (eds.), *Plato and the Divided Self* (Cambridge: Cambridge University Press), 128–49.

Wilburn, Josh (2012), "Akrasia and Self-Rule in Plato's *Laws*," *Oxford Studies in Ancient Philosophy* 43: 25–53.

Wilburn, Josh (2013a), "Tripartition and the Causes of Criminal Behavior in *Laws* ix," *Ancient Philosophy* 33: 111–34.

Wilburn, Josh (2013b), "Moral Education and the Spirited Part of the Soul in Plato's *Laws*," *Oxford Studies in Ancient Philosophy* 45: 63–102.

Wilburn, Josh (2014a), "*Akrasia* and the Rule of Appetite in Plato's *Republic* and *Protagoras*," *Journal of Ancient Philosophy* 8/2: 57–91.

Wilburn, Josh (2014b), "Is Appetite Ever 'Persuaded': An Alternative Reading of *Republic* 554b–c," *History of Philosophy Quarterly*, 31.3: 195–208.

Wilburn, Josh (2014c), "The Spirited Part of the Soul in Plato's *Timaeus*," *Journal of the History of Philosophy* 524: 627–54.

Wilburn, Josh (2015a), "The Problem of Alcibiades: Plato on Moral Education and the Many," *Oxford Studies in Ancient Philosophy* 49: 1–36.

Wilburn, Josh (2015b), "Courage and the Spirited part of the Soul in Plato's *Republic*," *Philosopher's Imprint* 15.26: 1–21.

Wilburn, Josh (2016), "Plato's Protagoras the Hedonist," *Classical Philology* 111/3: 224–44.

Williams, Bernard (1973), "The Analogy of City and Soul in Plato's *Republic*," in E. N. Lee, A. P. D. Mourelatos, and R. M. Rorty (eds.), *Exegesis and Argument* (Assan: Van Gorkum), 196–206.

Williams, Bernard (1993), *Shame and Necessity* (Berkeley: University of California Press).

Wilson, J. R. S. (1995), "Thrasymachus and the *Thumos*: A Further Case of Prolepsis in *Republic* I," *Classical Quarterly* 45/1: 58–67.

Wohl, Victoria (1999), "The Eros of Alcibiades," *Classical Antiquity* 18: 349–85.

Wolz, Henry G. (1967), "Hedonism in the *Protagoras*," *Journal of the History of Philosophy* 5: 205–17.

Woodruff, Paul (1999), "Rhetoric and Relativism: Protagoras and Gorgias," in A. A. Long (ed.), *The Cambridge Companion to Early Greek Philosophy* (Cambridge: Cambridge University Press), 290–310.

Woodruff, Paul (2000), "Socrates and the Irrational," in Nicholas D. Smith and Paul Woodruff (eds.), *Reason and Religion in Socratic Philosophy* (Oxford: Oxford University Press), 130–50.

Woods, Michael (1987), "Plato's Division of the Soul," *Proceedings of the British Academy* 73: 23–48.

Woolf, Raphael (2012), "How to See an Unencrusted Soul," in Rachel Barney, Tad Brennan, and Charles Brittain (eds.), *Plato and the Divided Self* (Cambridge: Cambridge University Press), 150–73.

Woozley, A. D. (1972), "Plato on Killing in Anger," *The Philosophical Quarterly* 22/89: 303–17.

Zaborowski, Robert (2018), "Plato's *Phaedrus* 253E5–255A1 Revisited: A Reappraisal of Plato's View on the Soul," *Organon* 50: 165–207.

Index Locorum

General Index